Hincmar of Rheims

Hincmar of Rheims

Life and work

EDITED BY RACHEL STONE AND CHARLES WEST

Manchester University Press

Copyright © Manchester University Press 2015

While copyright in the volume as a whole is vested in Manchester University Press, copyright in individual chapters belongs to their respective authors, and no chapter may be reproduced wholly or in part without the express permission in writing of both author and publisher.

Published by Manchester University Press
Altrincham Street, Manchester M1 7JA

www.manchesteruniversitypress.co.uk

British Library Cataloguing-in-Publication Data
A catalogue record for this book is available from the British Library

Library of Congress Cataloging-in-Publication Data applied for

ISBN 978 1 5261 0654 4 paperback

First published by Manchester University Press in hardback 2015

This edition first published 2016

The publisher has no responsibility for the persistence or accuracy of URLs for any external or third-party internet websites referred to in this book, and does not guarantee that any content on such websites is, or will remain, accurate or appropriate.

Typeset in 10.5/12.5 Minion Pro with Rotis Sans display by
Servis Filmsetting Ltd, Stockport, Cheshire
Printed by Lightning Source

To Edward and Ellie, and in memory of Richard

Contents

List of figures and tables	page ix
List of contributors	x
Preface and acknowledgements	xi
List of abbreviations	xii
Map of Frankish kingdoms	xiv
Genealogy of Carolingian rulers	xv

1	Introduction: Hincmar's world – *Rachel Stone*	1
2	Hincmar's life in his historical writings – *Janet L. Nelson*	44
3	To fight with words: the case of Hincmar of Laon in the Annals of St-Bertin – *Christine Kleinjung*	60
4	An unfortunate necessity? Hincmar and Lothar I – *Elina Screen*	76
	Appendix: The authenticity of the letters of Leo IV in the Collectio Britannica	85
5	'We are between the hammer and the anvil': Hincmar in the crisis of 875 – *Clémentine Bernard-Valette*	93
6	Hincmar's influence during Louis the Stammerer's reign – *Margaret J. McCarthy*	110
7	Hincmar and his Roman legal sources – *Simon Corcoran*	129
8	*Hincmar et la loi* revisited: on Hincmar's use of capitularies – *Philippe Depreux*	156

Contents

9   The bishop and the law, according to Hincmar's life of Saint Remigius – *Marie-Céline Isaïa*   170

10 Family order and kingship according to Hincmar – *Sylvie Joye*   190

11 'The praetor <u>does</u> concern himself with trifles': Hincmar, the polyptych of St-Remi and the slaves of Courtisols – *Josiane Barbier*   211
Appendix: The *nota* and the structure of the entry for Courtisols in the Paris manuscript   221

12 Hincmar's parish priests – *Charles West*   228

13 Heresy in the flesh: Gottschalk of Orbais and the predestination controversy in the archdiocese of Rheims – *Matthew Bryan Gillis*   247

14 Hincmar, priests and Pseudo-Isidore: the case of Trising in context – *Mayke de Jong*   268
Appendix: Letter from Hincmar of Rheims to Pope Hadrian II, spring 871   281

Bibliographies   289
Primary sources   289
Select bibliography of secondary literature   296
Index   300

Figures and tables

Figures

1 The Frankish kingdoms in 843 — *page* xiv
2 Simplified genealogy of Carolingian rulers — xv
3 Staatsbibliothek zu Berlin, Preußischer Kulturbesitz (SBB-PK), MS Phillipps 1741, fol. 191^r – extracts from the Breviary of Alaric written by different hands in a manuscript strongly associated with Hincmar (with permission of the Staatsbibliothek zu Berlin) — 134
4 *Nota* mark from Paris, BnF lat. 9903, fol. 21^r (redrawn) — 214
5 Reconstructed *nota* mark — 214
6 *Nota* mark from Carpentras, Bibliothèque Inguimbertine, MS 1779, fol. 277^r (redrawn) — 214
7 Bodleian Library, MS Eng Hist c.242, fol. 40^v – an early modern copy of the polyptych of St-Remi, showing a *nota* mark next to the list of the Courtisols witnesses (with permission of The Bodleian Library, University of Oxford) — 214

Tables

1 Structure of the *Vita Remigii* in the Bibliotheca Hagiographica Latina (BHL) — *page* 182
2 Structure of the *Vita Remigii* in Arras, BM MS 199 (189) — 183

Contributors

Josiane Barbier, Maître de Conférences, HDR, University of Paris Ouest-Nanterre-La-Défense
Clémentine Bernard-Valette, Associate Researcher, University of Lyon (Lumière, Lyon II)
Simon Corcoran, Senior Research Fellow, University College London
Philippe Depreux, Professor of Medieval History, University of Hamburg
Matthew Bryan Gillis, Assistant Professor, University of Tennessee, Knoxville
Mayke de Jong, Professor of Medieval History, Utrecht University
Christine Kleinjung, Wissenschaftliche Mitarbeiterin, Albert-Ludwigs University, Freiburg
Margaret J. McCarthy, independent scholar
Marie-Céline Isaïa, Maître de Conférences en Histoire Médiévale, Université Jean-Moulin Lyon3, CIHAM UMR 5648
Sylvie Joye, Maître de Conférences, Université de Reims Champagne-Ardennes and Institut Universitaire de France
Dame Janet L. Nelson, Emeritus Professor of History, King's College, London
Elina Screen, Departmental Lecturer in Early Medieval History, University of Oxford and College Lecturer in Medieval History, Trinity College
Rachel Stone, Postdoctoral Research Associate, King's College, London
Charles West, Senior Lecturer in Medieval History, University of Sheffield

Preface and acknowledgements

This book grew out of a series of sessions organised by the editors at the International Medieval Congress at Leeds in 2012, bringing together historians interested in Hincmar from across the world. The interest aroused by the sessions and the quality of the papers produced encouraged us to make more widely available this selection of some of the latest research on Hincmar. We thank all the contributors to this volume for agreeing to take part, and for smoothing the editing process.

We also wish to thank Hannah Probert for creating the map, and Nick Walsh for redrawing the *notae* marks in Josiane Barbier's chapter. We are grateful to the Presses Universitaires Paris Sorbonne for allowing us to include that chapter, a revised version of one originally published in French; to the Médiatheque of Rheims for permission to use our cover image; and to the Staatsbibliothek zu Berlin and the Bodleian Library, University of Oxford, for permission to reproduce pages from their manuscripts for illustrative purposes. Finally, we should like to thank Letha Böhringer, Andreas Öffner, Karl Heidecker and Phillip Wynn for their valuable contributions to the Hincmar panels at Leeds in 2012.

Rachel Stone and Charles West

Abbreviations

AB	*Annales Bertiniani*
BHL	Bibliotheca Hagiographica Latina
BM	Bibliothèque municipale
BnF	Bibliothèque nationale de France
CCCM	Corpus Christia norum Continuatio Mediaevalis
CCSL	Corpus Christianorum Series Latina
CSEL	Corpus Scriptorum Ecclesiasticorum Latinorum
DA	*Deutsches Archiv für Erforschung des Mittelalters*
Devisse, *Hincmar*	J. Devisse, *Hincmar, archevêque de Reims, 845–882*, 3 vols (Geneva, 1975–76)
Flodoard, *HRE*	Flodoard, *Historia Remensis ecclesiae*
Hincmar, *De raptu*	Hincmar of Rheims, *De coercendo et exstirpando raptu viduarum puellarum ac sanctimonalium*
J + no.	*Regesta Pontificum Romanorum ab condita ecclesia ad annum post Christum natum MCXCVIII*, ed. P. Jaffé *et al*
MGH	Monumenta Germaniae Historica
Capit.	*Capitularia regum Francorum*
Capit. Episc.	*Capitula episcoporum*
Conc.	*Concilia*
Epp.	*Epistolae (in Quart.)*
SRM	*Scriptores rerum Merovingicarum*
SS	*Scriptores (in Folio)*

Abbreviations

PG	*Patrologia Graeca*, ed. J.-P. Migne, 161 vols (Paris, 1857–66)
PL	*Patrologia Latina*, ed. J.-P. Migne, 221 vols (Paris, 1844–55)
s.a.	*sub anno*
SB	Staatsbibliothek
Schrörs, *Hinkmar*	H. Schrörs, Hinkmar, Erzbischof von Reims: sein Leben und seine Schriften (Freiburg im Breisgau, 1884)
Settimane	Settimane di studi del centro italiano di studi sull'alto medioevo
VR	Hincmar, *Vita Remigii episcopi Remensis*

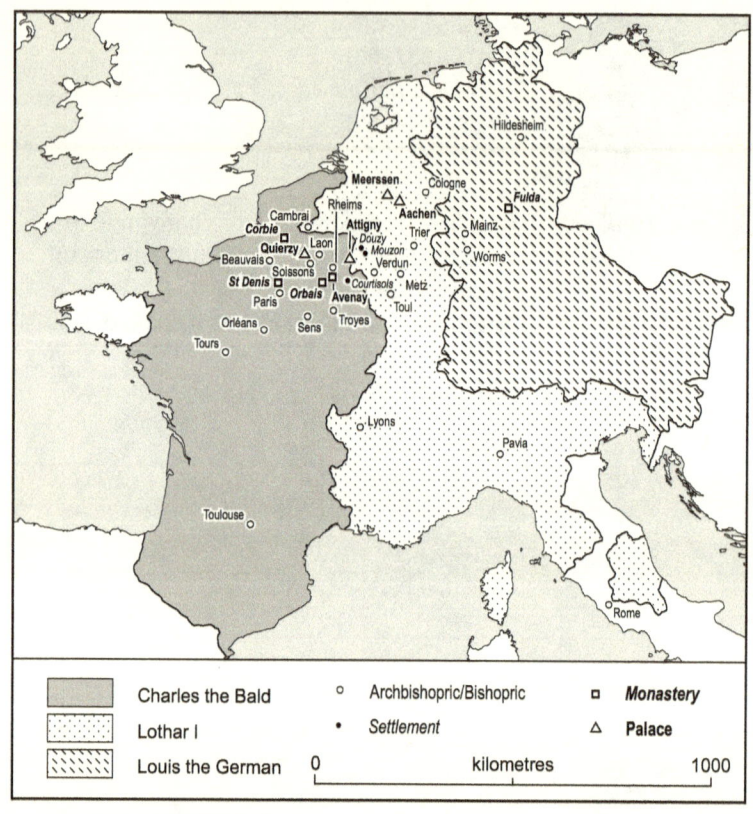

1 The Frankish kingdoms in 843.

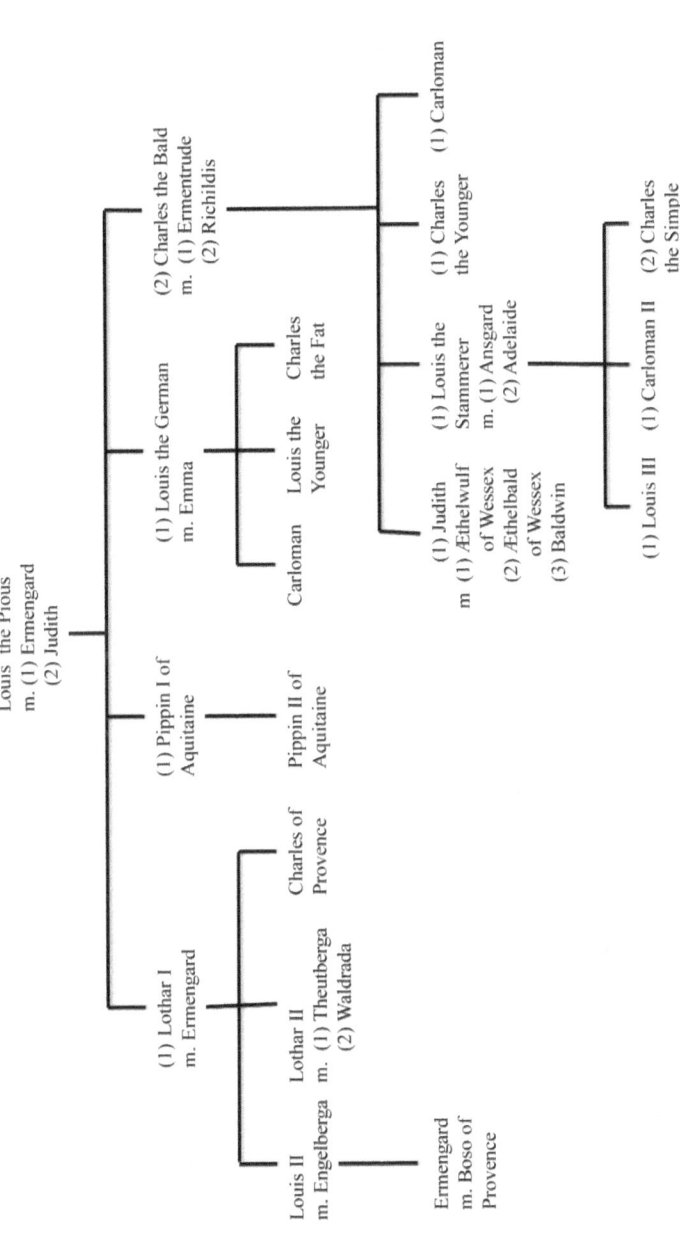

2 Simplified genealogy of Carolingian rulers.

1

Introduction: Hincmar's world

Rachel Stone

Life and times

When Flodoard, a canon of Rheims cathedral, came to write his history of the church of Rheims in the mid-tenth century, he had no doubt about the dominant figure in the see's story. It is not the numerous saintly bishops of Late Antiquity who take up most of the *Historia Remensis ecclesiae*, but a far less holy and more controversial figure: Hincmar, archbishop of Rheims between 845 and 882.[1] Hincmar's predominance is partly due to the large quantity of information about him that Flodoard had access to, above all Hincmar's numerous letters. It is mainly from Hincmar's own writings that Flodoard constructed his history of Rheims.

Our own view of the Carolingian empire is also greatly shaped by Hincmar's work. Hincmar was born within a decade of Charlemagne's acceptance of the imperial title in 800; he died in 882, six years before the death of the last undisputed Carolingian emperor, Charles the Fat. His long life therefore encompassed the greater part of the Frankish empire's existence. But Hincmar was not just a witness to the Carolingian ninth century. As archbishop of Rheims, he was one of its leading political figures, closely involved in most of the urgent issues of the time. Above all, he was one of the pre-eminent commentators of his day. His voluminous writing encompasses many genres: history (notably the Annals of St-Bertin between 861 and 882), theology, hagiography, political tracts, letters, moral treatises, regulations for the priests of his archdiocese, legal opinions, Church council *acta*, liturgical texts, administrative documents, poetry and exegesis.[2] Much of what we know about this period we know, directly or indirectly, from Hincmar;[3] as Janet Nelson comments, 'It has …

1

proved hard to view the ninth century other than through Hincmar's eyes'.[4]

Hincmar has therefore been a vital source for historians of the early Middle Ages. Indeed, given the scale of his production, almost anyone looking at ninth-century Francia engages with the archbishop at some point. His works are cited by studies on topics ranging from magically induced impotence via lordship to the legal right to confront one's accuser.[5] However, as a direct consequence of this breadth of interest, most historians consider only one element of Hincmar's activities, thereby breaking the coherence of his activities. The exceptions are two biographies of Hincmar: one by Heinrich Schrörs from 1884 and one by Jean Devisse published in three volumes in 1975–76.[6] Although these remain important resources, there has been much scholarship on Hincmar since Devisse, both drawing on neglected texts and re-examining some of Hincmar's well-known works.

This book therefore seeks to overcome the current fragmentation of scholarship by bringing together historians currently working on Hincmar in a range of fields. It is intended as a road-marker, showing how recent research has altered our understanding of the archbishop, and of the world he did so much to shape. Above all, as the subtitle indicates, it connects together Hincmar's life and work.

Hincmar's works are overwhelmingly anchored to a specific time, place and context: he wrote in response to events, not as an abstract theorist or secluded in a monastic cell. He was on the front line of politics, serving four successive rulers of western Francia (Louis the Pious, Charles the Bald, Louis the Stammerer and Carloman) and interacting with several more from the other Frankish kingdoms. His role as an archbishop was no sinecure: he was repeatedly embroiled in disputes both within his diocese and further afield, sometimes theological, but more often concerning practical matters of Church discipline and the preservation of Church property. Several of these disputes dealt with issues that touched him at a personal level, such as his claim to the archbishopric of Rheims and his bitter struggles with his nephew, Hincmar, bishop of Laon. To understand Hincmar and his work fully, therefore, we need an overview of the political and ecclesiastical worlds in which he moved,[7] so this first chapter concentrates on outlining Hincmar's career. It then looks briefly at what we can learn from him of Carolingian culture and society, and at Hincmar's legacy, as background for the more detailed studies in the rest of this book.

Early years: to 843

Hincmar was of noble birth and related to several counts, but we do not know exactly where or when he was born; suggested dates range from 802 to 810, and northern France is the most plausible location for his birthplace.[8] Hincmar himself states that he was 'raised from the beginnings of infancy' at the monastery of St-Denis.[9] He was probably a child oblate, and thus may have been barely weaned when he first entered religious life.[10]

Hincmar obviously won favour with the abbot of St-Denis, Hilduin, who took him to Emperor Louis the Pious's court, where Hilduin was arch-chaplain (head of the palace clergy), to continue his education.[11] This was at some point during the early or mid-820s, a formative moment in Hincmar's life, when he met figures like Adalard, Charlemagne's cousin, who died in 826.[12] He may also have witnessed Louis's voluntary public performance of penance at Attigny in 822 to atone for the blinding of his nephew Bernard of Italy;[13] Hincmar's later writings are certainly full of reported conflicts over the meanings of royal gestures, as well as moralising over the significance of rituals.[14]

At Attigny, Louis's confession brought a response from the bishops highlighting their own sins and negligence.[15] A political theory was developing in the mid-820s which stressed the interaction of the emperor, bishops and 'people', rather than focusing solely on secular rulers. Each social group (*ordo*) had its own *ministerium* (divinely bestowed office or function), but also shared in the emperor's *ministerium* of caring for the Church and empire. The bishops in particular saw themselves as jointly overseeing the empire; indeed, they not only shared power with the ruler, but their responsibility was even greater than his, since they were answerable to God for the sins of all those in their flocks, commoners and kings alike.[16] This theory found its fullest expression in the Council of Paris in 829, and Hincmar frequently repeated its key messages throughout his life.[17]

In 830, Louis the Pious's sons Pippin and Lothar led a revolt against their father, but Louis was soon able to regain control of his empire. Hilduin, who had supported the rebels, was briefly sent into exile in Saxony in 831.[18] Hincmar's precise activities are difficult to establish in this period. He claimed to have been Louis the Pious's confidant for eight years, but although he spent at least two periods at court, the dates are very uncertain.[19] In a letter to Pope Nicholas of July

867, Hincmar says vaguely that, after a period at the royal court, he returned to St-Denis:

> After the brothers in the monastery of St-Denis, where I had been raised, had converted to a regular life and habit, I dwelled there for a long time, fleeing the world without hope or appetite for a bishopric, or any prelateship. Taken from there by friends for the service of the emperor and the meetings of the bishops, serving from the obedience alone that was enjoined to me, after some years I sought again the quiet of the monastery. But the anchoring line with which I had negligently bound myself in port was broken, as my sins demanded, and, persuaded by exhortations in the guise of the salvation of the many, by those whom I trusted more readily than I perhaps should have, I was thrown back to the tempests of the huge and wide sea, in great peril.[20]

Flodoard is more specific, saying that Hincmar worked with Hilduin and Louis to restore monastic life in St-Denis, and that he accompanied Hilduin into exile. Hincmar then managed to gain favour with Louis and his magnates, and helped ensure Hilduin's recall. However, a charter from Louis the Pious in 832 concerning reform at St-Denis makes no specific mention of Hincmar.[21] Hincmar's return to St-Denis, therefore, may have been as early as 829 or as late as 832, either interrupted by Hilduin's exile or following it, and his exact role in the reform of St-Denis is not clear.

Nor does Hincmar say anything to Pope Nicholas about the next events in which he was almost certainly involved: those surrounding the second rebellion of Louis the Pious's sons Lothar, Pippin and Louis the German against their father, in 833/834.[22] This time, Louis was formally removed from his throne and made to carry out a 'voluntary' penance that prevented him acting as a ruler. Louis's deposition was ceremonially reversed when support for the rebels ebbed away and he regained power. Although Hilduin again supported the rebels, Flodoard states that Hincmar refused to abandon his loyalty to the emperor, even when Pope Gregory IV, who had come to Francia in support of Lothar, appealed to him.[23] Hincmar's close relations with both Louis the Pious and Charles the Bald makes this statement plausible, and Hincmar may not have wished to mention in his letter of 867 this dubious involvement of a pope in Frankish politics.

Another outcome of the second rebellion was to have long-term consequences for Hincmar. Archbishop Ebbo of Rheims was made a scapegoat for the penance that the bishops had imposed on Louis. He was forced to confess to a capital crime at the Council of Thionville in February 835 and resigned from his office of archbishop as 'unworthy'.[24] The procedural complications and irregularities around his resignation or deposition, however, meant that his claim to the province of Rheims was not conclusively extinguished. No successor to the see was appointed for ten years, and Ebbo remained a problem for Hincmar even beyond the grave.[25]

Hincmar does not seem to have drawn immediate political advantage from his loyalty to Louis the Pious in 833–34. His activities in the later 830s are hard to trace, although his comments to Nicholas imply that he returned to St-Denis again and a list of monks from there in 838 includes his name.[26] Flodoard says that he was responsible for care of the relics (*custos sacrorum pignerum*) and Hincmar may have assisted Hilduin in promoting the cult of St Denis and contributed to the writing of the *Miracula sancti Dionysii*.[27] He also probably continued acquiring a formidable knowledge of patristic authors: he claimed to have read the letters of Pope Leo many times in this period.[28]

On Louis's death in 840, a civil war broke out between his surviving sons, Lothar, Louis the German and Charles the Bald; Lothar claimed the whole empire and attacked Louis and Charles in turn. Hincmar's role during the war is unclear: Nithard, our most detailed source for the events of the war, makes no mention of him.[29] Hincmar presumably remained loyal to Charles the Bald, who at some time between 840 and 845 gave him control of one or more monasteries.[30] He was clearly affected emotionally by the civil war, recalling more than thirty years later the particularly bloody battle of Fontenoy.[31] He may also have made a more intellectual response to the conflict. The mid-ninth-century manuscript Paris BnF lat. nouv. acq. 1632A contains a collection of patristic citations known as the *Capitula diversarum sententiarum pro negociis rei publice consulendis* (CDS) on the topics of warfare and the duties of princes. This compilation has usually been attributed to Jonas of Orléans, though Phillip Wynn, who is currently editing the text, has suggested that it may have been produced by Hincmar, possibly in the spring of 842, as part of Charles's attempts to justify his actions against Lothar.[32]

The events of 840–43 also had several major effects on the ecclesiastical province of Rheims. Firstly, while Lothar controlled the area, Ebbo returned briefly to his archbishopric and ordained a number of clerics before fleeing again. The legitimacy of the ordination of

'Ebbo's clerics' remained a problem for Hincmar for decades to come.[33] Secondly, the division of the empire into three by the Treaty of Verdun in 843 meant that the province of Rheims now lay across a border: the majority of it was in West Francia (held by Charles the Bald), but part of it, including the whole diocese of Cambrai, lay within Lothar's Middle Kingdom.[34] There was also property belonging to the church of Rheims in East Francia (held by Louis the German) and in Aquitaine, which Pippin II still claimed to rule. This meant that any archbishop of Rheims needed an outlook that extended beyond the West Frankish kingdom. Finally, while the see had been left vacant, Charles the Bald had given away some of its property to reward his followers.[35] These events laid the foundations for three key themes of Hincmar's archepiscopate: arguments about the status of some of the clergy within his province, a concern for peace between rival Carolingian kings and an obsession with Church property.

An intellectual in religious politics, 843–855

As Janet Nelson has shown, the Treaty of Verdun did not end Charles the Bald's struggles within West Francia. Pippin II remained a threat: a major defeat inflicted on Charles's army in the Angoumois in June 844 meant that in 845 Charles had to agree to Pippin's continuing lordship in Aquitaine.[36] Periodically there were also severe difficulties with the Bretons and with Viking raiders, while the existence of rival kingdoms gave powerful magnates the ongoing possibility of switching allegiances.[37]

Charles was only in his early twenties, but already had considerable political experience and showed himself keen to recruit scholars to support his rule.[38] Hincmar's early involvement in such politically-motivated scholarship has also been suggested. Nelson argues that his hand can be detected both in the capitulary produced at Coulaines in 843 and in the *capitula* of Toulouse from 844.[39] Hincmar certainly played a prominent role in the Council of Ver in December 844, although the *capitula* from this meeting were written up by Lupus of Ferrières.[40] One of the demands at Ver was that the see of Rheims, 'destitute' and 'despoiled', should be given a bishop.[41] Charles responded by appointing Hincmar four months later.

Hincmar's first years in his see were difficult. He had to attempt to restore property of Rheims lost during the long episcopal vacancy (835–45); several early letters request assistance in this from Empress

Ermengard (wife of Lothar I) and Pippin II of Aquitaine.[42] He also needed to ensure the effective management of property still held. Josiane Barbier provides evidence that Hincmar took a personal interest in ensuring that Rheims dependants remained tied to their existing unfree status and were not allowed to escape from the Church's control.[43]

Hincmar also needed to negotiate treacherous post-war politics. Emperor Lothar I had previously supported the attempt of Ebbo to return to Rheims, and was therefore not well disposed to Ebbo's would-be replacement. As Elina Screen shows, Hincmar was eventually successful in cultivating Lothar's favour as well as Charles's, but Hincmar was never able to monopolise influence at any royal court.[44] Indeed, he was theoretically opposed to a ruler's favour being monopolised in such a way.[45]

Ebbo's direct threat to Hincmar's position was soon greatly lessened, but Hincmar's authority in his own province came under threat from a different source after 848: the controversial Saxon monk Gottschalk.[46] Although initially an oblate of Fulda in the eastern kingdom, Gottschalk had become a monk at Orbais in the diocese of Soissons in the early 830s and has been ordained as a priest by a chorbishop of Rheims while the see was vacant. As a result, Archbishop Hrabanus of Mainz was able to argue that he was Hincmar's responsibility, and so Gottschalk arrived in Rheims in 848. Gottschalk's views on predestination posed intellectual challenges that Hincmar could not ignore, and he produced three different works on the topic: *Ad reclusos et simplices in Remensi parrochia contra Gothescalcum* in 850, a now-lost treatise in 856 and finally *De praedestinatione Dei* in 859–60.[47]

In attempting to deal with Gottschalk, Hincmar probably alienated himself from many of the other intellectuals active at the same time. Prudentius of Troyes, John Scottus Eriugena, Lupus of Ferrières and Ratramnus of Corbie all ended up proposing views contrary to Hincmar's. Indeed, there seems to have been an overlap between opponents of Hincmar over predestination and supporters of the clerics ordained by Ebbo.[48] Ebbo of Grenoble, for example, the nephew of Ebbo of Rheims, was prominent at a council held in Valence in Lotharingia in 855 which condemned the Council of Quierzy's statement on predestination.[49]

Other bishops developed theories that attacked Hincmar's status in a different way. Theutgaud of Trier claimed, probably around

852/53, that he should be the primate over the province of Rheims. He based this on the argument that Trier, as the capital of the former Roman province of *Belgica prima*, was superior to Rheims, the capital of *Belgica secunda*.[50] It is not clear how seriously Theutgaud's claims were taken, but they were based on what became an important authority in disputes involving the province of Rheims: the Pseudo-Isidorian forgeries. It now seems clear that some version of this set of forgeries was being created at Corbie in the mid-830s, in reaction to the deposition of Ebbo, but the process of forgery was a long one, extending past 847.[51] Eric Knibbs has recently reasserted the traditional argument that Hincmar was a specific target of the forgers; certainly several of Hincmar's opponents, such as Rothad of Soissons and Hincmar of Laon, made use of the texts.[52]

Nevertheless, by the early 850s Hincmar could begin to feel more secure. Ebbo died in 851, and the Council of Soissons in April 853 decreed as invalid the orders of all clerics ordained by him after his deposition in 835.[53] At Quierzy in June 853 Charles the Bald, Hincmar and some of the other West Frankish bishops agreed a four-point formula on predestination, which they hoped would put an end to the problems caused by Gottschalk.[54] As for Pseudo-Isidore, the breadth of topics covered makes a targeted attack on Hincmar unlikely, and he cited the texts himself on occasions.[55] Indeed, although Hincmar of Laon was one of the most determined users of Pseudo-Isidorian texts, his subordinate clerics also used them against him.[56]

From the 850s onwards, Hincmar was able to focus more on ensuring correct religious practice within the province of Rheims. He restored the church of St-Remi and organised the translation of the body of St Remigius in 852. Marie-Céline Isaïa has also suggested that Hincmar may have begun work on a first version of the *Vita Remigii* in this period.[57] It was also now that Hincmar produced his first two sets of diocesan statutes. The many chapters concerning expectations of priests in his province confirm Hincmar's attention to detail and his concerns with the practicalities of parish life. Much of his time was still taken up with trying to enforce discipline locally.[58] Letters from throughout Hincmar's years in office discuss a wide variety of administrative, pastoral and legal questions, from his arranging the election of suffragan bishops to his attempts to block the remarriage of Lothar I's *vassus* Fulcric.[59] A letter to Bishop Lupus of Châlons-en-Champagne, for example, discusses a man who had mistakenly supported his own child at confirmation, and thus according to the

Carolingian understanding of godparenthood as creating kinship ties, was now incestuously married to his own wife.[60] Other letters concern the penance for a monk who had committed homicide and Hincmar's attempts to discipline a runaway *ministerialis*.[61]

Province and kingdom, 855–860

In 855, Lothar I died and his kingdom was divided between his three sons. The eldest, Louis II, held onto the kingdom of Italy, which he had controlled since around 840. Lothar's second son, Lothar II, received the northern part of the kingdom, while the youngest brother, the sickly teenager Charles, received Provence. Lothar I's Middle Kingdom, which had stretched from Frisia down to Italy, was no longer a threat to Charles the Bald. Instead Charles and Louis the German sought parts of it for themselves, or were able to cross through the region in order to attack each other.

Hincmar was more prominent among Charles's advisers from 856 onwards than he had been during the first decade of his episcopacy.[62] He composed a coronation *ordo* for Charles's daughter, Judith, on her marriage to King Æthelwulf of Wessex, and also produced several texts for Charles on a topic that particularly concerned the archbishop: ecclesiastical property.[63] The *Collectio de raptoribus*, promulgated by the Council of Quierzy in 857, collected biblical, patristic and canonical quotes to condemn those who misappropriated Church property.[64] The *Collectio de ecclesiis et capellis* from 857/58 was a much longer and more complex work, which tried to untangle different rights over churches.[65] As often with Hincmar, it may also reflect more personal quarrels. The two opponents of Hincmar's views mentioned in the preface are Prudentius of Troyes (with whom Hincmar had quarrelled over predestination) and Rothad of Soissons, one of Hincmar's suffragans, whom Hincmar deposed in 861 after years of tension.

Charles the Bald's concerns about orderly control of Church property came at a time when he himself was facing major political difficulties. While he and Lothar II were besieging a Viking army in Oissel in Normandy in the summer of 858, his brother Louis the German, invited by magnates of Charles's own kingdom, invaded. Some bishops went over to Louis on his invasion, most notably Wenilo of Sens. In contrast, Hincmar was among the most prominent of those resisting him. Louis summoned the West Frankish bishops to a synod at

Rheims in November 858; they met at Quierzy instead, and Hincmar drafted a long letter to Louis on their behalf. In this the bishops politely declined to become Louis's *fideles*, while exhorting him to restore the status of the Church and to consider the divine punishment that awaited someone who attacked an anointed king (like Charles).[66] These delaying tactics meant that Louis was unable to legitimise his coup, and gave Charles time to rally his supporters. Louis was forced to retreat in January 859 and Charles celebrated the restoration of his kingdom.[67]

Hincmar's prestige and influence were further increased by the events of 858, and he played a prominent part in subsequent diplomatic negotiations between Charles, Louis and Lothar II, who was acting as a peacemaker. These negotiations dragged on until a meeting at Koblenz in June 860, but meanwhile, a new matter was dominating attention. Soon after their marriage, Lothar II had become alienated from his wife, Theutberga. He 'put her aside' in 857, and accused her of incest with her brother Hubert. Forced to take her back in 858, after her champion had successfully endured the ordeal of boiling water, Lothar tried again in 860.[68] She confessed – almost certainly under coercion – to 'unnatural' intercourse with Hubert and asked at a synod to be allowed to retire to a monastery to do penance.

Although the case did not concern events in his province, Hincmar became involved because some Lotharingian bishops appealed for his advice on the case. The result was his treatise *De divortio Lotharii regis et Theutbergae reginae*, a complex piece of work built up in several phases during 860 and tackling a wide range of legal, penitential and moral questions.[69] Hincmar's opinions on the divorce were by no means automatically accepted, but the commission shows an appreciation of Hincmar's expertise beyond his own province. At the Council of Tusey in the autumn of 860 Hincmar was asked for his advice on two other long-running marital disputes: Count Stephen of the Auvergne; and Engeltrude, who had abandoned her husband, Boso.[70]

Hincmar was not, however, the most senior churchman to consider Engeltrude's case: Pope Nicholas I had already sent several letters to the synod concerning her.[71] Nicholas I was not the first pope to be involved in Engeltrude's case or the first with whom Hincmar had contact, but his interventions in Francia were to become far more frequent and far-reaching than those of his predecessors, and he and Hincmar often clashed.

Introduction: Hincmar's world

The archbishop and the pope, 861–867

From 861 onwards much of our basic historical narrative is supplied by Hincmar himself, who took over writing the *Annales Bertiniani* (the most substantial historical work from the period) after Prudentius's death in 861.[72] We are thus very well informed both about Carolingian family politics and Frankish relations with the papacy for 861–82, but we often see them predominantly through Hincmar's eyes, and he may conceal as much as he reveals.[73]

Conflicts within East Francia lessened the direct threat that Louis the German posed to Charles the Bald after 859.[74] He was therefore able to go more on the offensive and attempted unsuccessfully to take over the kingdom of the sickly Charles of Provence in 861.[75] Charles the Bald also tried to exploit Lothar II's marital difficulties. Lothar, however, had now gained enough support from his own bishops to hold a synod in Aachen in April 862; this decided that he could repudiate Theutberga and marry Waldrada and he did so later that year.[76]

Lothar in turn tried to take advantage of problems with West Frankish royal marriages. In 862, three of Charles the Bald's children attempted to marry without his permission. Judith eloped with Count Baldwin; Charles the Younger, still under age, married 'the widow of Count Humbert' and Louis the Stammerer married Ansgard, sister of Louis's favourite Odo.[77] The fate of Charles the Younger's marriage is not known; Charles himself was badly injured in an accident in 864 and died in 866 from his injuries.[78] Louis the Stammerer remained married to Ansgard for long enough to produce at least three children. At some point, however, he repudiated her, either voluntarily or under pressure from his father. Hincmar's role in accepting or even justifying this repudiation has been suspected, but cannot be proved.[79] At the very least, Hincmar made no sustained protest about Louis's second marriage.[80]

Hincmar was definitely deeply involved in Baldwin and Judith's case, which turned on a social topic of major concern to him: *raptus*, the abduction of women for the purpose of marriage.[81] Charles had Baldwin condemned by a secular judgment and then anathematised by his bishops, while Hincmar wrote letters warning people not to receive Baldwin.[82] At a meeting of Charles the Bald, Louis the German and Lothar II at Savonnières in late 862, Hincmar records Charles denouncing Lothar both for his own marriage to Waldrada and for his support of Baldwin and Engeltrude.[83] A year later, however,

Charles allowed Baldwin and Judith to marry, thanks to the intercession of Pope Nicholas on their behalf. Theutberga too appealed to Nicholas for support in regaining her position as Lothar II's wife.[84]

Nicholas I (r. 858–67) was one of the most significant popes of the early Middle Ages. His determined view of the extent of papal authority led him to become involved in long-running conflicts with both eastern and western churches,[85] but his own political position remained vulnerable, since it depended on the current ruler of Italy. Louis II briefly took military control of Rome in 864.[86] Louis could also restrict travel to and from Rome: in 864 he refused permission to Nicholas to send legates to Charles the Bald, and Hincmar describes at one point sending messengers disguised as pilgrims to Rome, so that they would not be intercepted.[87]

The papacy's role in ninth-century politics was essentially reactive: responding to those appealing for the pope's judgment in what could be seen as ecclesiastical matters, which included marriage disputes. Nicholas, however wanted to push such authority further. He claimed the right to judge bishops, even if there had not been an explicit appeal to Rome, and the exclusive right to call or confirm Frankish synods.[88] Both these claims were opposed by Hincmar, who argued that conciliar canons established only more limited rights for the papacy on such matters.[89]

Hincmar also clashed with Nicholas and his advisers over the more general question of the relative priority to be given to papal decretals (letters setting out the pope's decisions on matters of Church order) as against conciliar canons.[90] While Nicolas claimed the right to amend the decisions even of ecumenical councils, Hincmar argued that the texts of decretals had less authority than that of conciliar canons, comparing decretals to the Old Testament law and councils to the gospels.[91]

Papal claims to authority in judicial matters rested largely on the general grounds of being successors to St Peter.[92] Frankish bishops, such as Hincmar, in turn claimed to be the successors to the apostles, and did not therefore automatically regard themselves as bound to blind obedience to the pope.[93] Two different concepts of the Church are visible: the Roman view tended towards a papal monarchy; the view taken by Hincmar and other Frankish bishops instead stressed the autonomy and authority of metropolitans and the theoretical importance of consensus in decision-making (although Hincmar in practice had just as many absolutist tendencies towards his own subordinates as Nicholas had towards his).[94]

Although appeals by clerics and laypeople at all levels to the papacy multiplied in the second half of the ninth century, the mechanisms for papal judgments remained rudimentary.[95] Papal legates were regularly sent to Francia but they could be ineffective or subverted. There were also worries about letters to and from popes being intercepted or forged.[96] Yet the alternative, holding synods at Rome to deal with cases, was not necessarily more satisfactory. As Hincmar pointed out, dealing with cases in the provinces made it easy to produce witnesses, while it was extremely hard to assemble both parties to a case in Rome simultaneously.[97]

Papal interventions in Francia ultimately relied on the pope's authority being accepted both in theory and practice, which had more to do with politics than purely legal arguments; nor was it a simple matter of the theoretical 'power' of the parties concerned. For example, Engeltrude successfully avoided Nicholas's attempts to make her return to her husband, but the pope was able to force Lothar, at least temporarily, to take Theutberga back. Nicholas also deposed two archbishops (Gunther of Cologne and Theutgaud of Trier) for their role in Lothar's divorce.[98]

Hincmar was thus not the only archbishop to have bruising encounters with Nicholas, but his relations with the pope were peculiarly complex, as shown by a long letter of Hincmar to Nicholas in early 864.[99] In turn, the letter discusses the case of the bishopric of Cambrai, Baldwin and Judith's marriage, the deposition of Rothad of Soissons and Gottschalk's heresy. Nicholas's interest in Gottschalk confirms just how long-running a problem the monk was for Hincmar.[100] In contrast, Nicholas supported Hincmar over the election of a new bishop for Cambrai, rejecting Lothar II's choice of Hilduin, the brother of Archbishop Gunther of Cologne. It was only in 866, however, that an alternative bishop to Hincmar's liking was finally installed.[101]

Hincmar's dealings with Nicholas over Baldwin and Rothad were less satisfactory for him. Hincmar expressed unhappiness at Nicholas's decision that Baldwin should not have to do penance for his elopement with Judith, but was nevertheless forced to accept it.[102] The case of Rothad of Soissons, however, brought Hincmar into major conflict with Nicholas, because it concerned papal intervention in how Hincmar dealt with the bishops of his own province

– his understanding, in other words, of what it was to be an archbishop.

Rothad was a senior bishop, who had probably anointed Hincmar himself in 845, but long-term disagreements between them came to a head in 861, when Rothad deposed a priest for unknown reasons.[103] The priest appealed to Hincmar, who ordered him to be reinstated. Rothad's refusal to do so eventually led to him being deposed at the Council of Soissons in June 862. Before the sentence of this synod was pronounced, Rothad appealed to Nicholas I. Hincmar, however, claimed that Rothad in fact had later withdrawn his appeal, and that the whole matter was being stirred up by his own opponents in Lotharingia, who were angry with Hincmar for having opposed Lothar's divorce.[104]

Hincmar may also not have had the full support of his other suffragans, as subsequent events showed.[105] Nicholas ordered Hincmar to reinstate Rothad and to send him to Rome along with his accusers. Rothad reached Rome in the summer of 864. but no accusations were formally made; Nicholas therefore ceremonially reinstated him as a bishop and then cleared him of charges.[106] The papal envoy Arsenius subsequently brought Rothad to Charles the Bald and had him restored to his see in mid-865, 'not according to the rules, but according to an arbitrary and overbearing decision' as Hincmar put it.[107]

Once again, royal politics intersected with more specifically ecclesiastical matters. Charles and Louis the German had made an alliance directed against Lothar in early 865, with Hincmar as one of its guarantors.[108] Another action of Arsenius in West Francia was collecting Theutberga, whom he then restored to her role as Lothar II's queen, thus obstructing Lothar's efforts to ensure his succession. Johannes Haller argued that Charles the Bald accepted Rothad's restoration precisely because he wanted Nicholas I's support against Lothar.[109]

Hincmar had made enough enemies to be vulnerable, and he could not invariably count on Charles's support. He was still used by Charles to produce key royal documents, such as the Capitulary of Pîtres in June 864, a detailed discussion of government practice, coinage reform and the military measures to be taken against the Vikings. It was also at Pîtres that Pippin II was condemned to death, and Hincmar drew up the indictment against him.[110] But Hincmar was not the only powerful churchman whom Charles found useful, and that led to the archbishop facing a potentially far more dangerous conflict with Nicholas over Wulfad of Sens.[111]

Introduction: Hincmar's world

Wulfad was one of 'Ebbo's clerics', those ordained during Ebbo's reclamation of the see in 840–41. Their ordinations had been declared invalid by the Council of Soissons in 853, but Wulfad had continued to seek advancement and had become a favourite of Charles the Bald. In 866 Charles was anxious to make Wulfad archbishop of Bourges in order to strength his own control of Aquitaine; the validity of Wulfad's ordination was thus raised again. Despite the fact that he had confirmed the decisions of the first Council of Soissons, Pope Nicholas ordered Hincmar to re-open the case. A second Council of Soissons in 866 proposed a compromise: that the ordinations of Wulfad and the other should be graciously accepted as valid, but without overthrowing the decisions made in 853. Nicholas, however, now made ominous threats that Ebbo's deposition thirty years previously might not have been valid, raising questions about Hincmar's own position.[112] It was only shortly before Nicholas's death in December 867 that he was finally reconciled to Hincmar.[113]

These ecclesiastical disputes were not easily settled by 'canon law' – a misleading term, since it suggests modern concepts of a legal system, with an established framework of fixed legislation and formal procedures. Although canons (rulings on Church organisation) had been promulgated from the third century, in the Carolingian period there was still no agreed corpus of canons or consensus on what types of sources could be counted as canonical.[114] A number of different collections of canons circulated and the texts of the canons themselves were not necessarily fixed.[115] Vaguely worded canons were interpreted flexibly by all parties.[116] There was also no settled court procedure or system of appeals; instead, elements from penitential practice and more formal legal proceedings were blended together. Ebbo, for example, had supposedly not been judged but had voluntarily withdrawn from his office as unworthy.[117] Few judgments were definitive: decisions made by one pope could be reversed by his successor.[118] While it is unlikely that Nicholas in 866 actually wanted Hincmar deposed, he may have wanted the chance graciously to allow a humiliated Hincmar to remain as archbishop.

Charles the Bald still valued Hincmar's abilities: at the end of the Council of Soissons in 866, Charles's queen Ermentrude was ritually consecrated by Hincmar and the other bishops, perhaps in the hope of her bearing further healthy sons.[119] But Charles also expected to get his way, regardless of ecclesiastical judgments. The Council of Troyes in October 867 declared that in future no bishop would be deposed without consultation with the pope.[120] In their letter to Nicholas I, however, probably written by Hincmar himself, the bishops also asked for the *pallium*, a ceremonial vestment, to be sent to Wulfad, who had already been ordained as archbishop at Charles's command.[121] Control of bishoprics, and their large resources of land and men, was too important to rulers to be left as a purely internal Church matter.

Towards empire, 868–877

In the late 860s, Hincmar again asserted his rights as archbishop over his suffragans, eventually falling into bitter conflict with his own nephew, Bishop Hincmar of Laon.[122] Hincmar of Rheims initially supported his nephew when, in June 868, Charles the Bald summoned the bishop of Laon to answer charges of depriving men of their benefices unfairly. The older Hincmar at this point wrote several treatises, collectively known as *Pro ecclesiae libertatum defensione*, arguing for the defence of Church property and against the idea that a cleric could be summoned to appear in person before a secular court.[123] By the summer of 869, however, the two Hincmars were at loggerheads and Hincmar of Laon produced one or more canonical collections drawing on Pseudo-Isidore, arguing for severe restrictions on bishops being accused or judged, including by their metropolitans.[124]

This struggle was however overshadowed – or perhaps intensified – by a new factor. In mid-August 869, Charles the Bald heard that King Lothar II had died in Italy; Louis the German was also seriously ill. Charles seized his opportunity and took over Lotharingia. He was crowned at Metz on 9 September by Hincmar of Rheims. Charles's wife Ermentrude died on 6 October and six days later Charles was betrothed to Richildis, sister of Boso, a prominent Lotharingian magnate; Hincmar angrily referred to Richildis as Charles's concubine.[125]

Louis the German, once recovered from his illness, threatened war if Charles did not leave Lotharingia. Charles's son Carloman was also hoping to secure control of part of Lotharingia, possibly keen to secure his position before any rival half-brothers were born from the new marriage.[126] At an assembly at Attigny in May–June 870, Louis and Charles agreed to divide Lotharingia between themselves; the assembly also deprived Carloman of his many abbacies and imprisoned him, and forced Hincmar of Laon to swear an oath of loyalty to Charles the Bald and Hincmar of Rheims.[127]

Introduction: Hincmar's world

Carloman continued to rebel; imprisoned on various occasions, in 873 he was deposed from clerical office, then given the death penalty and finally 'mercifully' blinded. Hincmar probably helped justify Carloman's sentence, writing the *De regis persona et regio ministerio* at this time.[128] This text included several sections arguing for the severe punishment by kings of wrongdoing, including even executing their own relatives. Hincmar's key source for this work was Augustine, via a collection of patristic texts made in the late 830s, possibly by Hincmar himself.[129]

Hincmar of Laon, meanwhile, was accused of multiple offences by both Charles the Bald and Hincmar in 871 and deposed at a synod in Douzy.[130] In 873 he was taken prisoner by Boso of Provence and two years later blinded.[131] Although his blinding was unprecedented, Hincmar of Laon's deposition has parallels with earlier cases such as Rothad (and even Ebbo). His sophisticated use of Pseudo-Isidorian forgeries could not withstand the combined opposition of his king and his archbishop. Charles the Bald also dealt firmly with Pope Hadrian II when he tried to intervene, angrily asserting royal rights over ecclesiastical property and implicitly threatening the pope.[132]

Without the leverage offered by Lothar II's possible divorce, Hadrian had far less influence on Frankish politics than his predecessor. He was also concerned about the future of Italy, since Louis II had only one child, a daughter; in 872 the pope sent assurances to Charles that he was his choice as successor to the empire.[133] Hincmar, however, was less successful in his own interventions with Hadrian II, failing to prevent the translation of Actard of Nantes to the archbishopric of Tours in 872.[134]

Hincmar became less important to Charles after 873, with royal favour instead being given to other bishops and also to a new breed of lay abbots and quasi-lay abbots.[135] His varying tasks as a conscientious archbishop remained demanding, however: his fourth and fifth episcopal capitularies date from 874 and he also played a leading role at the Council of Douzy 874, which condemned incestuous marriage and attacks on Church property, and also passed judgment on a nun called Duda.[136]

Hincmar again proved his worth to Charles the Bald the next year. Louis II died in August 875 and Charles promptly headed for Italy. So did his rival for the imperial succession, Louis the German's son Carloman, whom Louis II had made his heir. Meanwhile, Louis the German himself invaded West Francia, as he had done in 858.[137]

Hincmar was hostile to Charles's attempt on Italy and, following Louis's invasion of West Francia, he wrote *De fide Carolo regi servanda*, a circular letter to the bishops of his archdiocese, discussing their response. Clémentine Bernard-Valette argues that rather than implicitly accepting Louis's invasion, as has sometimes been claimed, the document represents an earlier deliberative stage, trying to establish the principles of how bishops might fulfil their key task of ensuring peace, but without labelling Louis the German outright as a usurper.[138]

Charles himself, having been crowned emperor in Rome on Christmas Day 875 by Pope John VIII, was soon back in West Francia, and Louis retreated. Lawrence Nees suggests that around this time Hincmar gave Charles a gift of ivory carvings depicting Hercules, which formed a coded warning about the dangers of imperial pride.[139] Charles was certainly influenced by his new position: he held a synod at Ponthion in June–July 876, during which he made his *fideles* swear a new oath of obedience to him. Hincmar objected to the wording, wanting the episcopal oath to promise in fidelity only what was appropriate to the bishop's *ministerium*.[140] His attitude sprang from a concern to emphasise the mutual responsibility of king and bishop; it also probably had much to do with the fact that Charles had had Ansegis of Sens appointed as primate and papal vicar for Francia. Hincmar's new subordination was graphically symbolised by Ansegis being seated nearer to Charles at the synod than his former superior. Hincmar's annal for the year is scathing both about the synod and Charles' unsuccessful attack on East Francia after Louis the German's death in August 876.[141]

When Charles planned a second trip to Italy, Hincmar drew up one or more memoranda in his name for presentation to John VIII on dealing with misbehaving priests.[142] However, Charles's detailed arrangements for his absence, in the Capitulary of Quierzy from June 877, did not include Hincmar in the group of Charles' confidants overseeing Louis the Stammerer's actions.[143] Perhaps that is why Hincmar dwells with relish on Charles's death in Italy in October before meeting the pope, recounting how the emperor died in 'a wretched little hut' and discussing the stench of his corpse.[144] Probably in late 877, Hincmar wrote an account of a vision of the afterlife allegedly seen by a man called Bernold: Charles (called king rather than emperor) was being gnawed by worms, because he had not listened to Hincmar's good advice.[145]

Introduction: Hincmar's world

The wise old man, 877–882

Unfortunately for Hincmar, Charles's successors did not consistently listen to him either. Louis the Stammerer seems to have sought Hincmar's advice early on in his reign, and Hincmar played an important role in Louis's coronation in December 877. But Louis had a number of other counsellors, and decisions he made (such as not to intervene in Italy as John VIII wanted) may have been influenced by factors other than Hincmar's advice.[146] When Louis became seriously ill by the summer of 878 and died in April 879, Hincmar was not among those appointed as guardians of his sons, Louis III, then aged between fourteen and sixteen, and Carloman, aged thirteen. Hincmar probably also played little part in the arrangements by which the succession of Louis III and Carloman was ensured, and his account of these events is misleading: he accuses Gauzlin, abbot of St-Denis, of treachery in turning to Louis the Younger, when Gauzlin was actually ensuring that both brothers received a share in the kingdom.[147]

If Hincmar had lost the role in diplomatic negotiations he had kept until 878, he was still keen to advise the young kings and to ensure the Church was run correctly. The letter he composed to Louis from the Council of Fismes in April 881 has been described as his political testament, summarising Hincmar's ideas on the relations of the two powers, kings and bishops, and setting up a contrast between wise old counsellors, such as Hincmar, and the young king.[148] Hincmar also provoked a crisis by his actions at this synod concerning the vacant see of Beauvais. The clergy and people of Beauvais had chosen several unsuitable candidates in succession; Hincmar now planned, on dubious canonical authority, for a commission of bishops to select a new candidate. When Louis III instead installed Odacer in the see, Hincmar was able to force the new bishop out.[149]

Hincmar had lost none of his combativeness in his old age, nor his enthusiasm for writing: two texts from 882 sum up his preoccupations. As Isaïa shows, Hincmar's *Vita Remigii*, the final version of which was completed at this point, summarises Hincmar's views on theology and Church order, in the figure of the bishop as lawmaker.[150] Hincmar's last work, *De ordine palatii*, was written for Carloman in the autumn of 882, after his brother Louis III had died and he had succeeded to the whole of West Francia. Hincmar presents a vision of the ideal court (with a prominent role for a cleric like himself as arch-chaplain) and claimed to have learned about such matters from Adalard, sixty years earlier.[151]

Hincmar here consciously played on being a link to an earlier, better time, reflected also in his preference for citing the capitularies of Charlemagne and Louis the Pious over those of later kings.[152] His last actions, as described in his own annals, show his determined quality: since the church of Rheims' own armed contingent were away supporting Carloman, when the Vikings attacked Rheims, he had to escape the city by night, taking with him two vital resources: the relics of Remigius and the treasure of Rheims. Although Hincmar was so weak he had to be carried in a portable chair, he was still writing until he died in December 882.[153] Nothing less than death was able to stop Hincmar from expressing his opinions.

Hincmar's world

The arrangement of chapters in this volume corresponds broadly to key themes in previous research on Hincmar. His activities as an annalist and historian have long been analysed.[154] Janet Nelson, who has studied Hincmar's political thought for more than forty years, reflects on the complex links between his historical ideas and his personal history, arguing for the historical feeling behind many of Hincmar's texts. She sees the *Annales Bertiniani* specifically as bursting out of the annalistic genre to become something more artful.[155] Christine Kleinjung, meanwhile, shows us a more awkward side of the *Annales Bertiniani* for the modern historian, revealing how much the annals hide about one specific controversy in Hincmar's life: his conflict with his nephew Hincmar of Laon.[156]

Hincmar's political role is treated in the next three chapters, building on numerous earlier studies. Scholarly interest in Hincmar has traditionally focused on his political writings, seen as proving the capacity of Carolingian authors for theoretical analysis and as prefiguring later discussions of the relations between the state, the 'national' Church and the papacy.[157] His role in Lothar II's divorce has been examined in detail;[158] studies of Charles the Bald's reign also invariably feature him prominently.[159] The chapters here deal with less familiar royal relationships and political texts. Elina Screen and Margaret McCarthy show Hincmar at two ends of his career: the newly made archbishop having to negotiate his way between two masters, and the old but underappreciated statesman of Louis

Introduction: Hincmar's world

the Stammerer's reign.[160] They provide important case studies on how Hincmar tried, successfully or unsuccessfully, to gain and use political influence and show the highly contingent factors involved. Hincmar was not the only political player in the circle of these rulers, and events outside his control could also have a major impact.

Clémentine Bernard-Valette reveals Hincmar in the act of political deliberation, discussing the two invasions by Louis the German of Charles's kingdom in 858 and 875 and the texts Hincmar produced in response. Hincmar's text *De fide Carolo regi servanda* from 875 has been little studied; Bernard-Valette provides the first detailed analysis of it, arguing for it as a work in progress, trying to define rules for the situation in which Hincmar and the other bishops found themselves.[161]

The probable status of *De fide* as a work in progress links this text to another frequent concern of scholarship on Hincmar: his use of sources and especially normative sources. Devisse dedicated large parts of his research on Hincmar to tracing Hincmar's references, and recent editions of Hincmar's works have carried out similar explorations.[162] There has long been interest in his falsification of texts;[163] recent studies have also demonstrated how he collected extracts from historical, patristic and legal sources and then repeatedly reworked them.[164]

Three chapters of the book reflect this scholarly interest in Hincmar's use of 'law' in its broadest sense of authoritative norms. Simon Corcoran explores the difficulties Hincmar had in acquiring access to sources of Roman law; he also indicates briefly how Hincmar used or misused them to further his own ends.[165] Philip Depreux updates Devisse's study of Hincmar's citation of capitularies, looking at the specific contexts in which Hincmar chose to use either 'old' or contemporary texts.[166]

Marie-Céline Isaïa's chapter shows a different form of 'law', again indicating how porous the boundaries of genre can be. Hincmar's *Vita Remigii* is not simply an imaginative work of hagiography. It is also a handbook of theology, a 'mirror for a bishop' and a demonstration of the bishop as law-maker, able to go beyond existing norms to reflect God's will.[167]

Jean Devisse saw Hincmar as a profound analyst of social problems,[168] and one recent strand of research has explored Hincmar's reaction to a variety of aspects of lay life.[169] Sylvie Joye's chapter highlights one aspect of this, developing recent work on marriage and gender which draws on Hincmar's treatise *De raptu*.[170] This treatise has sometimes been considered in isolation;[171] Joye instead connects it to Hincmar's wider concerns about kingship. She shows how tightly the authority of kings and fathers was linked, the personal becoming profoundly political. Josiane Barbier highlights a different aspect of Hincmar's concern about the problems of this world: his determination to ensure the effective administration of Church property. There has been considerable recent interest in Carolingian administration and the use of polyptychs (estate surveys) as administrative documents.[172] Barbier adds to our knowledge of Hincmar as an administrator by showing him personally as a reader and user of this survey.[173]

The final section of the book deals with Hincmar and the Church, and this too touches on all levels of society. Charles West reveals Hincmar's concerns with the nitty-gritty of individual parish life both in theory and practice, demonstrating how the parish mattered to Hincmar in a way that it did not to later Church reformers.[174] Mayke de Jong discusses a disciplinary case that connects such local concerns to the papacy itself: the affair of the murderous priest Trising, who appealed to Hadrian II. De Jong also provides her own contribution to the recently renewed study of the origins and impact of the Pseudo-Isidorian forgeries.[175]

Hincmar's theological views have also been of considerable interest to scholars.[176] Matthew Gillis's chapter concentrates on one controversy in which he became involved: Gottschalk of Orbais' teachings on double predestination. David Ganz brought scholarship on Gottschalk out of the purely theological realm, connecting his teaching with the charged political atmosphere of the time.[177] Gillis now builds on this and other recent studies of Gottschalk to give us the latest understanding of this controversial man, demonstrating how difficult Hincmar and the Frankish Church found it to deal with a real-life heretic.[178] The personal and the political, Hincmar's life and his thought, are once again closely entangled.

Carolingian culture

The individual chapters in this book thus provide insights into many different aspects of Hincmar's life and work. Perhaps more important, however, is what the connections between the chapters show us about Hincmar and his society. Readers are likely to be struck by a number of recurring themes: this introduction will highlight a few.

Introduction: Hincmar's world

Firstly, discussions of surviving manuscripts (and their copies) show how Hincmar used the same working practices across many different types of text: the same note marks appear in the polyptych of St-Remi as in manuscripts where Hincmar was highlighting key theological or legal passages.[179] Corcoran suggests that Hincmar may not have had long-term access to some manuscripts, which would explain his concern to compile handy dossiers.[180] Hincmar's use and re-use of material continued throughout his career. Isaïa discusses Hincmar's copying of sections on predestination written more than twenty years earlier in the *Vita Remigii*, while the Council of Fismes in 881 drew on material Hincmar had collected for a work of his on attacks on Church property in 857.[181]

Hincmar was also a notoriously creative user and reworker of texts. Depreux points out how his choice of whether to cite older or more recent capitularies depends on the effect he wants to have on royal recipients, while Corcoran describes Hincmar as using texts like a lawyer, to ensure the outcome that he wanted.[182] Hincmar was hardly the only ninth-century intellectual to do so: the Pseudo-Isidore corpus was put to inventive use by a number of different parties.[183] Letters attributed to Leo IV were probably tampered with or forged by supporters of Hincmar, but also by his opponents.[184] This book reinstates Hincmar within a wider context of scholarly men 'fighting with words', sometimes unscrupulously. It shows us a world with multiple sources of authority, which ingenious individuals might be able to play off against one another.

Studies of Carolingian political culture have been transformed by Mayke de Jong's work on the 'penitential state'. Her research goes beyond polarised views – seeing ninth-century Francia as marked by either ideological conflicts or simple *Realpolitik* – to emphasise how shared norms of correct political conduct could be used as propaganda weapons, with each side in the civil wars of the 830s endeavouring to claim the moral high ground.[185] Hincmar, too, knew how to make use of such widely accepted norms. Kleinjung demonstrates how he sought to exploit expected standards of episcopal behaviour to position Hincmar of Laon as a 'bad bishop';[186] and the 'Quierzy letter' from 858 shows how skilfully Hincmar could use biblical norms about good kingship to block Louis the German's attempted takeover of West Francia.[187]

Many of Hincmar's disputes, however, were not solely concerned with the manipulation of well-established norms. The ninth century was a fruitful period for the creation of new models for particular social roles, such as bishops or married couples, but other issues were still being worked out.[188] Bernard-Valette shows Hincmar considering how bishops should deal with the *fait accompli* of a usurping king.[189] West discusses how Hincmar developed new norms for parish life, explaining away previous canonical prohibitions on burial within church.[190] And in the *Vita Remigii*, Hincmar shows us the saint as a man who can move beyond the letter of the law (on clerics doing penance) because of his holiness.[191]

Such creative interpretations of previous precedents could be vital to political, theological and legal battles. The case studies in this book give us a new insight into how claims to authority could be created and deployed. It was not only Hincmar who endeavoured to justify his actions via examples from the past. Battles of texts are visible with Hincmar of Laon and Gottschalk, with acrimonious accusations on all sides of the incorrect interpretation of key passages. Hincmar was particularly prone to switching between claiming that his opponents were ignorant and accusing them of being too clever by half.[192] Histories were created and recreated: the Pseudo-Isidore complex of forgeries imagined an entire previous history of the papacy and its decisions. Some areas of history, such as the events surrounding the deposition of Ebbo, were repeatedly contested, while Hincmar literally rewrote history when he got his hands on Prudentius's copy of the Annals of St-Bertin.[193]

Historical justifications, however, could also take forms beyond the purely textual. There was an important role for exemplary figures: Hincmar drew heavily on historical precedents and eventually became himself almost a living history lesson. In the 870s and 880s he could talk about Charlemagne and Louis the Pious in a way that few other people could.[194] He could reach back even further, to predecessor bishops as examples: Ambrose of Milan, St Remigius and the apostles themselves.[195] Yet Hincmar's self-identification with previous Christian leaders could potentially be trumped by his opponents; the pope was the successor to St Peter himself, as Nicholas I repeatedly pointed out. Most audacious of all such identifications, however, was Gottschalk's attempt to imitate the martyrs Crispin and Crispinian, by undergoing an ordeal similar to theirs.[196] Demonstrating his personal holiness in this dramatic but explicable way offered Gottschalk the prospect of bypassing all conventional structures of authority.

Gottschalk's offer reminds us of the intensely personal nature of Carolingian political culture. Other chapters show us the same aspect in less dramatic ways. McCarthy and Screen demonstrate the importance of both physical proximity to the ruler and letters sent either directly or via a helpful intermediary.[197] Hincmar's political networks were extensive throughout the Frankish kingdoms, but could not be taken for granted.[198] Screen suggests that by 852 he needed to extend his connections to a new generation of contacts, and in the 870s Charles the Bald and Louis the Stammerer were increasingly looking to other advisers besides Hincmar.[199] Networks sustaining and connecting Hincmar's opponents are also sometimes visible, such as the connections between Gottschalk's supporters and the clerics disputably ordained by Ebbo.[200] Opposition to Hincmar could be notably long-lasting: Gottschalk and Hincmar of Laon still had supporters even after their official downfall.[201]

Yet we should not reduce political effectiveness to a simple matter of individuals' personalities. Lothar I's acceptance of Hincmar after his initial hostility had more to do with events in Italy than any newly formed appreciation of Hincmar's character.[202] Charles the Bald's changing relationship with Hincmar was not simply a matter of the king failing to appreciate Hincmar's 'principled' stand on particular issues. Alliances and policies were not static: kings and popes reacted speedily to new opportunities, such as death or disaster befalling another ruler, and would-be royal advisers had to be ready to provide appropriate moral advice for all situations.

Carolingian society

Hincmar's political activities and his vast written output both had the broad aim of preserving a social order that he saw as divinely inspired. This was a patriarchal, hierarchical system that put noble male clerics like himself near the top of the social pyramid.[203] What is noteworthy is how much concern Hincmar had for all levels of this social order. Small things mattered to him, such as ensuring that the monastic estate of Courtisols recorded the status of all the unfree on the estate and retained their labour.[204] Although Hincmar may have had a direct material interest in that case, he was equally concerned to prevent the abduction of young women and to ensure that suitable priests were provided for relatively minor parish churches.[205] Why did such trivia matter to a man who corresponded with popes and kings?

One answer was that kings and popes themselves might become involved in such affairs, as with the delinquent priest Trising.[206] More significant, however was the fact that Carolingian religious and social theories linked together the actions of all members of society. The parish and its priest was a microcosm of the diocese with its bishop.[207] Fathers were analogous to kings and must have their rights over their dependants upheld in the same way.[208] The bishop himself was answerable to God for the salvation of all the Christian people in his care, including the king.[209]

It is this inextricable linking of the whole of society that explains both Hincmar's obsession with parish order and Carolingian fears of heresy. Gottschalk's theological theories might turn his 'simple' hearers away from the good works on earth that helped to ensure their place in heaven. Hincmar could not tolerate those who led others astray or brought the Church into disrepute, just as Gottschalk, in turn, could not cease proclaiming the message of God that had been entrusted to him.[210] Moral responsibility could never be delegated: the sins of subordinates were held against kings as well as bishops. This intense moral concern with the whole of society is already visible under Charlemagne and is also characteristic of Louis the Pious' penitential state.[211] As West points out, it contrasts with a far more *laissez-faire* attitude to the lower-level structures of the Church and parish life by the time of the eleventh-century reforms.[212]

Despite Hincmar's emphasis on the superiority of bishops to kings and the laity generally, his view of society retained a key role for lay noblemen and he could be surprisingly positive towards them and secular life generally. His network of correspondents included a number of *illustri viri* and he was happy to acknowledge laymen's proprietary rights in churches and their judgments on certain matters, such as matrimonial disputes.[213] Hincmar also accepted the Church's role in supplying troops to the army, even if there is little evidence that he himself led them into battle, as some other bishops and abbots did.[214] In a world where the earthly and heavenly cities were intermixed, Hincmar could refer to imperial laws with which he agreed as 'sacred' and his discussions could blur the lines between synods and assemblies.[215]

The Carolingian social and political order was maintained partly through such regular meetings, which Hincmar discusses in *De ordine palatii*.[216] Contemporary political ideology often saw social order as maintained via personal bonds formalised through rituals. The values

Introduction: Hincmar's world

of *fides* (faith) and consensus, with the use of the oath, supposedly linked members of society at all levels, from the married couple to the agreements of kings and magnates.[217] Hincmar repeatedly recorded the texts of oaths (and argued about their content); he stressed the binding force of an agreement that a king had made with his own hand.[218] Disorder and disobedience had to be combated wherever they were found, from the serf to the ruler.

Hincmar's obsession with demanding order may reflect the practical difficulty in achieving this. Elite men from popes and kings downwards could find it surprisingly hard to enforce their will in practice, especially at a distance. Gottschalk demonstrated the problems in dealing effectively with long-running defiance of episcopal authority.[219] Kings, too, were vulnerable to swings of fate, as Charles the Bald's career showed. Yet there was also a peculiar sort of equilibrium in ninth-century Frankish politics. During the nearly sixty years of Hincmar's active political life (c. 825–882), despite repeated infighting within the dynasty, only one Carolingian ruler was ever permanently removed from his kingdom;[220] reversals of fortune and restorations were far more frequent.

The increasing involvement of the papacy north of the Alps also made the permanent settlement of disputes more difficult. An appeal to Rome might involve months of travel and negotiations. Moreover, since the average length of a papal reign between 827 and 882 was only around eight years,[221] there was often the opportunity for a party disappointed by one pope to appeal to his successor.[222] The emphasis on consensus and reconciliation in Carolingian politics should not be seen as indicating a lack of conflict; statements about consensus were themselves often political propaganda.[223] Formal reconciliations may have been a necessary way of putting a positive gloss on situations where the balance of power allowed few complete victories. Hincmar's urge to settle scores with dead opponents probably reflects the frustration he felt at seldom being able to end any matter to his complete satisfaction during their lifetime.[224]

Hincmar's legacy

Hincmar dominated the second half of the ninth century (or at least the Hincmar-centred view we have of it), but his long-term impact was surprisingly slight, beyond his influence on Flodoard. His tomb, placed near to the body of St Remigius at his own command, is long lost;[225] supposed details of its sculpture are now seen instead as twelfth-century work.[226] A number of manuscripts commissioned or owned by Hincmar survive.[227] However his own works were relatively neglected and few later copies survive, although he did find some distinguished readers.[228]

Only two of his texts found wider circulation: *De cavendis vitiis*, the lay mirror he wrote for Charles the Bald, and the *Vita Remigii*.[229] The most likely reason for this relative lack of success is that Hincmar's works are so much of his time that they were difficult to detach from it. Unlike an author like Alcuin, who dealt in eternal (if banal) pieties, Hincmar's works largely dealt with specific, contemporary problems. Even the *Vita Remigii* survived only in versions that removed some of Hincmar's most distinctive contributions: it was wanted as straightforward hagiography, not as the wide-ranging hybrid of saintly life and clerical handbook that Hincmar had created.[230]

Some aspects of Hincmar's work did remain significant: certain of his (sometimes dubious) citations of canons and decisions on cases became incorporated into the canon law that developed from the eleventh century.[231] More than that, he has profoundly shaped our view of the early Middle Ages itself: much scholarship on Charles Martel, for example, has been influenced by Hincmar's negative description.[232] Similarly, St Remigius may overshadow Hincmar in the history of Rheims, but it is often Hincmar's image of Remigius that is celebrated.[233] Hincmar's 'historical' ideals were also preserved via rituals. As Janet Nelson observed, 'In 1825, Charles X, the last of the Bourbons, was anointed at Rheims with the holy oil which Hincmar had been the first to record as heaven-sent; and the coronation-prayer used was Hincmar's.'[234] Hincmar's legacy is as much the image of the early medieval world he created as any specific political and religious achievements of his own. For this reason, as well as looking through Hincmar's texts, we need also to look more carefully at Hincmar himself. It is only by connecting together his life and work that we can more fully understand the world he depicts so vividly.

Notes

1 Flodoard, *HRE*. The third book of four is entirely dedicated to Hincmar and occupies more than 40% of the pages in the MGH edition. On Flodoard and his history, see M. Sot, *Un historien et son église au X*^{e}

Introduction: Hincmar's world

siècle: Flodoard de Reims (Paris, 1993); pp. 486-739 are predominantly about Flodoard's account of Hincmar.

2 The register of Schrörs, *Hinkmar*, pp. 512-88 remains basic for the detailed chronology, even though some of his dating has now been questioned. See also M. Stratmann, 'Briefe an Hinkmar von Reims', *DA*, 48 (1992), 37-81.

3 On Frankish history writing in general, see Y. Hen and M. Innes, eds, *The Uses of the Past in the Early Middle Ages* (Cambridge, 2000); R. McKitterick, *History and Memory in the Carolingian World* (Cambridge, 2004).

4 J. L. Nelson, 'Ninth-century knighthood: the evidence of Nithard', in C. Harper-Bill, C. J. Holdsworth and J. L. Nelson, eds, *Studies in Medieval History presented to R. Allen Brown* (Woodbridge, Suffolk, 1989), pp. 255-66 at p. 256.

5 C. Rider, *Magic and Impotence in the Middle Ages* (Oxford, 2006), pp. 31-42; C. West, 'Lordship in ninth-century Francia: the case of Bishop Hincmar of Laon and his followers', *Past and Present*, 226 (2015), 3-40; F. R. Herrmann and B. M. Speer, 'Facing the accuser: ancient and medieval precursors of the confrontation clause', *Virginia Journal of International Law*, 34 (1993-94), 481-552.

6 H. Schrörs, *Hinkmar, Erzbischof von Reims: sein Leben und seine Schriften* (Freiburg im Breisgau, 1884) [hereafter Schrörs, *Hinkmar*]; J. Devisse, *Hincmar, archevêque de Reims, 845-882*, 3 vols (Geneva, 1975-76) [hereafter Devisse, *Hincmar*].

7 On the overlap of such issues, see e.g. Hincmar's letter to Nicholas I cited below, p. 13.

8 On his family, see Schrörs, *Hinkmar*, pp. 9-10; Devisse, *Hincmar*, II, pp. 1096-7; Nelson, Chapter 2, pp. 46, 52. On Hincmar's life before 840, see Schrörs, *Hinkmar*, pp. 10-25; Devisse, *Hincmar*, II, pp. 1089-94; L. Böhringer, 'Einleitung', in Hincmar of Rheims, *De Divortio Lotharii regis et Theutbergae reginae*, ed. L. Böhringer, MGH *Conc.* IV, Supplementum 1 (Hanover, 1992), pp. 1-98 at pp. 1-2; Nelson, Chapter 2, pp. 44-5.

9 Hincmar, Epistola 198, ed. E. Perels, MGH *Epp.* 8, p. 210.

10 On oblates, see M. de Jong, *In Samuel's Image: Child Oblation in the Early Medieval West* (Leiden, 1996).

11 On Hilduin, see Ph. Depreux, *Prosopographie de l'entourage de Louis le Pieux (781-840)* (Sigmaringen, 1997), pp. 250-6; A. L. Taylor, *Epic Lives and Monasticism in the Middle Ages, 800-1050* (New York, 2013), pp. 55-63.

12 On Adalard, see B. Kasten, *Adalhard von Corbie: die Biographie eines karolingischen Politikers und Klostervorstehers* (Düsseldorf, 1986).

13 M. de Jong, *The Penitential State: Authority and Atonement in the Age of*

Louis the Pious, 814–840 (Cambridge, 2009), pp. 122–31. On Hincmar's possible presence at Attigny, see Böhringer, 'Einleitung', p. 1, Nelson, Chapter 2, pp. 44–5.

14 P. Buc, 'Text and ritual in ninth-century political culture: Rome, 864', in G. Althoff, J. Fried and P. J. Geary, eds, *Medieval Concepts of the Past: Ritual, Memory, Historiography* (Cambridge, 2002), pp. 123–38, S. MacLean, 'Ritual, misunderstanding, and the contest for meaning: representations of the disrupted royal assembly at Frankfurt (873)', in B. Weiler and S. MacLean, eds, *Representations of Power in Medieval Germany 800–1500* (Turnhout, 2006), pp. 97–119.

15 de Jong, *Penitential State*, p. 126.

16 S. Patzold, *Episcopus: Wissen über Bischöfe im Frankenreich des späten 8. bis frühen 10. Jahrhunderts* (Ostfildern, 2008), pp. 105–84.

17 Patzold, *Episcopus*, pp. 149–68; de Jong, *Penitential State*, pp. 176–84. On Hincmar's political theories, see below, p. 39, n.157.

18 de Jong, *Penitential State*, p. 43.

19 *Juramentum quod Hincmarus Archiepiscopus edere jussus est apud Pontigonem, PL* 125, col. 1128: 'pater vester ... qui mihi per octo circiter annos secreta sua indubitanter credidit.' Böhringer, 'Einleitung', p. 1, points out that the eight years could include periods both before and after 829–30, rather than referring to a single extended stay at court.

20 Hincmar, Epistola 198, MGH *Epp.* 8, p. 210: 'Conversis autem ad regularem vitam et habitum fratribus in monasterio sancti Dionysii, ubi nutritus fueram, in illud saeculum fugiens sine spe vel appetitu episcopatus aut alicuius praelationis diutius degui et exinde adsumptus familiaribus obsequiis praefati imperatoris ac episcoporum conventibus pro sola oboedientia mihi iniuncta inserviens post aliquot annos monasterii quietem repetii. A quo peccatis meis exigentibus rupto anchorae fune, quo me in portu neglegenter devinxeram, sub obtentu salutis plurimorum persuasus hortamentis eorum, quibus facilius, quam mihi necesse foret, credidi, ad tempestates maris magni et spatiosi periculosissime sum reiactatus.'

21 Flodoard, *HRE* III-1, pp. 190–1; Sot, *Un historien*, p. 490.

22 de Jong, *Penitential State*, pp. 46–51, 214–52.

23 Flodoard, *HRE* III-1, p. 191.

24 de Jong, *Penitential State*, pp. 252–9; C. M. Booker, *Past Convictions: the Penance of Louis the Pious and the Decline of the Carolingians* (Philadelphia, 2009), pp. 183–203. Hincmar was present at this event: see Böhringer, 'Einleitung', pp. 1–2.

25 See below, p. 15.

26 Devisse, *Hincmar*, II, p. 1092.

27 Flodoard, *HRE* III-1, p. 191; J.-F. Goudesenne, 'La musique de l'ancien office de saint Remi retrouvée (VIIIe-IXe siècles)', in M. Rouche, ed.,

Clovis, histoire et mémoire, 2 vols (Paris, 1997), II, pp. 103–28 at p. 111; Devisse, *Hincmar*, II, p. 1007.
28 Devisse, *Hincmar*, II, p. 1094.
29 Nithard, *Historiarum libri quattuor*, ed. P. Lauer, *Nithard, Histoire des fils de Louis le Pieux* (Paris, 1964).
30 Flodoard, *HRE* III-1, p. 191 says he was given control (*regimen*) of both Notre-Dame in Compiègne and St-Germer-du-Fly near Beauvais. The former is implausible, since it was only founded later; the latter is confirmed by a letter of Hincmar to Charles the Bald (Flodoard, *HRE* III-18, p. 256).
31 Nelson, Chapter 2, p. 56, n.13. On Fontenoy, see J. Gillingham, 'Fontenoy and after: pursuing enemies to death in France between the ninth and eleventh centuries', in D. Ganz and P. Fouracre, eds, *Frankland: the Franks and the World of the Early Middle Ages: Essays in Honour of Dame Jinty Nelson* (Manchester, 2008), pp. 242–65.
32 On the manuscript, see G. Laehr, 'Ein karolingischer Konzilsbrief und der Fürstenspiegel Hincmars von Reims', *Neues Archiv der Gesellschaft für ältere deutsche Geschichtskunde*, 50 (1935), 106–34; H. H. Anton, *Fürstenspiegel und Herrscherethos in der Karolingerzeit* (Bonn, 1968), pp. 221–31. My thanks to Phillip Wynn for discussions on this text and sending me copies of his forthcoming work.
33 Patzold, *Episcopus*, pp. 316–21; Nelson, Chapter 2, pp. 47–8; Gillis, Chapter 13, pp. 258–60.
34 On the geography and divisions of the province of Rheims, see Sot, *Un historien*, pp. 17–42.
35 J. L. Nelson, 'Public *Histories* and private history in the work of Nithard', *Speculum*, 60 (1985), 251–93 at 281.
36 J. L. Nelson, *Charles the Bald* (London, 1992), pp. 135–44.
37 *Ibid.*, p. 142.
38 J. L. Nelson, 'The intellectual in politics: context, content and authorship in the capitulary of Coulaines, November 843', in L. Smith and B. Ward, eds, *Intellectual Life in the Middle Ages: Essays Presented to Margaret Gibson* (London, 1992), pp. 1–14 at p. 5.
39 Nelson, Chapter 2, pp. 45–6. Wilfried Hartmann (in his introduction to Council of Coulaines, 843, MGH *Conc.* III, no. 3, p. 10) rejects Hincmar's involvement in Coulaines, but this makes too much of Hincmar's vague statement (see above, p. 4) that he had remained in St-Denis after service with Louis the Pious; as Lupus' involvement with Charles shows, the boundaries of monastic life could be fairly flexible.
40 Nelson, 'Intellectual in politics', at p. 11; Council of Ver, 844, MGH *Conc.* III, no. 7, p. 36.
41 Council of Ver, 844, MGH *Conc.* III, p. 42, c. 9.
42 Hincmar, Epistolae 4, 12, 13, MGH *Epp.* 8, pp. 2, 4–6. Hincmar's new

position as archbishop meant that he in turn was approached by Lupus of Ferrières seeking help in reclaiming the cell of St Josse (Lupus, Epistolae 42, 44, ed. E. Dümmler, MGH *Epp.* 6, pp. 49-52).
43 Barbier, Chapter 11, pp. 218-21.
44 Screen, Chapter 4, pp. 80-3.
45 Hincmar, *De ordine palatii*, ed. T. Gross and R. Schieffer, MGH *Fontes iuris* 3 (Hanover, 1980), p. 66, c. 18, stresses the need for royal advisers to come from a variety of regions.
46 Gillis, Chapter 13.
47 Hincmar, *Ad reclusos et simplices in Remensi parrochia contra Gothescalcum*, ed. W. Gundlach, 'Zwei Schriften des Erzbischofs Hinkmar von Reims', *Zeitschrift für Kirchengeschichte*, 10 (1889), 258-310; Hincmar, *De praedestinatione Dei*, PL 125, cols 65-474. On the lost treatise, see Devisse, *Hincmar*, I, pp. 214-219.
48 Nelson, Chapter 2, p. 47.
49 Council of Valence, 855, MGH *Conc.* III, no. 33, p. 347.
50 D. Jasper and H. Fuhrmann, *Papal Letters in the Early Middle Ages* (Washington DC, 2001), pp. 173-4; O. Schneider, *Erzbischof Hinkmar und die Folgen: der vierhundertjährige Weg historischer Erinnerungsbilder von Reims nach Trier* (Berlin, 2010), p. 87; Hincmar, Epistola 58, p. 33.
51 de Jong, Chapter 14, pp. 273-5; Jasper and Fuhrmann, *Papal Letters*, p. 170.
52 E. Knibbs, 'The interpolated Hispana and the origins of Pseudo-Isidore', *Zeitschrift der Savigny-Stiftung für Rechtsgeschichte, Kanonistische Abteilung*, 99 (2013), 1-71 at 62-3; de Jong, Chapter 14, p. 276.
53 Council of Soissons, 853, MGH *Conc.* III, no. 27, pp. 253-93.
54 Gillis, Chapter 13, p. 258.
55 Fuhrmann, 'The Pseudo-Isidorian forgeries', at pp. 170-7.
56 de Jong, Chapter 14, pp. 276-7.
57 M.-C. Isaïa, *Remi de Reims: mémoire d'un saint, histoire d'une Église* (Paris, 2010), pp. 419-31, 452-64. On Hincmar's liturgical and poetic composition for these events see also Goudesenne, 'Musique', at pp. 110-20.
58 M. Stratmann, *Hinkmar von Reims als Verwalter von Bistum und Kirchenprovinz* (Sigmaringen, 1991); C. van Rhijn, *Shepherds of the Lord: Priests and Episcopal Statutes in the Carolingian Period* (Turnhout, 2007).
59 Bishops: H. G. J. Beck, 'The selection of bishops suffragan to Hincmar of Rheims, 845-882', *Catholic Historical Review*, 45 (1959), 273-308; Stratmann, *Hinkmar als Verwalter*, pp. 14-19; Fulcric: R. Stone, '"Bound from either side": the limits of power in Carolingian marriage disputes, 840-870', *Gender and History*, 19 (2007), 467-82; Screen, Chapter 4, pp. 82-3.
60 Hincmar, Epistola 79, MGH *Epp.* 8, p. 40 from 845-56. On Carolingian

Introduction: Hincmar's world

  ideas of godparenthood, see J. H. Lynch, *Godparents and Kinship in Early Medieval Europe* (Princeton, 1986).
61 Monk: Hincmar, Epistolae 190–1, MGH *Epp.* 8, p. 201, from 858–67; *ministerialis*: Epistolae 53–4, p. 32.
62 Devisse, *Hincmar*, I, pp. 354–60, II, p. 725, wanting to stress Hincmar's independent nature, sees Hincmar as having only short periods of closeness to Charles, but this is contradicted by the frequent tasks he carried out for the king. J. L. Nelson, 'The "Annals of St Bertin"', in M. T. Gibson and J. L. Nelson, eds, *Charles the Bald: Court and Kingdom*, 2nd revd edn (Aldershot, 1990), pp. 23–40 at pp. 37–8, sees only brief periods of criticism and estrangement from Charles in 865–66 and 876, while N. Staubach, *Das Herrscherbild Karls des Kahlen: Formen und Funktionen monarchischer Repräsentation im früheren Mittelalter* (Münster, 1982), pp. 98–9 argues for Hincmar's influence on Charles's 'foreign' policy in 858–69. As McCarthy, Chapter 6, pp. 110–12, 123 shows, the question of the influence of any individual is not a straightforward one.
63 On Hincmar's coronation ordines and ideas of royal ritual generally, see R. A. Jackson, ed., *Ordines coronationis Franciae. Texts and Ordines for the Coronation of Frankish and French Kings and Queens in the Middle Ages*, 2 vols (Philadelphia, 1995–2000), I, pp. 73–123; J. L. Nelson, 'Early medieval rites of queen-making and the shaping of medieval queenship', in A. Duggan, ed., *Queens and Queenship in Medieval Europe*, Proceedings of a conference held at King's College London, April 1995 (Woodbridge, Suffolk, 1997), pp. 301–15; J. L. Nelson, 'Hincmar of Reims on king-making: the evidence of the Annals of St Bertin, 861–882' in *Rulers and Ruling Families in Early Medieval Europe: Alfred, Charles the Bald and Others* (Aldershot, 1999), XVII, pp. 16–34.
64 Council of Quierzy, 857, MGH *Conc.* III, no. 38, pp. 392–6; Devisse, *Hincmar*, I, pp. 294–303.
65 Hincmar, *Collectio de ecclesiis et capellis*, ed. M. Stratmann, MGH *Fontes iuris*, 14 (Hanover, 1990). C. West, *Reframing the Feudal Revolution: Political and Social Transformation Between Marne and Moselle, c. 800–c. 1100* (Cambridge, 2013), p. 71, describes the Collectio as 'an extended gloss on *potestas episcopi*'. On the text, see also Ph. Depreux and C. Treffort, 'La paroisse dans le *De ecclesiis et capellis* d'Hincmar de Reims. L'énonciation d'une norme à partir de la pratique?', *Médiévales*, 48 (2005), 141–8; S. Wood, *The Proprietary Church in the Medieval West* (Oxford, 2006), pp. 804–12.
66 Council of Quierzy, 858, MGH *Conc.* III, no. 41, pp. 403–27; Bernard-Valette, Chapter 5, pp. 94–5; Devisse, *Hincmar*, I, pp. 313–27, and Staubach, *Herrscherbild*, pp. 103–13, give extended discussions of the letter.
67 Nelson, *Charles the Bald*, pp. 188–90; E. J. Goldberg, *Struggle for Empire:*

Kingship and Conflict under Louis the German, 817–876 (Ithaca, 2006), pp. 250–8.
68 *AB* s.a. 857, 858, 860, pp. 74, 78, 82 (trans. Nelson, pp. 84, 87, 92). On the case, see S. Airlie, 'Private bodies and the body politic in the divorce case of Lothar II', *Past and Present*, 161 (1998), 3–38; K. Heidecker, *The Divorce of Lothar II: Christian Marriage and Political Power in the Carolingian World*, trans. T. M. Guest (Ithaca, 2010); *On the Divorce of King Lothar and Queen Theutberga, by Hincmar of Rheims*, trans. R. Stone and C. West (Manchester, forthcoming).
69 Hincmar, *De divortio Lotharii regis et Theutbergae reginae*, ed. L. Böhringer, MGH *Conc.* IV, Supplementum 1 (Hanover, 1992).
70 Hincmar, Epistolae 135–6, MGH *Epp.* 8, pp. 81–107; Council of Tusey, 860, MGH *Conc.* IV, no. 3, pp. 12-13. On the cases see Stone, 'Bound'; Stone and West, *On the Divorce of King Lothar*.
71 Council of Tusey, 860, MGH *Conc.* IV, no. 3, p. 13.
72 Nelson, 'Annals'.
73 Kleinjung, Chapter 3.
74 Goldberg, *Struggle*, pp. 264-79.
75 Hincmar in *AB* s.a. 861, p. 87 (trans. Nelson, p. 96) condemns Charles's actions.
76 Heidecker, *Divorce*, pp. 100–19.
77 *AB* s.a. 862, pp. 87–8, 90–1 (trans. Nelson, pp. 97–100).
78 Nelson, *Charles the Bald*, pp. 209–10.
79 See C. Brühl, 'Hinkmariana II: Hinkmar im Widerstreit von kanonischen Recht und Politik in Ehefragen', *DA*, 20 (1964), 55–77; McCarthy, Chapter 6, pp. 112–14.
80 The attempts by Devisse, *Hincmar*, I, pp. 436–9, to justify Hincmar's behaviour are unconvincing. Flodoard, *HRE* III-19, p. 261, reports how Hincmar sent a letter to Louis's sons by his first mother, Louis III and Carloman, explaining: 'quare Ansgardim uxorem abiectam eum [Louis the Stammerer] recipere non coegerit et Adelaidim ab eo retineri non prohibuerit.'
81 See Joye, Chapter 10. I now accept Böhringer's argument ('Einleitung', pp. 68–71) on *De raptu* as dating from before 860, against R. Stone, 'The invention of a theology of abduction: Hincmar of Rheims on *raptus*', *Journal of Ecclesiastical History*, 60 (2009), 433–48 at 437.
82 *AB* s.a. 862, p. 88 (trans. Nelson, pp. 97–8); Hincmar, Epistolae 155–6, MGH *Epp.* 8, p. 120.
83 *Hludowici, Karoli et Hlotharii II. conventus apud Saponarias, 862*, MGH *Capit.* II, no. 243, pp. 159–65; Staubach, *Herrscherbild*, pp. 139–45.
84 *AB* s.a. 863, p. 98 (trans. Nelson, p. 110); Heidecker, *Divorce*, p. 100.
85 On Nicholas see J. Haller, *Nikolaus I. und Pseudoisidor* (Stuttgart, 1936); Y. Congar, 'S. Nicholas Ier (d. 867): ses positions ecclésiologiques',

Introduction: Hincmar's world

Rivista di storia della chiesa, 21 (1967), 393–410; R. Davis, *The Lives of the Ninth-century Popes (Liber pontificalis): the Ancient Biographies of Ten Popes from A.D. 817–891* (Liverpool, 1995), pp. 189–247; S. Scholz, *Politik – Selbstverständnis – Selbstdarstellung. Die Päpste in karolingischer und ottonischer Zeit* (Stuttgart, 2006), pp. 185–211.

86 *AB* s.a. 864, pp. 105–11 (trans. Nelson, pp. 112–16); see also Buc, 'Text and ritual'.
87 *AB* s.a. 864, 867, pp. 112, 138 (trans. Nelson, pp. 117–18, 140).
88 H. J. Sieben, *Die Konzilsidee des lateinischen Mittelalters (847–1378)* (Paderborn, 1984), pp. 31–41.
89 *Ibid.*, pp. 91–7, 100–7.
90 Congar, 'Nicholas Ier', at 398–402; Sieben, *Konzilsidee*, pp. 47–54, 69–70, 107–11.
91 Sieben, *Konzilsidee*, pp. 110–11.
92 H.-W. Goetz, 'Auctoritas et dilectio. Zum päpstlichen Selbstverständnis im späteren 9. Jahrhundert', in *Gedenkreden auf Ludwig Buisson (1918–1992): Ansprachen auf der Akademischen Gedenkfeier am 7. Januar 1993* (Hamburg, 1993), pp. 27–58 at 34–41; Scholz, *Politik*, pp. 198–9.
93 G. H. Tavard, 'Episcopacy and apostolic succession according to Hincmar of Reims', *Theological Studies*, 34 (1973), 594–623.
94 Y. Congar, *L'ecclésiologie du haut Moyen âge: de Saint Grégoire le Grand à la désunion entre Byzance et Rome* (Paris, 1968), pp. 164–77, 206–16.
95 de Jong, Chapter 14, pp. 272–3, 279–81.
96 On letters to and from Hincmar being intercepted or lost, see *AB* s.a. 867, p. 138 (trans. Nelson, pp. 140); J. L. Nelson, 'Literacy in Carolingian government', in R. McKitterick, ed., *The uses of literacy in early mediaeval Europe* (Cambridge, 1990), pp. 258–96 at 294 (citing Hincmar, Epistola 169, MGH *Epp.* 8, pp. 158–9). Nicholas, Epistola 79, ed. E. Perels, MGH *Epp.* 6, pp. 415–18 accuses Hincmar of tampering with the *acta* of the Council of Soissons in 853.
97 Hincmar, Epistola 169, MGH *Epp.* 8, p. 154; *Liber Pontificalis*, ed. L. Duchesne, 2 vols (Paris, 1886–92), *Vita Nicolai I*, c. 58, II, p. 162 (trans. Davis, pp. 234–6) records how no accuser against Rothad appeared at Rome.
98 Stone, 'Bound', at 475–6; Heidecker, *Divorce*, pp. 159–72.
99 Hincmar, Epistola 169, MGH *Epp.* 8, pp. 144–63; Sot, *Un historien*, pp. 517–27. Haller, *Nikolaus I*, p. 107 thinks this letter may never have been delivered.
100 Gillis, Chapter 13, p. 261. The portion of the letter dealing with Gottschalk is translated in V. Genke and F. X. Gumerlock, *Gottschalk and a Medieval Predestination Controversy: Texts Translated from the Latin* (Milwaukee, 2010), pp. 174–9.
101 Beck, 'Selection', at 283–6.

102 Hincmar, Epistola 169, MGH *Epp.* 8, pp. 144-6.
103 On Rothad, see P. R. McKeon, *Hincmar of Laon and Carolingian Politics* (Urbana, 1978), pp. 57-61; M. Stratmann, 'Wer weihte Hinkmar von Reims?', *DA*, 46 (1990), 164-72; Scholz, *Politik*, pp. 195-9; Devisse, *Hincmar*, II, pp. 583-600.
104 Hincmar, Epistola 169, MGH *Epp.* 8, p. 149.
105 E. Boshof, 'Odo von Beauvais, Hinkmar von Reims und die kirchenpolitischen Auseinandersetzungen im westfränkischen Reich', in D. Berg and H.-W. Goetz, eds, *Ecclesia et regnum: Beiträge zur Geschichte von Kirche, Recht und Staat im Mittelalter: Festschrift für Franz-Josef Schmale zu seinem 65. Geburtstag* (Bochum, 1989), pp. 39-59, at 48.
106 *Liber Pontificalis, Vita Nicolai I*, cc. 58-63, II, pp. 162-3 (trans. Davis, pp. 234-8).
107 *AB* s.a. 865, p. 118 (trans. Nelson, p. 123): 'non regulariter sed potentialiter'.
108 *Annales Fuldenses*, ed. F. Kurze, MGH *SRG* 7 (Hanover, 1891) s.a. 864, p. 62 (trans. T. Reuter, *The Annals of Fulda*, Manchester, 1992, p. 52); *Hludowici et Karoli pactum Tusiacense*, 865, MGH *Capit.* II, no. 244, pp. 165-7.
109 Haller, *Nikolaus I*, pp. 101-6.
110 Nelson, *Charles the Bald*, pp. 207-9; Hincmar, Epistola 170, MGH *Epp.* 8, pp. 163-5.
111 On Wulfad's background, see J. Marenbon, 'Wulfad, Charles the Bald and John Scottus Eriugena', in M. T. Gibson and J. L. Nelson, eds, *Charles the Bald: Court and Kingdom* (Oxford, 1981), pp. 375-83.
112 On the case, see Devisse, *Hincmar*, II, pp. 600-28; Patzold, *Episcopus*, pp. 325-46.
113 Devisse, *Hincmar*, II, pp. 628-30.
114 See above p. 12 on the contested position of papal decretals.
115 L. Kéry, *Canonical Collections of the Early Middle Ages (ca. 400-1140): a Bibliographical Guide to the Manuscripts and Literature* (Washington DC, 1999); A. Firey, 'Mutating monsters: approaches to "living texts" of the Carolingian era', *Digital Proceedings of the Lawrence J. Schoenberg Symposium on Manuscript Studies in the Digital Age*, vol. 2, no. 1 (2010), 1-14, at 4.
116 For example, see the conflicting interpretations by Nicholas I and the Frankish episcopate (Nicholas, Epistola 71, MGH *Epp.* 6, pp. 396-7) of Innocent I's statement to Victricus of Rouen (Epistola II, s. 6, *PL* 20, col. 473 (J286)) that 'majores causas' are to be referred to the papacy.
117 See above, pp. 4-5.
118 See e.g. Heidecker, *Divorce*, pp. 176-9, on the changed attitude to Lothar II's divorce under Hadrian II; Nicholas, Epistola 59, MGH

Introduction: Hincmar's world

Epp. 6, p. 365, confirmed the acta of the Council of Soissons 'salvo tamen Romanae sedis in omnibus iussu atque iudicio'.
119 *Coronatio Hermintrudis reginae*, 866, MGH *Capit.* II, no. 301, pp. 453–5.
120 Council of Troyes, 867, MGH *Conc.* IV, no. 24 A, p. 237: 'ita ut nec vestris nec futuris temporibus praeter consultum Romani pontificis de gradu suo quilibet episcoporum deiciatur'.
121 *Ibid.*, pp. 237–8.
122 Kleinjung, Chapter 2; McKeon, *Hincmar of Laon*.
123 McKeon, *Hincmar of Laon*, pp. 64–8 on the early disputes; Hincmar, *Expositiones ad Carolum regem pro ecclesiae libertatum defensione*, PL 125, cols 1035–70.
124 McKeon, *Hincmar of Laon*, pp. 69–70; Hincmar of Laon, *Materialsammlungen vorwiegend pseudoisidorischen Inhalts*, ed. R. Schieffer, *Die Streitschriften Hinkmars von Reims und Hinkmars von Laon 869-871*, MGH *Conc.* IV, supplementum 2 (Hanover, 2003), pp. 1–2.
125 *AB* s.a. 869, p. 167 (trans. Nelson, p. 164); On Boso of Provence, see S. Airlie, 'The nearly men: Boso of Vienne and Arnulf of Bavaria', in A. J. Duggan, ed., *Nobles and Nobility in Medieval Europe: Concepts, Origins, Transformations* (Woodbridge, Suffolk, 2000), pp. 25–41, at 32–8; S. MacLean, 'The Carolingian response to the revolt of Boso, 879–887', *Early Medieval Europe*, 10 (2001), 21–48.
126 On Carloman see J. L. Nelson, 'A tale of two princes: politics, text and ideology in a Carolingian annal', *Studies in Medieval and Renaissance History*, 10 (1988), 105–41, at 106–15.
127 Council of Attigny, 870, MGH *Conc.* IV, no. 33, pp. 380–95.
128 Hincmar, *De regis persona et regio ministerio ad Carolum Calvum regem*, PL 833–56; Anton, *Fürstenspiegel*, pp. 286–7; Devisse, *Hincmar*, II, pp. 710–17.
129 See above, p. 5.
130 Council of Douzy, 871, MGH *Conc.* IV, no. 37, pp. 410–572; McKeon, *Hincmar of Laon*, pp. 132–51; Kleinjung, Chapter 2, pp. 66–8.
131 John VIII, Epistola 101, ed. E. Caspar, MGH *Epp.* 7, pp. 94–5; *Annales Vedastini*, ed. B. von Simson, MGH *SRG* 12 (Hanover, 1909), s.a. 878, p. 43 says that the blinding was done by Boso.
132 J. L. Nelson, '"Not bishops' bailiffs but lords of the earth": Charles the Bald and the problem of sovereignty', in D. Wood, ed., *The Church and Sovereignty c.590-1918: Essays in Honour of Michael Wilks* (Oxford, 1991), pp. 23–34. On Hadrian II see H. Grotz, *Erbe wider Willen: Hadrian II., 867-872, und seine Zeit* (Vienna, 1970); Scholz, *Politik*, pp. 212–24.
133 Nelson, *Charles the Bald*, p. 238.

134 M. E. Sommar, 'Hincmar of Reims and the canon law of episcopal translation', *Catholic Historical Review*, 88 (2002), 429–45.
135 Nelson, *Charles the Bald*, pp. 233–4, 241–2.
136 Council of Douzy, 874, MGH *Conc.* IV, no. 40, pp. 579–96.
137 Nelson, *Charles the Bald*, pp. 239–43; Goldberg, *Struggle*, pp. 328–33.
138 Bernard-Valette, Chapter 5.
139 L. Nees, *A Tainted Mantle: Hercules and the Classical Tradition at the Carolingian Court* (Philadelphia, 1991), p. 235; pp. 147–257 give a detailed discussion of the *Cathedra Petri* and Hincmar's possible motives in giving Charles the carved ivory plaques to add to this. On Hincmar's relations with Charles in this period, see also S. Patzold, 'Konsens und Konkurrenz: Überlegungen zu einem aktuellen Forschungskonzept der Mediävistik', *Frühmittelalterliche Studien*, 41 (2007), 75–103 at 78–81.
140 *Juramentum quod Hincmarus Archiepiscopus edere jussus est apud Pontigonem*; see C. E. Odegaard, 'The concept of royal power in Carolingian oaths of fidelity', *Speculum*, 20 (1945), 279–89 at 283–7.
141 *AB*, s.a. 876, pp. 201–10 (trans. Nelson, pp. 190–8).
142 de Jong, Chapter 14, pp. 272–3.
143 McCarthy, Chapter 6, p. 114.
144 *AB*, s.a. 877, p. 217 (trans. Nelson, pp. 202–3).
145 M. van der Lugt, 'Tradition and revision: the textual tradition of Hincmar of Reims' "Visio Bernoldi" with a new critical edition', *Archivum latinitatis medii aevi* 52 (1994), 109–49; P. E. Dutton, *The Politics of Dreaming in the Carolingian Empire* (Lincoln NE, 1994), pp. 183–93. Bernold also observed the sufferings of Ebbo in the afterlife.
146 Devisse, *Hincmar*, II, pp. 966–78; McCarthy, Chapter 6, pp. 115–21.
147 *AB*, s.a. 879–80, pp. 234–42 (trans. Nelson, pp. 215–20); K. F. Werner, 'Gauzlin von Saint-Denis und die westfränkische Reichsteilung von Amiens (März 880). Ein Beitrag zur Vorgeschichte von Odos Königtum', *DA*, 35 (1979), 395–462; MacLean, 'Carolingian response'.
148 Council of Fismes, 881, MGH *Conc.* V, no. 15, pp. 166–200. On Hincmar's difficult relationship with Louis III, see also Devisse, *Hincmar*, II, pp. 979–97; Patzold, 'Konsens und Konkurrenz', at 83–7.
149 Council of Fismes, 881, MGH *Conc.* V, no. 15B, pp. 197–200; G. Schmitz, 'Hinkmar von Reims, die Synode von Fismes 881 und der Streit um das Bistum Beauvais', *DA*, 35 (1979), 463–86.
150 Hincmar, *VR*; Isaïa, Chapter 9.
151 Hincmar, *De ordine palatii*, ed. T. Gross and R. Schieffer, MGH *Fontes iuris* 3 (Hanover, 1980). Debates about the relationship of Hincmar's text to a possible earlier work by Adalard are summarised by R. McKitterick, *Charlemagne: the Formation of a European Identity* (Cambridge, 2008), pp. 142–55 and Patzold, 'Konsens und Konkurrenz', at 77, n.6.
152 Depreux, Chapter 8, p. 158.

Introduction: Hincmar's world

153 *AB*, s.a. 882, pp. 249-51 (trans. Nelson, pp. 225–6).
154 J. M. Wallace-Hadrill, 'History in the mind of Archbishop Hincmar', in R. H. C. Davis and J. M. Wallace-Hadrill, eds, *The Writing of History in the Middle Ages: Essays presented to Richard William Southern* (Oxford, 1981), pp. 43–70, Nelson, 'Annals'; M. Meyer-Gebel, 'Zur annalistischen Arbeitsweise Hinkmars von Reims', *Francia*, 15 (1987), 75–108; Nelson, 'Two princes'; Schneider, *Erzbischof Hinkmar*.
155 Nelson, Chapter 2.
156 Kleinjung, Chapter 3.
157 Anton, *Fürstenspiegel*, pp. 281–355; Devisse, *Hincmar*, II, pp. 671–723; J. L. Nelson, 'Kingship, law and liturgy in the political thought of Hincmar of Rheims', *English Historical Review*, 92 (1977), 241–79; Staubach, *Herrscherbild*, pp. 98–152.
158 See most recently Heidecker, *Divorce*; Stone and West, *On the Divorce of King Lothar*.
159 J. Calmette, *La Diplomatie carolingienne: du Traité de Verdun a la mort de Charles le Chauve (843–877)* (Paris, 1901); Nelson, *Charles the Bald*.
160 Screen, Chapter 4; McCarthy, Chapter 6.
161 Bernard-Valette, Chapter 5.
162 J. Devisse, *Hincmar et la loi* (Dakar, 1962); Devisse, *Hincmar*, III, pp. 1237–514; on the recent editions, see K. Brunner, 'Ein Krieg mit Texten. Anmerkungen an Stelle fälliger Rezensionen', *Mitteilungen des Instituts für Österreichische Geschichtsforschung*, 113 (2005), 392–8.
163 H. Fuhrmann, 'Fälscher unter sich: zum Streit zwischen Hinkmar von Reims und Hinkmar von Laon', in Gibson and Nelson, *Charles the Bald*, 2nd revd edn, pp. 224–34. J. P. Clausen, 'Spuren Hinkmars von Reims in einer Urkunde Ludwigs des Frommen (BM² 801)', *Archiv für Diplomatik*, 53 (2007), 81–98 discusses an interpolated charter of Louis the Pious probably reworked by Hincmar; p. 86, n.13 provides references to many other studies of Hincmar's forgeries and alleged forgeries.
164 L. Böhringer, 'Der eherechtliche Traktat im Paris. Lat. 12445, einer Arbeitshandschrift Hinkmars von Reims', *DA*, 46 (1990), 18–47; K. Heidecker, 'Gathering and recycling authoritative texts: the importance of marginalia in Hincmar of Reims' treatise about king Lothar's divorce', in M. Mostert, ed., *Organizing the Written Word: Proceedings of the First Utrecht Symposium on Medieval Literacy, Utrecht 5-7 June 1997* (Turnhout, forthcoming); M. Hartmann, '"Collectio contra haereticos et de privilegiis multarum sedium": ein bislang übersehenes Werk Hinkmars von Reims in der Centuriatoren-Handschrift ÖB Basel O II 29', in A. Mentzel-Reuters and M. Hartmann, eds, *Catalogus und Centurien: Interdisziplinäre Studien zu Matthias Flacius und den Magdeburger Centurien* (Tübingen, 2008), pp. 211–31.

165 Corcoran, Chapter 7.
166 Depreux, Chapter 8.
167 Isaïa, Chapter 9.
168 Devisse, Hincmar, II, pp. 1129–36.
169 See e.g. R. Stone, *Morality and Masculinity in the Carolingian Empire* (Cambridge, 2011); West, 'Lordship'; G. Calvet, '*Cupiditas, avaritia, turpe lucrum*: discours économique et morale chrétienne chez Hincmar de Reims (845–882)', in J.-P. Devroey, L. Feller and R. Le Jan, eds, *Les élites et la richesse au Haut Moyen Âge* (Turnhout, 2011), pp. 97–112. On Hincmar's moral thought more generally, see also D. Nachtmann, 'Einleitung' in Hincmar, *De cavendis vitiis et virtutibus exercendis*, MGH Quellen zur Geistesgeschichte des Mittelalters 16 (Munich, 1998), pp. 1–98; F. Sedlmeier, *Die laienparänetischen Schriften der Karolingerzeit: Untersuchungen zu ausgewählten Texten des Paulinus von Aquileia, Alkuins, Jonas von Orleans, Dhuodas und Hinkmars von Reims* (Neuried, 2000), p. 451–518.
170 Joye, Chapter 10.
171 See e.g. Stone, 'Invention'.
172 On administration see Nelson, 'Literacy'; Stratmann, *Hinkmar als Verwalter*. The Carolingian Polyptyques website (www.le.ac.uk/hi/polyptyques/index.html) provides an overview of these texts for students.
173 Barbier, Chapter 11.
174 West, Chapter 12.
175 de Jong, Chapter 14.
176 See e.g. Devisse, *Hincmar*, I, pp. 115–279; B. Taeger, 'Zum "Ferculum Salomonis" Hinkmars von Reims', *DA*, 33 (1977), 153–67; G. H. Tavard, *Trina deitas: the Controversy between Hincmar and Gottschalk* (Milwaukee, 1996); C. M. Chazelle, *The Crucified God in the Carolingian Era: Theology and Art of Christ's Passion* (Cambridge, 2001), pp. 165–299.
177 D. Ganz, 'The debate on predestination', in Gibson and Nelson, *Charles the Bald*, 2nd revd edn, pp. 283–302.
178 Gillis, Chapter 13.
179 Barbier, Chapter 11 p. 218.
180 Corcoran, Chapter 7, p. 144.
181 Isaïa, Chapter 9 p. 175; Council of Fismes, 881, MGH *Conc.* V, no. 15, p. 170.
182 Depreux, Chapter 8, pp. 158–9; Corcoran, Chapter 7, p. 144.
183 de Jong, Chapter 14, pp. 273–9.
184 Screen, Chapter 4, pp. 85–6.
185 de Jong, *Penitential State*. The same rhetoric of penitence and sin was taken up by Gottschalk in his conflicts: Gillis, Chapter 13, p. 249.

186 Kleinjung, Chapter 3, pp. 67–9.
187 Bernard-Valette, Chapter 5, pp. 94–5.
188 Patzold, *Episcopus*; Joye, Chapter 10, pp. 193–4, 198.
189 Bernard-Valette, Chapter 5, pp. 96–102.
190 West, Chapter 12, p. 231.
191 Isaïa, Chapter 9, pp. 179–81.
192 See e.g. Gillis, Chapter 13, p. 259.
193 Nelson, Chapter 2, pp. 49–50.
194 Nelson, Chapter 2, p. 54; Depreux, Chapter 8, p. 158.
195 Bernard-Valette, Chapter 5, pp. 98–100; Isaïa, Chapter 9, p. 171.
196 Gillis, Chapter 13, p. 254.
197 Screen, Chapter 4, pp. 79, 82–3; McCarthy, Chapter 6, pp. 119–20.
198 Nelson, Chapter 2, pp. 46–7. We rarely glimpse Hincmar's non-political networks, but Isaïa, Chapter 9, pp. 173–4, hints at the existence of a textual community around the *Vita Remigii* and its commemoration of the saint.
199 Screen, Chapter 4, p. 83; McCarthy, Chapter 6.
200 Nelson, Chapter 2, p. 47.
201 Gillis, Chapter 13, pp. 259–62; Kleinjung, Chapter 3, p. 70.
202 Screen, Chapter 4 pp. 80–2.
203 R. Stone, 'Gender and hierarchy: Archbishop Hincmar of Rheims (845–882) as a religious man', in P. H. Cullum and K. J. Lewis, eds, *Religious Men and Masculine Identity in the Middle Ages* (Woodbridge, Suffolk, 2013), pp. 28–45.
204 Barbier, Chapter 11, pp. 218–21.
205 Joye, Chapter 10; West, Chapter 12, pp. 230–1.
206 de Jong, Chapter 14, p. 268.
207 West, Chapter 12, p. 238.
208 Joye, Chapter 10, pp. 194–200.
209 Patzold, *Episcopus*, pp. 179–80.
210 Gillis, Chapter 13, p. 253.
211 J. L. Nelson, 'The voice of Charlemagne', in R. Gameson and H. Leyser, eds, *Belief and Culture in the Middle Ages: Studies Presented to Henry Mayr-Harting* (Oxford, 2001), pp. 76–88; de Jong, *Penitential State*.
212 West, Chapter 12, p. 239.
213 On Hincmar's letters to laymen, see Flodoard, *HRE*, III–26, pp. 330–46 and Sot, *Un historien*, pp. 594–608; West, Chapter 12, p. 233; Joye, Chapter 10, pp. 195–6.
214 J. L. Nelson, 'The church's military service in the ninth century: a contemporary comparative view?', in W. J. Sheils, ed., *The Church and War. Papers read at the Twenty-First Summer Meeting and the Twenty-Second Winter Meeting of the Ecclesiastical History Society* (Oxford, 1983), pp. 15–30.

215 Corcoran, Chapter 7, p. 141; Depreux, Chapter 8, pp. 160-1.
216 Hincmar, *De ordine palatii*, pp. 82-6, cc. 29-30.
217 Joye, Chapter 10, pp. 199-200; Bernard-Valette, Chapter 5, pp. 100-2.
218 Depreux, Chapter 8, pp. 159-60; L. Morelle, 'La main du roi et le nom de Dieu: la validation de l'acte royal selon Hincmar, d'après un passage de son "De Divortio"', in J. Hoareau-Dodinau and P. Texier, eds, *Foi chrétienne et églises dans la société politique de l'Occident du Haut Moyen Age: IVe-XIIe siècle* (Limoges, 2004), pp. 287-318.
219 Gillis, Chapter 13, pp. 256-61.
220 Pippin II in 864: see above, p. 14.
221 We know of Hincmar's interactions with the seven popes from Gregory IV (r. 827-44) to John VIII (r. 872-82).
222 See above, p. 36, n.18, on Lothar II's approaches to Hadrian II; and Gillis, Chapter 13, p. 261 on Gottschalk and Nicholas I.
223 Patzold, 'Konsens und Konkurrenz'.
224 Nelson, Chapter 2, p. 50; Dutton, *Politics*, pp. 171-94.
225 Flodoard, *HRE* III-30, pp. 362-3.
226 L. Nees, 'The fastigium of Saint-Remi ("the Tomb of Hincmar") at Reims', in R. A. Maxwell, ed., *Representing History, 900-1300: Art, Music, History* (University Park PA, 2010), pp. 31-52.
227 Devisse, *Hincmar*, III, pp. 1467-514; J. J. Contreni, '"Building mansions in heaven": the *Visio Baronti*, Archangel Raphael, and a Carolingian king', *Speculum*, 78 (2003), 673-706 at 696-706; F. Dolbeau, 'Ex dono Hincmari. Livres donnés par Hincmar (845-882) à Saint-Remi de Reims', in M. Coumert *et al.*, eds, *Rerum gestarum scriptor: Histoire et historiographie au Moyen Age: Mélanges Michel Sot* (Paris, 2012), pp. 601-14. See also Chazelle, *Crucified God*, pp. 239-54, 266-99, on Hincmar as the possible patron of the Utrecht Psalter and the ivory cover of the Pericopes of Henry II. Several Rheims manuscripts from the Carolingian period have been digitised and can be viewed online via the Europeana Regia project (www.europeanaregia.eu/en/historical-collections/bibliotheca-carolina).
228 Devisse, *Hincmar*, I, pp. 9-28; R. Schieffer, 'Nikolaus von Kues als Leser Hinkmars von Reims', in J. Helmrath and H. Müller, eds, *Studien zum 15. Jahrhundert: Festschrift für Erich Meuthen*, 2 vols (Munich, 1994), I, pp. 341-54; M. Stratmann, 'Zur Wirkungsgeschichte Hinkmars von Reims', *Francia*, 22 (1995), 1-43.
229 Nachtmann, 'Einleitung', at pp. 42-80; Hincmar, *Vita Remigii episcopi Remensis*, ed. B. Krusch, MGH *SRM* 3, (Hanover, 1896), pp. 244-50.
230 Isaïa, Chapter 9, pp. 181-4.
231 Corcoran, Chapter 7, pp. 143-4; J. Gaudemet, 'Indissolubilité et consommation du mariage: l'apport d'Hincmar de Reims', *Revue de droit canonique*, 30 (1980), 28-40; M. Stratmann, 'Zur Rezeption Hinkmars

von Reims durch Bernhard von Hildesheim und Bernold von Konstanz', *DA*, 44 (1988), 170–80.
232 P. Fouracre, *The Age of Charles Martel* (Harlow, 2000), pp. 123–5, 135, 183–4.
233 Chapter 13 of Isaïa, *Remi de Reims*, pp. 417–64, covering the period of Hincmar's episcopacy, is entitled 'Un nouveau saint Remi'.
234 Nelson, *Charles the Bald*, p. 146; on this holy oil, see now N. Staubach, '*Regia sceptra sacrans*. Erzbischof Hinkmar von Reims, der heilige Remigius und die "Sainte Ampoule"', *Frühmittelalterliche Studien*, 40 (2006), 79–101.

2

Hincmar's life in his historical writings
Janet L. Nelson

Hincmar was given to *multiloquium*, much-speaking. He excused himself by invoking Augustine, who had boldly asked the Almighty to excuse his own much-speaking, on the grounds that 'Loqui multum non est nimium, si tamen est necessarium' ('much-speaking is not excessive, as long as it is necessary').[1] Of course it was very often necessary. Even Jean Devisse, for whom 'after so many years of life together' (!) Hincmar remained 'un être attachant' ('a lovable being'), was moved by reading the *Collectio de ecclesiis et capellis* to exclaim: 'Incorrigible Hincmar! … chaque morceau est intéressant mais … la longueur est excessive' ('each bit is interesting but the whole thing is excessively long').[2]

Writing of the 820s

I will return presently to the *Collectio de ecclesiis*. But to get an entrée to Hincmar's life at the earliest possible date, we have to go back to August 822. Hincmar, as a youthful canon at St-Denis, had followed his *nutritor* Hilduin, abbot of St-Denis and imperial arch-chaplain, to the court of Louis the Pious and the great assembly of Attigny.[3] Hincmar recalled a marital dispute brought before the emperor there. Though he can only have been at most twenty when he was an eye-witness of what occurred, and though he was writing nearly forty years later an extremely lengthy and complicated legal opinion, he focused on the events in the manner of a historian, succinctly and in sequence, then coolly stated his retrospective approval of the bishops' handing-over of the case to 'noble laymen who were cognisant of such affairs and possessed very expert knowledge in the laws of the world' and who gave 'a lawful judgment' in an exemplary instance of 'limits laid down by your forefathers, not to be transgressed' (quoting Proverbs 22: 28).[4] Attigny gave Hincmar his first experience of observing power at close quarters: power wielded in different ways, competed for, negotiated and cleverly co-ordinated, at once masked and on display. Then, as later, Hincmar's view was cool, detached. When he wanted to, he could dispense with much-speaking, and cut to the chase.

In 829, Hincmar was assigned by Louis the Pious the task of helping Hilduin install the Benedictine Rule at St-Denis.[5] Writing in the mid-tenth century, with the benefit of the Rheims archive, Flodoard noted at this point that Hincmar, 'to fulfil by deed what he had recommended by word, also submitted himself to monastic life along with the rest, chastening his own body and subduing himself in spirit'.[6] This was a young man determined not just to talk the talk but to walk the walk: things not so easy to combine in a life that from 829 until 845 oscillated between court and more than one cloister.[7]

Two capitularies of the 840s

Any claim that Hincmar's life in these years is relevant to my present theme has to depend on stretching the definition of historical writings. The first of two cases in point is the Capitulary of Coulaines, produced in November 843.[8] It reflected, and reflected on, recent tumultuous events: civil war, peace of a kind and continuing political tensions. It was an imaginative attempt at an account of decision-making and action that can also be read as contemporary history. It was not the work of a committee but has the flavour of single authorship by someone familiar with the works of St Augustine. It was written to Charles the Bald's requirements, and incorporated the input and approval of the king and his counsellors, together with an acknowledgement in the opening *adnuntiatio* that vestiges of preceding conflicts were still harboured by 'nos et viri ecclesiastici necnon et in rei publicae nostrae solaciatores' ('us, and ecclesiastical men, and also those who provide us with support in our *respublica*').[9] It recorded a *bona convenientia*, a good meeting of men and of minds and wills, based on *pacta sinceritas*, agreed straightforwardness, which had overcome private and sectional interests. Its self-referential concern with consensus politics echoed that of a work that Hincmar had read at the court of Louis the Pious, Adalard of Corbie's *De ordine palatii*.[10] Hincmar was the capitulary's probable author. Later, when he archived it and cited it, he used it as retrospective commentary on his own life and the life of the realm.

The second capitulary that can, at a stretch, be categorised as historical writing was issued at Toulouse in June 844.[11] Charles the Bald had journeyed south to deal with Bernard of Septimania, 'who had long ago thirsted for the heights of power'.[12] Bernard also had political ties from long ago with Pippin II of Aquitaine, one of the two Carolingian contenders defeated at the battle of Fontenoy in 841.[13] Formally excluded from the division of Verdun in 843, Pippin had continuing support from some powerful people in Toulouse and the south-west. Bernard was captured and 'on Charles's orders was executed for treason, by judgment of the Franks', at (probably) Limoges early in 844.[14] Charles seized the chance to move much further south, hoping to take Toulouse and so eliminate Pippin II for good. Once Charles and his men were encamped around Toulouse and settling in to besiege the city, he found himself besieged by all kinds of people with grievances, such as monastic communities who claimed their lands were being 'plundered' by the followers of local magnates. The complainants were people who had not seen any king in a long time and were now keen to get justice against various oppressors in the region, including Bernard and his men.[15]

The *capitula* of Toulouse show that the oppressors also included bishops, and those who complained about them were the priests of 'little churches' (*ecclesiolae*). The author of the preamble, writing in the king's name, tried to keep a balance between the *necessitates* (needs) of bishops and the *possibilitates* (resources, means) of priests; but the responses in the *capitula* sketched a long history of abuses of power. My suggestion is that Hincmar was the author, and that his sympathies were with the priests. On 12 August 844, Charles, evidently on his way back north, granted 'the priest Hincmar' some lands in the Auvergne.[16] Such a grant was uncommon, but in this case it rewarded uncommon service, while signalling confidence in future services. The count of Toulouse in the 860s and 870s was Bernard, a relative (*propinquus*) of Hincmar's. There is no evidence as to whether Bernard, and perhaps Hincmar too, had prior connections in Septimania and/or Aquitaine, or whether each owed his receipt of favours there to the king, or whether both types of connection could be inferred. In Hincmar's case, a further type of connection was created in 845, when Charles chose him for election as the archbishop of Rheims. Thanks to a very long history of endowments, the post brought with it important landed interests and responsibilities in Aquitaine. To protect these interests, the archbishop needed to maintain a managerial infrastructure and to activate political support in the region, as his letters attest.[17]

The *Collectio de ecclesiis* of the 850s

The *Collectio de ecclesiis et capellis*, which Hincmar wrote in 857 or early 858 at the request of King Charles the Bald, purported to be an expert legal opinion on proprietary churches. Strictly speaking, this was not historical writing any more than capitularies were. But it was driven by certain historic pressures inherent in Hincmar's life as archbishop, namely those arising from the lordship of churches that Rheims held in the dioceses of other bishops. The *De ecclesiis*, which cited some of the same canon-law texts as the Toulouse *capitula*, addressed the friction between such lordly rights, *dominium*, which were extra-territorial, and the territorially circumscribed power held by each bishop in his see. In particular, the *De ecclesiis* was a polemic against Bishop Prudentius of Troyes who had challenged Hincmar's rights in Rheims' churches in the diocese of Troyes. These included rights over priests, analogous to the rights of lay *domini*, whether men or women (!), over *their* priests.[18] Hincmar thought that Prudentius, and other bishops on Prudentius's side, interpreted the law *inconvenienter*, inappropriately.[19]

Hincmar v. Prudentius

Predating by some years the rift over proprietary churches were two other contests that had pitted Hincmar against Prudentius: the debate over the validity of Archbishop Ebbo of Rheims' deposition in 834, followed by his brief restoration, and his deposition again, in 840–41; and the debate over predestination. The same men seemed to take up positions on the same sides in both disputes: if you supported Ebbo (and those clergy consecrated by him in 840–41) then you dissented from Hincmar's line on predestination, and vice versa.

Prudentius was among those Frankish bishops who felt sympathy for 'Ebbo's *clerici*'. For Hincmar, what was at stake in the Ebbo imbroglio was the legality of his own position as Ebbo's successor at Rheims. During a four-year vacancy at Rheims during 841–45, the temporal lordship of the see, which included proprietary churches, had been commended 'by us', said Charles the Bald in a charter, 'through great necessity and in all respects unwillingly (*magna necessitate ac per omnia inviti*) to our *fideles* [these included the king's doctor, his jester and a priest who was Hrabanus Maurus's nephew] as some reward for their service'.[20] In the post-war crisis year 845, when the king picked Hincmar to head a very important see, he accepted the need for restitutions.

And then there was predestination. It is a long time since David Ganz took the modern historiographical debate away from theologians, and looked to explain the doctrinal choices of those he termed 'the intelligentsia' in terms of factional politics and personal dispositions: 'the pessimism of humanists such as Lupus ... and Radbertus was accentuated by events' such as Viking and Saracen attacks.[21] But events took humanists different ways: some were for Gottschalk's teaching that some were predestined to salvation and others to damnation, while others were against. Ganz's attempt at refocusing the debate was valiant, but stymied by sheer lack of biographical data on most of those involved. In Hincmar's case, though, we can get more sense of a life in its time. Gottschalk was condemned for heresy by successive East and West Frankish Church councils in 848 and 849, with Hincmar leading the pack in the west. At the council at Quierzy in March 849, Gottschalk was 'publicly flogged and compelled to burn the books containing his teachings'.[22] He was held in custody thereafter in the monastery of Hautvillers near Épernay just 35 km south of Rheims – no ordinary monastery this, but one firmly in the archiepiscopal grip, and amply resourced with a scholarly library and a scriptorium that had not long before produced the Utrecht Psalter.[23] Did Hincmar hope to 'turn' Gottschalk and, even, exploit his learning? That indeed would have been *dominium*! Prudentius was present at the 849 council, and, despite earlier sympathy for Gottschalk, he went along with the official line, which was Hincmar's line. Thereafter, Prudentius increasingly distanced himself from the king: a fact that emerges clearly from the critical remarks about Charles in a continuation of the *Royal Frankish Annals*, the so-called *Annals of St-Bertin*, written by Prudentius, first as a palace cleric, then as bishop of Troyes, between 835 and 861.

Hincmar, after the 849 council, wrote a short diocesan letter, known now as *Ad reclusos et simplices*, addressed 'dilectis filiis simplicibus huius sanctae sedis' ('to his beloved children, the simple believers of this see'), warning them against Gottschalk's heretical teachings, and assuring them that there was but one predestination, 'a copious redemption of the human race through the blood of the Redeemer, and through the free grace of God'.[24] Hincmar sent a copy of this letter to Hrabanus Maurus together with Gottschalk's statement of his views, and a statement from Prudentius in effect endorsing Gottschalk.[25] Hrabanus approved Hincmar's hard line. In 853, at yet another council at Quierzy, Gottschalk's writings were condemned. Prudentius was there, no doubt with gritted teeth, when the assembled bishops agreed four summary points on predestination which Hincmar had prepared and presented.[26]

Annals

All the above forms the real-life context in which Hincmar became an author of historical writing – or as he preferred to put it, a recorder of *gesta regum*, the deeds of kings.[27] The *Annales regni Francorum* were carried on at the imperial court, probably (with intermissions) under Hilduin's supervision, roughly until the death of Louis the Pious in 840. Thereafter, during the ensuing three or four decades, there were independent continuations of those annals in the western, middle and eastern Frankish kingdoms. From the 840s until the late 880s, the so-called *Annals of Fulda* were produced in the orbit of the archbishop of Mainz; the so-called *Annals of Xanten* were written for much of that period at, perhaps, Ghent, then Cologne by the one-time court librarian, Gerward; and the *Annals of St-Bertin* were written by Bishop Prudentius at his see of Troyes until 861, when he died, as it were, pen in hand, leaving his single copy to fall into the hands of the king, and then into Hincmar's.[28] Hincmar very quickly assumed the annal writer's task anonymously but unmistakably. It was an opportunity to continue Hilduin's work. It was a taking-up of a responsibility to king and kingdom. 'Hincmar saw History as counsel.'[29]

It was also a takeover, and a settling of scores, in no uncertain terms: among other things, an act of revenge – Hincmar's *antapodosis*. In a copy made in 1638 of a now-lost early medieval manuscript of the *Annals of St-Bertin*, a marginal note beside the passage in the 859 annal, in which Prudentius attributed to Pope Nicholas I views on predestination that accorded with his own, may well have been written by Hincmar himself: 'Here Bishop Prudentius wrote concerning Nicholas what he [Prudentius] wished was the case, but in saying that it *was* so, he said what was not true'.[30] After the first few lines of the 861 annal comes the following passage:

> Prudentius bishop of Troyes originally named Galindo, a Spaniard by birth, was at first a most learned man: it was he who some years ago had resisted the predestinationist Gottschalk. But later, excited by bitter feelings, he became a very keen defender of that heresy against certain bishops who had previously been allied with him in resisting the heretic. Then he died, still scribbling away at things that were mutually contradictory and contrary to Faith: thus, though racked by a long illness, he put an end at the same time both to living and to writing (*indeque non modica inter sese diversa et fidei adversa scriptitans, moritur; sicque ... ut vivendi ita et scribendi finem fecit*).[31]

Incorrigible Hincmar! – still unable to let pass an opportunity to condemn and correct the errors of his old opponent, still desperate to convince readers – and perhaps, even more so, himself – that his own views coincided with those of the pope.[32] Similar motives may lie behind what was arguably a Hincmarian interpolation in the passage about the Council of Quierzy in the 849 annal.[33] Perhaps the 853 entry on the four-part correct definition of predestination is another possible interpolation, and likewise the indignant passage about the assembly in 846 at Épernay (a particularly valuable cluster of Rheims estates where the recovery of alienated Church property was a major issue) where the king rejected episcopal advice on restitutions. Another interpolation may be the curiously detailed statement under the year 856 about the consecration and coronation by 'Hincmar bishop of Rheims' of Charles the Bald's daughter Judith on her marriage to King Æthelwulf of the western English.[34] It seems, then, that Hincmar saw his first task as continuator of *gesta regum* as correcting Prudentius's historical record by filling in some gaps on matters which were of specific concern to Hincmar.

A more fundamental and long-running duty as perceived by the new historiographer royal was to provide a narrative of actions he judged exemplary of good or ill. By 861, as Hincmar embarked on his annalistic stint, Charles the Bald's 'restoration' in 859 after a serious rebellion had begun to look convincing. The king had regained vital political support and was turning the tide against Viking attacks. He was able to legislate on the coinage.[35] He was listening to Hincmar's advice. In the 860s, the *Annals of St-Bertin* became something they had not been in Prudentius's hands: more or less court-centred.

Hincmar's audience, starting with himself, grew to include not just a coterie (at Rheims) but the assemblies where the elite of the realm so frequently met.

In August 869, news of the death of Charles's nephew Lothar II – without a legitimate male heir – fortuitously coincided with the serious illness of Charles's older brother Louis the German. Charles's long-maturing plan to take over Lothar's kingdom seemed suddenly about to be realised when he secured sufficient support to stage an imposing accession ceremony at Metz on 9 September, with Hincmar as actor–manager. Hincmar's own speech justifying Charles's extended rule over the Franks was a key part of this great set-piece, in which Frankish history since Clovis and St Remigius was connected both to Rheims and to the glittering present of *Francia Media*. It was accompanied by a full record of Charles's winning of Frankish consensus and his consecration with heaven-sent oil 'of which', Hincmar said, in a tiny phrase with a very long afterlife, 'we still have some' (*unde adhuc habemus*). All this makes the 869 annal the longest in the whole work, and considerably longer than any entry in other contemporary historical writing.[36] Like the rest of Hincmar's annals, this account is a tissue of selective truth and misrepresentation and wishful thinking, of much-wordiness and significant silences. But with Hincmar, there is a transparency about the constructed narrative that makes it somehow innocent, and makes the genre something more than annals. Charles's apparent success was Hincmar's finest hour as counsellor and as historian. Aachen beckoned, and with it the throne of Charlemagne.

Within exactly a month, counsel had turned into dire warning. Hincmar's supply of precise dates constituted a coded message of heavenly disapproval and earthly foreboding. The news of the death of Charles's wife Ermentrude reached him on 9 October, St Denis's day – the feast of Charles's patron. The king's acquiring of a new partner, Richildis, and their dash to Aachen immediately after, occurred with a haste that was more than unseemly. Hincmar's authorial tone darkened. No new supporters were won over at Aachen. When Charles moved south-westwards to the palace of Gondreville near Toul for St Martin's day (11 November) – the feast of the other great patron of the Franks and their king – he received, not more support, but instead papal envoys threatening that the consequence of 'invading' Lothar's kingdom would be excommunication. Hincmar's almost-final word on 869 was written with hindsight: 'Charles was deceived by the vain persuadings of false messengers that his brother Louis [the German] was near death.'[37] Even harsher criticism of Charles was to be conveyed in a similar code when Hincmar wrote up his account of Charles's disastrous defeat by Louis the German's son and successor at Andernach on 7 October 876, and its aftermath, the premature birth of a baby son.[38]

Other distinctive features of Hincmar's section of the *Annals of St-Bertin*, 861–82, show the historian of contemporary politics raising the annalist's sights. First, the increase in the sheer quantity and quality of the information here compared with Prudentius's annals shows a consistent attempt to cover Charles's whole kingdom, as well as the wider Frankish world. Examples are the reports of the diplomatic activities of Empress Engelberga, wife of Emperor Louis II 'of Italy': Hincmar the annalist is the sole source for details of her efforts in 872 to negotiate over the imperial succession, successively with Charles the Bald through envoys, then in person with Louis the German.[39] Count Bernard of Toulouse rates six mentions in the context of politics in Aquitaine and the far south, and this can perhaps be linked to Hincmar's continuing contacts with his *propinquus* and ongoing interests in the region of Toulouse where he gained the royal favour that was the prerequisite to promotion to the archbishopric of Rheims.[40] Count Bertram of the Tardenois, an area in Champagne quite near Rheims, is similarly identified as Hincmar's *propinquus*, and in contexts such as the taking of oaths from men of the *pagus* which show him active as Hincmar's lay adjunct.[41] Apart from these kinsmen, Hincmar wrote to no fewer than twenty-eight *viri illustres*, most of them counts, in the West Frankish kingdom, as well as half a dozen others in the Middle Kingdom and Italy, and others in East Francia – and there were many more ecclesiastical correspondents, again including several in Italy.[42] Hincmar's political networks were as extensive as his antennae were sensitive to affairs of the two cities, of God and of this world, that were always, to borrow Augustine's term, *permixtae*, 'thoroughly mixed up'.[43]

Second, while Prudentius had been concerned to record Scandinavian activity, Hincmar's annals show a more thoroughly informed interest in the strategy and tactics of the Northmen, and in connections between events. In the dedicatory letter of his third treatise on predestination to Charles the Bald, Hincmar refers in passing to his military service, which as an archbishop he was bound to offer – and proud to offer – against the Northmen on the Seine, confirming the concerns and knowledge so often expressed in the annals.[44] Hincmar was also interested in the acculturation of Northmen into Frankish politics. Roric, Scandinavian lord of Frisia and Christian convert, was among the *viri illustres* to whom Hincmar wrote letters urging his intervention in reconciling a dangerous dispute within the royal family: Charles's daughter Judith, widowed in Wessex, had refused to settle for chaste incarceration, deciding instead on remarriage to Baldwin, a young noble on the make, and if necessary threatening to seek refuge with Roric. Hincmar displayed a strong professional interest in that affair for it went to the heart of politics at court and on the frontier.[45]

Third, and nearest not just to the heart of politics but to Hincmar's heart, *gesta regum* became most obviously the annals' theme. This was because Hincmar himself, like the business of Church and court that preoccupied him, was both *ecclesiasticus* and *palatinus*. He had been nurtured at the palace of Louis the Pious in the 820s. During most of the two decades when he was keeping up the *gesta regum*, he was a royal counsellor, a man with more or less great influence at the West Frankish court of Charles the Bald, and then of his son and grandsons.

Old age

Hincmar's view of old age, despite various ailments, I think resembled Augustine's: 'senecta ista iuvenilis est, senecta ista virilis est, semper virebit' ('this old age is youthful, this old age is manly, it will ever be vigorous').[46] Increasingly, in the 870s, he found himself having to share influence with, or even be displaced in royal favour by, younger men and natural rivals for the king's ear, like Archbishop Ansegis of Sens, the Count of the Palace Adalard or the Arch-chancellor Gauzlin.[47] Yet the latter part of Hincmar's *gesta regum* shows that he never lost his political *nous*, nor his appetite for political life; and he retained his wide interests, notably in Italy, with whose elites he had long-standing contacts. He was an intellectual in politics not just in the 840s, not just in the 860s, but right to the end of his life.

In late summer 877, after Charles the Bald's death, Hincmar gladly received a summons from the new king, Louis the Stammerer, and eagerly tendered his counsel and aid. In a letter, he recalled for Louis's benefit that despite the difficulties surrounding every such transition, kings had always managed to come through safely – with the help of good counsellors.[48] In 881, Louis died aged thirty-two, leaving the West Frankish kingdom to be divided between his two sons. In August 882, the elder son also died, aged only twenty-one. Hincmar, undaunted by the string of succession crises, again offered counsel, this time in the form of a substantial treatise, to Louis's younger son Carloman, now ruler of a reunited West Frankish realm. Hincmar addressed, not the king directly, but:

> the good and wise men of a younger generation. You have called on my humbleness, because I am of such old age and because I have so long been in holy orders. I am someone who played my part in the affairs of the Church and of the palace as these were being prosperously conducted when the empire was at its greatest extent and unified, and I heard the counsels and teaching both of those who ruled the Church in holiness and justice and those who in those past times oversaw prosperously the empire's solid structure, and by the teaching of those men I learned what had been handed down by their ancestors.[49]

Now, casting himself as the *bajulus* or tutor to Charles the Bald's grandson, and aspiring to fill Adalard's place as *primus inter primos consiliarios* – a wise Leonidas to the young king's Alexander – Hincmar at a great assembly at Quierzy on 9 September (the same date that Charles the Bald had been crowned at Metz) presented his updated version of Adalard's *De ordine palatii*.[50]

In 882 the annals ended, abruptly, *in medias res*. There is no sense of the author's having run out of steam: on the contrary, characteristic of Hincmar's later annals were attempts at a more thematic treatment and the writing of sequences of events *en bloc* after outcomes had become known.[51] The 882 annal is something of a triumph in this regard. Though Northmen were ravaging the area around Rheims, the keeping of the record was maintained. Only when Hincmar learned that Rheims itself was threatened with attack while the fighting-men of the see were away with the king fighting against other marauders did he decide to flee: his entourage were able to carry him away in a portable chair to the safety of Épernay, together with the body of St Remigius and the treasures of his church. He died, probably on 23 December 882.[52] Like his annalist-predecessor Prudentius, Hincmar had, so to speak, had the pen in his hand virtually to the last moment, still *multiloquens*, still incorrigibly offering counsel in *gesta regum*. He had served a long stint. His personality, his abiding self-confidence enhanced by age and experience, had stamped both his political life and his historical writing. With him, annals burst their genre-buttons and acquired the look and feel of history.*

* My thanks go to Rachel Stone and Charles West for their editorial help and patience, and to them and the audience at the Leeds Hincmar-session in 2012 for many thoughtful comments.

Notes

1 Hincmar to Nicholas I, in Flodoard, *HRE* III–13, pp. 222–35 (a very long letter), at p. 222. Anyone interested in Hincmar is deeply indebted to Martina Stratmann for her exemplary edition of Flodoard's text.
2 Devisse, *Hincmar*, II, p. 843. The critic himself was given to much speaking: his Hincmar runs to 1,585 pages. Cf. *ibid.*, II, p. 1135: 'Déconcertant Hincmar, moderne par tant d'aspects, ... si irrémédiablement carolingien par tant d'autres côtés' ('Disconcerting Hincmar – so modern in so many ways, yet in so many others, so incurably Carolingian'). See further the penetrating review of Devisse's work by David Ganz, *Revue belge de philologie et d'histoire*, 57 (1979), pp. 711–18.
3 Flodoard, *HRE* III–1, p. 190. See H. Schrörs, *Hinkmar*, p. 12; Devisse, *Hincmar*, II, p. 1089.
4 This was the hearing of the case of Northild at the Council of Attigny: Hincmar, *De divortio*, Responsio 5, pp. 141–2. See now J. L. Nelson, 'Hunnish scenes – Frankish scenes: a history that stands still?', in J. L. Nelson, S. Reynolds and S. Johns, eds, *Gender and Historiography: Studies in the Earlier Middle Ages in Honour of Pauline Stafford* (London, 2012), pp. 175–90, at 176–7, 184–5.
5 O. G. Oexle, *Forschungen zu monastischen und geistlichen Gemeinschaften im westfränkischen Bereich* (Munich, 1978), p. 32.
6 Flodoard, *HRE* III–1, pp. 190–1.
7 Hincmar supported, but perhaps also restrained, his *nutritor*, Hilduin, through the tortuous events of the early 830s: see Flodoard, *HRE* III–1, p. 191, with n.21. He was consistently loyal to Louis and present at Louis's ritual restoration at St-Denis in 834; thereafter he seems to have divided his time between serving as a cleric at court and continuing his duties at St-Denis and at St-Germer-de-Fly, a monastery given him by Louis: Flodoard, *HRE* III–1, p. 191.
8 The remainder of this paragraph restates my arguments in J. L. Nelson, 'The intellectual in politics: context, content and authorship in the capitulary of Coulaines, November 843', first published in L. Smith and B. Ward, eds, *Intellectual Life in the Middle Ages: Essays Presented to Margaret Gibson* (London, 1992), pp. 1–14, reprinted in J. L. Nelson, *The Frankish World 750–900* (London, 1996), pp. 155–68, with

some revisions that owe a good deal to A. Krah, *Die Entstehung der 'potestas regia' im Westfrankenreich während der ersten Regierungsjahre Kaiser Karls II.* (840–877) (Berlin, 2000), esp. pp. 205–30, 250–55, to B. Apsner, *Vertrag und Konsens im frühen Mittelalter: Studien zu Gesellschaftsprogrammatik und Staatlichkeit im westfränkischen Reich.* Trierer historische Forschungen, 58 (Trier, 2006), esp. pp. 42–55, and to the precisely focused comments of S. Patzold, *Episcopus: Wissen über Bischöfe im Frankenreich des späten 8. bis frühen 10. Jahrhunderts.* (Ostfildern, 2008), pp. 296–8, 300–1.

9 *Respublica* occurs in Hincmar, *De ordine palatii,* pp. 46, 50, cc. 8, 9 and often, especially in the phrase *reipublicae ministri,* in Hincmar's works: Devisse, *Hincmar,* II, p. 679, n.38.

10 See above, n.9, and below, n.49. For the theme of *convenientia,* see Apsner, *Vertrag und Konsens,* pp. 73–88.

11 *Capitulare Septimanicum apud Tolosam datum, June 844,* now edited as Council of Toulouse, 844, MGH *Conc.* III, no. 4, pp. 18–23. See H. Mordek, *Bibliotheca Capitularium regum Francorum manuscripta: Überlieferung und Traditionszusammenhang der fränkischen Herrschererlasse* (Munich, 1995), pp. 59–69, esp. p. 65. For the discussion here of the *capitula* of Toulouse, see Nelson, 'Making ends meet: wealth and poverty in the Carolingian church', in W. J. Shiels and D. Wood, eds, *The Church and Wealth. Papers read at the 1986 Summer Meeting and the 1987 Winter Meeting of the Ecclesiastical History Society* (Oxford, 1987), pp. 25–35, reprinted in J. L. Nelson, *Frankish World,* pp. 145–55.

12 *AB* s.a. 844, p. 45 (trans. Nelson, p. 57). The *Annals of St-Bertin,* so called because the earliest manuscript was written at St-Bertin, were a continuation of the *Annales regni Francorum (Royal Frankish Annals),* the second part of which had been written by Prudentius as a palace cleric, then as bishop of Troyes, between 835 and 861. See *AB* trans. Nelson, Introduction, pp. 2, 6–16.

13 Hincmar wrote of the internecine bloodshed of Fontenoy in 877, in a letter to Louis the Stammerer written immediately after Charles the Bald's death: Hincmar, *Novi regis instructio ad rectam regni administrationem, PL* 125, cols 983–90, at col. 986, c. 4: 'tantum malum et tam grande periculum in Fontanido devenerit quantum inter Christianos non accidit ex eo tempore quo primum Carolus cum Raganfredo in Vinciaco pugnavit' ('such evil and such huge danger befell at Fontenoy [in 841] that nothing like it had happened since the time when Charles [Martel] fought Raganfred [and the Neustrians] at Vinchy [in 717]'). Hincmar offered an impressively long historical view of the conflict surrounding Carolingian royal successions, generation after generation, and the role of aristocratic interests therein: *boni barones* had preserved peace after Pippin's death in 768, despite the dangers of a realm divided between two

brother-kings; but later successions had evoked *invidia* and *cupiditas*, and finally *discordia*. Cf. the comment of Devisse, *Hincmar*, II, p. 969, evidently reading aristocratic interests as at least in part class interests: 'L'analyse nous paraît singulièrement forte chez un homme de 70 ans qui n'a pas lu Marx!' See below, pp. 53–4.

14 *AB* s.a. 844, p. 45 (trans. Nelson, p. 57): 'maiestatis reus Francorum iudicio, iussu Karoli in Aquitania capitalem sententiam subiit'.

15 See J. L. Nelson, 'The contexts of Dhuoda', in L. Jégou, S. Joye, T. Lienhard and J. Schneider, eds, *Faire lien – aristocratie, réseaux et échanges compétitifs: mélanges en l'honneur de Régine Le Jan* (Paris, 2015).

16 *Recueil des actes de Charles II le Chauve, roi de France*, ed. A. Giry, M. Prou and G. Tessier, 3 vols (Paris, 1943–55), I, no. 57, pp. 161–3. This charter survives in the original.

17 M. Stratmann, *Hinkmar von Reims als Verwalter von Bistum und Kirchenprovinz* (Sigmaringen, 1991), pp. 46, 59; see now Stratmann's fine edition of Flodoard, *HRE* III–13, p. 235 (referring to *mansiones nostras super fluvium Ligerim secus confinium regni Aquitanie*); III–21, pp. 271, 286, to an archbishop and a bishop; III–26, p. 338, to counts, esp. Bernard of Toulouse).

18 Hincmar, *Collectio de ecclesiis et capellis*, pp. 86–8. See also Stratmann, Introduction to *De ecclesiis*, pp. 8–14, 18–20; S. Wood, *The Proprietary Church in the Medieval West* (Oxford, 2006), pp. 804–12; Nelson, 'Church properties and the propertied Church: donors, the clergy and the church in medieval Western Europe from the fourth century to the twelfth', *English Historical Review*, 125 (2009), pp. 355–74, at 362–70.

19 Flodoard, *HRE* III–18, p. 253: 'Contra dispositionem Prudentii Trecasini episcopi', and cf. *Collectio de ecclesiis et capellis*, p. 76, where Hincmar criticises Prudentius and his allies for 'inappropriately interpreting' (*inconvenienter interpretantes*) canonical texts (these are Orléans I (511), c. 17, Toledo III (589), c. 19, an African canon cited in the Dionysio-Hadriana, c. 65).

20 *Recueil des actes de Charles le Chauve*, vol. I, no. 75, pp. 210–13, at 213.

21 D. Ganz, 'The debate over predestination', in M. T. Gibson and J. L. Nelson, eds, *Charles the Bald: Court and Kingdom*, 2nd revd edn (Aldershot, 1990), pp. 283–302, at 286.

22 *AB* s.a. 849, p. 57 (trans. Nelson, p. 67); W. Hartmann, *Die Synoden der Karolingerzeit im Frankenreich und in Italien* (Paderborn, 1989), pp. 227–8.

23 K. van der Horst, 'The Utrecht Psalter: picturing the Psalms of David', in K. van der Horst, W. Noel and W. C. M. Wüstefeld, eds, *The Utrecht Psalter in Medieval Art: Picturing the Psalms of David* ('t Goy, 1996), pp. 23–84, at 23, 73.

24 Hincmar, *Ad reclusos et simplices in Remensi parrochia contra*

Gothescalcum, ed. W. Gundlach, 'Zwei Schriften des Erzbischofs Hinkmar von Reims', *Zeitschrift für Kirchengeschichte*, 10 (1889), pp. 258-310, at 258, 269-70.

25 R. Kottje, 'Zu den Beziehungen zwischen Hinkmar von Reims und Hrabanus Maurus', in Gibson and Nelson, *Charles the Bald*, pp. 235-40.
26 Council of Quierzy, 853, MGH *Conc.* III, no. 28, pp. 294-7.
27 Hincmar, Epistola 187, ed. E. Perels, MGH *Epp.* 8, p. 196.
28 See for the so-called *Annals of Fulda*, the late Tim Reuter's Introduction to his translation, *The Annals of Fulda* (Manchester, 1992), pp. 1-9; for the so-called *Annals of Xanten*, H. Löwe, 'Studien zu den *Annales Xantenses*', *DA*, 8 (1951), pp. 59-99; for the so-called *Annals of St-Bertin*, see above, n.12, and *AB* trans. Nelson, pp. 2-16.
29 So, J. L. Nelson, 'History-writing at the courts of Louis the Pious and Charles the Bald', in A. Scharer and G. Scheibelreiter, eds, *Historiographie im frühen Mittelalter* (Vienna, 1994), pp. 435-42, at p. 442; see also J. L. Nelson, 'The "Annals of St-Bertin"', in Gibson and Nelson, *Charles the Bald*, pp. 23-40.
30 Levillain, Introduction to *AB*, pp. xviii-xxi; *AB* trans. Nelson, pp. 10-11, and s.a. 859, p. 91, n.13.
31 *AB* s.a. 861, pp. 84-5 (trans. Nelson, p. 94).
32 See Nelson, 'Annals', pp. 31-2.
33 *AB* s.a. 849, p. 57 (trans. Nelson, p. 67), with Nelson, p. 14.
34 *AB* s.a. 846, p. 52, (trans. Nelson, pp. 62-3), and s.a. 856, p. 73 (trans. Nelson, p. 83).
35 See Nelson, *Charles the Bald* (London, 1992), pp. 188-96; on coinage, *Constitutio Carisiacensis de moneta*, 861, MGH *Capit.* II, no. 271, pp. 301-2.
36 *AB* s.a. 869, pp. 152-68 (trans. Nelson, pp. 152-65).
37 *AB* s.a. 869, p. 168 (trans. Nelson, p. 165). On Hincmar's narrative at this point, and coded criticism of Charles which was repeated in 876, see Nelson, 'History-writing', pp. 441-2.
38 *AB* s.a. 876, pp. 208-10 (trans. Nelson, pp. 197-8).
39 *AB* s.a. 872, pp. 185-86 (trans. Nelson, pp. 177-8).
40 See Flodoard, *HRE* III-26, p. 338, and above, p. 46.
41 Flodoard, *HRE* III-26, p. 342.
42 Flodoard, *HRE* III-26, pp. 330-46; cf. also III-27, pp. 346-52, which cites or gives full texts of letters to royal women - including Queen Ermentrude (p. 348), though her request that he fast for her was apparently confided orally (p. 283), but, interestingly, not including Empress Engelberga - and to clergy, III-21 to 25, pp. 269-330.
43 Augustine, *De civitate Dei*, ed. B. Dombart and A. Kalb, CCSL 47-48, 2 vols (Turnhout, 1965) I, 35: 'Perplexae quippe sunt istae duae civitates in hoc saeculo invicemque permixtae, donec ultimo iudicio dirimantur'.

R. Markus, *Saeculum: History and Society in the Theology of St Augustine* (Cambridge, 1970), p. 62, translates *perplexae ... invicemque permixtae* as 'inextricably interwoven and mingled with each other'.
44 Hincmar, *De praedestinatione Dei*, dedicatory letter to Charles the Bald, Epistola 131b, MGH *Epp.* 8, pp. 70–73 at p. 72; cf. Flodoard, *HRE* III–16, p. 250.
45 See Nelson, *Charles the Bald*, pp. 203–4.
46 Augustine, *Enarrationes in Psalmos*, ed. E. Dekkers and J. Fraipont, CCSL 38–39, 2 vols (Turnhout, 1956), 91, 11, cited by Markus, *Saeculum*, p. 23, n.3.
47 See Nelson, *Charles the Bald*, pp. 241–51.
48 See above, p. 56, n.13, and *Novi regis instructio*, PL 125, col. 985, c. 1.
49 Hincmar, *De ordine palatii*, prologue, p. 32.
50 *Ibid.*, p. 54, c. 12: 'Adalardum senem et sapientem domni Karoli magni imperatoris propinquum et monasterii Corbeiae abbatem, inter primos consiliarios primum, in adolescentia mea vidi. Cuius libellum de ordine palatii legi et scripsi'. The editors comment, p. 55, n.101, that Hincmar must have become acquainted with *De ordine palatii* between 822 and 826 when Adalard died. Note Hincmar's identifying Adalard as Charlemagne's *propinquus* (in fact they were first-cousins). Propinquity was something to celebrate.
51 For the *AB* in these latter years, see M. Meyer-Gebel, 'Zur annalistischen Arbeitsweise Hinkmars von Reims', *Francia*, 15 (1987), pp. 75–108.
52 *AB* s.a. 882, pp. 245–51 (trans. Nelson, pp. 223–6); for the date of Hincmar's death, see K. F. Werner, 'Gauzlin von Saint-Denis und die westfränkische Reichsteilung von Amiens (März 880). Ein Beitrag zur Vorgeschichte von Odos Königtum', *DA*, 35 (1979), pp. 395–462, at 453, n.186.

3

To fight with words: the case of Hincmar of Laon in the Annals of St-Bertin[1]

Christine Kleinjung

At least six formal episcopal depositions were discussed in councils in Western Francia and Lotharingia after 835. Archbishop Hincmar of Rheims was involved in every one.[2] However, the deposition of one of them, Bishop Hincmar of Laon, proved one of the most awkward episodes in his career. As a young man, Hincmar of Laon seemed very promising; his uncle Hincmar of Rheims must have been proud of him.[3] The future bishop of Laon was educated by Hincmar of Rheims, who played the role of a mentor. In his twenties in 858, the younger Hincmar was elected bishop of Laon – not without the assistance of the metropolitan of Rheims, who introduced him to the inner circle of the court of Charles the Bald.[4] Without any doubt Hincmar of Laon benefited from the high and influential political position of his uncle. However, the fall soon came and the relationship between the two Hincmars changed for the worse.

Other than Hincmar of Laon himself, the main actors in this conflict were King Charles the Bald and Archbishop Hincmar of Rheims, who was uncle and metropolitan of the accused.[5] As discussed below, between 868 and 871 Hincmar of Laon[6] came into conflict with King Charles the Bald over the king's sovereignty in matters of Church property.[7] From 869, Hincmar of Rheims was also drawn into the conflict, which became ever more intense, eventually leading to the deposition of Hincmar of Laon at the Council of Douzy in 871. Removed from episcopal office, Hincmar of Laon was blinded a short time afterwards, allegedly by Boso, count of Vienne and son-in-law of Charles the Bald, one of the most powerful *fideles*.[8] In August 878 he was partly rehabilitated by Pope John VIII at the Council of Troyes but not restored to his see. He died one year later.

Hincmar of Laon's fall may have been part of a wider political conflict. Another blinding occurred in the West Frankish kingdom in the 870s: that of Carloman, the son of Charles the Bald.[9] This blinding was a commutation of the death sentence originally pronounced.[10] None of our sources mentions complicity between the rebellious son of the king, Carloman, and the accused Bishop Hincmar of Laon, but it may be more than a coincidence that Hincmar of Laon's case was negotiated at the Council of Attigny in 870, where he was forced to swear an oath of loyalty to Charles,[11] and that Carloman was arrested at the palace of Attigny at the same time. The Annals of Saint-Bertin mention the declaration of fidelity and in the same breath the imprisonment of Carloman.[12] Finally, both Carloman and Hincmar suffered the same punishment: Carloman was blinded at the Council of Senlis in 873,[13] and Hincmar, arrested in the same year and turned over to the ministrations of Count Boso, endured the same fate two years later.[14]

Defining offences against order

The course of events in the case of Hincmar of Laon has been discussed extensively. This chapter, therefore, does not focus on the characters and personalities of the protagonists, but on their ways of making sense and defining rules in a conflict situation. In the ninth century, bishops were a prominent political and social group with a claim to leadership. What happened if one of them offended against the standards defined by the group itself? As bishops also had significant political power at their disposal, this was by no means just a question for the ecclesiastical sector. It was, rather, an explosive, highly political act, in which the king was involved. The bishops, together with the king, had responsibility for the overall political programme. Clashes like this between kings and bishops – and among bishops – allow us to examine the ruptures of political structures and the efforts made by contemporaries to manage them.[15]

What is regarded as being an offence against order depends on time and social context. Just as dependent on time is the question of which groups claim for themselves the prerogative of interpretation (*Deutungshoheit*) of the political and social order. An offence against norms that was detected would be punished, in the case of bishops by deposition. But who defined an offence against the norm? In the second half of the ninth century this was an open process in which several interest groups were involved and the papacy increasingly also asserted a claim for recognition. And all of these actors wrote and wrote.

The production of these textual weapons is significant for the character of the conflicts among the secular and clerical elites and around episcopal depositions in the ninth century. How do intellectuals resolve conflicts? They write! In their texts they refer to their norms and interpret rituals. The texts are written when the rules are challenged, when players offend against the expectations of the dominant group. The texts are not only words; they are objects with a physical materiality. And they were used at synods and assemblies where questions of political order concerning kingship, episcopal office and Church property were discussed. The authors of such texts, however, could not expect their papers to be strong enough to be successful in every case. They just tried to present texts in different situations and for different audiences. The Carolingian courts can be identified as one important centre of intellectual debates, and the court audience, as well as a synodal audience, was supposed to be addressed by these texts.[16]

In the case of Hincmar of Laon, as different concepts of order clashed together, each party prepared itself for the battle with texts. In this quarrel, texts were used – as shown by Karl Brunner – as media ('als Medien') and their physical presence was deployed in disputes and rituals.[17] Apart from the extensive council records of Douzy[18] and the records on the Council of Attigny,[19] we have letters and the polemical treatises (the famous *Streitschriften*, such as the *Opusculum LV capitulorum*,[20] the *Pittaciolus*[21] and the *Rotula prolixa*) of both parties – what Karl Brunner called 'products of a battle of the texts'.[22]

The Annals of St-Bertin

We also have, however, a historiographical account of the case, because Hincmar of Rheims dealt with it in his Annals of St-Bertin over several years, and it is on this account that I want to concentrate.[23] As well as the case of his nephew, Hincmar presented three other cases of a bishop's *deposition* in which he was personally involved: Rothad of Soissons, Gunther of Cologne and Theutgaud of Trier.[24] I want to ask what part the public and private work of Hincmar of Rheims' historiographical writing played in this context of conflicts between bishops. Are there intertextual references between the different groups of texts? How did Hincmar of Rheims deal in this work with his rebellious nephew?

Hincmar of Rheims had several very different ways of composing this text. Some annals were written down from year to year, while in some other cases he wrote and rewrote history, composing his annals coherently as a whole text.[25] According to a detailed study of the entire Annals of St-Bertin, it seems unlikely that Hincmar of Rheims retrospectively rewrote single entries following a change in his own perceptions.[26] He used the annals as media to express his opinion and interpretation. We know that Hincmar did not write the annals as a sort of personal diary, but for an audience which consisted of himself, the clergy of Rheims and presumably the Carolingian West Frankish kings. The annals may have been used to spread criticism of the behaviour of the kings in public.[27]

In his annals Hincmar of Rheims tells a story. The presentation differs fundamentally from the form of the synodal sources. In the historiographical records he presents his perceptions, he deals with silence and with new correlations. Not only is the truth disputed, but likewise the means of its creation and representation. I now want to examine what statements from the canonistic-legal context are extracted in Hincmar's history. Is there a shift of emphasis? Are central statements presented in abridged or sharpened form?

The first entry in the Annals of St-Bertin dealing with Hincmar of Laon is to be found in the report for the year 868:

> Charles travelled on by way of the royal *villae* situated in the county of Laon. Without the prior knowledge of any bishop of his province, he ordered Hincmar bishop of Laon to come to answer a case in his own courts, in other words summoned him to secular judgment, because he had taken away benefices from certain of Charles' men. But Bishop Hincmar protested that he did not dare to come, as he had been ordered, to a secular judgment, leaving aside that of the ecclesiastical courts.[28]

This beginning of the story of Hincmar of Laon gives no hint of the later turn of events. It is by no means about an unworthy and bad bishop. The topic is rather one of those that determined the pulse of the age: dealing with ecclesiastical property and the relationship of secular and spiritual power. Hincmar of Laon had refused to give the king the entire control over the distribution of the property of the see of Laon.

Hincmar of Rheims was determined to restore the Church property of Rheims that had been lost in the war between the sons of Louis the Pious. In accordance with this fundamental political concept, in the matter of Hincmar of Laon the archbishop at first clearly took a stand in favour of his nephew and suffragan, and supported him publicly against King Charles at the meeting of the royal court at Pîtres:

> Archbishop Hincmar of Rheims took Hincmar of Laon with him and went with other bishops to the king at Pîtres. Using written texts and oral arguments, he showed what great prejudice both episcopal authority and the universal Church were suffering through such a judgment.[29]

The attitude of Hincmar of Rheims is clear: it is a matter of responsibilities, the separation of the spiritual and secular spheres, and an appropriate procedure. Bishops have to pass judgment on their fellow bishops, and the king must not.

Hincmar of Laon defies the king

But at the end of the report of the year 868 we glimpse a first sign of less sympathy for his nephew's behaviour: Hincmar of Rheims comments that his nephew provoked the king more than 'befits the episcopal dignity' (*amplius quam episcopalis gravitas postulat*)[30] by his appeal to Rome and his refusal to come to the king:

> He [Charles the Bald] was angry with Hincmar bishop of Laon because he had sent to Rome without the king's permission and obtained letters on which Charles had not agreed. He was in fact absolutely furious with the bishop for resisting him so contumaciously.[31]

And Hincmar of Rheims continues in the annal of 869: 'now the bishop, though summoned through the other bishops to come to the king, still declined to obey the royal command'.[32] What Hincmar does not mention here in his annals is his dissatisfaction with the invocation of papal authority, which threatened his position as metropolitan and his authority over the bishop of Laon.

The system of values of Hincmar of Rheims becomes very clear at this point. Contrary to his initial expectations, his nephew's actions were not completely living up to this system of values, because Hincmar of Laon did not accept the authority of his uncle and metropolitan, and still refused to appear before the king, even after the other bishops had called upon him to do so. Only after this failed attempt by the other bishops did Charles take drastic steps in 869 and summon Hincmar of Laon before the Council of Verberie.[33] Hincmar of Rheims mentions that Hincmar had to appear at Verberie,[34] but he keeps quiet in the annals about the later events after Verberie. We know about them from his letters and later polemical treatises: Hincmar of Laon had sent to Rome at the end of the year 868, but the bishops assembled at Verberie did not allow this appeal to the apostolic see.[35]

Furthermore, in preparation for Verberie, Hincmar of Laon had rounded up his clergy, instructed them about the power of binding and loosing, and announced that he would impose the severest form of interdict over his diocese in the case of his arrest.[36] The interdict meant that any church service and even the administering of sacraments would be forbidden in the diocese of Laon. Hincmar was not arrested at Verberie, but he was arrested shortly afterwards in May 869. The interdict then entered into force. A delegation of the clergy of the diocese of Laon appeared before Hincmar of Rheims to plead for revocation of the interdict. They asked him to imagine how much danger the interdict brought to the people of the diocese.[37] Yet in the Annals of St-Bertin he does not mention these dramatic events at all.

In the following year, Hincmar of Laon was brought before the Council of Attigny.[38] Hincmar of Rheims did not attend this synod because he was suffering from gout. But he presented his *Opusculum LV capitulorum*[39] in reaction to Hincmar of Laon's *Pittaciolus*.[40] Hincmar of Laon came to the synod, bringing some collections of Pseudo-Isidorian forgeries with him.[41] The assembled bishops were on the side of Hincmar of Rheims, and Hincmar of Laon escaped from the synod at night, in fear of his uncle and of Charles the Bald. After the synod he presented his own way of interpretation in a letter called the *Rotula prolixa*.[42] In the Annals of St-Bertin there is a loud silence. Hincmar of Rheims does not mention the polemical treatises. Instead he focuses on the oath – and on the arrest of Carloman at the palace of Attigny.

Hincmar v. Hincmar

Here we now learn for the first time in the Annals of St-Bertin that there was also talk of the younger Hincmar's disobedience towards his archbishop, though the quarrel had begun several months before. The rebellious bishop was said to have been called to account because of this, and because of his refusal to submit to royal power. In response to the reproaches of the bishops at the synod, Hincmar of Laon is said to have presented a written document signed in his own hand and to have read it publicly. This oath and the voluntary performance meant so much to Hincmar of Rheims that he copied out the wording in the annals:[43]

> I, Hincmar, bishop of the church of Laon, shall be faithful and obedient now and henceforth to the lord my superior (*domnus senior meus*) King Charles, according to my office, as a man ought to be to his superior and any bishop ought in rightness to be to his king, and I profess myself willing to obey as far as I know and can the privilege of Hincmar metropolitan of the province of the church of Rheims, according to the sacred canons and the decrees of the apostolic see promulgated in accordance with the sacred canons. And he subscribed this.[44]

At that point the case had escalated into a struggle not only between Hincmar of Rheims, Charles the Bald and the rebellious Hincmar of Laon but also between the bishop of Laon and his own clergy. The interdict declared by Hincmar of Laon led to many problems.[45] The unjustified interdict and the abuse of his episcopal office later became one of the main charges of Hincmar of Rheims against his nephew. Yet it is not emphasised in his historiographical report.

The case of Hincmar of Laon was finally treated at the Council of Douzy in August and September 871.[46] There, Charles the Bald accused Hincmar of Laon of infidelity and betrayal. Hincmar of Rheims focused on the disregard of the authority of the metropolitan of Rheims, which Hincmar of Laon had deliberately ignored by proclaiming an unjustified interdict over his diocese.[47] Hincmar of Rheims presented a *Libellus expostulationis* against his nephew and he himself composed the text of the synodal records; he did so in presenting the decision of every single participant bishop, allegedly in their own words.[48] Further we have minutes from the synod – more evidence for the care exercised in this case.

Hincmar's annals did not refer to the interdict, and left the distress of the clergy of Laon unmentioned, along with all the polemical treatises – the whole battle with texts. However, his report of the Council of Douzy in the Annals of St-Bertin makes it clear that there had definitely been a radical change in his mood by then. His presentation of his nephew in the text is scathing:

Hincmar of Laon in the Annals of St-Bertin

Hincmar of Laon, bishop of Laon in name only, an exceptionally arrogant man, rebelled against his king contrary to the truth of the Gospel and to apostolic and ecclesiastical authority. Without showing respect for anyone he raged against the neighbouring clergy and laity and those committed to him, and scorned to pay any attention to his metropolitan when, as the rules lay down, he warned him about his behaviour. He roused the king, his archbishop and the bishops of the whole realm to such fury against him that the king summoned a synod to meet at Douzy in August, to pass judgment there on Hincmar's depravities.[49]

Here we now have a clear shift of emphasis in his historiographical writing. In his work Hincmar of Rheims referred to private and public matters, and they included a disobedient nephew who would not pay attention to the admonitions of his metropolitan and uncle.

Economy with the truth?

The brief reference in the annals to the fact that Hincmar of Laon bore only the name of a bishop opens the door to a great ideological programme. The office of bishop meant very much more than just bearing the name. Here we no longer find any understanding for the nephew who had always chosen provocation, who (even after the oath sworn in Attigny) was not prepared to accept the established forms – of agreement, finding consensus and dispensing justice – and who, as we shall see, had put up massive resistance to his uncle on central points.

From Hincmar of Rheims's report of the Council of Douzy we learn a great deal, but much of it remains vague compared to the synodal records of Douzy itself and Hincmar's polemical writings. Hincmar of Laon acted, according to his uncle, against evangelical truth and apostolic authority. Through this depiction, Hincmar of Rheims wanted to suggest the complete isolation of Hincmar of Laon, who had violated the core competence of his office: a bishop must always stand on the side of evangelical truth and apostolic authority. When he opposed his king, he had his archbishop and all his fellow bishops against him. By the acts of violence 'committed against the clergy and laity entrusted to him' is meant the interdict that Hincmar of Laon imposed on his diocese with the aim of suppressing the opposition to him and forcing the clergy and people to be loyal to him in the conflict with the king.

Of course we hear nothing of Hincmar of Laon's argument in the

Annals of St-Bertin, but we also learn just as little about the specific charges made or about the proceedings. The deposition is mentioned briefly and there is a remarkable intertextual reference to the synodal records that were also edited by Hincmar of Rheims himself:

> [Bishop] Hincmar [of Laon] came to the synod in the end, but in a most arrogant fashion. There a petition was presented by King Charles following the ecclesiastical rules, and Hincmar, having been accused and convicted on clearly proven charges according to the statutory procedures, received the statutory sentence of deposition. All this is contained in the official records of the synod, as sent by the synod itself to the apostolic see through the venerable Bishop Actard who had been present at it.[50]

The rightful judgment is contained in the records and they were sent to the apostolic see; the procedure was observed. Hincmar kept quiet in the Annals about his own role in the proceedings. He mentioned the common decision of all the bishops, and named the bishop sent to Rome, in both cases to demonstrate the independent judgement of the assembly at Douzy and to cover up his own decisive role as well as that of the king.

In Hincmar's report about Attigny and Douzy in the annals, the nephew Hincmar of Laon appears as a rebel against his king. After Douzy the presentation in the annals is nearly always hostile. Yet all activities of Hincmar of Laon concerning Church property in 868 and 869 were presented as justified in the annals by Hincmar of Rheims himself. In the annals we have Hincmar's own narrative reproduced with a structure of its own. There is a great compression of events which we can reconstruct in much more detailed form from the legal texts, because there are statements in these texts that are like the minutes of proceedings. Evidently Hincmar did not subsequently modify his early positive statements about his nephew in the Annals of St-Bertin after the end of the story.

This is evidence for Hincmar's different ways of writing his annals.[51] Perhaps this was in order to show that he, Hincmar of Rheims, had pursued the same aim right from the outset: the defence of episcopal *auctoritas* and metropolitan authority which must be protected against the king and laity, but also against abuse by office holders. And he tried to secure his own position as important adviser to the king. His annals are a medium of communication to convey this message.

There is clear setting of priorities in the Annals of St-Bertin: Hincmar of Laon's conflict with Charles the Bald is very much to the fore. By contrast, the reproaches of the metropolitan Hincmar, with regard to disrespect for the position of the metropolitan and abuse of episcopal *auctoritas*, become less important – contrary to the legal texts. In his annals Hincmar is obviously starting out from the assumption that this audience has to be convinced in a different manner from the readers of or listeners to his synodal reports. The synodal records were written for the archive of the diocese of Rheims, for Hincmar himself and for presentation at royal assemblies and synods, especially among the clerical elites. The case of the annals is not so clear, but they may have been written not only for Hincmar himself but also for the king, and maybe for a court audience and secular elites as well. This court audience played an important role in conflicts like the one presented here because questions of moral behaviour and identity concerning kingship and episcopal office were discussed at this intellectual and political centre.[52]

The narrative of the annals stands beside the synodal record; it is not possible to build a united or coherent story from the different sources. Looking at the proceedings, opposition to the king on its own was not the only charge against the bishop of Laon and was not even decisive – though Hincmar suggested precisely this with his account in the annals. On the contrary, he even holds against the nephew in retrospect that the latter had sworn an oath of allegiance to the king in 869 without the knowledge of the metropolitan or the provincial bishops![53] Hincmar of Laon did not accept the system of norms composed and interpreted by his uncle. And Hincmar of Rheims was not willing to have the privilege of interpretation of the *ministerium episcopalis* wrested away from him, or even to allow this to be doubted.

Rather than this struggle over interpretation of norms, however, Hincmar of Rheims's history of Hincmar of Laon shows him simply in breach of widely shared norms, such as 'apostolic authority'. In his uncle's view as presented in the annals, Hincmar of Laon proved himself to be unworthy and the older Hincmar shows him as a rebel against royal power. In the Annals of St-Bertin he relates the history of a rebellion – against the king, but also against ecclesiastical order.

Yet, though Hincmar of Laon was not only deposed but also made incapable of office by blinding in 875 or shortly afterwards, there is no word about this from Hincmar of Rheims. This may hint at some differences between Hincmar's aim to judge the bishop of Laon according to the canons (in his own interpretation) and the punishment of blinding ordered probably by Charles the Bald. In fact, we learn of the punishment of blinding only retrospectively in the annals, from the entry for the year 878, when Hincmar of Laon was partly rehabilitated by Pope John VIII at the Council of Troyes. Hincmar states:

> When Hincmar's supporters heard what Pope John had said, namely that Hincmar, though blinded, could if he wished chant the Mass, and that the king had given his agreement to Hincmar's receiving a share in the episcopal revenues of Laon, the bishops of other provinces and also the metropolitans of other regions unexpectedly, and without having any orders from the pope, led Hincmar, clad in his priestly robes, into the papal presence; and from there, chanting, they brought him away and led him into the church and had him give the sign of blessing over the people. With that, the synod was brought to a close.[54]

The blind Hincmar was clothed by his supporters and led to the altar – without any command by the pope, as Hincmar of Rheims emphasises.

Hincmar of Laon thus did have supporters, the existence of whom Hincmar of Rheims keeps quiet about for the whole time in the annals. He is also silent on the political implications of the punishment. Blinding is not really the style in which conflicts among intellectuals were resolved in the West, but it was a punishment for political treason. Hincmar of Laon was blinded as a rebel against the king and the political order – one may recall the rebellion of Bernard of Italy. Blinding as commutation of capital punishment in treason cases was a Byzantine practice imported to the west in the sixth and seventh centuries.[55] We do not know whether capital punishment was discussed in the case of Hincmar of Laon, as it was for Carloman, the rebellious son of Charles the Bald.

Conclusion

How should a bad bishop be treated? There is no clear or simple answer. Treason, abuse of office and misuse of episcopal authority always have more than one dimension: there are secular and ecclesiastical norms. In the case of the rebellious Carloman, who had been a cleric of the church of Sens, Hincmar of Rheims refers to the ecclesiastical standard when he writes that Carloman's capital punishment was commuted into blinding so that 'Carloman could do penance'.[56] In the case of Hincmar of Laon, different norms are also discussed: Charles the Bald and Hincmar of Rheims have different points of view. The differences between them are very clear in the annals for the year 868 and the beginning of 869. The shift of emphasis thereafter may be connected with an enhanced relationship between Hincmar of Rheims and Charles the Bald from the summer of 869.[57]

Hincmar presents one possible view in his annals, and a different or modified one in his synodal records. He did not rewrite the whole story of his nephew Hincmar of Laon after the end of the case. So the story is not presented as fully coherent – except in the aim to consolidate Hincmar of Rheims' own position as metropolitan and at court. In the annals from 869 to 873 he shows great sympathy for Charles the Bald, sympathy that we should not take for granted. He does not express any disapproval of the royal actions against the rebel Hincmar of Laon. But he does not mention the blinding at all, and we do not hear of it in the annals until 878. Hincmar of Laon was defeated and banned from office, and Hincmar of Rheims could not guess that the Pseudo-Isidorian decretals used in this case foreshadowed the future.

In Hincmar's annals, king and archbishop are a team, acting together for the benefit of the realm. Hincmar does not present questions of canon law, he does not mention his own polemical treatise and he is silent about the arguments of Hincmar of Laon. This presentation may be explained by fact that the annals were addressed to a court audience and by the specific function of historiographical writing, which has to demonstrate clarity and freedom from ambiguity (even when the conflict actually was ambiguous). We know the whole story neither from the synodal sources nor from the annals.[58] Silence is a significant weapon in historiographical writings, and so it is in the case of Hincmar of Laon in the Annals of St-Bertin.

Notes

1 This contribution corresponds to the paper given at Leeds in July 2012 with only a few additions and annotations. I am currently preparing a study on the depositions of bishops in the ninth and tenth century in the Western Frankish kingdoms where the case of Hincmar of Laon will be discussed in detail. I am very grateful to the editors and the co-contributors at Leeds for helpful comments on my paper.

2 The deposition cases are: Ebbo of Rheims in 835, Wenilo of Sens in 859, Rothad of Soissons in 862, Gunther of Cologne and Theutgaud of Trier (in 863) as well as Hincmar of Laon. Around the time of the condemnation of Ebbo, some other bishops suffered exile or loss of office because of their role in the opposition to Louis the Pious. On rebellious bishops see S. Airlie, '"Not rendering unto Caesar": challenges to early medieval rulers', in W. Pohl and V. Wieser, eds, *Der frühmittelalterliche Staat – europäische Perspektiven* (Vienna, 2009), pp. 489–501, on Hincmar of Laon pp. 496–7, on the bishops banned from office during the reign of Louis the Pious, p. 494; see also C. M. Booker, 'The public penance of Louis the Pious: A new edition of the Episcoporum de poenitentia, quam Hludowicus imperator professus est, relatio Compendiensis (833)', *Viator*, 39 (2008), 1–19, at p. 4 with n. 12; Ph. Depreux, *Prosopographie de l'entourage de Louis le Pieux (781–840)* (Sigmaringen, 1997), pp. 406–8.

3 For the life of Hincmar of Laon see P. R. McKeon, *Hincmar of Laon and Carolingian Politics* (Urbana, 1978).

4 The circumstances of this election became one of the issues in the later struggle between uncle and nephew. See Hincmar, *Opusculum LV capitulorum*, ed. R. Schieffer, *Die Streitschriften Hinkmars von Reims und Hinkmars von Laon 869–871*, MGH *Conc.* IV, supplementum 2 (Hanover, 2003), pp. 99–361, Praefatio, pp. 145–6; for the charge of nepotism see c. 42, p. 306. For the introduction to Charles's inner circle, see K. Zechiel-Eckes, *Rebellische Kleriker?: eine unbekannte kanonistisch-patristische Polemik gegen Bischof Hinkmar von Laon in Cod. Paris, BNF, nouv. acq. lat. 1746*, MGH Studien und Texte 49 (Hanover, 2009), pp. 40–3.

5 This complex conflict was not just a struggle for power but a controversy about episcopal behaviour. As C. West, 'Evaluating conflict at court: a West Frankish perspective', in M. Becher and A. Plassmann, eds, *Streit am Hof im frühen Mittelalter* (Gottingen, 2011), pp. 317–30, at p. 329, points out, Carolingian courts 'were after all intellectual centres almost as much as political ones'.

6 For details of the conflict and the fall of the bishop see McKeon, *Hincmar of Laon*; Zechiel-Eckes, *Rebellische Kleriker*, pp. 43–54; H. Fuhrmann, 'Fälscher unter sich: zum Streit zwischen Hinkmar von Reims und Hinkmar von Laon', in M. T. Gibson and J. L. Nelson, eds, *Charles the Bald: Court and Kingdom*, 2nd revd edn (Aldershot, 1990), pp. 224–34; H. Fuhrmann, *Einfluß und Verbreitung der pseudoisidorischen Fälschungen: von ihrem Auftauchen bis in die neuere Zeit*, 3 vols (Stuttgart, 1972–74); J. Devisse, *Hincmar*, II, pp. 766–85; Schrörs, *Hinkmar*, pp. 315–53.

7 J. Nelson, '"Not bishops' bailiffs but lords of the earth": Charles the Bald and the problem of sovereignty', in *The Frankish World 750–900* (London, 1996), pp. 133–43; G. Bührer-Thierry, 'Épiscopat et royauté dans le monde carolingien', in W. Fałkowksi and Y. Sassier, eds, *Le*

monde carolingien: bilan, perspectives, champs de recherches (Turnhout, 2009), pp. 143–55, at p. 145 on Church property.
8 *Annales Vedastini*, s.a. 878, ed. B. von Simson, MGH *SRG* 12 (Hanover, 1909), p. 43.
9 *AB* s.a. 873, p. 190 (trans. Nelson, p. 181).
10 M. McCormick, *Eternal Victory: Triumphal Rulership in Late Antiquity, Byzantium and the Early Medieval West* (Cambridge, 1986), pp. 313, 334; on the punishment of blinding, see G. Bührer-Thierry, '"Just anger" or "vengeful anger"? The punishment of blinding in the early medieval West', in B. H. Rosenwein, ed., *Anger's Past: the Social Uses of an Emotion in the Middle Ages* (Ithaca, 1998), pp. 75–91.
11 Council of Attigny, 870, MGH *Conc.* IV, no. 33, pp. 380–95; on the oath, pp. 387–8; on the Carolingian councils mentioned in this chapter, see generally W. Hartmann, *Die Synoden der Karolingerzeit im Frankenreich und in Italien* (Paderborn, 1989). On oath-taking in West Francia, see Bernard-Valette, Chapter 5.
12 Hincmar's record in the Annals includes the oath *verbatim*: *AB* s.a. 870, pp. 169–71 (trans. Nelson, p. 167).
13 J. L. Nelson, *Charles the Bald* (London, 1992), p. 227. Hincmar of Laon's uncle does not mention it in his Annals but he writes about the blinding of Carloman in 873: *AB* s.a. 873, p. 190 (trans. Nelson, p. 181).
14 Hincmar of Laon refers to the imprisonment and blinding in his letters. McKeon, *Hincmar of Laon*, p. 162.
15 Airlie, 'Not rendering', p. 496; On the study of conflict and ritual see generally P. Buc, 'Text and ritual in ninth-century political culture: Rome 864', in G. Althoff, J. Fried and P.J. Geary, eds, *Medieval Concepts of the Past: Ritual, Memory, Historiography* (Cambridge 2002), pp. 123–38, esp. 124–8, 135–8.
16 See West, 'Evaluating conflict'.
17 On the use of texts in rituals see K. Brunner, 'Ein Krieg mit Texten. Anmerkungen an Stelle fälliger Rezensionen', *Mitteilungen des Instituts für Österreichische Geschichtsforschung*, 113 (2005), 392–8 at 396.
18 Council of Douzy, 871, MGH *Conc.* IV, no. 37, pp. 410–572.
19 See above, n.11.
20 See above, n.4.
21 Hincmar of Laon, *Pittaciolus*, ed. Schieffer, *Streitschriften*, pp. 57–97.
22 Brunner, 'Krieg', p. 395.
23 J. L. Nelson, 'History-writing at the courts of Louis the Pious and Charles the Bald', in A. Scharer and G. Scheibelreiter, eds, *Historiographie im Frühen Mittelalter* (Vienna, 1994), pp. 435–42; J. L. Nelson, 'The "Annals of St. Bertin"', in M. T. Gibson and J. L. Nelson, eds, *Charles the Bald: Court and Kingdom* (Oxford, 1981), pp. 15–36, reprinted in J. L. Nelson, *Politics and Ritual in Early Medieval Europe* (London, 1986), pp. 173–94.

24 S. Patzold, *Episcopus: Wissen über Bischöfe im Frankenreich des späten 8. bis frühen 10. Jahrhunderts* (Ostfildern, 2008), pp. 405–6. Hincmar of Rheims was involved in four or more of the cases: see above, n.2.
25 M. Meyer-Gebel, 'Zur annalistischen Arbeitsweise Hinkmars von Reims', *Francia*, 15 (1987), 75–108; on Hincmar of Laon at 96, 106.
26 Nelson, 'Annals', p. 28 ('a series of subjective and more or less instanteous perceptions'); Meyer-Gebel, 'Annalistische Arbeitsweise', 104–5.
27 Nelson, 'History-writing', p. 441 with a revision of her older opinion ('private work') in Nelson, 'Annals'.
28 *AB* trans. Nelson, p. 150, n.14.
29 *AB* s.a. 868, p. 150 (trans. Nelson, pp. 150–1).
30 *AB* s.a. 868, p. 152 (trans. Nelson, p. 152).
31 *Ibid*. Hincmar of Laon used the Pseudo-Isidorian forgeries to give a reason for his appeal to Rome: Fuhrmann, *Einfluß und Verbreitung*, I, pp. 219–24.
32 *AB* s. a. 869, p. 152 (trans. Nelson, p. 152).
33 Council of Verberie, 869, MGH *Conc*. IV, no. 29, pp. 325–36. Fuhrmann, *Einfluß und Verbreitung*, III, pp. 632, 649, 652, 707; McKeon, *Hincmar of Laon*, pp. 31, 36, 182–3, 279–80.
34 *AB* s.a. 869, p. 152 (trans. Nelson, p. 153).
35 Hincmar, *Opuscula et epistolae*, PL 126, cols 526–31 at col. 531 (Schrörs, *Hinkmar*, Reg. 237, see also Reg. 234, 235). The bishops assembled at Verberie did not allow this appeal.
36 Zechiel-Eckes, *Rebellische Kleriker*, pp. 43–4. This is only known from Hincmar's letters.
37 McKeon, *Hincmar of Laon*, p. 33; Hincmar, *Opusculum LV capitulorum*, pp. 261, 269, 272–8, cc. 27, 29, 30. The clergy of Laon wrote a polemical treatise against their bishop, ed. Zechiel-Eckes, *Rebellische Kleriker*, pp. 55–84.
38 See above, n.11.
39 See above, n.4.
40 See above, n.21.
41 Hincmar of Laon, *Materialsammlungen vorwiegend pseudoisidorischen Inhalts*, ed. Schieffer, *Streitschriften*, pp. 1–55; McKeon, *Hincmar of Laon*, pp. 173, 283–4.
42 Hincmar of Laon, *Rotula prolixa*, ed. Schieffer, *Streitschriften*, pp. 363–408.
43 The oath is also inserted *verbatim* in Hincmar's *Libellus expostulationis* for the Council of Douzy 871 (Hincmar, *Libellus expostulationis*, MGH *Conc*. IV, no 37B, pp. 420–87, at p. 477, c. 22) and the part of the oath concerning the king is also inserted in the charge of Charles the Bald against Hincmar of Laon at Douzy (*Anklageschrift Karls des Kahlen gegen Hinkmar von Laon*, MGH *Conc*. IV, no. 37A, pp. 417–20 at 418–19).

44 *AB* s.a. 870, p. 169 (trans. Nelson, p. 167). Hincmar of Rheims refused to swear a similar oath to King Charles the Bald in 876 allegedly because Charles could not be the *senior* of the older Hincmar. The background may be Hincmar's anxiety about his slipping influence at the court: see H. H. Anton, *Fürstenspiegel und Herrscherethos in der Karolingerzeit* (Bonn, 1968), pp. 320–25; S. Patzold, 'Konsens und Konkurrenz. Überlegungen zu einem aktuellen Forschungskonzept der Mediävistik', *Frühmittelalterliche Studien*, 41 (2007), 75–103 at 79–80; Schrörs, *Hinkmar*, pp. 363–4.
45 The clergy of Laon tried to defeat Hincmar of Laon with the weapon of the pseudo-Isidorian decretals which the latter used himself against his uncle: Zechiel-Eckes, *Rebellische Kleriker*, pp. 52–4.
46 Council of Douzy, 871, MGH *Conc.* IV, no. 37, pp. 410–572.
47 *Ibid.*, pp. 410–11.
48 *Antworten der Bischöfe*, MGH *Conc.* IV, no. 37C, pp. 488–502.
49 *AB* s.a. 871, p. 181 (trans. Nelson, p. 174).
50 *AB* s.a. 871, pp. 181–2 (trans. Nelson, p. 174).
51 Meyer-Gebel, 'Annalistische Arbeitsweise'.
52 On Carolingian intellectuals and their debates at court see C. Wickham, *The Inheritance of Rome: a History of Europe from 400 to 1000* (London, 2009), pp. 405–27; on Carolingian court audiences, see Nelson, Chapter 2, pp. 50–3.
53 Hincmar, *Libellus expostulationis*, MGH *Conc.* IV, no. 37B, pp. 429–30, c. 10.
54 *AB* s.a. 878, p. 229 (trans. Nelson, pp. 211–12).
55 McCormick, *Eternal Victory*, pp. 313, 334.
56 *AB* s.a. 873, p 190 (trans. Nelson, p. 181): 'So that he might have time and opportunity for doing penance, however, yet not have the power to commit the still worse offences he was planning, the death sentence was commuted, by the public assent of all present, to a sentence of blinding'.
57 Schrörs, *Hinkmar*, pp. 302–7, speaks of a new harmony between Hincmar of Rheims and Charles the Bald in summer 869. In September 869 Hincmar managed the coronation of Charles at Metz. On the influence of the political situation on Hincmar's writing, see Nelson, Chapter 2.
58 During the Council of Attigny, before swearing his oath Hincmar of Laon spoke to his uncle in private and tried to make a deal with him. We know about this event only from the account of Hincmar of Rheims in his *Libellus expostulationis*, MGH *Conc.* IV, no. 37B, pp. 478–9, c. 23; W. Hartmann, 'Gespräche in der "Kaffeepause" – am Rande des Konzils von Attigny 870', *Annuarium historiae conciliorum*, 27/28 (1995/96), 137–45.

4

An unfortunate necessity? Hincmar and Lothar I

Elina Screen

A relationship remembered

In 867, Hincmar wrote to Pope Nicholas I, looking back over the long drawn-out saga of the deposition of his predecessor, Archbishop Ebbo, and the fate of the clerics Ebbo had ordained. He summed up his relations with Emperor Lothar I, ruler of the Middle Kingdom from 843 until his abdication on 23 September 855, as follows:

> at the start of my episcopate the lord Lothar of happy memory, on account of his conflict over the kingdom with his brother, the lord Charles, to whose service I adhered faithfully, did enough for me [in that regard] with Sergius and afterwards with his successor Leo; but later, inspired by God, he repented, and sent letters addressed to the apostolic see, in which he took care to correct his fault.[1]

In hindsight, therefore, Hincmar recalled his relationship with Lothar as one of imperial recalcitrance, caused by Lothar's disputes with his brother, the ruler of West Francia, followed by satisfactory imperial amendment.

The Treaty of Verdun in 843, which left the archbishopric of Rheims divided between the West Frankish and Middle Kingdoms, meant that Hincmar could not avoid contact with Lothar. Rulers and ruled alike, accustomed to a political system which valued loyalty to a single lord above all, faced a new reality: now the interests of the great ecclesiastical and lay magnates crossed political boundaries, and the elite needed to manage connections with more than one Carolingian ruler.[2] How did Hincmar – faced with the unfortunate necessity of acknowledging a second Carolingian master alongside Charles the Bald – negotiate this relationship in practice? Hincmar's relationship with Lothar fell into distinct phases: a first tentative phase up to 847, the turning point of 847, a more direct relationship from 847 onwards (albeit with continuing points of dispute) and then a final change occurring in 855.[3] The reasons for Lothar's change in attitude towards Hincmar have been especially debated. The role of personality and the political context have previously been emphasised,[4] but I shall argue that religious factors were also significant in the evolving relationship, which was central to the first part of Hincmar's career, from 845 to 855.[5]

Hincmar's long subsequent career has left complex, partisan and largely retrospective evidence for his relationship with Lothar.[6] Hincmar had firm ideas on the roles of bishops and rulers, seen both in his later relationships with Louis the German and Charles the Bald, and in his comments on past precedents such as Ambrose's dealings with Theodosius I.[7] It is not possible to establish whether Hincmar's relationship with Lothar contributed to the formation of these ideas, but Hincmar's ideals are certainly likely to have coloured his memory of the relationship. Furthermore, Hincmar's appointment and his attempts to depose the clerics Ebbo had ordained met with strong opposition.[8] After Lothar's death in 855, Hincmar remained under pressure to confirm the legitimacy of his actions, and his assertion of his powers as metropolitan triggered opposition from Hincmar of Laon and Rothad of Soissons.[9] These continuing pressures led to the falsification and forgery of documents for and against Hincmar.[10] Flodoard's tenth-century *Historia Remensis ecclesiae*, upon which we depend for much of Hincmar's correspondence, then further shaped the evidence.[11] Debates over the quality of the evidence thus strongly mark all contributions on Hincmar's relationship with Lothar, from Émile Lesne's important article responding to the work of Robert Parisot and Joseph Calmette, to Klaus Herbers' ground-breaking study on Leo IV.[12]

Early challenges

Hincmar faced daunting challenges upon his consecration as archbishop of Rheims on 3 May 845.[13] The archdiocese was divided:[14] the bishopric of Cambrai, held by Theoderic, a supporter of Lothar, lay within the Middle Kingdom, while Rheims itself and Hincmar's other suffragans – some of whom, like Prudentius, had reservations about the new archbishop[15] – were in Charles the Bald's kingdom. Moreover,

Rheims held lands right across the newly divided Carolingian empire, from Aquitaine (largely under Pippin II's *de facto* control in 845) to the Wormsgau. Many were in lay hands as a result of royal grants, by Lothar and Charles the Bald among others, making restoration of these alienated lands a priority for Hincmar.[16] Carolingian family politics, and Charles the Bald's often difficult relationships with his brothers Lothar and Louis the German, and nephew Pippin II, also affected Hincmar's ability to achieve his aims of restoring the lands and authority of his archdiocese, affirming the legitimacy of his position, removing the clerics Ebbo had consecrated and asserting his rights as metropolitan.[17] Over time, theological and pastoral challenges that straddled the ecclesiastical and political frontiers also arose, including the debate over predestination and Fulcric's unlawful remarriage.[18]

Hincmar's position with Charles the Bald was established, but he needed to work out how to accommodate Lothar's claims for loyalty and service in respect of those lands and that part of the archdiocese that lay in the Middle Kingdom. A relationship with Lothar was an especial necessity, given the emperor's ability to intervene at Rome and Hincmar's desire for papal confirmation of his measures. In the aftermath of the civil war, however, Lothar seems to have adopted a 'with me or against me' approach to the elite, complicating a *rapprochement* for Hincmar.[19] Nevertheless, the events of 844–45 suggest that Lothar was not completely ill-disposed to Hincmar at the outset.

In 844 Lothar had supported the Council of Yütz, which expressed concern at the ravages caused to the Church by the civil war, and the second chapter of the council's acts had recommended that episcopal vacancies should be ended.[20] The fact that Lothar, who at the start of 844 still strongly supported Ebbo's claims for reinstatement as archbishop of Rheims, had completely dropped Ebbo by the end of the year greatly assisted Hincmar's position in 845. (Hincmar later reported to Pope Nicholas that Ebbo had infuriated Lothar by refusing to go to Constantinople as an envoy, a decision made more understandable by Ebbo's apparent foot problems.)[21] In 845, Louis the German installed Ebbo as bishop of Hildesheim, a safely remote backwater, again helping make way for Hincmar.[22] Lothar's tacit acceptance of Hincmar's appointment showed a willingness to co-operate with his brothers and the Frankish Church in religious matters, as befitted a Christian ruler; care for the Church was, after all, one of the key concerns for an emperor. A significant gulf remained for Hincmar to bridge before he could achieve a working relationship, however, as the events of 846–47 showed.

Hincmar's response to his challenges in general, and to the problem of finding a way to work with Lothar in particular, was to set about immediately developing the empire-wide network of contacts through which the Carolingian powerful worked. Hincmar had started his career at court in 822, serving first Hilduin of St-Denis and then Louis the Pious.[23] Hincmar thus knew all the key figures at Louis the Pious's court, who formed the first post-Verdun generation of lay and clerical magnates. These useful connections and Hincmar's loyalty help explain why Charles selected Hincmar for the important – but politically very tricky – see of Rheims in 845. Hincmar's residence at Louis the Pious's court meant that he would also have known Lothar, either directly or indirectly, though his staunch partisanship of Louis and Charles the Bald are unlikely to have recommended him to the emperor.[24]

Indeed, in 845–47 Hincmar did not write to Lothar directly, but carefully approached those around him.[25] Hincmar's earliest letters after his consecration were to key figures in Lothar's kingdom: to Hetti, archbishop of Trier, Drogo, archbishop of Metz, and Ermengard, Lothar's empress, praising her religious fervour and promising to pray for her.[26] Amolo, the archbishop of Lyons, was soon added to Hincmar's contacts.[27] Hincmar was clearly making efforts to build a relationship with Lothar, but the constraints imposed by Hincmar's loyalty to Charles the Bald also complicated matters. Hincmar's second letter to Empress Ermengard – written in 846–47 at a time of particularly bad relations between Lothar and Charles the Bald, and which Flodoard summarised and quoted at some length – is particularly important here.[28]

The abduction of Lothar's (unnamed) daughter at the start of 846 by a certain Giselbert had triggered the downturn in relations. Although Charles and Louis the German publicly disclaimed all knowledge of this in March 846, and the fugitives fled to Pippin II in Aquitaine, not to Charles,[29] the kidnap offered Lothar a good pretext to take advantage of the significant setbacks Charles the Bald had experienced against Pippin II, the Bretons and the Vikings since mid-844.[30] In 846–47, Lothar was thus making strong efforts to assert his authority in Charles's kingdom through supporters in the Breton march, including Lambert, and those linked with Lothar's daughter Bertha, the abbess of Avenay, in the archdiocese of Rheims.[31]

Events also exposed Hincmar to attack:[32] in 846 Lothar sought a general council, held under papal auspices, to resolve 'the accumulated questions surrounding the persons of Ebbo and Hincmar'.[33] Lothar's ability to intervene at Rome in support of Ebbo's clerics, and to complicate papal authorisation of the acts of the Council of Paris (held in late 846 to confirm Ebbo's dismissal from Rheims), also threatened Hincmar's position.[34]

It was at this time that Ermengard wrote to Hincmar to accuse him of attacking Avenay and abstracting a certain *mansus*.[35] In his reply, denying these accusations, Hincmar was anxious to emphasise that he was faithful to Lothar, his lord.[36] Ermengard also suggested that Hincmar demonstrate his fidelity to Lothar by sending a *missus* to Lothar; Hincmar, however, was evasive on this point, because it would compromise his service to Charles.[37] The aim of Ermengard's letter was apparently to press Hincmar to acknowledge his fidelity to Lothar more visibly, on Lothar's terms, and to re-open the dispute over the lands of Avenay that had been settled to Hincmar's satisfaction by Charles the Bald's *missi*. In return, Hincmar offered a vision of two Carolingian masters, to both of whom he was faithful, despite all the pressure applied by Lothar's supporters. But could Hincmar's vision of two masters offer a practicable model in better times?

The turning point of 847

Giselbert's abduction of Lothar's daughter continued to affect Charles the Bald's relationship with Lothar until November 848, when envoys of Louis the German eventually reconciled Lothar and Giselbert. Lothar's relations with Charles the Bald finally and fully recovered at their meeting at Péronne in 849.[38] However, 847 already saw a decided thaw when the three brothers met at Meerssen in February; Louis the German reported that Lothar had ordered his supporters to end their activities against Charles, and Avenay is no longer mentioned in Hincmar's correspondence (indeed Bertha may have returned to the Middle Kingdom).[39] Hincmar also benefited from this meeting: soon thereafter Lothar wrote to the pope, withdrawing his support for Ebbo, forwarding the acts of the Council of Paris that confirmed Hincmar as archbishop, asking for the *pallium* to be bestowed on Hincmar, and requesting the pope to welcome Hincmar when he came to Rome.[40]

What lay behind this sudden change, which signalled an acceptance of Hincmar's position as archbishop? Among the suggestions put forward, personality – Lothar's or Hincmar's – and the significance of their personal encounter at Meerssen have tended to come to the fore. The older literature saw Lothar's change of mind as a mark of his personal and political inconstancy and changeability.[41] For Devisse, the meeting allowed Lothar 'to take the measure of the personality of Hincmar and [Lothar] passed from indifference to sympathy'; the letter to the pope in 847 was 'the simple administrative regularisation of a situation that had remained in suspense, on account of the dispute between Charles and Lothar, until the meeting at Meerssen'.[42] According to Schrörs, Lothar had a different motive: at Meerssen, Lothar recognised Hincmar had the 'energy and adroitness' that Drogo, archbishop of Metz, lacked.[43] Lothar hoped to harness these qualities by securing a new grant of the papal vicariate for Hincmar.[44] Klaus Herbers has shown that the evidence for this request for a new vicariate is very uncertain, however, and – as Parisot already observed – it seems implausible that Lothar would have sought such a grant for Hincmar, especially at a time when relations with Charles the Bald remained frigid.[45] (See Appendix, pp. 85–6 below, on the problematic evidence for the vicariate.) While personality is undoubtedly an important factor in the success or failure of political relationships, I believe events in Italy and Francia in 847 help make Lothar's sudden acceptance of Hincmar more explicable. In particular, the impact of the Saracen attack on Rome in August 846 upon Lothar's actions has not been brought out strongly enough in discussion.[46]

Following an initial assault on Ostia, the Saracens attacked and looted Rome and St Peter's itself on 27 August 846.[47] News of this rapidly reached Francia. It mattered deeply to Lothar: he had been crowned at St Peter's in 823, and his picture hung in the church, a symbol of the ongoing special relationship between the Carolingians and Rome.[48] Lothar responded by holding an assembly in Francia in the autumn of 846, at which he resolved to build walls around St Peter's, and to raise money from his own and his brothers' kingdoms for this purpose. A substantial army was also to muster in Italy in January 847 to launch a campaign against the Saracens.[49] The capitulary simultaneously put in hand the classic Carolingian measure against military defeat, namely addressing possible causes of God's disfavour:

> No one doubts that it is because our sins and iniquities deserve it that so great an ill has befallen Christ's Church that even the very Roman

church which is the head of Christendom has fallen into the hands of infidels, and throughout all the borders of our realm and that of our brothers the people of the pagans has prevailed. Therefore we have firmly judged it necessary that with the help of God's mercy we amend everything in which we know he is particularly offended by us, and that by making fitting satisfaction we may endeavour to placate the divine justice, so that we can have him placated whom we realise to be angry.[50]

These concerns make Lothar's emphasis on the recovery of the Church and the promotion of peace in his communiqué at Meerssen in February 847 rather less disingenuous:

> To us and to my brothers it seemed right that we should join ourselves together, so as to seek after the will of God, how the holy Church can be repaired and how both we, and you, and that [whole] Christian populace can have peace.[51]

Collecting money from Charles the Bald's kingdom for Rome's walls would also require the support of key councillors such as Hincmar.[52]

The evidence thus suggests that in February 847 Lothar had the state of the Church on his mind, and perhaps therefore a willingness to tackle his sins of omission and commission against Rheims. Finally, in February, Lothar was about to visit Italy: a *placitum* places Lothar in Pavia on 12 May 847.[53] With the risks of his absence in mind, Lothar's imminent departure to Italy would also encourage him to improve relations with his brothers. Hincmar thus may have benefited in 847 from Lothar's need to secure human and divine goodwill before embarking on a risky journey to Italy and a significant project for the good of the Church.

Emperor and archbishop (almost) as one

Whatever the reasons for the change, in the period after 847, Hincmar's relationship with Lothar certainly improved. Hincmar began to address letters to Lothar directly, and not just to potential intermediaries such as Ermengard. In 847, Hincmar wrote to Lothar concerning Fulcric, Lothar's excommunicated *fidelis*, who had taken refuge in the province of Trier.[54] Hincmar also served as envoy between Charles the Bald and his brothers in the run-up to either the 849 meeting at Péronne or the 851 meeting at Meerssen, another indication that he was now an accepted intermediary for all parties.⁵⁵ It seems likely that Hincmar gained the restoration of some of Rheims' alienated lands within the Middle Kingdom in the period after 847.⁵⁶

In 852, Fulcric's second excommunication and Hincmar's attempts to restore the alienated revenues from the estate of Douzy triggered another round of letters from Hincmar to recipients in the Middle Kingdom. It is striking that these letters addressed a different set of intermediaries at Lothar's court, including the otherwise unknown *ministerialis* Wulfing.⁵⁷ Some of Hincmar's earlier generation of correspondents had died,⁵⁸ but another factor may be that, after the meeting at Meerssen in 847 and serving as Charles's envoy in 849/51, Hincmar had gained access to key figures at Lothar's court, such as Hilduin, Lothar's arch-chancellor, who also acted as an intermediary for Amolo of Lyons.⁵⁹ Hincmar thus had new contacts who could promote his cause in the Middle Kingdom. His correspondents included Eberhard of Friuli, but not apparently other key *ministeriales* such as Matfrid, Liutfrid or Adalhard.⁶⁰ I have suggested elsewhere that 852–53 saw a shift in the balance of power in the south of Lothar's kingdom; Hincmar's choice of correspondents might provide some further tantalising hints about internal groupings within Lothar's kingdom.⁶¹

If Hincmar had suffered from Lothar's hostility to Charles the Bald in 846–47, both he and Charles reaped rewards from the good relationship cemented with Lothar in 852–53. Charles was able to tonsure Pippin II after meeting Lothar in 852,⁶² and Hincmar finally demoted the clerics Ebbo had ordained at the Council of Soissons in 853, with Bishop Theoderic of Cambrai, Lothar's supporter, playing a central role in the proceedings.⁶³ There were, however, limits to Lothar's support: despite Hincmar's efforts to secure the emperor's ear, others also had access to Lothar. Fulcric, for example, took letters from Lothar and Louis the German to Rome and gained papal absolution.⁶⁴ Although Hincmar had his own contacts with the papacy, such as Bishop Leo of Silva Candida, the appeal of Ebbo's clerics – together with Lothar's opposition, expressed by Bishop Peter of Spoleto – led to the failure of Hincmar's first two attempts to secure Leo's confirmation of the acts of the Council of Soissons.⁶⁵ Lothar retained significant influence at Rome, which meant that Hincmar, who required papal support to legitimise his actions relating to Ebbo's clerics and to buttress his position as metropolitan against his opponents, needed to court the emperor.⁶⁶

In Lothar's final year of life, however, the tone of the relationship seems to change again. Lothar was very ill in January 855 and from that point onwards a sense of the impending end may have coloured his actions.[67] Hincmar wrote to Lothar on his recovery and admonished him on the care of his soul; Flodoard implies that Hincmar wrote more than once in Lothar's final months on the subject of the emperor's soul.[68] By July, Lothar had changed his mind regarding the acts of the Council of Soissons and intervened on Hincmar's behalf.[69] The emperor abdicated and entered the monastery of Prüm, dying as a monk on 29 September 855. It is perhaps these months that Hincmar chose to dwell upon when looking back on the relationship, when his admonitions bore most fruit and his vision of the emperor listening to the archbishop came closest to reality.

Conclusion

The relationship between Hincmar and Lothar developed over time, from Hincmar's cautious initial approaches via intermediaries, to much more direct and robust contacts. For Hincmar, a good relationship with Lothar was necessary from the outset because of Rheims' extensive lands in the Middle Kingdom, and to avert interventions on behalf of his opponents. Lothar's ability to influence the pope on affairs close to Hincmar's heart, such as Fulcric's excommunication and the confirmation of the acts of the Councils of Paris and Soissons, also meant that Hincmar needed to cultivate this relationship. Later on, the better relations between Charles and Lothar allowed Hincmar finally to remove Ebbo's clerics and to make some headway in dealing with Fulcric. Hincmar acknowledged that he was a subject of Lothar's, as well as Charles the Bald, from the first;[70] the problem seems to have been that Hincmar's vision of dual loyalty was not acceptable to Lothar prior to 847. Hincmar's loyalty to Charles, and the preponderance of his responsibilities in the West Frankish kingdom, meant that Lothar had no realistic prospect ever of subverting Hincmar.

From 847, Lothar seems to have accepted the necessity of acknowledging Hincmar and establishing a working relationship with the archbishop, although often continuing to deploy his influence at Rome against Hincmar. It is hard to know what part Hincmar's personal contacts with Lothar, at Meerssen in 847, and later on as an intermediary between the brothers in either 849 or 851, may have played in bringing about this transition; the passing of time and the realisation that the division of Verdun could not easily be overturned, surely also contributed to Lothar's changing attitude.

However, Hincmar's need to turn to Lothar on certain matters was in itself a useful expression of the emperor's status and position. Co-operating with Hincmar also represented the restoration of right order in the Church, a particular Carolingian concern, expressed in the decrees of the 851 meeting at Meerssen, for example.[71] I have argued that this duty to the Church took on especial significance for Lothar in the aftermath of the attack on Rome in 846, and helped stimulate Lothar's *rapprochement* with Charles and Hincmar. Mutual concern for the Church perhaps offered Lothar and Hincmar safe shared ground, whereas the familiar language of loyalty and *fides* sometimes divided rather than united. By the end of his life, Lothar seems to have accepted Hincmar as one source of salutary admonition, alongside Hrabanus Maurus and the pope. Achieving a working relationship with Lothar was always a necessity for Hincmar, though it was perhaps only in the final year of Lothar's life that the relationship approached Hincmar's retrospective vision of a repentant emperor responding to archiepiscopal advice.

Appendix: The authenticity of the letters of Leo IV in the *Collectio Britannica*

Did Lothar ask for the daily pallium for Hincmar, and did Hincmar excommunicate Lothar?

The largest collection of letters of Pope Leo IV is transmitted in British Library Additional MS 8873, generally known as the *Collectio Britannica*.[72] The *Collectio Britannica* contains letters of eight popes, ranging in date from Pope Gelasius (r. 492–96) to Urban II (r. 1088–99), and two substantial sections of excerpts from assorted legal sources.[73] Exactly when and where the manuscript was copied is uncertain: perhaps in Italy, after 1095.[74] Twenty-six of the forty-five letters of Leo IV entered on fols 159^v–171^r are otherwise unknown. These unique letter fragments include two in which Leo refuses Lothar's request to grant Hincmar the vicariate over all Francia, but grants Hincmar daily use of the *pallium*;[75] and two directed to the bishops of Francia and Lothar, in which the pope condemns Hincmar for excommunicating Lothar and Charles the Bald.[76] In all, the authenticity of eight of the forty-five letters of Leo IV in the *Collectio Britannica*, including the four relating to Lothar and Hincmar, has been doubted.[77]

Earlier scholarship on the letters concerning Leo IV's grant to Hincmar of the daily use of the *pallium* was divided, with Parisot and Calmette arguing the letters were false, and Lesne making a strong case for their authenticity.[78] Klaus Herbers has provided the first detailed analysis of Leo IV's letter fragments as a whole.[79] He concluded that crucial words on the *pallium*'s daily use may have been interpolated within Hincmar's circle into a standard grant of the *pallium*; the letters were certainly available to Flodoard in the tenth century at Rheims, and might have been interpolated by 866, when Pope Nicholas accused Hincmar of incorrect use of his *pallium*.[80] This conclusion adds further grounds to doubt Lothar's apparent request for Hincmar to receive the vicariate of Francia; at the very least, this must be considered not proven.[81] Hincmar's later hostility to any intermediary between the metropolitan and the pope lessens the likelihood that he would have been interested in such a charge.[82] Herbers also offers additional linguistic arguments for regarding the letters on the excommunication of Lothar and Charles the Bald, which have long been considered suspect, as forgeries, perhaps linked to an effort by Ebbo's clerics to blacken Hincmar.[83] The failure of any contemporary sources to mention such a significant event, when for example Prudentius' *Annales Bertiniani* criticised Lothar on moral grounds in 853, seems to me conclusive.[84]

All four letters related to Hincmar and Lothar in the *Collectio Britannica* are thus interpolated, falsified or forged. They therefore reflect the heated conflicts over the status of the clerics that Ebbo had consecrated and Hincmar had deposed, and Hincmar's efforts to assert the primacy of his metropolitan see, rather than reflecting Hincmar's and Lothar's relationship in 845–55.

Notes

1 Hincmar, Epistola 198, ed. E. Perels, MGH *Epp.* 8, pp. 204–17, at p. 207: 'Sic enim bonae memoriae domnus Hlotharius in initio ordinationis meae apud Sergium et post apud successorem ipsius Leonem pro contentione regni, quam erga fratrem suum habebat domnum Karolum, cuius obsequiis fideliter adhaerebam, sategit. Unde postea Deo inspirante paenitentiam egit et litteris ad sedem apostolicam missis quod excesserat corrigere studuit.'

2 The decrees of the second meeting at Meerssen in 851, esp. c. 4, reported in *AB* s.a. 851, pp. 60–3, at p. 61 (trans. Nelson, pp. 70–3, at pp. 70–1), express rulers' concerns on this point.
3 E. Lesne, 'Hincmar et l'empereur Lothaire', *Revue des questions historique*, NS 34 (1905), pp. 5–58, esp. 19, 55; Devisse, *Hincmar*, I, pp. 31–113, esp. 34–40. Schrörs, *Hinkmar*, pp. 50–71, also has an important discussion of the relationship.
4 See p. 81 below.
5 For Devisse, *Hincmar*, I, pp. 29–113, the years 845–55 were Hincmar's 'apprenticeship' (p. 113). A marked generational shift followed in 855–61, leaving Hincmar among Charles the Bald's oldest advisers (p. 104).
6 K. Herbers, *Leo IV. und das Papsttum in der Mitte des 9. Jahrhunderts. Möglichkeiten und Grenzen päpstlicher Herrschaft in der späten Karolingerzeit* (Stuttgart, 1996), pp. 338–9.
7 See Bernard-Vallette, Chapter 5, on the crisis of 875 and the model of Ambrose, and Isaïa, Chapter 9, on relations between kings and Remigius in Hincmar's *Vita Remigii episcopi Remensis*.
8 For a detailed account of the processes against Ebbo and his clerics, see Devisse, *Hincmar*, I, pp. 31–113, esp. pp. 71–97.
9 See Kleinjung, Chapter 3, and P. R. McKeon, *Hincmar of Laon and Carolingian Politics* (Urbana, 1978), on Hincmar of Laon; and Devisse, *Hincmar*, I, pp. 101–2, on Rothad of Soissons.
10 Most notably the pseudo-Isidorian forgeries: see D. Jasper and H. Fuhrmann, *Papal Letters in the Early Middle Ages* (Washington DC, 2001), pp. 135–95, and de Jong, below, pp. 273–9. For forged and falsified letters relating to Lothar I and Hincmar, see below, pp. 85–6.
11 Flodoard, *HRE*: on Flodoard's portrayal of Hincmar, see M. Sot, *Un historien et son église au Xe siècle: Flodoard de Reims* (Paris, 1993). Flodoard's decision to summarise Hincmar's letters in categories such as letters to important laymen and queens (Flodoard, *HRE*, III-26 to 27, pp. 330–52), complicates the dating of Hincmar's letters. The correspondence with Lothar follows that with Pope Leo IV, in III-10 (pp. 207–9), and is discussed by Sot, *Flodoard*, pp. 503–6.
12 Lesne, 'Hincmar et l'empereur Lothaire'; R. Parisot, *Le Royaume de Lorraine sous les Carolingiens (843–923)* (Paris, 1899), pp. 737–42; J. Calmette, *La Diplomatie carolingienne: du Traité de Verdun à la mort de Charles le Chauve (843–77)* (Paris, 1901), pp. 187–90; Herbers, *Leo IV*, esp. pp. 336–53.
13 Devisse, *Hincmar*, I, p. 31; M. Stratmann, *Hinkmar von Reims als Verwalter von Bistum und Kirchenprovinz* (Sigmaringen, 1991), p. 5.
14 See Sot, *Flodoard*, pp. 26–7 and map 4, for the division.
15 Devisse, *Hincmar*, I, p. 112; *AB*, trans. Nelson, p. 9, and Nelson, Chapter 2, pp. 47–50.

16 Hincmar, *De iure metropolitanorum*, PL 126, cols 189–210, at c. 22, col. 201; Devisse, *Hincmar*, I, pp. 105–13, and Stratmann, *Hinkmar als Verwalter*, pp. 45–53. Lands in Aquitaine: Hincmar, Epistola 13, MGH *Epp.* 8, p. 6; in the Wormsgau: Flodoard, HRE, III–26, p. 332 (Schrörs, *Hinkmar*, Reg. 520). For Hincmar's concern to recover the slaves of Courtisol, see Barbier, Chapter 11.

17 See n.9 above, n.54 below and Devisse, *Hincmar*, I, pp. 102–3, on Hincmar's relations with other Church provinces.

18 On Gottschalk, see Gillis, Chapter 13. On Fulcric, see Devisse, *Hincmar*, I, pp. 36–7, 39–40; R. Stone, '"Bound from either side": the limits of power in Carolingian marriage disputes', *Gender and History*, 119 (2007), 467–82, and below, pp. 82–3.

19 Nithard, *Historiarum libri quattuor*, ed. P. Lauer, *Nithard, Histoire des fils de Louis le Pieux* (Paris, 1964), IV, 4, p. 132 reports that Lothar had already begun removing those hostile to himself in 842.

20 Council of Yütz, 844, MGH *Conc.* III, no. 6, pp. 31–2, c. 2. Yütz is near Thionville.

21 Hincmar, Epistola 198, MGH *Epp.* 8, p. 211; Lesne, 'Hincmar et l'empereur Lothaire', p. 8. On Ebbo's long-standing foot problems, see *Narratio clericorum Remensium* in *Concilium Ingelheimense*, 840, MGH *Conc.* II, 2, no. 61, appendix 3, pp. 806–14, at 807 and 812.

22 *Ibid.*, p. 812.

23 Schrörs, *Hinkmar*, pp. 12–24, and Nelson, Chapter 2, pp. 44–5.

24 Hincmar, unlike Hilduin, remained with Louis at the Field of Lies in 833: Schrörs, *Hinkmar*, p. 23. The civil war also left deep scars: J. L. Nelson, 'The search for peace in a time of war: the Carolingian Brüderkrieg, 840–843', in J. Fried, ed., *Träger und Instrumentarien des Friedens im hohen und späten Mittelalter* (Sigmaringen, 1996), pp. 87–114. Lesne, 'Hincmar et l'empereur Lothaire', p. 30, suggests Lothar never felt personal hostility to Hincmar.

25 Devisse, *Hincmar*, I, p. 52.

26 Hincmar, Epistolae 2 (Hetti), 3 (Drogo), MGH *Epp.* 8, p. 2; Epistola 4 (Ermengard), p. 2: 'Irmingardi augustae scribens congratulatur audito religionis ipsius fervore, asserens se in precibus assidua pro ea dependere munia.' Lesne, 'Hincmar et l'empereur Lothaire', p. 9, suggests Ermengard was hostile to Ebbo, having received his abbeys (Lothar removed Bobbio and Stablo from Ebbo: Hincmar, Epistola 198, p. 211).

27 Hincmar, Epistola 10, MGH *Epp.* 8, p. 4, after June 846.

28 Hincmar, Epistola 12, MGH *Epp.* 8, pp. 4–5.

29 *Annales Fuldenses*, s.a. 846, ed. F. Kurze, MGH *SRG* 7 (Hanover, 1891), p. 36 (trans. T. Reuter, *The Annals of Fulda* (Manchester, 1992), pp. 24–5).

30 *AB* s.a. 844–45, pp. 46–51 (trans. Nelson, pp. 58–60). F. Lot and L. Halphen, *Le Règne de Charles le Chauve (840–77)* (Paris, 1909), p. 149,

note that Pippin paid homage to Charles as his overlord as part of the treaty of 845. This technicality may have offered a pretext for Lothar's hostility to Charles.

31 Bertha: Hincmar, Epistola 11, MGH *Epp.* 8, p. 4; Lambert: Lot and Halphen, *Charles le Chauve*, p. 167.
32 On the impact upon Rheims, see Lesne, 'Hincmar et l'empereur Lothaire', pp. 10–11, and Calmette, *La Diplomatie carolingienne*, p. 11.
33 Devisse, *Hincmar*, I. p. 35; Hincmar, Epistola 198, MGH *Epp.* 8, p. 210: 'Emenso autem anno post ordinationem meam [=846] Hlotharius imperator, ut praedixi, causa fratris sui erga me commotus epistolas a Sergio papa exegit, sicut postea mihi innotuit, pro refricando concilio de Ebonis depositione, quasi discordia esset in Remensi ecclesia pro mea ordinatione, quod nullatenus constitit.'
34 See Devisse, *Hincmar*, I, p. 36, on the Paris synod; on the context and the preceding, abortive synod of Trier, see Lesne, 'Hincmar et l'empereur Lothaire', pp. 11–16.
35 Hincmar, Epistola 12, MGH *Epp.* 8, pp. 4–5.
36 *Ibid.*, p. 5: 'domnus meus Hlotharius, potest veraciter cognoscere, quia non tantum illi, nulli homini in mundo sum infidelis.'
37 *Ibid.*, 'quantam merito domno meo velim servare fidelitatem.' See Lesne, 'Hincmar et l'empereur Lothaire', p. 29; compare Devisse, *Hincmar*, I, pp. 37–8, n.32, suggesting that Hincmar might in fact be referring to Lothar at this point in the letter.
38 *Annales Fuldenses*, s.a. 848, pp. 37–8 (trans. Reuter, pp. 27–8); *AB* s.a. 849, p. 56 (trans. Nelson, pp. 66–7).
39 Adnuntiatio domni Hludowici, c. 4, in *Hlotharii, Hludowici et Karoli conventum apud Marsnam primus*, 847, MGH *Capit.* II, no. 204, pp. 68–71, at p. 70. Bertha was certainly at Lothar's court in 852 (*Die Urkunden Lothars I. und Lothars II.*, ed. T. Schieffer, MGH Diplomatum Karolinorum III (Berlin, 1966), nos. 118 and 124, pp. 270–1 and 283–5); see E. Screen, 'Lothar I: the man and his entourage', in M. Gaillard, M. Margue, A. Dierkens and H. Pettiau, eds, *De la mer du Nord à la Méditerranée. Francia Media, une région au cœur de l'Europe (c.840–c.1050): actes du colloque international (Metz, Luxembourg, Trèves, 8–11 février 2006)* (Luxemburg, 2011), pp. 255–74, at p. 266.
40 Lothar, Epistola 46, ed. A. von Hirsch-Gereuth, MGH *Epp.* 5, pp. 609–11. On the dating of the letter to April–May 847, Lesne, 'Hincmar et l'empereur Lothaire', pp. 20–1, is convincing.
41 Devisse, *Hincmar*, I. p. 38.
42 *Ibid.*, pp. 38–9.
43 Schrörs, *Hinkmar*, p. 57: 'die Anerkennung, die Drogo sich nicht zu verschaffen vermocht, hoffte der Kaiser durch Hinkmars Thatkraft und Gewandtheit erreicht zu sehen.'

44 Schrörs, *Hinkmar*, p. 57, and Lesne, 'Hincmar et l'empereur Lothaire', p. 44, drawing upon Leo IV, Epistola 12, ed. A. von Hirsch-Gereuth, MGH *Epp.* 5, pp. 590–1 (J2607).
45 Herbers, *Leo IV*, pp. 344–8; Parisot, *Le Royaume de Lorraine*, p. 739. On the authenticity of the key letters, see below, pp. 85–6.
46 Lot and Halphen, *Charles le Chauve*, mention the attack upon Rome, pp. 171–2, but as an expression of Lothar's weakness, rather than a stimulus for collective action.
47 *AB* s.a. 846, pp. 52–3 (trans. Nelson, p. 63); *Liber Pontificalis*, ed. L. Duchesne, 2 vols (Paris, 1886–92), *Vita Sergii II*, cc. 44–7, II, pp. 99–101 (trans. Davis, pp. 93–6). R. Davis, *The Lives of the Ninth-century Popes (Liber pontificalis): the Ancient Biographies of Ten Popes from A.D. 817–891* (Liverpool, 1995), p. 96, n.92, reconstructs the complex course of events.
48 *Annales regni Francorum*, s.a. 823, ed. F. Kurze, MGH *SRG* 6 (Hanover, 1895), pp. 160–1; *Liber Pontificalis*, ed. Duchesne, *Vita Leonis IV*, c. 33, II, p. 114 (trans. Davis, p. 124).
49 Synod 'in Francia', 846, MGH *Conc.* III, no. 12, pp. 133–9. A date of 847 has also been suggested for the assembly, but 846 is more probable: H. Zielinski, 'Reisegeschwindigkeit und Nachrichtenübermittlung als Problem der Regestenarbeit am Beispiel eines undatierten Kapitulars Lothars I. von 847 Frühjahr (846 Herbst?)', in P.-J. Henig, ed., *Diplomatische und chronologische Studien aus der Arbeit an den Regesta Imperii* (Cologne, 1991), pp. 37–49. On Lothar's part in the building of the Leonine wall, see *Liber Pontificalis*, ed. Duschesne, *Vita Leonis IV*, c. 69, II, p. 123 (trans. Davis, pp. 139–40) and p. 138, n.49 for the inscription evidence; Herbers, *Leo IV*, pp. 138–9, and S. Gibson and B. Ward-Perkins, 'The surviving remains of the Leonine wall', *Papers of the British School at Rome*, 47 (1979), 30–57, at 31–3.
50 Synod 'in Francia', 846, MGH *Conc.* III, no. 12, p. 135, c. 2: 'Nulli dubium est, quod peccatis nostris atque flagitiis merentibus tantum malum in ęcclesia Christi contigerit, ut et ipsa Romana ęcclesia, quę capud est christianitatis, infidelium minibus traderetur et per omnes fines regni nostri fratrumque nostrorum paganorum populus prevaleret. Idcirco necessarium valde iudicavimus, ut omnia, in quibus maxime deum a nobis offensum esse cognoscimus, ipsius adiuvante misericordia corrigamus, et ut per satisfactionem congruam divinam studeamus placare iusticiam, quatinus, quem iratum sensimus, placatum habere possimus.' Trans. Davis, *Lives of the Ninth-century Popes*, p. 96, n.90.
51 *Adnuntiatio Hlotharii, Hlotharii, Hludowici et Karoli conventum apud Marsnam primus*, 847, MGH *Capit.* II, no. 204, p. 70: 'Nobis et fratribus nostris visum fuit, ut ad Dei voluntatem querendam, qualiter sancta

ecclesia recuperata esse possit et pacem et nos ac vos et iste populus christianus habere possimus, nos simul coniungeremus'; unpublished trans. by R. Pollard.
52 All three brothers did indeed pay up: *Liber Pontificalis*, ed. Duchesne, *Vita Leonis IV*, c. 69, II, p. 123, 'Ad quam ipse cum suis fratribus non modicos argenti libras direxit' (trans. Davis, p. 140).
53 H. Zielinski, 'Ein unbeachteter Italienzug Kaiser Lothars I. im Jahre 847', *Quellen und Forschungen aus italienischen Archiven und Bibliotheken*, 70 (1990), 1–22.
54 Hincmar, Epistola 18, MGH *Epp.* 8, p. 7. Hincmar's response seems a harbinger of his later attempts to assert the authority of his province against Trier's claims to primacy under Theutgaud: see Herbers, *Leo IV*, p. 341, and Devisse, *Hincmar*, I, p. 102.
55 Hincmar, Epistolae 41–2, MGH *Epp.* 8, p. 25.
56 *Die Urkunden Lothars I.*, ed. Schieffer, no. 198 (*deperditum*), p. 353, granting *Meuravallis*, *Termedo* (Termes) and *Roserolis*. Schieffer dates this grant to 845–55. See Sot, *Flodoard*, p. 505, on these lands.
57 Hincmar, Epistolae 49, 63, MGH *Epp.* 8, pp. 30–1, 35. On Douzy, see Devisse, *Hincmar*, I, p. 111, and Stratmann, *Hinkmar als Verwalter*, p. 47.
58 Hetti of Trier died on 27 May 847 and Ermengard on 20 March 851; see n.5 above on the generational change.
59 Hincmar, Epistola 50, MGH *Epp.* 8, p. 31; Hilduin intervened for Amolo in *Die Urkunden Lothars I.*, ed. Schieffer, no. 125, p. 286.
60 Hincmar, Epistolae 49, 69, MGH *Epp.* 8, pp. 26, 36–7; on Lothar's *ministeriales*, see Screen, 'Lothar I', pp. 262–5.
61 Screen, 'Lothar I', pp. 269–70. Certainly under Lothar II, Matfrid's kin supported his daughter Engeltrude against Hincmar from 856 onwards: see Stone, 'Bound', esp. pp. 474–6.
62 *AB* s.a. 852, pp. 64–5 (trans. Nelson, pp. 74–5).
63 See Devisse, *Hincmar*, I, pp. 75–96, on Theoderic's role.
64 Leo IV, Epistola 22, ed. A. Hirsch-Gereuth, MGH *Epp.* 5, pp. 598–9 (J2614); Stone, 'Bound', pp. 471–3; Herbers, *Leo IV*, pp. 339–40.
65 Hincmar, Epistola 72, MGH *Epp.* 8, p. 38; Herbers, *Leo IV*, pp. 348–51.
66 Herbers, *Leo IV*, pp. 349–50: 'Die Unterstützung des Kaisers war besonders wichtig.' Devisse, *Hincmar*, I, pp. 50–2, goes too far in suggesting that Pope Leo expected Hincmar to communicate via Lothar.
67 *AB* s.a. 855, p. 70 (trans. Nelson, p. 80). Lothar made three grants for his soul in 855: *Die Urkunden Lothars I.*, ed. Schieffer, no. 136 (St Mary's, Aachen), pp. 304–7; and nos. 137, 139 (Prüm), pp. 307–8, 310–11.
68 Hincmar, Epistola 75, MGH *Epp.* 8, p. 39; Flodoard, *HRE* III-10, p. 209: 'Et alia nonnulla eidem scripsit.'
69 Herbers, *Leo IV*, p. 350; Lesne, 'Hincmar et l'empereur Lothaire', p. 19.

70 Lesne, 'Hincmar et l'empereur Lothaire', p. 44.
71 *AB* s.a. 851, c. 5, pp. 61–2 (trans. Nelson, p. 71).
72 P. Ewald, 'Die Papstbriefe der Brittischen Sammlung', *Neues Archiv der Gesellschaft für ältere deutsche Geschichtskunde*, 5 (1880), 275–414 and 503–96, remains the only complete study of the manuscript. Robert Somerville (with Stephan Kuttner), *Pope Urban II, The Collectio Britannica, and the Council of Melfi (1089)* (Oxford, 1996), pp. 3–21 provides an updated description of the manuscript and its history.
73 Ewald, 'Die Papstbriefe', pp. 278–9; Somerville, *Pope Urban II*, pp. 4–5.
74 Somerville, *Pope Urban II*, pp. 11–12. On the *terminus post quem* for the contents, see Herbers, *Leo IV*, p. 56.
75 Leo IV, Epistolae 12–13, MGH *Epp.* 5, pp. 590–2 (J2607–8).
76 Leo IV, Epistolae 36–7, MGH *Epp.* 5, pp. 604–6 (J2618–9).
77 See also W. Ullmann, 'Nos si aliquid incompetenter... (Some observations on the register fragments of Leo IV in the Collectio Britannica)', reprinted in his *The Church and the Law in the Earlier Middle Ages* (London, 1975), VII, pp. 3–11, arguing against the pope's authorship of Leo IV, Epistolae 19, 21 and 41, MGH *Epp.* 5, pp. 597–8, 607 (J2613, 2615, 2647); and J. L. Nelson, 'The problem of King Alfred's royal anointing', reprinted in her *Politics and Ritual in Early Medieval Europe* (London, 1986), pp. 309–28, arguing that Epistola 31, p. 602 (J2643), is a forgery of the 1060s or 1070s.
78 Lesne, 'Hincmar et l'empereur Lothaire', pp. 34–49; Parisot, *Le Royaume de Lorraine*, pp. 737–9; Calmette, *La Diplomatie carolingienne*, pp. 187–90.
79 Herbers, *Leo IV*, pp. 48–91, esp. 53–8, summarising the debates, and pp. 79–88 analysing the letter fragments; see Jasper and Fuhrmann, *Papal Letters*, pp. 108–10, for a good English-language summary of the debates prior to the appearance of Herbers, *Leo IV*.
80 Herbers, *Leo IV*, pp. 344–8.
81 Parisot, *Le Royaume de Lorraine*, p. 739; Herbers, *Leo IV*, pp. 345–6.
82 Hincmar, *De iure metropolitanorum*, PL 126, col. 206, c. 31; noted by Lesne, 'Hincmar et l'empereur Lothaire', pp. 44–5.
83 Parisot, *Le Royaume de Lorraine*, pp. 740–2, and Lesne, 'Hincmar et l'empereur Lothaire', pp. 51–4, both reject these letters; see Herbers, *Leo IV*, pp. 342–3. But Devisse, *Hincmar*, I, pp. 41–2, accepts the excommunication.
84 *AB*, s.a. 853, p. 67 (trans. Nelson, p. 77).

5

'We are between the hammer and the anvil': Hincmar in the crisis of 875

Clémentine Bernard-Valette

Historiography has taught us to see Archbishop Hincmar as a supporter of rules, of the law. In his book *Hincmar et la loi*, devoted to the legal background of Hincmar's thought and its application, Jean Devisse showed how keen the archbishop of Rheims was to resolve conflicts and controversies between clergymen, magnates (*primores regni*) and kings in the most rightful way.[1] By 875, Hincmar was well known as a master of canon law. He had been a leader in many important cases: predestination; King Lothar II's divorce, which ultimately gave the Lotharingian throne to Charles the Bald; the translation of Actard, bishop of Nantes, to Tours; and the conflict with Hincmar of Laon about episcopal power and freedom. In all these cases, Hincmar's writings underlined his attachment to the rules established by canonical authorities: conciliar texts, decretals and papal letters, and patristic texts. Hincmar's purpose was always to define a rule that would be suitable for any situation.

In 875, when Charles the Bald left his kingdom for Rome and the imperial crown, Hincmar was faced by a new invasion of Charles's kingdom by his brother, Louis the German.[2] This was in some ways a repeat of 858, when Louis the German had first invaded his brother's kingdom, with the difficulties it had involved: disorder, plots and uncertainty.[3] Faced with these awkward circumstances, Hincmar had to devise an answer that followed the rules. We do not know if he sent a letter to Louis as he had in 858, but we do have a text that shows Hincmar trying to fulfil his task by defining a rule. This chapter will try to show how the resulting treatise *De fide Carolo regi servanda* is, consequently, more work-in-progress than a normative text.[4]

Prolegomena

To better grasp the issues at stake in 875, we must look back to Louis the German's first invasion of Charles's kingdom in 858. When Louis invaded his brother's kingdom on that occasion, he summoned the bishops to a synod in Rheims at the end of November 858 in order to secure his leadership of his brother's kingdom. Charles's bishops prevented this initiative and decided to hold a meeting in Quierzy a few days before Louis's synod. Hincmar and other bishops from the provinces of Rheims and Rouen decided to warn Louis, and sent him a letter to persuade him not to usurp his brother's throne.[5]

The bishops' 858 letter had three purposes: it announced that they refused to meet Louis at a council where the latter wanted to see his plans ratified by Charles's *primores regni*;[6] it reminded Louis of the necessity of protecting the confraternity regime and the conditions of peace between Louis the Pious's sons and heirs, as ratified by Lothar, Louis and Charles in Verdun in 843;[7] it also tried to obtain from Louis a guarantee of protection for Church properties (*res et facultates ecclesiasticae*), for the wealth, money and land possessed and administered by the Frankish Church was coveted by both parties in the conflict.[8] In a nutshell, in 858 the bishops tried to remove from Louis each and every tool that could enable him to lead the kingdom in spite of Charles.

In their letter, the bishops used both kindness and harshness. They did not hesitate to threaten Louis by insisting on his impending death, warning that he would be assaulted by devils on his deathbed.[9] They also referred to Louis's forefather, Charles Martel, who was damned because he had misused Church property (*res ecclesiasticae*).[10] On the other hand, the bishops also kept a respectful attitude towards Louis and they fully assumed their charge (*ministerium episcopale*) by giving advice on the right way to lead the palace, guide subordinates and manage estates. The chapters of the letter following the terrifying *Visio Eucherii* – in which Bishop Eucherius of Orléans sees Charles Martel's torments – review the conduct of all members of both palace and Church. This kind of admonitory and advisory discourse would be reused and renewed in one of the final treatises of the archbishop, *De ordine palatii*, written in 881.[11]

It is beyond the scope of this chapter to discuss this letter's influence on the regulation of this first invasion of Louis the German. However, we can see that the bishops were on the front line whenever a major upheaval in the political situation in the Carolingian world occurred, and this for several reasons. First of all, they administered the assets of the diocese and had to ensure the redistribution of the land's income. They were faced with problems of wealth distribution between the two kings, but also between the *primores regni* who depended on one or the other.[12] Another problem was the violence that people faced during these invasions; the clergy in particular were often already the victim of other types of invasions or raids. In 858, Viking raids on northern and eastern Neustria had reached an unprecedented scale, and Charles's bishops complained about these attacks.[13]

In 858, Hincmar and his colleagues believed that they had, in practice, to keep playing their role as source of advice and assistance by making proposals to Louis, so that he should act in accordance with the behaviour expected from a Christian king. Their use of imperative verbs in the letter demonstrated the *consilium* they were giving to Louis. Underlining the independence of the episcopate from royal power, they stated that the bishops were the ones who should summon a synod; they should not be summoned to one by Louis, even if the latter were king.[14] The legitimacy of Louis's invasion was not discussed; the bishops only complained about the trouble it created.[15] The bishops felt entitled to advise only on what concerned them directly, primarily Church property. The threat of damnation addressed to Louis the German concerned his misuse of such property, not all of his actions. Thus the bishops positioned themselves in this letter with great skill: they are less the subjects of Charles the Bald than the guarantors of a social and economic order rendered unstable by Louis's invasion. This support for order can be seen in the last sentence of the letter, a demand that peace and security must replace worry and trouble.[16] Overall, their letter presented an update of the themes of the Council of Paris of 829.[17] Finally, the letter is based on the authority *par excellence*, that is to say, the Bible – the bishops scarcely use the Church Fathers to support their point. The synod report gives forty-three biblical quotations, but very few references to the Church Fathers.[18]

875: disorder in the kingdom?

In 875, when history repeated itself or seemed to be doing so, Hincmar was no longer the influential and respected adviser he had been in the 850s and 860s. He did not share Charles's enthusiasm for the imperial project.[19] He had contributed greatly to his coronation as king of Lotharingia in 869, but now it seemed to be Pope John VIII who, from his headquarters in Rome, could help Charles reach the pinnacle of glory with the imperial crown.

Charles no longer had to fight for his kingdom, as in 858. He was a powerful king: he had won the inheritance of Lotharingia and was about to be crowned as the fourth Carolingian emperor. The situation was absolutely different from 858. Charles's palace was dangerously empty, and the bishops and magnates were again left alone to face the ambitions of Louis the German. This time, however, Charles had not fled, but had rather set out to conquer a new kingdom. And, when Louis arrived, he was not awaited by the magnates of the western kingdom.

Louis the German was also powerful, even if he had been badly ill in 870.[20] He shared his brother's ambitions, though not necessarily for himself: he wanted his son Carloman to become emperor and was unhappy with his brother's coronation. Besides, Louis remembered how he had been able to persuade his brother to share Lotharingia with him in 870.[21] He thus remained a fearsome neighbour for Charles.

The situation of the ecclesiastical province of Rheims had also changed since 858. With the coronation of Charles the Bald as king of Lotharingia, the province was once again at the centre of the Carolingian area. This position brought hardships to the archbishop, especially in 875. Being close to the kingdom's borders, Hincmar was the first to face Louis the German's invasion. Though Hincmar was not involved in Charles's Italian expedition, he was among the advisers who stayed with Richildis and Louis the Stammerer to help them govern in the king's absence.[22] This peculiar situation explains the nature of the letter he wrote in 875, a treatise that seemed to respond to the situation in 858 yet was radically different in both aim and argument.

Looking for order: a deliberative treatise

Published in the Patrologia Latina under the title *De fide Carolo regi servanda*,[23] the treatise again took the form of a letter, this time addressed to the bishops of the ecclesiastical province of Rheims by their metropolitan. It was written at their request, or the request of some of them, which shows the level of concern felt by the bishops of the north-east, who had most to fear from Louis's march on the kingdom.[24] Though this was not a letter sent privately and discreetly to the bishops, it was internal to the sphere of higher ecclesiastics, primarily bishops (who were also abbots of important monasteries and nobles of Charles's kingdom). Hincmar knew the letter could be read by kings or their familiars, but its public nature does not change the fact that it was written to and for the bishops; and this had several implications for how the letter was written.[25] First, as the text was not sent directly to either king, Hincmar does not respond to specific claims: this text does not belong to the literature of negotiation, whereas the 858 letter does. Primarily, Hincmar gives advice and tries to inform the bishops of his province on the role they can or should play to best fulfil the mission entrusted to them when they were placed at the head of their diocese.[26]

The major novelty is the form taken by the text: a long deliberation in which the various alternatives are examined in turn, weighed up, and yet no position is explicitly asserted. The vocabulary of deliberation is constantly present in the treaty: the verb *consulo* ('I advise') is used twice in anaphora (stylised repetition) to enjoin the bishops to discuss among themselves and with the magnates.[27] In addition, the injunctive or deliberative subjunctive marks the stages of Hincmar's reflection at the beginning of chapters.[28] Finally, anaphors and parallel structures regularly discuss alternatives, and the formulation of successive and contradictory assumptions allows the consideration of all scenarios.[29]

The bishops addressed by Hincmar are concerned by rapidly changing political events and their uncertain impact on the bishops' ministry. The result is a work in progress, a treatise that considers different ways out of the crisis and therefore different attitudes that can be adopted according to the changing situation. It seems to me that this inconclusive character has not been sufficiently considered by Hincmar's modern readers, which has sometimes led to too clear-cut interpretations that read the letter as effectively expressing Hincmar's support for Louis, without taking into account the essential indeterminacy of the treatise that has been shown here.[30]

Its indeterminacy might also make the *De fide* an interesting witness to the nature of the deliberations that could occur in a synod. Normally we see only the outcome, namely the text emanating from these meetings, but the *De fide* shows the intermediate step – consideration before the result of consultation – which was carefully written down and sent to the trouble-making King Louis.[31]

The flexibility of the bishops is another dimension of the deliberative character of the *De fide*. The bishops had means of action, thanks to the military troops they maintained and through their control of significant territories, but they also possessed a strong moral influence that they could exert over their contemporaries. This moral influence should certainly not be exaggerated, but the Carolingian dynasty as a whole remained sensitive to potential threats and messages from clerics when their conduct was not in conformity with the laws of Christianity. The Frankish episcopate had developed under Louis the Pious, to the point where it could submit the emperor to public penance. This episcopal influence was not diminished during the reigns of Charles the Bald and his brothers.[32]

However, seldom had the bishops' situation been so complicated. It is in this context that Hincmar turned to a proverb: 'Inter malleum et incudem sumus' ('We are between the hammer and the anvil').[33] The proverb summarised the uncertainty of the episcopal position, and Hincmar used it to convey the difficulties and dangers facing the bishops caught between two kings, two loyalties and (especially) two armies, but also the opportunities that this 'impossible' situation represented. The image of the metal forged between hammer and anvil initiates a series of biblical images based on metal and the forging action; from the simple image of a smith, Hincmar comes to a metaphoric representation of the bishop as instrument of God. Stuck as they were, the bishops had no choice but to bend, to break or to be reshaped into a moral model that would influence events by encouraging kings to imitate them.[34] The proverb was used both to describe a situation and to be a starting point for the bishops to reflect on the attitude they could adopt to resolve the deadlock.

Episcopal order against royal disorder

To be influential, however, it was necessary to build a discourse that could affect the sovereign and would make him willing to listen to the advice of the episcopate. To find light in such a dark context, Hincmar was armed with awareness that other bishops had faced similar events before him. He therefore made significant use of the 'doctrina et exemplum maiorum' ('the doctrine and example of the elders'). As if he was getting ready to enact a rule, Hincmar first resorted to authorities that were unquestioned and unquestionable, such as the Bible and the Church Fathers, as the basis and source for his argument.[35] Walking alongside the great bishops of the past, Hincmar and his fellow bishops could find the right way. More remarkable is the fact that in this treatise, the Church Fathers are more than textual authorities; their lives are vivid examples showing a way to safety.[36] It is only afterwards that he draws practical conclusions from these texts. The Fathers who are cited, mostly bishops themselves, offered multiple paths, multiple ways to tackle dangerous political situations. Hincmar proceeds by establishing small sequences of texts from the patristic tradition or canon law to find one or more solutions to problems caused by the superimposition of two conflicting political powers. These sequences constitute subsets in the treatise and sometimes stray to some extent from the text's framework, in order to focus as fully as possible on the leeway available to the bishops.

The greatest bishop for Hincmar in the *De fide* is definitely Ambrose of Milan. Every reaction, every choice in his confrontation with imperial power is examined. Three circumstances of Ambrose's life are highlighted: relations with the usurper Maximus between 383 and 388; the conflict with Valentinian II about the Milanese basilica during the Arian controversy; and the confrontation with the usurper Eugenius between 392 and 394.[37] In the treatise, Hincmar first reminds his reader of Ambrose's strong opposition to the imperial claim of Valentinian II that the Arians be allowed church access. But he also shows Ambrose defending Valentinian's power against Maximus. The treatment of this historical character is very instructive: Hincmar's judgement of Maximus's behaviour is ambivalent. Maximus's faith is orthodox, a positive element among the faults of the usurper. Hincmar condemns the sovereigns not for their political actions, but for their religious failure. Consequently, Eugenius cannot be positively judged because he promoted pagan cults. This was a clever way of not taking a position in the emerging conflict between Charles and Louis: like Valentinian II, Maximus and even Eugenius were sometimes good, sometimes bad, for Ambrose and the Milanese community, but as Christians not as kings. This argument enabled Hincmar to avoid showing Louis the German as necessarily the bad usurper.

A longer discussion follows of the reaction that one could expect from a bishop: to stay in his city and die a martyr, or to leave. Augustine advocated staying to face the Vandals; although he agreed with bishops leaving their dioceses in desperate circumstances, he promotes resistance in his letter to Bishop Honoratus.[38] In the seventeenth chapter, there is a long enumeration of famous bishops from the fourth and fifth centuries who serve as examples. This enumeration is based on the anaphora 'Sic fecit' to form a body of proofs supporting a defensive attitude from the bishops. Augustine's attitude is followed by the holy bishops (and also saints) Nicaisius of Rheims, Lupus of Troyes, Anianus of Orléans, Remigius of Rheims[39] and Martin of Tours, who all chose to associate with usurping rulers without compromising themselves.

A related question is then considered: how to associate with a usurper without sinning? Hincmar offers the twin examples of Ambrose and Martin. Like Ambrose, Martin stayed in his city and faced the usurper Maximus.[40] Their examples are supported by two quotations from Augustine to show firstly that communication with a king without being contaminated by his sin is possible, and secondly that it is not his usurpation that is held against him, but the sacrileges of which it is the cause.[41] As the Carolingian Empire was Christian, there was little risk of bishops being prosecuted and led to martyrdom. As a consequence, Martin and Ambrose are more effective examples because they stay, as recommended by Augustine, but without compromising themselves, for they keep episcopal authority (*apostolica auctoritas*).[42] That is to say, they are able to assume their charge of spiritual *consilium* for the personal salvation of the political leader.

The possibility of damnation, which had already been cited in 858 through the example of Charles's forefather, Charles Martel, reappears here. In a properly deliberative perspective, Hincmar cites texts in favour of excommunication, but also statements that the punishment of the wicked is inevitable without any need for excommunication.[43] These chapters form an extended excursus in the third section of the treatise. The precise deliberation about the merits of excommunicating a sinning king shows the real purpose of the letter, that is, to find a common answer of the episcopate to Louis's project of invasion.

Fides

The discussion concerns above all not the means of action, but rather the principles in whose name the bishops could act. The first principle is the conservation of *fides*, which means faith as well as fidelity.[44] The call for the episcopate to be a power of opposition is based on respect for *fides* as a bond between Christians, a bond which alone guarantees the preservation of social order. Hincmar quotes a biblical episode that states respect for civil power as a maxim, even when it is guilty of sacrilege; he summarises 1 Samuel 16–24, the biblical story of David's persecution by Saul and the absolute respect David showed on every occasion for the anointed king, 'unctus Domini'.[45] Practising *fides* does not admit any exception.

The biblical lesson is therefore applied to the contemporary situation, as an historical lesson. Hincmar, quoting Gregory the Great, compares kings and subjects to Saul and David:[46] Gregory used the term *subditi* ('subjects') for bishops in order to reaffirm the nature of the ties that bound the king to the *primores ecclesiae* ('ecclesiastical magnates') of his kingdom. Fidelity had to be be understood more as a religious act which imitates faith in God, not purely political loyalty. The bishops have to keep their *fides* untouched to be worthy of their episcopal charge.

But preservation of *fides* is not reserved to the bishops alone; it must be practised by kings as well, in their relationships with magnates and other kings. Hincmar therefore reminds Charles and his brother of the oaths they have taken on several occasions.[47] Louis the German has no right to disturb the organisation that comes from a confirmed oath (*sacramentum*), nor may Charles act against the general interest, for kings have obligations too. The same theory of *fides* as absolute, and of the unbreakable nature of an oath, lay behind the oaths sworn at Strasbourg in 842 (between Charles the Bald, Louis the German and their supporters) and the reciprocal oath between Charles the Bald and his subjects at Quierzy in 858.[48] Hincmar's description of relationships based on *fides* is also implicitly applicable to the relationship between the two kingly brothers. In 875, as in 858, the problem was that fidelity had been breached by Louis the German and his projects in Charles's kingdom.

However, the lack of explicit condemnation of Louis's action and the use of the *exemplum* of Martin of Tours together meant that Hincmar's recipients were not compelled to desperate, and perhaps unnecessary, resistance to Louis. The problem, according to Hincmar, was not the invasion itself, but a much more serious situation: the breach of the peace guaranteed by *fides*. The royal power, to which one is bound by oath, cannot be betrayed, as this could have adverse consequences for the people and property for which the bishops are responsible, in case of retaliation at each change of allegiance.[49]

The end of the treatise confirms that Hincmar was seeking to refocus the debate on this vital point. This call to fidelity answers the only goal that Hincmar keeps in mind throughout this treatise: the maintenance of peace among Christian people. Peace is the necessary prerequisite to living according to Christ's teaching, and that is why it is the basis for Hincmar's text. He quotes Augustine's *De civitate Dei*: 'For the peace that is our own we enjoy now with God by faith, and will enjoy in eternity with him by sight'. Highlighting the importance of peace, the link between *fides* and *pax* is very clear. Fidelity is the means which leads to the end, that is to say, peace.[50]

In reality, in this treatise we see taking shape between the lines the idea of a Christian society which has everything to lose in these internal conflicts. Hincmar says: 'Let us, bishops and magnates of the king, according to our *ordines*, observe in the doctrine or examples of the forefathers what we should follow and what we should avoid.'[51] In this sentence, the bishops and the magnates unite to find the right means of action. The concept of *ordo* shows that Hincmar considers the Carolingian whole as an organised society, whose order comes from a division of charges through the Gelasian theory of the two powers.[52] It is perhaps less the recurring conflicts between the sovereigns of the Carolingian dynasty than the presence of 'pagans and false Christians' (Vikings and Bretons) which lead Hincmar to this sense of a Christian unity governed by members of one family.[53]

Conclusion: rules displaced

For Janet Nelson in her biography of Charles the Bald, Hincmar and some of his colleagues had already chosen Louis against Charles in 875. Undoubtedly, there was an exhortatory dimension to this treatise that sought to encourage the bishops of the ecclesiastical province of Rheims to be cautious. Yet more important was a perhaps rather unexpected openness on Hincmar's part to what the future could bring in the short term. An element of criticism of Charles and his policies was not hidden, but the issue was less one of political co-operation with Louis and more a question of peacekeeping in respect to the situation established in 843 at Verdun. Fraternity was still an ideal dear to Hincmar, in spite of the disappointments Charles had inflicted on him. This fidelity was thus linked not so much to a man as to an idea, a political system that, despite its many faults, allowed a Christian people to live not exactly in peace, given the violence of the attacks of the Vikings, but at least only in a legitimate war between the faithful and the pagans. The text highlighted the definition of royal and episcopal authority, definitions which Hincmar worked on numerous times, whether on his own initiative, at the request of sovereigns, or to enlighten these sovereigns in the absence of any request.[54] If Hincmar seemed to be going out of his way to avoid giving a simple solution to an immediate problem, it was because he was trying to resolve an even more important one.

Notes

1 J. Devisse, *Hincmar et la loi* (Dakar, 1962). Hincmar searched constantly for legislative texts during his archiepiscopate, as he sought to strengthen his argumentation in political and theological conflicts with authoritative references. See Corcoran, Chapter 7.

2 The testimony of Hincmar in the *Annales Bertiniani* is clear on the responsibility of Louis the German. See *AB* s.a. 875, pp. 198–9 (trans. Nelson, pp. 188–9): 'Hludouuicus uero, persuadente Engilramno ... cum hoste et filio ac aequiuoco suo Hludouuico usque ad Attiniacum uenit. Ad quem obsistendum primores regni Karoli, iubente Richilde regina, sacramento se confirmauerunt, quod non adtenderunt, sed ex sua parte regnum Karoli pessumdantes, hostile more deuastauerunt. Similiter et Hludouuicus cum suo exercitu idem regnum in pessum dedit; sicque Natiuitatem Domini in Attiniaco agens, per placitamenta primorum, regni Karoli depraedatione facta, cum quibusdam comitibus ex Karoli regno qui ad eum se contulerant rediit'.

3 *AB* s.a. 858, pp. 78–9 (trans. Nelson, pp. 88–9): 'Interim comites ex regno Karli regis Ludoicum Germanorum regem quem per quinque annos inuitauerant, adducunt, qui kalendis septembris Ponteonem regiam uillam adueniens, per Catalaunos et Cupedenses Aiedincum Senonum peruenit. ... Ludoicus uero, receptis his qui a Karlo defecerant, Augustam Tricorum adit, ibique distribuens inuitatoribus suis comitatus, monasteria, uillas regias atque proprietates, ad Attiniacum palatium reuertitur'.

4 Hincmar, *De fide Carolo regi servanda*, *PL* 125, cols 961–84. I have prepared a new edition for my PhD thesis: Clémentine Bernard-Valette, 'Gouverner le peuple chrétien: édition critique, traduction et commentaire des traités royaux d'Hincmar, archevêque de Reims (845–882)', under the direction of Pr. Paul Mattei, Université Lumière-Lyon II.

5 Quierzy letter, edited as Council of Quierzy, 858, MGH *Conc.* III (Hanover 1984), no. 41, pp. 403–27.

6 *Ibid.*, p. 408, c. 1: 'Sed nos ad placitum illud occurrere non potuimus et propter incommoditatem et brevitatem temporis et propter inconvenientiam loci et, quod est lugubrius, propter confusionem tumultus exorti.'
7 *Ibid.*, p. 408, c. 2: 'Sed et tractatum de restauratione sanctae dei ecclesiae et statu ac salute populi christiani, quod nunc vos nobiscum habere velle dicitis, iustius et rationabilius illud haberi potuisset, si nostris, quin potius divinis consiliis et observationibus atque obtestationibus superno respectu obtemperare voluissetis.'
8 *Ibid.*, p. 413, c. 7: 'Et si ecclesiam dei, sicut nobis scripsistis, quaeritis restaurare, debita episcopis et sibi commissis ecclesiis privilegia intemerata, sicut divinitus constituta sunt, custodite. Praecepta et inmunitates et honorem earum, sicut avus et pater vester conservaverunt, conservare curate.'
9 *Ibid.*, p. 410, c. 4: 'quando anima vestra de corpore exiet, ante mentis oculos ponite, ...et videbit omnia peccata sua et sentiet videns diabolos se constringentes et coartantes et, quicquid contra caritatem et fidem debitam cogitavit, parabolavit et fecit in isto saeculo et per dignos poenitentiae fructus non emendavit, ante oculos semper habebit et effugere volebit et non valebit.'
10 *Ibid.*, p. 414, c. 7: 'Quia vero Carlus princeps, Pippini regis pater, qui primus inter omnes Francorum reges ac principes res ecclesiarum ab eis separavit atque divisit, pro hoc solo maxime est aeternaliter perditus.'
11 *Ibid.*, pp. 418–23, cc. 8–14; Hincmar, *De ordine palatii*. On this text, see Stone, Chapter 1, pp. 19–20.
12 Council of Quierzy, 858, MGH *Conc.* III, no. 41, p. 414, c. 7: 'Quapropter ... illae [res et facultates] sub consecratione immunitatis sunt, de quibus debent militare vasalli, et pari tuitione a regia potestate in ecclesiarum usibus debent muniri'.
13 J. L. Nelson, *Charles the Bald* (London, 1992), p. 187. Council of Quierzy, 858, MGH *Conc.* III, no. 41, p. 411, c. 5: 'quae calamitatem et miseriam, quam a paganis patimur'; p. 413, c. 6: 'et qui fugiunt a facie paganorum, cum in illas partes venerint, in quibus degitis, refugium tranquillum inveniant'.
14 *Ibid.*, p. 408, c. 1: 'in tam angusto tempore archiepiscoporum litteras non valuimus de conventu habere'.
15 *Ibid*: 'propter confusionem tumultus exorti'.
16 The bishops' support for order can be seen in the last sentence of the 858 letter, that peace and security must replace worry and trouble, *Ibid.*, p. 427, c. 15: 'studebimus, ut quantotius pro sua ineffabili pietate evigilet et imperet ventis et mari, id est tempestatibus diabolicis et inquietudinibus saecularium hominum, et redeat quantulacunque tranquillitas, gratia

et misericordia eiusdem domini nostri Iesu Christi, cui est et sit potestas et honor et gloria et imperium in saecula saeculorum'.
17 *Concilium Parisiense*, 829, MGH *Conc.* II, 2, no. 50D, pp. 605–80.
18 Only Gregory the Great is cited, in Council of Quierzy 858, MGH *Conc.* III, no. 41, p. 411, c. 4, but without giving an explicit quotation from the text of his homily. The influence of the Church Fathers can be seen nonetheless in the vocabulary used by the bishops, like 'paxillus' (*Ibid.*, p. 420, c. 12), which is borrowed from the Pseudo-Cyprian treatise, *De XII abusiuis saeculi*. See *Pseudo-Cyprianus: De XII abusivis saeculi*, Texte und Untersuchungen zur Geschichte der Altchristlichen Literatur, 3rd Reihe, Bd. 4, Heft 1, ed. S. Hellmann (Leipzig, 1909), p. 44, c. 6.
19 Devisse, *Hincmar*, II, p. 805: 'Le choix impérial est donc une faute inadmissible, aux yeux du prélat, contre le royaume, contre les fidèles, contre les conseillers, contre l'archevêque de Reims!'
20 *AB* s.a. 870, p. 175 (trans. Nelson, p. 170).
21 *AB* s.a. 870, pp. 171–4 (trans. Nelson, pp. 167–9).
22 *De fide*, col. 963, c. 3: 'primores ... qui jussione uxoris suae, cum filio suo Ludovico, regnum suum ab omnibus tam Christianis quam paganis hostibus, cum consilio et auxilio episcoporum ac ceterorum consiliariorum suorum defendant'.
23 The title in the unique surviving manuscript (Basel Universtätsbibliothek 0 II 29) is 'Commonitio et exhortatio Hincmari ad episcopos ac totius regni primores ut fidem intemeratam seniori suo Karolo servare debeant, quando Romam perrexit'. The title we use now was given by the modern editors, Jan Buys and Jacques Sirmond.
24 *De fide*, col. 961, c. 1: 'De communi anxietate nostra, de qua exiguitatem meam dilectio vestra consuluit, proponens mihi verba sancti Bonifacii papae, ... quae donante Domino ex doctrina Patrum nostrorum sentio scriptis vestrae charitati respondeo'.
25 *Ibid.*, col. 963, c. 2: 'Quatenus si rex noster ea legerit quae de illo dicuntur, si vera sunt illa corrigat, si autem vera non sunt, de caetero admittere caveat. Si autem et frater ejus dominus Ludovicus ea legerit, quae de fratre illius dicuntur notabilia caveat, et quae de illo laudabilia promittuntur exsequi studeat.'
26 *Ibid.*, col. 963, c. 4: 'Qua de re nobis episcopis satis agendum est, ne in consilio, quod a nobis reipublicae ministri secundum domni regis mandatum petierint, a nostro ministerio excidamus, et ne de auxilio, quantum Deus unicuique nostrum posse dederit, abscedamus.'
27 *Ibid.*, col. 980, c. 35: 'Consulamus etiam ... sociis et commilitionibus nostris.'
28 *Ibid.*, col. 965, c. 7: 'Exhibeamus etiam unusquisque nostrum', which is not the only example of the exhortative style Hincmar uses.
29 *Ibid.*, col. 984, c. 42: 'Si denique rex noster fuerit, annuente Deo, reversus,

recipiamus eum cum gaudio, et de sibi ac Ecclesiae atque regno necessariis in postmodum procurare episcopaliter illum commoneamus, et prosperitati suae congaudeamus. Si vero, quod non optamus, aliter judicio Dei contigerit, devotionem ac fidem debitam erga illum sinceriter custodientes, sicut scriptum est, dicamus corde, dicamus et ore Domino: "Exsultaverunt filiae Judae", id est confessionis humillimae, "in omnibus judiciis tuis, Domine" [Psalm 96:8].'

30 Nelson, *Charles the Bald*, pp. 239, '"Keeping Faith', his circular letter to the bishops and lay magnates of his province, combined lukewarm counsels of loyalty with scalding criticisms of Charles (unconvincingly attributed to 'others'), and in effect made the case for yielding to Louis". Similarly, Eric Goldberg states: 'Hincmar circulated a letter to the bishops and nobles of his archdiocese, ostensibly urging them to remain loyal to Charles the Bald but in fact voicing harsh criticism of him, thus effectively sanctioning capitulation to Louis': E. Goldberg, *Struggle for Empire: Kingship and Conflict under Louis the German, 817–876* (Ithaca, 2006), p. 331.

31 This is the precise aim of the Quierzy synod: Council of Quierzy 858, MGH *Conc*. III, no. 41, Introduction, p. 408: 'Haec, quae sequuntur, capitula miserunt episcopi provinciarum Remensis et Rotomagensis a Carisiaco palatio, quo convenerant, ... Hludowico regi in Attiniaco palatio consistenti.'

32 É. Delaruelle, 'En relisant le *De institutione regia* de Jonas d'Orléans: l'entrée en scène de l'épiscopat carolingien', in C. E. Perrin, ed., *Mélanges d'histoire du moyen âge: dédiés à la mémoire de Louis Halphen* (Paris, 1951), pp. 185–92; S. Patzold, *Episcopus: Wissen über Bishöfe im Frankenreich des späten 8. bis frühen 10. Jahrhunderts* (Ostfildern 2008).

33 *De fide*, col. 965, c. 8: 'apud nationes tritum vulgi sermone: "Inter malleum sunt et incudem" legimus'. The proverb comes from the Jerome translation of a passage of the Homilies on the Book of Jeremiah by Origen, but Hincmar does not seem to know its source; he takes it for a popular proverb. See Origen, *Homiliae in Jeremiam*, 3:1, 304, *PG* 13, cols 253–543 at 526; Jerome, *Translatio homiliarum Origenis in Jeremiam et Ezechielem*, *PL* 25, cols 583–786 at 607. Cf. R. Tosi, *Dictionnaire des sentences latines et grecques: 2286 sentences avec commentaires historiques, littéraires et philologiques*, trans. R. Lenoir (Grenoble 2010), p. 520.

34 *De fide*, col. 967, c. 13: 'Verum quia, ut praediximus, inter malleum et incudem positi sumus, et quod inter malleum et incudem ponitur, aut frangitur vel conquassatur, vel producitur et formatur, sicut in Numerorum libro legimus [Numbers 10:1]. ... Quaeramus tubas argenteas inter malleum et incudem productas, id est eloquia Domini'.

35 Hincmar uses quotations from Ambrose, Augustine, Gregory the Great, Jerome, Leo the Great and Gelasius I.

36 He refers many times to the Church Fathers as instructive examples: *De fide*, col. 963, c. 2: 'in majorum doctrina seu exemplis'; col. 964, c. 5: 'Patrum innitentes vestigiis'; col. 969, c. 15: 'sancti praedecessores nostri'; col. 969, c. 15: 'dicta et exempla'.
37 *De fide*, col. 964, c. 5; cols 968-9, c. 14; col. 969, c. 15; col. 973, c. 21; cols 974-5, c. 24; col. 978, c. 32; cols 981-2, c. 38; cols 982-3, c. 39. Hincmar quotes Ambrose's works as well as hagiographical or historical texts whose main character is Ambrose, like the *Historia tripartita* or the *Vita* written by Paulinus of Milan.
38 *Ibid.*, col. 970, c. 16, citing Augustine, Epistola 228, ed. A. Goldbacher, *S. Aureli Augustini Hipponiensis episcopi epistulae*, CSEL 34, 44, 57-58 (Vienna, 1895-1923), IV, p. 486: 'Nam qui fugiunt, vel suis devincti necessitatibus fugere non possunt, si comprehensi patiuntur, pro seipsis non pro fratribus utique patiuntur. Qui vero propterea patiuntur quia fratres, qui eis ad Christianam salute indigebant, deserere noluerunt, sine dubio suas animas pro fratribus ponunt'.
39 *De fide*, col. 971, c. 17.
40 *Ibid.*, cols 972-6, cc. 19-27.
41 *Ibid.*, cols 974-6, cc. 22-7.
42 *Ibid.*, col. 972, c. 19.
43 *Ibid.*, cols 976-8, cc. 27-31.
44 Many occurrences of the *fides* word family can be found in the treatise: 'infidelitatis', col. 965, c. 9; 'fideles', 'infidelitate', col. 966, c. 11; 'fidem', col. 967, c. 13; 'fide', 'fidem', col. 969, c. 15; 'fidem Christi', col. 971, c. 17; 'fide', 'contra fidem agree', col. 972, c. 19; 'de fidelium gloria', col. 973, c. 20; 'oblitus fidei suae', col. 973, c. 21; 'quae pars fideli cum infideli', col. 977, c. 29; 'in debitae fidei observatione', 'ab illius debita fide exorbitantes', col. 978, c. 32; 'salva in Deum fide, seniori nostro fidem non servaverimus', 'servans fideliter', col. 979, c. 33; 'ut fidem debitam erga eum observent', col. 980, c. 35; 'in conservatione fidei erga seniorem nostrum', 'ab orthodoxae fidei regula deviasse', col. 981, c. 37; 'Jubentur autem etiam servi Christiani, et boni fideles, dominis suis temporalibus aequanimiter fideliterque servire', col. 981, c. 38; 'fide quae in Deum est', col. 983, c. 40; 'vota fidelium', 'per fidem Dei', cols 983-4, c. 41; 'devotionem ac fidem debitam erga illum sinceriter custodientes', col. 984, c. 42.
45 *Ibid.*, cols 979-80, cc. 33-4.
46 *Ibid.*, cols 979-80, c. 34: Hincmar cites an extract from Gregory the Great, *Regula Pastoralis*, ed. B. Judic, F. Rommel and C. Morel, *Grégoire le Grand, Règle pastorale*, Sources Chrétiennes 381-2, 2 vols (Paris, 1992), III-4, vol. I, pp. 280-3: 'Quid enim per Saul nisi mali rectores, quid per Dauid nisi boni subditi designantur? ... Nam cum in praepositis delinquimus, ejus ordinationi qui eos nobis praetulit obviamus'.

47 *De fide*, col. 966, c. 11: 'Nunc autem qualiter regnum istud undique a Paganis et falsis Christianis, scilicet Britonibus, sit circumscriptum, et ut ita dicamus, viscerali commotione de his qui aliquamdiu in eo fideles ac utiles visi fuerant exstitisse, sit perturbatum: et quae conditio de regnis nepotum suorum inter illum et fratrem ejus sit sacramento firmata, utinam aut ignoraretur, aut inter eos ipsa conditio servaretur, et neque discordia Ecclesiarum praesules, et servi ac ancillae Domini inquietarentur, et Christianus populus affligeretur, ac inter regni primores viscerale bellum insurgeret, et rapinae ac depraedationes rerum ecclesiasticarum, atque divitum seu pauperum conflagrarent.'

48 On the consequences of the reciprocal oath between Charles the Bald and his subjects at Quierzy in 858, see É. Magnou-Nortier, *Aux origines de la fiscalité moderne: le système fiscal et sa gestion dans le royaume des Francs à l'épreuve des sources (V^e-XIe siècles)* (Geneva, 2012), pp. 642-5 and especially p. 642.

49 *De fide*, col. 965, c. 8: 'Nos quidem, quia non pastores sed mercenarii, et apud Deum et apud homines judicabimur : oves autem nobis commissae, quia sine pastore errabunt vel dispergentur, et facultates ecclesiasticae, quibus sustentari debent, velut relictae sine custodibus, diripientur ac vastabuntur, si defuerit virtus principis, cujus potestate defendantur, vel custodes, qui pro ovibus et earum alimoniis principi et defensori ac tutori ecclesiae suggerant.'

50 *De fide*, col. 984, c. 41: 'Pax autem nostra propria et hic est cum Deo per fidem, et in aeternum erit cum illo per speciem', quoting Augustine, *De civitate Dei*, 19, 27, ed. B Dombart and A. Kalb, CCSL 47-48, 2 vols (Turnhout, 1965), II, p. 697. The link between *fides* and *pax* is very clear: fidelity is the means leading to the end, that is to say the peace.

51 *De fide*, col. 963, c. 2: 'Nos autem episcopi et regni primores, secundum ordines nostros, in majorum doctrina seu exemplis, quid nobis sequendum, quidue cavendum sit, conspiciamus.'

52 Gelasius, Epistola, 12, c. 2, ed. A. Thiel, *Epistolae romanorum pontificum genuinae, et quae ad eos scriptae sunt a S. Hilario usque ad Pelagium II. Tomus I: A S. Hilario usque ad S. Hormisdam: Ann. 461-523* (Braunsberg, 1868), pp. 350-1 (J632).

53 *De fide*, col. 966, c. 11: 'Nunc autem qualiter regnum istud undique a Paganis et falsis Christianis, scilicet Britonibus, sit circumscriptum.'

54 Hincmar's royal works are numerous. They cover a large part of his time as archbishop, from the *De divortio Lotharii regis et Theutbergae reginae*, written in 860, to the *De cavendis vitiis*, composed on Charles's demand in 869, and the *De regis persona et regio ministerio*, a royal command of 873. The last years of Hincmar's life are full of exhortative treatises addressed to every Carolingian king: a treatise for Louis the Stammerer, *Novi regis instructio* in 877, a letter to Charles the Fat, *De institutione regia/Ad*

Carolum III imperitum in 879 and a diptych of advice to Carloman, the *De ordine palatii* and *Admonitio ad episcopos* in 882. See McCarthy, Chapter 6, and Stone, Chapter 1, pp. 19–20.

6

Hincmar's influence during Louis the Stammerer's reign

Margaret J. McCarthy

Introduction

King Louis the Stammerer succeeded Charles the Bald on the throne of West Francia in 877, inheriting both his father's kingdom and his father's advisers. Prominent among those advisers was Hincmar, archbishop of Rheims, who was the chief architect of Louis's coronation, composing and conducting the coronation ritual. A common narrative about Hincmar in the 870s is that he was losing favour near the end of Charles the Bald's reign,[1] but then Louis the Stammerer's accession provided another opportunity for Hincmar to become again an influential figure. It is clear from contemporary accounts such as the *Annales Bertiniani* that Hincmar's role in Louis's court was multifaceted and extremely interesting; the extent and nature of his influence is well worth investigating.

In this investigation, I am going to examine occasions upon which it is known that Hincmar intervened during Louis's reign. These occasions include the coronation ritual, the Council of Troyes in September 878, and other interactions during Louis's reign as well as Hincmar's pre-coronation letter *Novi regis instructio ad rectam regni administrationem*. I shall examine whether these documents and events demonstrate influence by Hincmar on Louis's actions and decisions. Was Hincmar able to establish an advisory role at Louis's court, and did he maintain any influence during the sixteen months of Louis's reign?

It is first necessary to decide how exactly to assess an adviser's influence. Is it even possible to tell from the existing records if Hincmar was influential? Did his opinions and advice have a noticeable effect on Louis's decisions and on events during Louis's reign? This question is complex and requires a serious investigation of the involvement of Hincmar alongside other factors in Louis's kingdom.

Based on the historical record provided by the annals and other documents, it is possible to identify events and decisions in which Hincmar was involved. However, to determine what effect Hincmar in particular had on Louis's actions and decisions and to measure to what extent the archbishop was involved in governing West Francia, more specific information may be required. The problem becomes that of finding any solid evidence to support an estimation of the *quantity* of Hincmar's influence; this is primarily because it is not possible to isolate occasions when Hincmar was a primary or unique influence on Louis's governmental policy. There are several reasons for this: first, it is difficult to separate Hincmar's role as a political adviser to the king from his position as archbishop of Rheims. Second, it may not be possible to differentiate Hincmar's contribution from the pressure of other powerful men at court, such as Louis's advisers Boso of Vienne and Hugh the Abbot. The decisions made by Louis were also affected by external events and Louis's own opinions.

Hincmar might have considered that exerting influence on the king was part of his duty as a bishop. Carolingian kings looked to their nobles and clergy for guidance. Hincmar himself believed in the value of wise counsel: he thought that kings should seek out counsellors to help them govern. This is made very clear in his *Novi regis instructio*, where he says that the kingdom requires good counsellors in order to be well governed: 'We read that good kings employed good counsellors for themselves, and by means of good kings and good counsellors the people of the kingdom enjoyed many benefits, and by means of bad kings and bad counsellors the people of the kingdom suffered many ills.'[2] Hincmar also quotes the Bible to make this point: 'There is no man who is so wise that he does not require the advice of another, just as is written: "The wise man who listens will become wiser and will possess wise counsel", and "He who trusts his own thoughts acts impiously".'[3]

The question of influence cannot be separated from that of motivation: why was Hincmar involved in the government of West Francia, and how did that affect when and how he sought influence? Hincmar believed that the duty of the archbishop was to help counsel the king.[4] In Hincmar's opinion, advisers could influence the king and were necessary for the safe guidance of the kingdom, especially when the king was young and inexperienced. The *Novi regis instructio* was not the only instance when Hincmar advised a king to seek advice: Hincmar wrote to Louis the German with advice as early as 858, and was still counselling the young Louis III, Louis the Stammerer's son, at the Council of St-Mâcre (Fismes) in 881.[5] Investigating Hincmar's motivations is particularly difficult because the majority of the sources were written by Hincmar himself and thus reflect his view of events. With many possible reasons for his actions, it is very difficult to isolate any one reason, and this chapter discusses those uncertainties. Several questions suggest themselves, however. Was Hincmar seeking increased personal power? Was he looking for more influence for Church leaders, given his position as a senior archbishop in the kingdom? Or was Hincmar altruistic, providing his advice for unselfish reasons and attempting to consider what would be best for West Francia?

Context

As shown in the other chapters in this volume, Hincmar had been politically active for years before Louis the Stammerer's accession. He had had a long career as a counsellor of Charles the Bald, Louis's father. He had been quite involved in Charles's councils but had lost influence and royal favour in the later years of Charles's reign, especially after 873; Hincmar's opposition to Charles's Italian ventures contributed to his marginalisation in the West Frankish court.[6] A member of the West Frankish elite since at least 844, Hincmar had known Louis the Stammerer since his birth, and had observed and recorded his earlier years as Charles's heir in West Francia.

Louis and Hincmar had several recorded interactions before Charles's death. In the summer of 875, while acting as co-regent during Charles's absence in Italy, Louis granted the villa of Neuilly away from the church of Rheims, an action with which Hincmar was not pleased.[7] Hincmar recovered this land for Rheims on Charles's return from Italy in 876. The *Historia Remensis ecclesiae* also lists a letter that Hincmar wrote to Louis in the summer of 877 about dealing with the Northmen, demonstrating that the two men did correspond before Charles's death.[8]

One of the most mysterious events in Louis the Stammerer's life was his divorce. Unfortunately, the exact circumstances and date of Louis's divorce and remarriage are uncertain, as is Hincmar's involvement in the matter. Louis's first wife was Ansgard, whom he married in Lent 862 in Neustria as part of his rebellion against his father. At the time, Louis was sixteen years old.[9] Ansgard was clearly an appropriate wife for Louis, as she came from a family with a strong political background and was also the sister of a friend of his;[10] but she had been Louis's own choice, not that of Charles the Bald, who could therefore have resented her. This marriage lasted long enough to produce two sons, Louis III and Carloman, and a daughter, Gisela. At some point during the 870s, Louis divorced Ansgard and married a woman named Adelaide.[11] Louis's divorce was not mentioned in the *Annales Bertiniani* and Hincmar's role is difficult to discern.[12]

Regino of Prüm places the responsibility for the divorce squarely on the shoulders of Charles the Bald, saying that Charles – because he had not given his consent to the marriage – forced Louis to divorce Ansgard and forbade Louis to consort with her any more.[13] Among the Franks, parental consent to a son's marriage was absolutely required before the age of fifteen,[14] and seems also to have been required after.[15] For example, Louis the German refused his consent to a match proposed by his son Louis the Younger, and the marriage did not occur.[16] This was not a satisfactory reason for annulling a marriage that had already taken place, however, as seen in the nearly identical (and contemporary) case of the elopement of Charles the Younger, Louis the Stammerer's brother: Pope Nicholas refused to grant Charles the Younger a divorce solely on the basis of lack of parental consent. The marriage was still canonically valid.[17]

As he was senior archbishop in West Francia, and had written so much on the divorce of Lothar II and Theutberga, it is difficult to believe that Hincmar was not involved in Louis's divorce.[18] One possibility is that this incident was omitted from the *Annales* because of Hincmar's 'connivance' in the divorce;[19] however, this would present a contrast to Hincmar's generally received views on divorce, which held marriage as indissoluble.[20] Louis's first marriage was mentioned in the *Annales Bertiniani* as an actual marriage and thus, in Hincmar's opinion, valid;[21] Hincmar states in the *Annales Bertiniani* that Charles the Bald recognised Ansgard as a legitimate wife in 862, as part of Louis's reconciliation with Charles after Louis's rebellion.[22] It is also possible that Hincmar did not protest too much at the time of Louis's divorce as he was worried about losing any influence he might have had with Charles the Bald at a time when he was generally out of favour; Gauzlin did take Hincmar to task later for his lack of public opposition to the divorce.²³ Unfortunately, the letter Hincmar wrote about the divorce has been lost, so it is impossible to know for certain his views on the subject.²⁴

Hincmar supported Louis's sons in the accession dispute after Louis the Stammerer's death. This, combined with his views on divorce, suggests that Hincmar was against Louis's divorce. However, Hincmar may have supported these sons from the first marriage in pragmatic preference to the alternative of under-age rulers, so we cannot necessarily infer his views about the divorce from his choice of sides in the dispute. More importantly, there is no direct evidence for Louis's own views on his divorce, although Regino suggests that he was unwilling.²⁵ So, while Hincmar opposing the divorce suggests that he was also in opposition to Charles's policy, there is no way to conclusively determine whether Hincmar was supporting Louis in this case. This divorce therefore does not prove that Hincmar had any influence on Louis before Charles's death.

In the summer of 877, Charles drew up the Capitulary of Quierzy, which provided for the government of West Francia during Charles's forthcoming visit to Italy. Among other provisions in this document, Charles the Bald left Louis under the guardianship of certain men, who may have been those whom Charles considered necessary for his son's support. These men included the bishops of Paris, Tournai, Beauvais and Soissons, as well as many abbots and counts.²⁶ The principal omission, in fact, is Hincmar himself, who did not have an official role in Louis's guardianship while Charles was absent in Italy. This was probably as a result of Hincmar's loss of influence in Charles's court by the late 870s, but it also indicates that Charles was not setting Hincmar up in the role of adviser to Louis. Hence these two survivors of Charles's reign did not have an official relationship established before Charles died, and Hincmar was not officially established as a counsellor for Louis the Stammerer during the summer regency of 877.

A few months after this capitulary was signed, Charles died on 6 October 877 in the Alps while returning to West Francia from Italy. This clearly caused a major upheaval in West Francia and is the logical starting point for a closer examination of the relationship between Louis the Stammerer and Hincmar of Rheims. With a new ruler taking over the government of West Francia, Hincmar had the opportunity to resume a primary role in West Frankish affairs, and he took it.

Hincmar's influence during Louis the Stammerer's reign

Hincmar's role in Louis's accession

The first major extant source that gives any insight into their relationship is a letter sent by the archbishop to the heir apparent, *Novi regis instructio ad rectam regni administrationem*. In this letter, written soon after Charles's death, Hincmar explains that Louis had sent a request to Hincmar asking for his counsel and support. Because Hincmar was unable to go to Louis himself, he instead sent this letter as a response to Louis's request.[27] The contents of this letter are the best clue to the circumstances in which it was sent. Hincmar said that Louis asked for his advice: if this is true, then Louis was looking for help in a very difficult situation as he attempted to solidify his grasp on West Francia at the onset of his reign, before his coronation.

Hincmar addressed this situation by devoting the first part of his letter to describing previous accessions. His advice to Louis, using these as examples, was extremely clear: attempt to get all the magnates, clergy and laity, working towards the same goal. Avoid dissent, because dissent will result in unrest and many other evils.[28] Hincmar recommended that Louis convene a large assembly of the counts of West Francia to confirm their agreement to the provisions of Quierzy; this would have the not negligible side effect of preventing the magnates from looting Frankish territory in the absence of an acknowledged ruler.[29] This suggestion was very relevant to the situation, as Louis needed to negotiate with his father's nobles in order to establish his position as king. He especially had to deal with those men who supported Richildis, Charles's widow and also sister of the important noble Boso of Vienne. Various meeting points were established among the magnates, and Louis and Richildis' eventual meeting at Compiègne was swiftly followed by Louis's coronation.[30]

The course that Hincmar had recommended was adopted and Louis was crowned and anointed as Louis had desired, but this is where the dilemma of influence becomes clear: was Hincmar's advice the major reason Louis chose to meet with the Frankish nobles, or did other factors play a part? Is it possible to determine the extent of Hincmar's influence in this situation? This letter and the recommendations in it do demonstrate that Hincmar was closely following the progress of the attempts to crown Louis and of the manoeuvres of the opposition.[31] Devisse takes this supposition a step further and maintains that the negotiations were 'clearly' conducted by Hincmar.[32] If he had conducted the negotiations that would indeed show that

Hincmar had significant influence, but there is very little evidence to support that hypothesis. Instead, the letter's existence implies that Hincmar was not with Louis to give him advice in person or help with the negotiations and that Hincmar was not necessarily available to provide guidance to Louis before his accession.

Whether or not Hincmar was solely responsible for these negotiations, his position with Louis is starting to become clear. At this point, the start of Louis's reign, Hincmar had a fair amount of influence; his absence from Louis's side did not mean that he lost the opportunity to recommend a course of action to the new king. Louis, in seeking his advice, viewed Hincmar as a good source of useful information about governing West Francia; in return, Hincmar was confident enough to preach to Louis. Almost too confident: the authoritarianism that had contributed to Charles the Bald's dissatisfaction with Hincmar's advice is on full view,[33] as the archbishop is both condescending and dictatorial in his letter. Louis followed the advice, but whether or not it was solely because Hincmar suggested it is debatable.

Within a month of Hincmar writing his letter, Louis was crowned king of West Francia. Hincmar both wrote the coronation ritual and performed the consecration and coronation; the archbishop of Sens also had a role in the ceremony.[34] Hincmar had written other rituals for the kings of West Francia, most recently the coronation of Charles the Bald in 869 as king of Lotharingia, which he used as a model for Louis's ceremony. In creating Louis's coronation ceremony, Hincmar also attempted to use the opportunity to seize recognition for his own see of Rheims, which was riding high on Hincmar's success.[35] Compiègne was in Rheims' archdiocese and thus Hincmar could claim the right to preside but, as the rival archbishop of Sens also played an important part in Louis's coronation,[36] the glory was not only Hincmar's. By the end of the coronation ceremony Hincmar had established himself as the pre-eminent religious adviser to Louis the Stammerer, but it is notable that Hincmar did not attempt to become Louis's only adviser. In fact, Hincmar had already recommended in his letter that Louis consult with other magnates, both church and lay: 'Therefore you should with haste send to Hugh and Gauzlin the abbots, and to the counts Boso, and Conrad, and Bernard, and the other Bernard.'[37]

This coronation ceremony offers a good opportunity to examine Hincmar's motivations in his interactions with Louis. Hincmar did not attempt to become sole counsellor to Louis but proposed instead the establishment of a governing council. Despite the omission of his own name from the list of advisers, Hincmar perhaps envisioned a role for himself as a senior member of the council, a pre-eminent adviser politically as well as religiously. He was working for the good of the kingdom, to establish a strong governing council and body of faithful advisers, which would help with the stability of the kingdom. He was also following the role of a bishop in promoting neutrality and discouraging factionalism, taking care not to incite dissension within the kingdom. Hincmar's duty and privilege as archbishop was to ensure that the king was properly crowned, but an additional motivation here was Hincmar's attempt to make Rheims pre-eminent; Hincmar used the ceremony to promote his own diocese, as was his duty as archbishop.

Hincmar and his rivals

Despite Hincmar's optimistic suggestions about promoting peace and concord, the first hint of factionalism during Louis's reign can already be seen in the events around Louis's accession. In the *Annales Bertiniani*, Hincmar recorded complaints about the distribution of *honores* prior to Louis's coronation: 'The magnates of the kingdom, as much the abbots as the counts, [were] indignant since he had given out some of these *honores* without their consent.'[38] This was connected to the negotiations, as Louis distributed favours to gain supporters, but it had the drawback of inciting dissent among those who had not been consulted or who had not received the gifts that they wanted. Hincmar had foreseen this in his letter and had warned Louis not to allow a small group of *fideles* to monopolise posts within the kingdom.[39]

As Hincmar had earlier suggested, Louis needed the support of all the great magnates to run the kingdom, namely Hugh the Abbot, Gauzlin and the counts Boso of Vienne, Conrad of Paris, Bernard of Autun and Bernard of Gothia.[40] In this situation, surrounded by powerful and ambitious men, Louis had to tread very carefully. The nobles split into two factions. Gauzlin, Conrad of Paris and Bernard of Gothia formed one faction, while Hugh the Abbot, Boso of Vienne and Bernard of Autun formed the other.[41] MacLean describes this as a division between the 'supermagnates' of Charles the Bald's reign – Hugh, Boso and Bernard – and a group of northern Frankish nobles who had been promoted by the Capitulary of Quierzy.[42] These were the men who would compete with Hincmar to advise and influence the new king during his reign. Although later in Louis's reign Hincmar was loosely allied with Gauzlin's faction, in the sources that Hincmar left he does not explicitly align himself with any group.[43] This may have been a strategy to protect his influence during Louis's reign, or a choice stemming from the duty of a bishop to promote peace in the kingdom (and hence discourage factionalism).

How did Hincmar influence Louis the Stammerer during his reign, especially while the king was surrounded by other strong personalities? Hincmar held the position of archbishop of Rheims, the most senior churchman in the *regnum*, which in and of itself brought a weight of power and influence in Church affairs and in related secular ones. In addition to this post, he also had the benefit of years of influence on Charles and of years of experience in the West Frankish political scene. He was not the only courtier who combined political experience with high ecclesiastical office. Hincmar was not archchancellor for Louis; the person who held that post was the abbot Gauzlin, continuing on from his appointment under Charles the Bald. Gauzlin was named in the Capitulary of Quierzy as a member of Louis's regency council, and was also one of the men whom Hincmar had suggested as advisers for Louis.

Physical proximity may also have been an important element for Hincmar in exerting influence over Louis. He was clearly with Louis the Stammerer at the coronation that signalled the start of his reign as accepted king, and his physical proximity to the new ruler as well as his role in composing and conducting the accession ceremony implies that he had the opportunity to influence the king at that point. His presence at court would have allowed him to advise Louis; given that Hincmar had duties to his archdiocese, it is difficult to believe that he would have remained in Compiègne after the coronation if he had no influence on the king.

However, Hincmar did not remain in Compiègne indefinitely, nor did he follow Louis's itinerant court. During the course of Louis's reign, Hincmar was absent from court regularly, presumably due to ecclesiastical responsibilities in Rheims. It is possible to reconstruct Hincmar's activity during Louis's reign from various sources. As previously stated, he was in Compiègne for Louis's coronation and stayed from November to early December of 877. At the beginning of 878, Hincmar was in Rheims in the winter and the Lenten season through to Easter of that year, during which time Louis was mainly hunting in the north of Francia.[44] Hincmar was with the king at the Council of Troyes in September 878. He almost certainly accompanied Louis to the council at Fouron with the eastern Carolingian King Louis the Younger in late November 878, before returning to Rheims at the end of the year. Hincmar remained in Rheims from Christmas through to Lent and Easter 879.[45] During this time, Louis was again hunting in the excellent woods in the north and east of his kingdom, near Rheims. But Louis's reign ended in April 879, when he died at Compiègne on Good Friday. It is not clear whether Hincmar was in attendance at Louis's deathbed; he may have been with Louis, but was more likely in Rheims.

Merely being away in Rheims does not mean that Hincmar had no way to communicate with the king; as long as Louis travelled in the region around Rheims, Hincmar could correspond with and influence him. Rheims was an important administrative centre and conveniently located near to Compiègne; from his archdiocesan seat Hincmar had helped Charles the Bald to govern,[46] though he had never been part of Charles's permanent court.[47] Rheims' proximity to Louis and Charles's favourite hunting grounds in the Ardennes meant that correspondence could easily travel from Hincmar to the king, wherever he was. The *Historia Remensis ecclesiae* records several letters sent from Hincmar to Louis during the winter of 878, so communications were clearly being exchanged when the two men were in different locations.[48] Through his correspondence, Hincmar was able to advise and guide Louis when they were in the same region, if not in the same city, just as he had done for Louis's father.

But in the summer of 878, when Louis was recovering at Tours from a life-threatening illness, Hincmar seems to have been absent. This absence possibly allowed other advisers to increase their influence over Louis. For example, during his convalescence, Louis granted charters to several institutions, such as those issued to St-Martin of Tours. Two charters were issued, one without an intercessor and the other at the request of the brothers.[49] As Louis was convalescing at this abbey his gratitude for their care and hospitality was certainly understandable and was expressed in the charters themselves, but it is also evident that Louis's physical proximity gave Abbot Hugh the opportunity to influence Louis in his favour in Hincmar's absence.[50] Another abbot, Abbo of St-Sauvin-sur-Gartempe, may have taken advantage of Louis's presence in Tours to request a charter for his institution.[51] Hugh's influence carried over to the Council of Troyes, when yet another charter was issued in favour of the abbey, this time a confirmation of previous charters made at Hugh's explicit request.[52] One solid form of political influence was the role of intercessor for an institution requesting a charter from the king. It is notable, in contrast, that Hincmar is not mentioned in any of Louis the Stammerer's existing charters as an intercessor, nor in any other way. Hincmar was very interested in property at Rheims,[53] so this was not due to any lack of interest in charters on Hincmar's part. One possible explanation is, of course, that Hincmar was losing political influence.

Diplomacy and Hincmar

The effects of this loss of influence – because of Hincmar's absence during Louis's convalescence – became clear at the Council of Troyes, in September 878, when Pope John VIII visited West Francia to hold an ecclesiastical council. Hincmar may well have been left out of Louis's deliberations with Hugh before this council. In the *Annales Bertiniani*, Hincmar grumpily describes various machinations leading to the excommunication of Bernard of Gothia and the distribution of *honores* to selected magnates as having been done in secret.[54] He meant 'secret from Hincmar': his reference to 'ipsorum consiliariorum suorum' rather clearly indicates that he was not among those men consulted. His absence from these negotiations signals a reduction of his influence in the political life of West Francia at this point.

Notwithstanding his exclusion from the people consulted about the redistribution of gifts, Hincmar's advice was still congruent with the decisions taken by Louis the Stammerer. Charles the Bald had been very interested in expanding into Italy, a policy which Hincmar had opposed.[55] Louis's actions in 878 were more in agreement with Hincmar's opinions: one of the principal reasons for the pope's trip to West Francia was to persuade Louis to become involved in transalpine affairs, lending John some support in his disputes with papal vassals in Italy, but Louis refused to leave West Francia to assist the pope.[56] Yet, though Louis followed Hincmar's policies in this matter, this was certainly not entirely due to Hincmar's influence. At this point Louis was convalescing from the life-threatening illness that had afflicted him in the summer; the council had been delayed several times and he had barely managed to make it to Troyes to meet the pope. He was in no fit state to become involved with foreign politics. Louis's original reason for heading to Tours in the spring had been a revolt of his nobles; and, though the redistribution of *honores* at Troyes was a result of the resolution of this revolt, he still must have been concerned about internal stability in the kingdom. In addition, repeated incursions by Northmen on the Atlantic coast were drawing on his military resources and personnel. In uncertain health and with other, more pressing domestic issues, Louis needed no urging from Hincmar to refuse the pope's request.

Despite his lack of involvement in secular matters, Hincmar did have significant influence in the ecclesiastical matters being debated at the Council of Troyes. As pre-eminent spokesman for the West Frankish bishops, he composed the bishops' declaration of faith and responded to the pope's statements at the council.[57] However, there is no evidence that ecclesiastical influence translated into political influence: Hincmar was not gaining political clout through these interactions, although they fell within his remit as archbishop of Rheims and surely helped reinforce his position of pre-eminence among his fellow priests and bishops.

The other major political event of 878 was the conference between Louis the Stammerer and Louis the Younger in late November, which resulted in the Treaty of Fouron. Hincmar's involvement is not directly mentioned but, given his detailed description of this council in the *Annales Bertiniani* and Fouron's proximity to his diocese, he was almost certainly in attendance. He would have been available for consultation with the king and could have offered guidance. The treaty included provisions promoting peace between the two kings, as well as an acknowledgement of the inheritance rights of Louis the Stammerer's two sons.[58] Both of these were policies that Hincmar promoted and could definitely indicate his influence on the composition of the agreement between the two neighbours. Hincmar had previous experience with diplomatic negotiations, such as those establishing peace between Charles the Bald and Louis the German in 859 after the latter's invasion of West Francia.[59] Hincmar's experience would have been extremely useful for Louis and, given that the terms of the treaty were two policies that Hincmar supported, his involvement here is plain.

Despite his successful diplomacy in the autumn of 878, Louis the Stammerer's ill health returned in the spring and he died shortly thereafter, in April 879. Notably, Hincmar was not named as a guardian for Louis's sons after his death. At the start of Louis's reign, Hincmar had suggested six men as counsellors for Louis during his reign (in addition to himself), but sixteen months later Louis named only three of them as guardians. Hugh and Boso's faction had managed to push aside Gauzlin and his supporters, the faction with which Hincmar was loosely allied. This triumph indicates that Hincmar was no longer in favour at Louis's court. Hincmar, of course, was also older and more tired; so some of this stepping back from court politics may have been an effort to concentrate his limited personal resources in his own diocese, or an unwillingness to travel because of old age. Yet he re-emerged on the political stage after Louis's death as a strong supporter of the inheritance rights of the teenage sons from Louis's first marriage. Hincmar may not have been able to resist the temptation to regain influence by supporting them against Adelaide's posthumous son, or he may simply have felt that his voice was needed to guide West Francia in the debate over the succession; he did not seem inclined to yield his role to a younger generation, and as mentioned he was advising Louis III as late as 881.

Conclusion

Hincmar's prestige as archbishop of Rheims did not diminish during Louis's reign; he was the most senior ecclesiastical figure in West Francia. His theological work and his eminence as a churchman were unquestioned, as shown by his presence in the records of the Council of Troyes. He deserved respect as one of the longest-serving royal counsellors, with a deep fund of knowledge of political divisions in West Francia – and Francia as a whole – that stretched back to the start of Charles the Bald's reign. This prestige and knowledge helped Hincmar and Louis during Louis's first months as king.

Hincmar definitely did exert influence over Louis the Stammerer at the start of the reign. This influence was at its height at Louis's coronation in November 877, when he wrote an important instructional letter and personally arranged and conducted the coronation for Louis. But this glory did not persist; his influence over Louis the Stammerer declined from November 877 to April 879. I believe that he was politically outmanoeuvred by a different network of noblemen, with others gaining influence and pushing Hincmar aside, rather than Hincmar resigning of his own volition or knowingly choosing actions that would lead to a loss of influence. The turning point was Louis's convalescence at Tours. Towards the end of the reign, and especially noticeable at the Council of Troyes in 878, Hincmar's advice was not consulted; it seems fairly clear that he had lost influence over Louis. Louis then turned to others for the political advice and experience that he had previously received from Hincmar, and Hincmar's unhappiness with this can be seen in the *Annales Bertiniani*. The fact that Hincmar was not named in the succession council confirms this loss of influence.

However, this is clearly a simplification of a complex problem. In addressing Hincmar himself, the roles that other people played are neglected; I have for the most part ignored Gauzlin, Boso, Hugh and other influences on Louis the Stammerer. The biggest issue, therefore, is the fundamental problem of judging supposed influence. I have discussed Hincmar's relationship with Louis the Stammerer and the interactions between king and archbishop, but how much these interactions actually resulted in changes to Louis's policy and how much Hincmar's opinions influenced Louis is much harder to determine. It is almost impossible to judge which consequence is the result of one specific person exercising influence versus others not doing so; it is easier to gauge the influence or presence of a faction than of an individual. There are no clear-cut points at which it is possible to say that Louis made a decision based entirely (or even mostly) on Hincmar's advice as opposed to the advice of many different advisers. It is easier to show where Louis's decisions went against Hincmar's advice, as in his assignment of *honores* at Troyes, than to show that any one policy stems directly from Hincmar's suggestion.

Hincmar's motivations are also difficult to discern: it is hard to ascertain whether or not he was acting out of altruism or self-interest and how far his involvement was influenced by his position as an archbishop. This makes it more difficult to determine whether he obtained any of his desired results as he interacted with the king and the court. Part of this problem results from the lack of evidence available, but it is also caused by the nature of that evidence and the lack of clear statements that indicate motivations, even in such a seemingly straightforward account such as Hincmar's *Annales Bertiniani*.[60]

This is not a problem that is unique to the relationship between Louis the Stammer and Hincmar of Rheims; it is a problem common to many such investigations. However, the examination of possible threads of influence is important in and of itself, even without arriving at any definite conclusion about the actual rationale behind the decisions made by historical figures. To ask what a source can tell us about influence and motivations may lead to more fruitful inquiries in the future. For now, investigating these causes and motivations leads us to a deeper understanding of the role of Hincmar in West Francia and the wider world, and a better picture of the man himself.

Notes

1 *AB* trans. Nelson, p. 203, n.19; Devisse, *Hincmar*, II, p. 802ff.
2 Hincmar, *Novi regis instructio ad rectam regni administrationem*, *PL* 125, cols 983–90, at 985, c. 1: 'Legimus quia boni reges constituti bonos sibi consiliarios adhibuerunt, et per bonos reges et bonos consiliarios regnorum populi multa bona habuerunt, et per malos reges et malos consiliarios regnorum populi multa mala sustinuerunt.'
3 *Ibid.*, col. 988, c. 8: 'Nullus enim homo est sic sapiens ut alterius non indigeat consilio, sicut scriptum est: "Audiens sapiens sapientior erit, et intelligens gubernacula possidebit" et "qui confidit cogitationibus suis impie aget" [Proverbs1:5 and 12:2].'
4 Devisse, *Hincmar*, II, p. 692: 'Leur *imposer* des conseillers sages – l'archêveque a, bien évidemment, vocation à jouer ce rôle! – fait partie du devoir d'Etat pour le métropolitain rémois.'
5 J. L. Nelson, *Charles the Bald* (London, 1992), p. 11 and n.19; Devisse, *Hincmar*, II, p. 692, referring to Council of Fismes, 881 c. 8, now edited in MGH *Conc.* V, no. 15A, pp. 178–96 at 194–6.
6 Nelson, *Charles the Bald*, p. 241: Hincmar had been 'displaced by ... Bishop Odo of Beauvais, Archbishop Actard of Tours ... and Archbishop Ansegis of Sens.' Devisse, *Hincmar*, I, p. 354ff; II, p. 725ff, p. 802ff.
7 *AB*, trans. Nelson, pp. 188–9, n.9; Hincmar, *De villa Noviliaco*, ed. H. Mordek, 'Ein exemplarischer Rechtsstreit: Hinkmar von Reims und das Landgut Neuilly-Saint-Front', *Zeitschrift der Savigny-Stiftung für Rechtsgeschichte, Kanonistische Abteilung*, 83 (1997), pp. 86–112, at 106, c. vii: 'Per quosdam ex nostris apud domnam Richildem reginam, et apud domnum Hludowicum, filium domni regis Karoli, obtinuerunt Donati et Landradae filii, ut villa Noviliacus cum suis appendiciis eis consignaretur'.
8 Flodoard, *HRE* III-19, p. 260.
9 *AB* s.a. 862, p. 91 (trans. Nelson, p. 100).
10 C. Brühl, 'Hinkmariana II: Hinkmar im Widerstreit von kanonischem Recht und Politik in Ehefragen', *DA*, 20 (1964), pp. 55–77, at 66.
11 Regino of Prüm, *Chronicon*, ed. F. Kurze, MGH *SRG* 50 (Hanover, 1890), s.a. 879, p. 114 (trans. S. MacLean, *History and Politics in Late Carolingian and Ottonian Europe: the Chronicle of Regino of Prüm and Adalbert of Magdeburg*, Manchester, 2009, p. 180): 'Eo [adulescentes filios Ludowici] quod iussu Caroli eorum genitrix spreta atque repudiata fuerit'; K. F.

Werner, 'Die Nachkommen Karls des Grossen bis um das Jahr 1000 (1.-8. Generation)', in W. Braunfels, ed., *Karl der Grosse: Lebenswerk und Nachleben*. Band IV: *Das Nachleben* (Düsseldorf, 1965), pp. 403-79 at 440.

12 K. Heidecker, *The Divorce of Lothar II: Christian Marriage and Political Power in the Carolingian World*, trans. T. M. Guest (Ithaca, 2010), pp. 98-9.

13 Regino, *Chronicon*, s.a. 878, p. 114 (trans. MacLean, p. 179): 'Habuit autem, cum adhuc iuvenilis aetatis flore polleret, quandam nobilem puellam nomine Ansgard sibi coniugii foedere copulatam ... Sed quia hanc sine genitoris conscientia et voluntatis consensu suis amplexibus sociaverat, ab ipso patre postmodum est ei interdicta et interposito iurisiurandi sacramento ab eius consortio in perpetuum separata. Tradita est autem eidem ab eodem patre Adalheidis in matrimonium'.

14 Heidecker, *Divorce*, pp. 114-15, following P. L. Reynolds, *Marriage in the Western Church: the Christianization of Marriage During the Patristic and Early Medieval Periods* (Leiden, 1994), p. 388, esp. n.12.

15 K. F. Drew, 'The family in Frankish law', in Drew, *Law and Society in Early Medieval Europe* (London, 1988), VI, pp. 1-11, at p. 4.

16 Heidecker, *Divorce*, p. 115, following *AB* s.a. 865, pp. 123-4 (trans. Nelson, p. 128).

17 Heidecker, *Divorce*, p. 158, following Nicholas I, Epistola 9, ed. E. Caspar, MGH *Epp*. 6, p. 275 (J2705).

18 See in particular Hincmar, *De divortio*.

19 See J. L. Nelson, 'The "Annals of St Bertin"', in M. T. Gibson and J. L. Nelson, eds, *Charles the Bald: Court and Kingdom*, 2nd revd edn (Aldershot, 1990), pp. 23-40 at 38, for an interesting discussion of the political motivations and reasons behind this possible deliberate omission, or 'Hincmargate'.

20 Devisse, *Hincmar*, I, pp. 402, 418; Hincmar, *De divortio*, Responsio 2, p. 126.

21 Devisse, *Hincmar*, I. p. 438.

22 *AB* s.a. 862, p. 92 (trans. Nelson, p. 101).

23 Heidecker, *Divorce*, p. 98; Flodoard, *HRE* III-19, p. 261. Heidecker connects this disapproval from Gauzlin to the dispute over the succession after Louis's death.

24 This letter is mentioned in Flodoard's catalogue, *HRE* III-20, p. 267: 'Item de duabus uxoribus ipsius Ludovici, filii Karoli, qualiter actum fuerit, et cetera.'

25 Regino, *Chronicon*, s.a. 878, p. 114 (trans. MacLean, p. 179).

26 *Conventus Carisiacensis*, 877, MGH *Capit*. II, nos. 281-2, pp. 355-63, at 359, c. 15: 'Qualiter et quo ordine filius noster in hoc regno remaneat, et qui debeant esse, quorum auxilio utatur, et vicissitudine cum eo sint;

videlicet ex episcopis assidue sint cum illo: aut Ingilwinus aut Reinelmus sive Odo seu Hildeboldus; ex abbatibus, sia alia necessitas non evenerit, assidue sint cum eo: Welpho, Gauzlinus et Folco; ex comitibus vero: aut Teudericus aut Balduinus sive Chuonradus seu Adalelmus; alternatim cum illo consistent et quanto saepius pro nostra utilitate potuerint, Boso et Bernardus. Si versus Mosam perrexerit, sint cum eo: Franco episcopus, Iohannes episcopus, Arnulfus comes, Gislebertus, Letardus, Matfridus, Widricus, Gotbertus, Adalbertus, Ingelgerus, Rainerus una cum praedictis; si ultra Sequanam perrexerit: Hugo abba, Waltherus episcopus, Wala episcopus, Gislebertus episcopus et ceteri nostri fideles illius partis una cum praedictis; sed et de aliis fidelibus nostris, secundum quod in unaquaque parte regni necesse fuerit.'

27 Hincmar, *Novi regis instructio*, col. 984, c. 1: 'Dominatio vestra mihi mandavit, ut ad vos festinarem venire, quia mecum de vestris, et sanctae Ecclesiae, ac regni utilitatibus tractare velletis: unde vobis humili ac certa responsione satisfactionem exhibeo'.

28 *Ibid.*, cols 984–5, c. 1: 'Legimus in antiquis historiis, quia saepe, quando reges constituti sunt, inter regni primores discordia orta est, quoniam aliqui sine aliorum consilio ejus constitutionem vindicare sibi votuerunt. Quae discordia non sine impedimento fuit pacificata.'

29 *Ibid.*, col. 987, c. 7: 'et petite, ut talem locum, sicut eis commodius visum fuerit, vobis et eis qui in istis partibus sunt, sed et ipsis qui in illis partibus sunt, convenire provideant, et vobis mandent ut illuc veniatis cum primoribus qui in istis partibus sunt. Et taliter quique conveniant ut regnum non depraedetur, nec devastetur, ut communi consilio de communi necessitate et utilitate tractetis, qualiter illa capitula, quae pater vester proxime in Carisiaco annuntiavit, ad effectum pervenire possint, quae interim relegite et vos et illi qui vobiscum sunt, et mente recondite.'

30 *AB* s.a. 877, pp. 218–19 (trans. Nelson, pp. 203–4).

31 L. Levillain, 'Les personnages du nom de Bernard dans la seconde moitié du IXe siècle', *Moyen Âge*, 42 (1946), pp. 197–242, at 220.

32 Devisse, *Hincmar*, II, p. 972.

33 Devisse, *Hincmar*, I, p. 416: by the 860s, Charles was tired of Hincmar's 'authoritarianism and intransigence'.

34 *AB* s.a. 877, p. 219 (trans. Nelson, p. 204): 'consecratus et coronatus est in regem Hludouuicus ab Hincmaro Remorum episcopo.'

35 R. A. Jackson, *Vive le Roi!: a History of the French Coronation from Charles V to Charles X* (Chapel Hill, 1984), p. 204; R. McKitterick, 'The Carolingian kings and the see of Rheims, 882–987', in R. McKitterick, *Frankish Kings and Culture in the Early Middle Ages* (Aldershot, 1995), pp. 228–49, at 228.

36 *AB* s.a. 877, p. 220 (trans. Nelson, p. 205).

37 Hincmar, *Novi regis instructio*, col. 987, c. 7: 'Propterea sub celeritate

mittite ad Hugonem et Gozlenum abbates, et ad Bosonem, et Conradum, et Bernardum, itemque Bernardum, comites'. *AB* trans. Nelson, p. 203, n.19 notes that Hincmar's suggested advisers were split into factions. See also O. G. Oexle, 'Bischof Ebroin von Poitiers und seine Verwandten', *Frühmittelalterliche Studien*, 3 (1969), pp. 138–210, at 200–2.
38 *AB* s.a. 877, p. 218 (trans. Nelson, p. 203): 'regni primores tam abbates quam comites indignatos quia quibusdam honores dederat sine illorum consensu'.
39 S. Thompson, 'The Kingdom of Provence and its rulers, c.870–c.950' (PhD dissertation, University of Cambridge, 2002), p. 68, citing Hincmar, *Novi regis instructio*, col. 987, c. 8.
40 See above, n.37. On these men, see S. Airlie, 'The political behaviour of the secular magnates in Francia, 829–879' (DPhil dissertation, University of Oxford, 1985), p. 238.
41 J. M. H. Smith, *Province and Empire: Brittany and the Carolingians* (Cambridge, 1992), p. 190.
42 S. MacLean, *Kingship and Politics in the Late Ninth Century: Charles the Fat and the End of the Carolingian Empire* (Cambridge, 2003), pp. 116–17.
43 M. J. McCarthy, 'Power and kingship under Louis II the Stammerer, 877–879' (PhD dissertation, University of Cambridge, 2012), pp. 74–7.
44 Devisse, *Hincmar*, II, p. 922.
45 *Ibid.*
46 *Ibid.*, I, p. 29: 'Reims est aussi un centre important pour l'administration du royaume et Charles compte sur le prélat pour l'aider à reprendre en mains un royaume plus ou moins rétif où l'anarchie aristocratique l'a emporté depuis dix ans.'
47 *Ibid.*, II, p. 919.
48 Flodoard, *HRE* III-19, p. 260; Schrörs, *Hinkmar*, Reg. 430, 431, 434.
49 *Recueil des actes de Louis II le Bègue, Louis III et Carloman II, rois de France (877–884)*, ed. F. Grat, J. de Font-Réaulx, G. Tessier and R.-H. Bautier (Paris, 1978), no. 12, pp. 28–33; no. 14, pp. 37–40. It is possible that a third charter was issued, but there is only fragmentary evidence for this; see no. 39, p. 101.
50 Oexle, 'Bischof Ebroin', pp. 200–1.
51 S. Perrault and G. Pon, 'Deux diplômes du IXe siècle pour Saint-Savin', *Bibliothèque de l'École des chartes*, 167 (2009), 179–95, at p. 194. Thanks to Charles West and Stuart Airlie for drawing this article to my attention.
52 *Recueil des actes de Louis le Bègue*, no. 15, pp. 40–6.
53 As shown during the dispute over the villa of Neuilly in Charles the Bald's reign: see above, n.7.
54 *AB* s.a. 878, pp. 229–30 (trans. Nelson, p. 212): 'et cum consilio ipsorum consiliariorum suorum dispertitus est honores Bernardi Gothiae

markionis per Theodericum camerarium et Bernardum comitem Aruernicum et per alios secrete dispositos.'

55 Devisse, *Hincmar*, II, p. 803ff.
56 *Ibid.*, II, pp. 975–6.
57 *Ibid.*, II, p. 976.
58 *AB* s.a. 878, pp. 231–2 (trans. Nelson, pp. 213–14).
59 Devisse, *Hincmar*, I, p. 344ff.
60 For more on the trustworthiness of the *Annales Bertiniani*, see Kleinjung, Chapter 3.

7

Hincmar and his Roman legal sources[1]
Simon Corcoran

Hincmar of Rheims is famous among writers from Carolingian Francia for the extent of his use of Roman legal sources. His explicit and *verbatim* quotations have themselves come to form a part of the textual history of the Theodosian Code, whose text generally rests on few witnesses. This does not mean, of course, that Hincmar's importance to our knowledge of Roman legal works and their early medieval use is matched by the importance of these works to Hincmar. Biblical, patristic, papal and conciliar texts were his predominant and preferred authorities.

Hincmar's use of Roman material, however, is still distinctive compared to most of his contemporaries, so that his usage is worth investigating. Scholars, whether primarily interested in Hincmar himself (Schrörs, Devisse),[2] in the Roman works he cited (Mommsen and Meyer),[3] or in their survival in the early medieval period (Conrat, de Wretschko),[4] have over the years searched out citations and analysed his engagement with these sources. Most prominent among these scholars is Jean Devisse, whose 1962 pamphlet *Hincmar et la loi* remains a fundamental starting point, albeit marred by some frustrating and disorientating misprints.[5] Finally, recent editions of Hincmar's works have been assiduous not only in specifying sources, but also in carefully distinguishing verbal borrowings by distinctive typography.[6]

Even so, identifying sources is not always easy, in part because of those cases where the references are general or vague, but also because there was so much textual recycling. This is always a hazard with legal sources, but the ninth century in particular witnessed much creative re-imagining of normative materials, especially into the Pseudo-Isidorian forgeries.[7] However, even the most honest use may rely upon material at several removes from the texts supposedly cited, and so give a misleading impression of the works available to a writer. Therefore, the aims of this chapter are, first, to describe as clearly as possible which Roman legal texts Hincmar cites and in what forms he knew them and, second, briefly to assess the status and function of these texts for Hincmar, based on his choice and manipulation of the material.

Hincmar's references to Roman law come in numerous forms and Devisse famously castigated predecessors for not distinguishing clearly enough between different types of citation. He himself divided the material between citations, allusions and vicarious quotations, which is a generally useful pattern for approaching Hincmar's practice.[8]

First, *verbatim* quotations of the Roman legal texts are relatively common. Sometimes these are attributed to a specific work or even to a book or title, suggesting authority and also guiding those readers who might be able to follow up the texts independently. Thus there are references to books and titles of the Theodosian Code (*CTh.*),[9] often by their numeration in the Breviary of Alaric (*Brev.*),[10] or to chapters from the Epitome of Julian (*Epit. Iul.*).[11] More often, for imperial laws, the quotations have the heading naming the emperors and perhaps recipients, and sometimes even the subscripts (the dating clause at the end). However, these descriptive or diplomatic elements are usually lacking, and on occasion quotations may not even be clearly signalled as such. The explanatory *interpretationes* added by the Breviary compilers to accompany their chosen texts are only rarely identified as such,[12] and indeed, being shorter and clearer, tend to be the default form of text quoted, unless there is a good reason to do otherwise.[13]

Second, texts may be identified, but their contents only paraphrased or briefly summarised.[14] Third, there may be broad allusions to laws, allusions which need not relate to a particular text and could simply be imprecise references to generally known rules. Thus Hincmar refers to Roman law requiring five, seven or ten witnesses for certain acts, taking the latter number from Ambrose, whereas the others could as easily have been dredged up from a half-remembered passage of Isidore of Seville as from detailed knowledge of the Breviary of Alaric.[15] Certainly Hincmar's apparently broad acquaintance with the Roman material does not mean that he is not recycling at second or third hand.

Nonetheless, the Roman law sources that can be clearly identified in Hincmar are:

The Theodosian Code, the post-Theodosian Novels and the *Sententiae* of Paulus, mostly in versions that can be attributed to the Breviary of Alaric or its epitomes; plus the Sirmondians.
The Epitome of Julian, containing summaries of the Novels of Justinian.
The *Lex Dei* or *Mosaicarum et romanarum legum collatio* ('Comparison of Mosaic and Roman Laws') (*LD*).[16]
Roman law texts such as the Gregorian or Justinian Codes (*CJ*), cited because embedded in the Church Fathers (Augustine, Gregory the Great).

Before we unpick this list, however, it needs to be explained that we are not dependent solely upon Hincmar's works for understanding his use of Roman law. It is fortunate that two key contemporary manuscripts associated with Rheims survive, namely Berlin SB Phillipps 1741 – hereafter Y (from Mommsen's Theodosian apparatus)[17] – and Paris BnF lat. 12445 (hereafter D).[18] Roman legal materials form only a minor part (10% or less) of these manuscripts, which are principally made up of canonical and other similar material.[19] However, there is a strong consonance between the texts they contain (both the Roman and the canon-law materials) and those cited by Hincmar, even to the sharing of specific textual variants. This has long been recognised (at least since Conrat), but it was Devisse who most emphatically characterised both of them as Hincmar's own manuscripts and suggested a complex history for them.

Judging from matching citations in Hincmar's writing, the major part of Y was copied piecemeal during the 850s.[20] Devisse suggested that there was already use of Y in the Second Episcopal Capitulary (852), based on a single Breviary citation.[21] In fact Roman sources are barely reflected before the *De praedestinatione Dei* (859),[22] although it is usually presumed that Hincmar was already assembling material for this from 856 onwards.[23] Perhaps, therefore, the later 850s are the most likely period for the Roman texts being copied into Y. A new portion was added at the beginning of Y in 868 with material relevant to the assembly at Pîtres in that year, although very little is Roman law.[24]

Y was also itself the key exemplar for D. Here Devisse's conclusions are rather more speculative, imagining that the major canon-law portion of **Y**, together with advice on episcopal administration, was copied out for presentation to the younger Hincmar at his consecration as bishop of Laon in 858.[25] The latter then copied further material into it during the 860s, primarily the sort of Pseudo-Isidorian texts avoided by his uncle.[26] A copy of Hincmar of Laon's subscription for his collection of sources of 8 July [869] even appears in the upper margin of fol. 166^v.[27] The manuscript was then reclaimed by the elder Hincmar and returned to Rheims after his nephew's fall in 871, with the main Roman law sequence from **Y** copied into it only now (**Y** fols 179–92 + Vat. Reg. Lat. 1283 fols 95–6 = **D** fols 187–202), because it had been either unwanted or still absent in 858. Further Roman materials absent from **Y** were added, concentrated in two main sections (**D** fols 210–14, 216–24), having been collected as a result of Hincmar's repeated involvement in the affairs of the younger Hincmar and his associated relations with Charles the Bald between 868 (the assembly at Pîtres) and 871 (Council of Douzy).

Böhringer sees Devisse's explanation of the Paris manuscript as overly fanciful and complicated.[28] Instead, she argues the whole of **D** was produced solely at Rheims for the elder Hincmar during his dispute with his nephew, therefore *c.*870, containing a broad variety of texts, significantly derived from **Y**, but with further material added, including the Pseudo-Isidorian, that was needed to engage with the bishop of Laon. This sober interpretation appears more plausible than Devisse's peripatetic one. The main Roman sequence from **Y** was copied quite carefully into **D**, making it appear as a fair copy, which even neatly incorporates marginalia from **Y** into its text.[29] The presence of marginalia noting textual divergences between several manuscripts present in two of the Roman law sections in **D**, but only in the main section in **Y** suggests that what is in **D** could originally have been in some now missing portion of **Y**, since such a careful task was surely conducted only once.[30] **Y** would thus be an even more important source for **D** than is immediately apparent. Whatever the exact history of the two manuscripts and their inter-relationship, both can be characterised as working manuscripts of Hincmar, representing repositories of source-texts collected to suit his interests and ready to be mined as needed. Their contents do suggest at least two key periods of assembling the Roman legal texts a decade or more apart (the later 850s and *c.*870).

What, therefore, are the Roman legal materials present in **Y** and

D? The core material common to both is what is generally called an augmented Breviary.[31] Imperial constitutions on religious affairs had been collected together and edited into the sixteenth and final book of the Theodosian Code (published in 437). When that Code and other Roman texts were recycled by Alaric II into his slimmed down Breviary in 506, little of Book 16 survived, since the Visigothic kingdom at that time was still Arian, and texts celebrating or privileging things Catholic were hardly to be favoured. Originally produced for the Roman subjects of the Visigothic kings, the Breviary, being both more handy and more intelligible than its source-texts (because of its explanatory *interpretationes*), became the preferred Roman legal work in the Catholic Frankish kingdoms, and indeed versions even more abbreviated were created.[32] For ecclesiastics in Gaul, however, Roman imperial laws on Church matters were a useful resource, and it is perhaps no surprise that, although the full Theodosian Code was no longer copied intact, the ecclesiastical constitutions of emperors from the Code and indeed elsewhere were taken and adapted.

Thus it was that the Breviary Book 16 came to be supplemented by constitutions taken from full Codes. Only one manuscript of the book completely restored in this fashion survives (the Ivrea Breviary),[33] but Y and its derivative D bear witness to a similar process, although with a much more selective approach. For instance, they take only eight out of sixty-six constitutions from title 5 'On heretics'. Also present are the first seven Sirmondian Constitutions, deriving from a Gallic ecclesiastical collection of imperial laws independent of the Theodosian Code, probably assembled in their current form in or near Lyons in the late sixth century and best known from a seventh-century manuscript which was certainly at Lyons in the ninth.[34] However, even with these additions, in neither manuscript does this process create an intact Book 16. Following on from the Book 16 selections, in both Y and D come the first title of the Breviary version of the Theodosianus Book 9 (on prosecutions), which is also found as a self-standing text elsewhere,[35] two texts from the first title of Book 1 (on imperial constitutions) – see Figure 3: Berlin MS Phillipps 1741 (Y) fol. 191^r, showing Bk 9 and Bk 1 extracts in different hands – and parts of Novels of Valentinian III and Marcian in their Breviary versions.

This was material originally copied into Y by 860. The later additions to Y do not include much new Roman law (principally a Breviary Novel of Valentinian), but the material added to D (whether or not

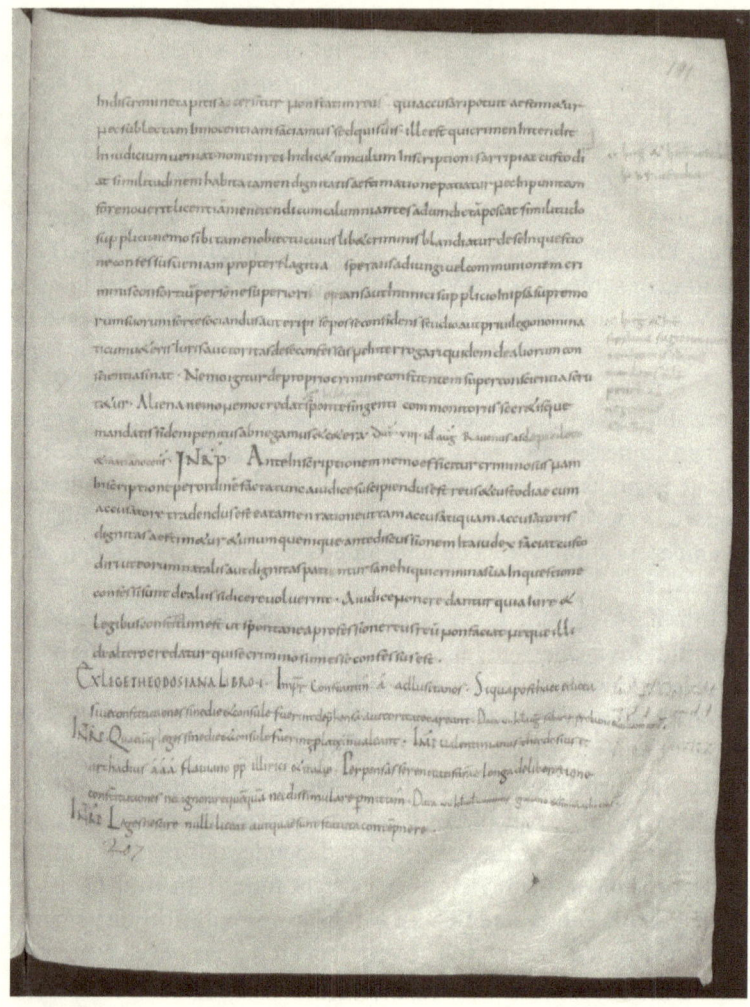

3 Staatsbibliothek zu Berlin, Preußischer Kulturbesitz (SBB-PK), MS Phillipps 1741, fol. 191ʳ – extracts from the Breviary of Alaric written by different hands in a manuscript strongly associated with Hincmar (with permission of the Staatsbibliothek zu Berlin).

any of it came from a now missing portion of Y) is more extensive if also rather miscellaneous, yet clearly focused on judicial procedure: extracts from the Breviary Theodosianus books 2, 4 and 11 and from the Breviary *Pauli Sententiae* Book 5 and, most unusually, two Novels of Valentinian (8.1–2) not from the Breviary selection, and so deriving from the full collection.[36] Finally, also unique to D, at the very end of the manuscript as it survives is a section which includes two chapters taken from the Epitome of Julian.

How, therefore, do these manuscripts relate to what Hincmar chose or was able to cite? Certainly they must be the source for the majority of Roman legal citations made by Hincmar, since the coincidence between their contents and what Hincmar quotes is remarkable. This can on occasion be confirmed by the presence of shared textual variants.[37] Further, the contents of the manuscripts, both the core 'augmented' Breviary texts in Y, later copied in D, and the second layer of material present especially in D, neatly match different phases of Hincmar's writings, the earlier contents already being used in the period up to 860, and the later reflecting the concerns of the period 868–871.

The most important feature to note is that almost all the non-Breviary Theodosian Code passages quoted by Hincmar are present in the two manuscripts. The only exceptions are *CTh.* 16.5.6 and 62, quoted in a sequence of imperial constitutions in *De praedestinatione Dei*.[38] This is best explained by part of the sequence having been taken from a parallel sequence in the canon-law *Collectio Quesnelliana* (CQ),[39] a compilation well attested in northern Francia, which Hincmar certainly knew and used elsewhere.[40]

Therefore, given that all Hincmar's Theodosian quotations can be traced to either Y or the *Collectio Quesnelliana*, we can ask the question: did Hincmar himself ever see an intact Theodosian Code? It is logical to presume that, for Hincmar to choose material for his working books, he had to gain access to larger texts from which to make his choices. This is most easily explained by suggesting that his source was a Breviary already furnished with a fully augmented Book 16 like that from Ivrea. It is possible that Y was simply copied exactly from a pre-existing selection, although the fact that the copyist of Y (fol. 181^r) noticed his own repetition of *CTh.* 16.2.2 – already copied as *Brev. Th.* 16.1.1 (fol. 179^v) – may suggest a mistake made during an active process of choosing constitutions.[41] Apart from Book 16, all other Theodosian material present in Y and D is confined to constitutions taken from the Breviary. Although a few Breviary texts used by Hincmar are not attested in the two manuscripts, there are no texts from the full Theodosian Code, other than those from Book 16, cited by Hincmar anywhere. Thus Hincmar probably had access, perhaps even repeated access, to an augmented Breviary, but never to a complete Code.

Pause for thought is offered by Janet Nelson's suggestion that Hincmar was a significant influence behind the Edict of Pîtres issued in June 864 by Charles the Bald, described by her as 'the most remarkable piece of legislation between Justinian's Novels and the 12th century'.[42] Although the only *verbatim* quotation of Roman law in this is from a Breviary *interpretatio*,[43] a whole series of texts from the Theodosian Code and the post-Theodosian Novels, going beyond what was available in the Breviary, must lie behind many of its provisions.[44] Certainly D also contains two non-Breviary Novels of Valentinian (8.1-2; fol. 210^{r-v}), demonstrating Hincmar's access to some fuller Novel material than was available in the Breviary, although neither is quoted elsewhere in Hincmar's works. Otherwise, however, the legal material behind the Edict of Pîtres is very different from that which we find in Y and D, or elsewhere in Hincmar's writings. Of course, Y and D represent bodies of material chosen and collected at various times and deliberately focused on the issues that most closely exercised Hincmar as a cleric. Counterfeiting coinage, as in the Edict, would not be the type of subject on which he would otherwise have been likely to pile up preparatory references.[45] Was he sufficiently flexible and knowledgeable of Roman legal materials to find what he (or the king) needed as and when required? Did this include accessing a complete Theodosian Code?

It is notable that some constitutions present in Y and D contain marginal *scholia* noting divergent (if not exactly significant) readings from three other manuscripts – see Figure 3: Berlin MS Phillipps 1741 (Y) fol. 191^r, with marginalia to *Brev. Th.* 9.1.11 – one perhaps a Breviary from St-Denis ('Dy'), a second a royal Breviary ('Reg'), while the third has been interpreted as being an intact Code ('intr' = 'integer'?), an uncertain inference.[46] Some readings appear to reflect closely those in the famous Vaticanus manuscript of the Theodosian Code (Vatican Reg. lat. 886), which, although probably written and used in Italy in the sixth century, is attested in Gaul by the early eighth.[47] While there is very little explicit evidence for Charles the Bald owning legal collections,[48] lesser Carolingians certainly did,[49] and such an ancient imperial volume graced with more prestige than use might have sat very nicely among the books of a king, especially one who came to see himself as a successor of earlier emperors and was as confident a manipulator of Roman legal texts as Hincmar himself.⁵⁰ There is no indication as to who wrote the notes in Y and D, but, as some are common to both and were probably copied from Y into D, they must have originally been added to Y in the late 850s or 860s and could well be by Hincmar himself. Unfortunately none of the relevant passages is quoted directly in Hincmar's writing, preventing us testing whether he might have adopted their readings. However, given that Hincmar sometimes appears to manipulate his texts, if generally on a minor scale (especially when contrasted to the wholesale confections of Pseudo-Isidore), this type of minute textual collation may have provided Hincmar with additional confidence in choosing or emending readings to suit his purposes. Nonetheless, while it is not impossible that Hincmar might have encountered a full Theodosianus at the royal court, it has left no discernible imprint upon his work. It certainly remains the more plausible option that Hincmar had access only to an augmented Breviary.

Such a Breviary could also have provided the Sirmondians (Ivrea contains just 1–3), although of the seven copied into Y and D Hincmar quotes only Sirmondian 3 in his works.⁵¹ A parallel is provided by Florus of Lyons, a slightly older contemporary (d. *c.*860), also considered notable for his engagement with Roman legal texts.⁵² As noted above, the sole manuscript (Berlin Phillipps 1745) containing the longer recension of Sirmondians 1–18 was at Lyons in the ninth century, where it was corrected by Florus himself. As part of the dispute between Louis the Pious and Bishop Agobard over the forced conversion of the slaves and children of the Jews of Lyons in the 820s, Florus compiled a set of authorities,⁵³ whose only Roman legal content comprised extracts from five of these Sirmondians (nos. 1, 3, 6, 11, 15) plus a sixth text (known as Sirmondian 20), possibly once present in this manuscript, but certainly known from another probable Lyons manuscript.⁵⁴ These same authorities, with the addition of Sirmondian 17 (= *CTh.* 1.27.1), were reused in Florus's later polemic against Bishop Modoin of Autun.⁵⁵ Like Hincmar, Florus was dependent upon, even limited by, key source manuscripts, but this also highlights the fact that what someone directly used need only be a part of what was available to him. Further, once a writer used material, he was likely to recycle the same texts he had used before, whether or not he revisited his source manuscript.

However, Y and D cannot explain all the material that Hincmar used. Some of his quotations of the Theodosian Code and *Pauli Sententiae* come from the versions in the Aegidian Epitome of the

Breviary (*Epit. Aegid.*).[56] A manuscript of this text, although probably copied at Bourges,[57] seems to have entered the library at Rheims early in Hincmar's episcopate, as the Aegidian Epitome passages are attested in earlier works (and indeed not much later on).[58] It is also pertinent to note that the Rheims library certainly and unsurprisingly contained manuscripts of Isidore's *Etymologies*, whose fifth book was often a source of rather garbled knowledge of Roman law.[59] Although this work was known to Hincmar, it is hard to demonstrate that he ever had to rely on it.

It should be noted here that the *Sententiae* of Paulus is the only work in the juristic tradition of Roman law (as opposed to that of the imperial constitutions) that Hincmar uses, but only because it belonged to the Breviary tradition and so was part of the *lex Theodosiana*.[60] It is not clear whether Hincmar appreciated the fact that the work was originally pagan, although he must have known that Paulus was a jurist.[61] Although the *Sententiae* were popular in the late empire, being summary, comprehensive and comprehensible, their absorption into the Breviary essentially superseded the full work,[62] and it is unlikely that Hincmar knew it directly, although not all his *Sententiae* citations can be closely sourced.[63] Some such works did sometimes survive, as with the Epitome of Ulpian, known only from a single ninth-century Frankish manuscript (Vatican Reg. lat. 1128),[64] so that access to now-lost texts is not inconceivable.

Next there is the Epitome of Julian. While only two passages from this are attested in D (see below p. 139), there are numerous quotations in Hincmar's works of some dozen chapters, although drawn from only two lengthy constitutions on ecclesiastical matters (*Epit. Iul.* CXV, CXIX). Justinian's codification, the Institutes, Digest and Code, had little purchase in Carolingian Francia, where it had never been promulgated. Some rare fragments of possible transalpine manuscripts are known, but they seem to have had almost no impact on contemporary writers.[65] Justinian's Novels were also little known, except in the form of the Epitome of Julian, which comprised summaries deriving from a Constantinople lecture-course of the 550s. This was the most widely copied and quoted Justinianic work in the early medieval west.[66] When Hincmar refers to *lex Iustiniana*, this is what he routinely means.[67]

He does cite two constitutions from the Justinian Code, each a couple of times (*CJ* 7.44.3, 7.48.4), but these are not direct uses and the exact nature of what he was ultimately quoting may not have been entirely clear to him.[68] He takes these Code extracts from the letter of Gregory the Great to the defensor John,[69] a letter famous as providing a rare early medieval example of detailed citation from the Justinianic corpus (Digest, Code, Novels). As it happens, for one of these Justinian texts there was a parallel Breviary passage present in D (fol. 213^v), but this was not in fact used by Hincmar and he does not seem to have made any connection between the two versions.[70] Gregory's letter also contains a passage from a Novel of Justinian (*Nov.* 90.9) in a Latin translation not elsewhere attested[71] and which Hincmar also quotes.[72] Hincmar, however, was well aware that here and elsewhere Gregory was weaving an authoritative web from Justinianic materials.

Furthermore, Hincmar chose to invoke Justinian's legal changes, which had finally set the period of prescription for ecclesiastical property at forty years (the period that needed to elapse before title became immune to a Church claim to take back property), on top of the thirty years already known under the older secular Theodosian law.[73] In fact manuscript D reveals the unstated knowledge that lies behind this usage, since it contains a passage (fol. 237^r) in which two relevant chapters from the Epitome of Julian, which attest to Justinian's final rulings on this point, are correctly identified and associated also with the apposite letter of Gregory the Great, specifically in connection with confusing claims of two ecclesiastical institutions against one another.[74] Here we can see that Hincmar knows more than he chooses to cite, since neither of the two Julian chapters is quoted explicitly anywhere in his surviving works and we might otherwise have been uncertain whether he knew the details of these texts. Indeed, on other occasions Hincmar specifically states that he is giving only a selection of relevant laws;[75] on the basis of what was available to him in Y and D at least, we can see his claim is no pretence. Given the concentration of his citations from one ecclesiastical constitution of the Epitome in particular (*Epit. Iul.* CXV), it is reasonable to wonder if he used some pre-existing focused selection. But such transalpine collections as are known show almost no overlap in the material chosen, nor do they tend to preserve the original constitution and chapter numbers that Hincmar sometimes quotes.[76] Thus, despite Devisse's doubts, especially regarding textual divergences,[77] it is easiest to suppose that Hincmar had direct access to a manuscript of the Epitome of Julian (with or without the *Lex Dei*, of which more later); and his citation of the Julianic *lex Iustiniana* at Douzy in 871 was perhaps the most explicit ever invocation of Justinianic law in Carolingian Francia.[78]

What is most clear, however, is that this explicit use is a feature of his later works from c.870. Stray earlier quotations are unascribed or misidentified, such as his apparently unknowing use of the Epitome in his Second Episcopal Capitulary (852).[79] Similarly, two passages close but not identical to Julian appear in the assembled authorities that follow the *De raptu*.[80] These two texts are attributed to the edicts of *pii* or *piissimi imperatores*, an ambiguous designation that is as suitable for ninth- as for sixth-century emperors.[81] The date of *De raptu* is uncertain, but is most likely to be c.860.[82] Thus straightforward derivation for those texts from the Epitome of Julian seems unlikely.

Further vicarious citation is provided by a constitution from the Gregorian Code quoted *verbatim*, the sole non-Christian imperial text so used, but only because it occurs in a passage of Augustine.[83] The full Gregorian Code is unlikely to have survived to the ninth century.[84] Even the Breviary Gregorianus finds no place in Hincmar's work, except as woven into Pseudo-Isidorian texts quoted at him by Hincmar of Laon.[85] Elsewhere Augustine's allusions to the content of imperial laws are quoted,[86] but only once does Hincmar claim that these can be read independently in the Theodosian corpus.[87]

Finally, there is the *Lex Dei* or *Mosaicarum et Romanarum legum collatio*, famously mentioned twice in the *De divortio* in 860 but nowhere else.[88] Since the *Lex Dei* always travels in the manuscripts with the Epitome of Julian,[89] it is perhaps surprising that it is mentioned only in this one work a decade before the flurry of explicit Epitome citations. Although Hincmar refers to two titles by name and number (*LD* 5 and 6), he does not quote any text *verbatim*; instead he states, perhaps optimistically, that anyone who cares, judges included, can read these for himself. However, the oddest thing for anyone reading Hincmar, with his interweaving of biblical and Roman legal texts, is that he characterises the work as 'Lex Romana'. Surely any reader of the *Lex Dei* (perhaps its original title; or more descriptively the 'Comparison of Mosaic and Roman Laws') is immediately struck precisely by the juxtaposition of the two types of material. This is an early attempt at comparative law and is far more akin to what Hincmar himself is doing than the other legal works on which he draws.[90] It is therefore surprising that he does not make more use of it. For instance, a passage from Papinian asserting the criminal liability of husbands who kill adulterous wives (*LD* 4.10.1) would seem especially pertinent and certainly manipulable for the purposes of *De raptu*, written at about the same time, in which uxoricide is a key topic.[91] Inasmuch as he does use it, Hincmar does seem to be emphasising the Roman law of the *LD* as pre-Christian. Why and how the *Lex Dei* came into Hincmar's orbit, only to pass out again after such limited impact, is a mystery.

Roman law and legal sources, or more generally secular law, are referred to by Hincmar in different ways – sometimes simply *leges*, or *leges Romanae, sacrae leges, leges publicae, lex Theodosiana* (for the Code/Breviary tradition), *lex Iustiniana* (for the Epitome of Julian).[92] These are not casually interchangeable designations and do not appear uniformly throughout Hincmar's *oeuvre*. Nonetheless, the default type of Roman text that Hincmar cites is an imperial pronouncement of a Christian emperor, for which by the 870s he comes to use the term *sacrae leges*,[93] already standard even for documents of contemporary rulers.[94] It is also significant, however, that such imperial laws are often quoted with the rider that they are ones which the Church has accepted or approved, and do not necessarily rest upon their own authority alone.[95]

For which purposes did Hincmar choose and use the Roman texts? In general substantive Roman law was of little interest compared to matters of procedure and jurisdiction. Any good lawyer knows that, while substantive law can be manipulated and interpreted, it is a point of procedure that can most easily sabotage or save a case. Thus, although Hincmar tackled substantive issues of marriage in *De divortio*, giving opinions that in theory Lothar could both divorce Theutberga and marry Waldrada, the fatal flaws for Lothar's case, as Hincmar presented them, were rather procedural, and particularly evidential.[96] For instance, Hincmar accepted Theutberga's exoneration by ordeal (857) and, despite it being a form of trial largely alien to the Roman legal tradition and with which the Church was uneasy,[97] he argued that Roman law allowed such a custom, if long established, to acquire thereby legal validity.[98] Hincmar's view of Theutberga's later spontaneous confessions before the bishops (860) was the opposite, especially as that process also involved the condemnation of her brother unheard and in his absence, which, barring exceptional circumstances, was against both Church and Roman law.[99] Some usages are especially imaginative, showing how normative texts can so easily be used in ways never envisaged by the original legislators. Thus

Hincmar, after asserting that earlier rulers had fostered Roman laws, then cites a Roman ruling that allowed someone's heirs to continue a legal action already initiated, basing upon this the argument that rulers are irreversibly bound by their predecessors' laws.[100] However, these uses of Roman law are often little more than supplements to other biblical or patristic texts, as different types of authority are lined up for mutual support. The key authority for the rules of evidence, for instance, is the story of Susannah in the Book of Daniel, whose interpretation and implications Hincmar teases out as would a jurist.[101] Ultimately, therefore, Susannah is more important than Theodosius.

It is the conflict around Hincmar of Laon, however, which brings out the most concerted use of Roman procedural law, from Hincmar's defence of the Church at Pîtres in 868 to the deposition of the younger Hincmar at Douzy in 871. Here issues of jurisdiction were especially important, such as 'Who can accuse whom? Who can try whom? Who can appeal to whom?' The elder Hincmar first used his nephew's case to assert ecclesiastical privileges in jurisdiction against the secular power (Pîtres 868)[102] but, as old disputes festered and new ones arose around the younger Hincmar, the uncle later switched to defending his own position as metropolitan against episcopal insubordination and papal interference. Terminology in Roman laws is adapted to context as the civil 'province' becomes the ecclesiastical,[103] and metropolitan becomes primate.[104] Often the legal point boils down to a fairly straightforward legal maxim or *regula iuris*, such as 'one witness is no witness'[105] or 'ignorance of the law is no defence'.[106] Two particularly important, related principles were that someone should not be tried and condemned in their absence nor without witnesses or other suitable evidence.[107] These were key weaknesses on which Hincmar had alighted in the case of Theutberga and her brother, Hubert,[108] and which later formed the background in setting out the rules for the trial of the priest Huntbert at the Council of Douzy in 874.[109] Yet this also raised the related question of the intractable defendant who refused to appear to answer charges, and could be condemned as contumacious after ignoring three summonses.[110] However, even though most of these principles are thoroughly Roman, Hincmar did not need to cite or only cite strictly Roman legal sources to support them. As noted above, conciliar or patristic 'approval' was the key to the current validity of Roman rules.[111]

Finally, even the most seemingly minor rules could be employed to try to trip up an opponent. Thus the rule about imperial laws without consular date lacking validity (*Brev. Th.* 1.1.1) was turned against the *sententiae* signed by Hincmar of Laon on 8 July 869, to which his clergy also subscribed, where the day and month had been specified, but apparently not the year.[112] It is undoubtedly true that it would be unusual for any properly executed document, intended to have legal effect, to lack a suitable and full dating clause, and this need not apply just to contemporary royal charters, where the practice is most clearly visible.[113] Hincmar's argument may therefore have carried some weight, or at least plausibility, in his struggle against a dangerous document that was tantamount to an indictment by Hincmar of Laon of his uncle's metropolitan tyranny.

Hincmar's quotations show numerous verbal variants from his sources. Many of these are simply the result of 'cut and paste' and have no substantial impact on meaning.[114] However, it has already been suggested that the textual variants noted in Y and D show Hincmar's interest in such matters, and a couple of well-known examples will demonstrate Hincmar's readiness to employ verbal manipulation, even in small ways.

First, *CTh.* 16.2.41 talks of the accusation of clerics as *laudabilis* (praiseworthy), which reading is attested in the Vatican Theodosianus, the Ivrea Breviary and also in Y and D. In these last two texts, however, a correcting hand (perhaps Hincmar himself) has changed the text from *laudabilis* to *inlaudabilis*. This is then reflected in all Hincmar's later uses of this passage.[115] Accusations against clerics, even those who deserved it, were clearly not to be characterised as intrinsically praiseworthy.[116] The emendation is not, in fact, unreasonable, as the constitution tries to tread an uncertain line between punishing for *calumnia* (false accusation) those who cannot prove their case against clerics and praising those who help to remove from the clergy those whose crimes defile it. However, Hincmar probably adopted the reading from its presence in the frequent manipulations of this passage across the Pseudo-Isidorian corpus.[117]

Under *CTh.* 16.2.8, an ecclesiastical privilege addressed by Constantius II to the clergy, no one is allowed to impose new public levies upon them (*sc.* the clergy) and their slaves (*mancipia*). As in the previous case, these are the Vatican and Ivrea readings, but in Y, D and Hincmar's citations this is changed to refer to estates (*fundos*) and slaves, a useful clarification or extension of the immunity granted.[118] This reading proved very influential, since it entered the *Collection in*

74 Titles (T.3 c.33),[119] whence it was taken up in other collections[120] and ended up in Gratian's *Decretum* (II, C.16. q.1 c.40).[121] Further, Hincmar attributes the law emphatically to Constantine the Great (so also Y and D) and adds this explanation: 'When he says '"no one", none is excluded, but even the prince's power is understood to be included.' This gloss would surely have surprised Constantius and was no doubt unwelcome to Charles the Bald.

Even where a quotation stops can be significant. Thus Hincmar cites the rule from the Epitome of Julian that a bishop cannot leave his province without leave of the metropolitan, ending with a canny *et reliqua*, which conceals the fact that the text continues by stating that the emperor (i.e. the secular power) also can grant leave.[122] In seeking to curb his nephew, he did not wish to endorse royal interference in ecclesiastical affairs. All these may be small textual manipulations, but they clearly show how Hincmar's prejudices colour his use of texts.

What, therefore, can we conclude about Hincmar and his Roman legal sources? First, he did not have at his command the same materials throughout his period of activity. Probably from the later 850s he used an 'augmented' Breviary, from which he created the core of Roman material in the Berlin manuscript (Y), but he also had access to the Aegidian Epitome. The 'Comparison of Mosaic and Roman laws' flitted into and out of his orbit in 860, whereas the Epitome of Julian became properly familiar to him only from around 870. Other texts he knew vicariously through patristic or other sources. Second, although he quotes Roman texts more widely than his contemporaries, much of this citation clusters in particular periods and works, the most continuous engagement being in 868–71. Because of the nature of the disputes in which he became embroiled, the law that interested him most often was procedural or jurisdictional and nearly always derived from Christian emperors. Even so, these authorities are usually of lesser importance than biblical or canonical texts. Finally, he often uses texts in imaginative ways, but he also quotes selectively and makes verbal emendations, sometimes trivial, but sometimes deliberately intended to shift the meaning or interpretation. He may have been encouraged by the realisation that different manuscripts already contained variant readings. Ultimately Hincmar is a clever lawyer, who wants to make the law work for him and knows how to extract something, anything, to bolster a case he is already determined to make. Yet the wholesale forgery of the Pseudo-Isidorian tradition represents a step too far for his taste.

Notes

1 I should like to thank Rachel Stone and Charles West for including me in the Hincmar sessions at Leeds in July 2012 and inviting me to contribute to this volume. Thanks are owed also to Michael Crawford, Abigail Firey, Matthew Gillis, Sylvie Joye, Wolfgang Kaiser and Benet Salway.
2 H. Schrörs, *Hinkmar*, pp. 409–15; Devisse, *Hincmar*.
3 *Theodosiani libri XVI cum constitutionibus Sirmondianis: et leges novellae ad Theodosianum pertinentes*, ed. T. Mommsen and P. M. Meyer, 2 vols (Berlin, 1905), I.1, lxxxix; II, lviii–lix; cf. *Mosaicarum et Romanarum legum collatio*, ed. M. Hyamson (London, 1913), pp. xiii–xiv, xxxi–xxxiv; R. M. Frakes, *Compiling the 'Collatio legum Mosaicarum et Romanarum' in Late Antiquity* (Oxford, 2011), pp. 35–6, 40–6.
4 M. Conrat, *Geschichte der Quellen und Literatur des römischen Rechts im frühen Mittelalter* (Leipzig, 1891), pp. 23–4, 255–6; M. Conrat, 'Ueber eine Quelle der römischrechtlichen Texte bei Hinkmar von Rheims', *Neues Archiv der Gesellschaft für ältere deutsche Geschichtskunde*, 24 (1899), 349–57; M. Conrat, 'Hinkmariana im Cod. Paris Sangerm. 12445', *Neues Archiv der Gesellschaft für ältere deutsche Geschichtskunde*, 35 (1910), 769–75; A. de Wretschko, 'De usu Breviarii Alariciani forensi et scholastico per Hispaniam Galliam Italiam regionesque vicinas', in Mommsen and Meyer, *Theodosiani libri XVI*, I.1, cccvii–ccclxxvii at cccxvi–cccxviii, cccxxxix–cccxli. Cf. J. Gaudemet, 'Survivances romaines dans le droit de la monarchie franque du Vème au Xème siècle', *Tijdschrift voor Rechtsgeschiedenis*, 23 (1955), 149–206 at 168–9.
5 J. Devisse, *Hincmar et la loi* (Dakar, 1962). Note that Devisse did not revise this work, which concerns only secular law, for his *magnum opus*, *Hincmar, archevêque de Reims*, although he did include a survey of Hincmar's canon-law sources in his Appendix III, vol. III, pp. 1395–1465.
6 Note in particular Letha Böhringer's edition of *De divortio* and *Die Streitschriften Hinkmars von Reims und Hinkmars von Laon 869–871*, ed. R. Schieffer, MGH *Conc*. IV, supplementum 2 (Hanover, 2003).
7 See K. Zechiel-Eckes, *Fälschung als Mittel politischer Auseinandersetzung. Ludwig der Fromme (814–840) und die Genese der pseudoisidorischen Dekretalen* (Paderborn, 2011) and de Jong, Chapter 14.
8 Devisse, *Hincmar et la loi*, pp. 14–33.
9 The standard edition of the Theodosian Code, Sirmondian Constitutions and the Novels is that of Mommsen and Meyer (see above, n.3).
10 For the Breviary of Alaric and its epitomes (including the Aegidian), see *Lex romana Visigothorum*, ed. G. Haenel (Leipzig, 1849), and below,

p. 133. Hincmar's references to book number (e.g. *Expositiones ad Carolum regem pro ecclesiae libertatum defensione*, PL 125, cols 1035–70 at 1039, 1045) cannot of themselves distinguish between Code and Breviary, but title numbers can (e.g. the reference in *De praedestinatione Dei*, PL 125 cols 401–2, c. 37.5 must be Code; in *Libellus expostulationis*, Council of Douzy, 871, MGH *Conc.* IV, no. 37B, pp. 420–87 at 458, should be Breviary); cf. the reference to *Pauli Sententiae* at *De praedestinatione Dei*, col. 389, c. 36. Allowance must always be made for the errors endemic in copying Roman numerals.

11 *Iuliani epitome latina Novellarum Iustiniani*, ed. G. Haenel (Leipzig, 1873). See e.g. Hincmar, *De presbiteris criminosis*, pp. 75, 107, cc. 10, 32; *Opusculum LV capitulorum*, ed. Schieffer, *Streitschriften*, p. 277, c. 30.

12 See e.g. *Expositiones ad Carolum regem*, PL 125, col. 1045.

13 See e.g. *Brev. Th.* 9.1.5, discussed below (n.103).

14 See e.g. Hincmar, *De raptu*, PL 125, col. 1021, c. 5.

15 Hincmar, *De divortio*, Responsio 12, pp. 191–2, citing Pseudo-Ambrose, *De lapsu virginis consecratae*, ed. I. Cazzaniga, *De lapsu Susannae (De lapsu virginis consecratae) incerti auctoris* (Turin, 1948), c. 20, pp. 10–11; or possibly *Brev. Th.* 4.4.1 and 3, *Brev. Gaius* 1.6.4, or Isidore of Seville, *Isidori Hispalensis Episcopi Etymologiarum sive originum libri XX*, ed. W. M. Lindsay, 2 vols (Oxford, 1911), 5.24.5–6.

16 Editions: *Collatio*, ed. Hymanson (with English translation); *Fontes iuris Romani antejustiniani. Pars altera, Auctores*, ed. J. Baviera, 2nd edn (Florence, 1940), pp. 541–89.

17 Devisse, *Hincmar et la loi*, pp. 50–4; Devisse, *Hincmar*, III, 1399–1407. A fragment from the same manuscript is also in the Vatican library (Vatican, Reg. lat. 1283).

18 Devisse, *Hincmar et la loi*, pp. 54–62; Devisse, *Hincmar*, III, 1399–1407; Conrat, 'Hinkmariana'; C. G. Mor, 'Un manoscritto canonistico francese del secolo IX', in *Scritti di storia giuridica altomedievale* (Pisa, 1977), 317–32; L. Böhringer, 'Der eherechtliche Traktat im Paris. Lat. 12445, einer Arbeitshandschrift Hinkmars von Reims', *DA*, 46 (1990), 18–47; Schieffer, *Streitschriften*, pp. 105–6. The manuscript can be viewed online at: http://gallica.bnf.fr/ark:/12148/btv1b9072677g.

19 Devisse, *Hincmar et la loi*, 51.

20 *Ibid.*, pp. 44–9, lists Roman law citations chronologically.

21 Hincmar, *Capitularia* II, MGH *Capit. Episc.* II, pp. 53–4, c. 21 citing *Brev. Th.* 16.1.6.*int.*

22 Hincmar, *De praedestinatione Dei*, PL 125, col. 65.

23 Devisse, *Hincmar et la loi*, pp. 44–5, dates this to 857/8; Devisse, *Hincmar*, I, 214, sees drafting as already begun in 856.

24 For a more recent view of what might have been added in 868, see Schmitz, *De presbiteris criminosis*, pp. 50–1.

25 Devisse, *Hincmar et la loi*, pp. 55–6; P. R. McKeon, *Hincmar of Laon and Carolingian Politics* (Urbana, 1978), p. 14 and Appendix I, nos. 3 and 5.
26 K.-G. Schon, *Die Capitula Angilramni*, MGH Studien und Texte 39 (Hanover, 2006), pp. 21–3.
27 McKeon, *Hincmar of Laon*, pp. 223 n.78, 286–7. For the uncertainties over Hincmar of Laon's various documents and which surviving texts represent which, see McKeon, *Hincmar of Laon*, pp. 172, 283–8; L. Kéry, *Canonical Collections of the Early Middle Ages (ca. 400–1140): a Bibliographical Guide to the Manuscripts and Literature* (Washington DC, 1999), pp. 175–6; Schieffer, *Streitschriften*; K. Zechiel-Eckes, 'Frühe Pseudoisidor-Rezeption bei Hinkmar von Laon', *DA*, 66 (2010), 19–54.
28 Böhringer, 'Der eherechtliche Traktat', pp. 20–1.
29 Thus the incorporation of *Brev. Nov. Marcian.* 1.*int.* into *Brev. Th.* 9.1.6 (Y fol. 190^v at D fol. 197^{r-v}; *Theodosiani libri XVI*, II, lix). Corrections to *CTh.* 16.2.41 are shared by both MSS (Y fol. 184^v; D fol. 191^v; apparatus criticus in *Theodosiani libri XVI*, I.2, 850).
30 Two of the three marginalia in Y (fols 190^v–191^r) are reproduced in D (fol. 198^r); *Theodosiani libri XVI*, I.1, xlv.
31 The Book 16 material in D is copied from and so matches that in Y, except for some constitutions missing through the loss of a folio (*Theodosiani libri XVI*, I.1, xc–xci).
32 J. Gaudemet, *Le Bréviaire d'Alaric et les Epitome* (Milan, 1965); M. Rouche and B. Dumézil, eds, *Le Bréviaire d'Alaric: aux origines du code civil* (Paris, 2008). On the *interpretationes*, see J. F. Matthews, 'Interpreting the *interpretationes* of the *Breviarium* of Alaric', in R. W. Mathisen, ed., *Law, Society, and Authority in Late Antiquity* (Oxford, 2001), 11–32.
33 Ivrea Bibl. Cap. XXXV(17) = E (Eporediensis); *Theodosiani libri XVI*, I.1, lxvii–lxviii, xc–xci. Some Theodosian constitutions are preserved in E alone.
34 The manuscript is now divided between Berlin and St Petersburg, but the key portion containing the Sirmondians is Berlin SB, Phillipps 1745, which contains eighteen constitutions. The history of the Sirmondians is obscure and uncertain, with some scholars suspecting forgery or at least interpolation. See O. Huck, 'Les constitutions sirmondiennes: introduction', in R. Delmaire, ed., *Les Lois religieuses des empereurs romains de Constantin à Théodose II*, 2 vols (Paris, 2005–09), II, 429–68 and below, p. 137.
35 Cologny Fondation Martin Bodmer, Cod. Bodmer 107 (late ninth century). See H. Mordek, *Bibliotheca capitularium regum Francorum manuscripta: Überlieferung und Traditionszusammenhang der fränkischen Herrscherlasse* (Munich, 1995), p. 115.

36 *Theodosiani libri XVI*, II, lix; Böhringer, 'Der eherechtliche Traktat', 27.
37 Such as the correction made to the Theodosian Code *(CTh.)* 16.2.41 in Y and D (*Theodosiani libri XVI*, I.2, 850) and present also in *Expositiones ad Carolum regem, PL* 125, col. 1046, *De presbiteris criminosis*, p. 70, c. 6 and *Libellus expostulationis*, MGH *Conc.* IV, no. 37B, p. 473, c. 30.
38 Hincmar, *De praedestinatione Dei, PL* 125, cols 401–2, c. 37.
39 *Collectio Quesnelliana (CQ), PL* 56, cols 353–746 at 681–4, c. 54. The sequence in both texts is *CTh.* 16.1.2, 16.4.2, 16.5.6, 16.5.62. Of the subsequent imperial texts quoted in *De praedestinatione dei* (*PL* 125, cols 402–3), some, which were never part of the Code tradition, should derive from the *CQ* cc. 14, 16, 28 (*PL* 56, cols 492–4, 551–4). Devisse, *Hincmar et la loi*, p. 24 cautiously suggests that the *Collectio Hispana* (*PL* 84, cols 93–848 at 176–7) is not an alternative source in these cases. Hincmar in this passage also cites *CTh.* 16.5.1 and 16.5.60, which ought logically also to have come from *CQ*, but they are absent from it as currently known. Both are present in Y. See Devisse, *Hincmar et la loi*, p. 23.
40 On the *CQ*, see Conrat, *Geschichte*, 145; Kéry, *Canonical Collections*, pp. 27–9; M. D. Elliot, 'New evidence for the influence of Gallic canon law in Anglo-Saxon England', *Journal of Ecclesiastical History*, 64 (2013), 700–30 at 707; for the use of it and the *Hispana* generally in Hincmar, see Devisse, *Hincmar*, III, 1407–13.
41 *Theodosiani libri XVI*, vol. I.1, xc.
42 J. L. Nelson, 'Translating images of authority: the Christian Roman emperors in the Carolingian world', in M. M. Mackenzie and C. Roueché, eds, *Images of Authority: Papers presented to Joyce Reynolds on the Occasion of Her Seventieth Birthday* (Cambridge, 1989), pp. 194–205. The text is edited as *Edictum Pistense*, 864, MGH *Capit.* II, no. 273, pp. 310–28.
43 *Brev. Novellae Valentiniani* 11. int.
44 Nelson's study builds on the earlier analysis of F. L. Ganshof, *Le Droit romain dans les capitulaires et dans la collection d'Ansegise*, Ius Romanum Medii Aevi, pars 1, 2 b cc α (Milan, 1969), 30–8. I am not sure that Nelson's ingenious suggestion can be correct that the thirty-seven chapters of the Edict (stressed by Hincmar in his report in *AB* s.a. 864, p. 113 (trans. Nelson, p. 118)) were intended to go just one further than the thirty-six of Valentinian's Novels. This numeration is that of the modern edition: the highest number recorded in the manuscripts being either 33 or 39, the latter only in a sequence including those of Theodosius II (*Theodosiani libri XVI*, II, xv–xvi).
45 Note that Hincmar deliberately omits reference to counterfeiting in his quotation of *Brev. Paul.* 5.25.1 in *De divortio*, Responsio 12, p. 192.
46 *Theodosiani libri XVI*, I.1, xlv, cv, re *CTh.* 4.18.1–2, 4.19.1, 4.20.3, 4.22.3,

9.1.15, 9.1.19. Caution may be wise, given that the three abbreviations are 'InDy', 'Inreg', 'Intr', so the last should rather denote a town or church beginning 'Tr' or 'T*r'.

47 For the *Vaticanus* in Gaul, see *Theodosiani libri XVI*, I.1, xlvi; L. Traube, *Theodosiani libri XVI cum Constitutionibus Sirmondianis et Leges novellae ad Theodosianum pertinentes. Tabulae et narratio tabularum* (Berlin, 1905), iv and Tab. V; also *Neues Archiv*, 31 (1906), 507. Parts of at least two other Code copies considered to be Gallic in origin do survive, although not preserving the relevant passages for comparison. See the discussion in B. Salway, 'The publication of the Theodosian Code and transmission of its texts: some observations', in S. Crogiez-Pétrequin and P. Jaillette, eds, *Sociéte, économie, administration dans le Code Théodosien* (Villeneuve d'Ascq, 2012), pp. 21–61 at 24–9.

48 Note R. McKitterick, 'Charles the Bald (823–877) and his library: the patronage of learning', *English Historical Review*, 95 (1980), 28–47 at 41 *re* Yale University, Beinecke MS 413 (Capitulary collection of Ansegis), which need not be associated with Hincmar either.

49 For Carolingian lay ownership of secular law books, note in particular the case of Eberhard of Friuli, Charles the Bald's brother-in-law: R. McKitterick, *The Carolingians and the Written Word* (Cambridge, 1989), pp. 245–50; P. J. E. Kershaw, 'Eberhard of Friuli, a Carolingian lay intellectual', in P. Wormald and J. L. Nelson, eds, *Lay Intellectuals in the Carolingian World* (Cambridge, 2007), pp. 77–105 at 85–7.

50 See J. L. Nelson, '"Not bishop's bailiffs, but lords of the Earth": Charles the Bald and the problem of sovereignty', in D. Wood, ed., *The Church and Sovereignty c.590-1918: Essays in Honour of Michael Wilkes* (Oxford, 1991), pp. 23–34.

51 Sirm. 3 is quoted in *Expositiones ad Carolum regem* (*PL* 125, col. 1045) and *De iure metropolitanorum*, *PL* 126, cols 189–210 at 209, c. 35. *PL* 125, col. 1047 reflects the text of *CTh.* 16.2.47 rather than the parallel at Sirm. 6. Hincmar, Epistola XV, *PL* 126, col. 95 contains an additional phrase describing the usurper John's legislation (*quos abdicata tyranni praesumptione*), which is absent from both the *CTh.* 16.2.47 and Sirm. 6 textual traditions. If not genuine, it is not clear to me why anyone should have bothered to interpolate this.

52 *Theodosiani libri XVI*, I.1, ccclxxviii–ccclxxix.

53 *Capitula ex lege et canone collecta*, *PL* 119, cols 419–22; see K. Zechiel-Eckes, 'Sur la tradition manuscrite des *Capitula ... De coertione Iudeorum*, ou Florus de Lyon au travail', *Revue bénédictine*, 107 (1997), 77–87.

54 *Corpus legum ab imperatoribus Romanis ante Iustinianum latarum, quae extra constitutionum codicas supersunt*, ed. G. Haenel (Leipzig, 1857), s.a. 1183. This constitution is dated to 430, but regarded as a

later forgery. See W. Kaiser, *Authentizität und Geltung spätantiker Kaisergesetze: Studien zu den Sacra privilegia concilii Vizaceni* (Munich, 2007), pp. 272–81 for the two versions of this text in Florus and pp. 212–20 on the probable Lyons manuscript (Paris, BnF lat. 12097).

55 K. Zechiel-Eckes, 'Florus' Polemik gegen Modoin: Unbekannte Texte zum Konflikt zwischen dem Bischof von Autun und dem Lyoner Klerus in den dreißiger Jahren des 9. Jahrhunderts', *Francia*, 25 (1999), 19–38.

56 For this epitome, see D. Liebs, *Römische Jurisprudenz in Gallien (2. bis 8. Jahrhundert)* (Berlin, 2002), pp. 111, 221–30. The text is printed in one of the parallel columns in Haenel's Breviary edition.

57 Leiden Universiteitsbibliotheek BPL 114. See F. M. Carey, 'The scriptorium of Reims during the archbishopric of Hincmar (845–882 AD)', in L. W. Jones, ed., *Classical and Medieval Studies in Honor of Edward Kennard Rand* (New York, 1938), pp. 41–60 at 57 (preferring a Rheims origin); Mordek, *Bibliotheca*, 502–7 (arguing for Bourges).

58 E.g. *Epit. Aegid. Paul.* 5.5.3 in *De praedestinatione Dei* (*PL* 125, col. 389) [859]; *Epit. Aegid. Th.* 1.2.7 in *De divortio*, Responsio 12, p. 187 [860].

59 Rheims, BM, 425 and 426. See Carey, 'The scriptorium of Reims', pp. 55–6; Devisse, *Hincmar*, III, 1497.

60 See above, n.10.

61 Manuscript D (fol. 219^r) records the *explicit* to the *Sententiae*, described as addressed by Julius Paulus to his son (Mor, 'Manoscritto', p. 326). Paulus is also mentioned in texts that Hincmar was likely to have known (*CTh.* 1.4.3 = *Brev. Th.* 1.4.1; Isidore of Seville, *Etymologiae* 5.14).

62 On the *Sententiae* tradition in Gaul, see Liebs, *Römische Jurisprudenz*, pp. 99, 118, 146–7.

63 See Devisse, *Hincmar et la loi*, p. 62; *De divortio*, p. 82; *De presbiteris criminosis*, pp. 101–2, c. 28.

64 W. Kaiser, 'Review of Martin Avenarius, Die pseudo-ulpianische liber singularis regularum', *Zeitschrift der Savigny-Stiftung für Rechtsgeschichte, Romanistische Abteilung*, 127 (2010), 560–603.

65 See C. M. Radding and A. Ciaralli, *The 'Corpus Iuris Civilis' in the Middle Ages: Manuscripts and Transmission from the Sixth Century to the Juristic Revival* (Leiden, 2007), pp. 49–51. Cf. W. Kaiser, 'Ein unbekanntes Zitat von Institutiones Iustiniani 3,6 pr.-8 in einer Abhandlung des Hrabanus Maurus zum Ehehindernis der Verwandtschaft', in H. Altmeppen, I. Reichard and M. J. Schermaier, eds, *Festschrift für Rolf Knütel zum 70. Geburtstag* (Heidelberg, 2009), pp. 513–57.

66 Discussed in detail by W. Kaiser, *Die Epitome Iuliani: Beiträge zum römischen Recht im frühen Mittelalter und zum byzantinischen Rechtsunterricht* (Frankfurt am Main, 2004).

67 *De presbiteris criminosis*, pp. 75, 79–80, 107, cc. 10, 13, 32; *Libellus expostulationis*, MGH *Conc.* IV, p. 457, c. 23.
68 *CJ* 7.44.3: *De presbiteris criminosis*, p. 69, c. 6; *Opusculum LV capitulorum*, pp. 268, 295, cc. 28, 36. *CJ* 7.48.4: *Expositiones ad Carolum regem* (*PL* 125, cols 1060, 1069); and *Collectio contra haereticos* in M. Hartmann, 'Collectio contra haereticos et de privilegiis multarum sedium: Ein bislang übersehenes Werk Hinkmars von Reims in der Centuriatoren-Handschrift ÖB Basel O II 29', in A. Mentzel-Reuters and M. Hartmann, eds, *Catalogus und Centurien: Interdisziplinäre Studien zu Matthias Flacius und den Magdeburger Centurien* (Tübingen, 2008), pp. 211–31 at 230.
69 Gregory the Great, *Regesta* 13.49[50], *Registrum epistularum*, ed. D. Norberg, CCSL 140–140A, 2 vols (Turnhout, 1982), pp. 1062, 1064.
70 *CJ* 7.48.4 = *Brev. Th.* 4.14.1 (*CTh.* 4.16.2). For only one of these passages (*PL* 125, col. 1060) does Hincmar not name Gregory as the source, and minor verbal variants confirm that all three citations derive from his letter; cf. W. Kaiser, 'Nachvergleichungen von Novellen- und Codexzitaten in einer frühmittelalterlichen Sammlung mit Exzerpten aus dem Register Gregors d. Gr. (Reg. 13,49 [50])', *Zeitschrift der Savigny-Stiftung für Rechtsgeschichte, Romanistische Abteilung*, 125 (2008), 603–44 at 637. Note that Hincmar quotes *CTh.* 16.2.31 (in Y and D) at *Expositiones ad Carolum regem*, *PL* 125, col. 1039 in a sequence of Theodosian constitutions, but never uses Gregory's extracts from the equivalent Justinian text (*CJ* 1.3.10).
71 Kaiser, 'Nachvergleichungen', 606–13.
72 *Opusculum LV capitulorum*, p. 268, c. 28.
73 *De iure metropolitanorum*, *PL* 126, col. 207, c. 32, alluding to Justinianic law and its citation by Gregory. For the thirty-year prescription, see *Brev. Nov. Val.* 8, present in both Y and D.
74 *Epit. Iul.* CIV c.366 and CXIX c.511, with an explicit reference also to Gregory the Great, *Regesta* 7.36, p. 500. For the details, see Mor, 'Manoscritto', p. 330 and Böhringer, 'Der eherechtliche Traktat', 32.
75 E.g. *Expositiones ad Carolum regem*, *PL* 125, cols 1039, 1060.
76 Thus the *Constitutiones de rebus ecclesiasticis* cannot be the source: on this text see Kaiser, *Epitome Iuliani*, pp. 419–60. The greatest overlap of chapters is with the contemporary north Italian *Lex Romana canonice compta*: see *Lex romana canonice compta: testo di leggi romano-canoniche del sec. IX pubblicato sul ms. paragino Bibl. Nat. 12448*, ed. C. G. Mor (Pavia, 1927).
77 Devisse, *Hincmar et la loi*, p. 63; *Hincmar*, II, 658.
78 Gaudemet, 'Survivances romaines', 168.
79 Hincmar, *Capitularia* II, MGH *Capit. Episc.* II, pp. 54–5, c. 21 quoting *Epit. Iul.* CXV c. 475.

80 Hincmar, *De raptu*, *PL* 125, col. 1035 quotes *Epit. Iul.* CXV c. 478 with an additional otherwise unattested section. Col. 1036 appears to be a paraphrase of *Epit. Iul.* CXV c. 428 (Devisse, *Hincmar et la loi*, pp. 38–9 is sceptical, but they do share the rare term *taxeota* for the *cohortales*, i.e. the provincial office-staff). The text is unlikely to be a direct adaptation from Justinian's original Novel 123, only attested in contemporary Frankish manuscripts by a version of its short preface (Paris BnF lat. 3838, 3846): see Kaiser, *Epitome Iuliani*, p. 423 n.36.

81 See e.g. Lothar II referring to Louis the Pious and Lothar I in Diplomata Lothar II, no. 4, *Die Urkunden Lothars I. und Lothars II*, ed. T. Schieffer, MGH Diplomatum Karolinorum III (Berlin, 1966), p. 388; Council of Valence, 855, MGH *Conc.* III, no. 33, p. 358, c. 9: *edictum piissimorum augustorum*. For Justinian as *piissimus*, see *Epit. Iul.* XXI c. 69, XXIII c. 88; cf. CVIII c. 382 (Constantine).

82 See Joye, Chapter 10, p. 190.

83 Antoninus (Caracalla) cited from Augustine, *De adulterinis coniugiis* 2.8, ed. J. Zycha, *Sancti Aureli Augustini opera sect. V, pars. III*, CSEL 41 (Vienna, 1900), pp. 347–410 at 389 by Hincmar, *De divortio*, Responsio 21, p. 225; cf. the allusion to the Emperor Julian in Epistola XV to Charles the Bald (*PL* 126, col. 95) taken from Gregory the Great, *Regesta* 3.64, p. 214.

84 The latest evidence for the Gregorianus in Gaul is the Breviary itself (506), since the later appendices added containing Gregorian material may have copied pre-existing selections. See Liebs, *Römische Jurisprudenz*, pp. 111, 115, 141–5.

85 *Brev. Greg.* 3.5.1 in *Ps.-Eusebii decreta* c. 11 and *Ps.-Symmachus, Decreta synodalia* 5, cited by Hincmar of Laon, *4. Untersammlung*, MGH *Conc.* 4, Supplementum 2, pp. 36, 38.

86 *Expositiones ad Carolum regem*, *PL* 125, col. 1051 quoting Augustine, *Tractatus* VI, 25, *In Iohannis Evangelium tractatus CXXIV*, ed. R. Willems, CCSL 36 (Turnhout, 1954), p. 66.

87 *Libellus expostulationis*, MGH *Conc.* IV, p. 468, c. 28, quoting Augustine, *In Iohannis Evangelium tractatus*, Tractatus VII, 11, p. 78. Hincmar does not actually identify the law, perhaps *Brev. Th.* 1.2.4 (*CTh* 1.2.6). The same passage without the Theodosian statement is quoted in *De divortio*, Responsio 12, p. 192.

88 *De divortio*, Responsio 12, pp. 178, 185.

89 There are three manuscripts, of which one is ninth-century and transalpine (Burgundy?) – Berlin SB. lat. fol. 269, on which see Hyamson, *Collatio* (including a facsimile of the *Lex Dei* section) and Kaiser, *Epitome Iuliani*, pp. 39–59.

90 For a recent discussion of the unknown fourth-century author and his

aims, see Frakes, *Compiling the Collatio*, who considers it a Christian work.
91 R. Stone, 'The invention of a theology of abduction: Hincmar of Rheims on *raptus*', *Journal of Ecclesiastical History*, 60 (2009), 433–48 and A. Pieniądz, 'Incmaro di Reims e i suoi contemporanei sull'uxoricidio: l'insegnamento della Chiesa e la pratica sociale', *Reti medievali rivista*, 12 (2011), 25–52.
92 Devisse, *Hincmar et la loi*, p. 76.
93 See e.g. *De presbiteris criminosis*, p. 69, c. 6; Epistola XXXVI (*PL* 126, col. 255); *Opusculum LV capitulorum*, p. 269, c. 29; *Libellus expostulationis*, MGH *Conc.* IV, p. 427, c. 5; *De ordine palatii*, p. 46, c. 8. Treason is judged by the 'sacred laws': *AB* s.a. 868, 873, pp. 150, 190 (trans. Nelson, pp. 151, 181).
94 See e.g. the confirmation by the Council of Paris in 846 (with Hincmar subscribing first) of the privileges of Corbie deriving from *sacrae litterae* of Louis the Pious, Lothar I and Charles the Bald: MGH *Conc.* III, no. 13, pp. 144–5.
95 See e.g., *Expositiones ad Carolum regem*, *PL* 125, col. 1063; *Opusculum LV capitulorum*, pp. 145, 201, *Praefatio*, c. 17; *Libellus expostulationis*, MGH *Conc.* IV, p. 427, c. 5.
96 K. Heidecker, *The Divorce of Lothar II: Christian Marriage and Political Power in the Carolingian World*, trans. T. M. Guest (Ithaca, 2010), pp. 82–3; A. Firey, *A Contrite Heart: Prosecution and Redemption in the Carolingian Empire* (Leiden, 2009), pp. 9–60.
97 Trial by ordeal was not usually approved, although sometimes supervised, by the Church at this time: see R. Bartlett, *Trial by Fire and Water: the Medieval Judicial Ordeal* (Oxford, 1986), especially pp. 70–5 on ninth-century critics; F. McAuley, 'Canon law and the end of the ordeal', *Oxford Journal of Legal Studies*, 26 (2006), 473–513.
98 *De divortio*, Responsio 9, p. 167, quoting *Epit. Aegid. Th.* 5.12.1 (rather than the Breviary version, missing from **Y** and **D**).
99 *De divortio*, Responsio 10, p. 169, referring to *leges publicae* (probably *Brev. Nov. Val.* 12.*int.*).
100 *De divortio*, Responsio 12, p. 187, quoting *Epit. Aegid. Th.* 1.2.7.
101 Firey, *Contrite Heart*, p. 44.
102 Hincmar selectively quoted numerous Theodosian laws in the *Expositiones ad Carolum regem*: *PL* 125, cols 1038–9, 1045–8, 1051, 1060–4, 1068–9; cf. Hincmar's own comments at *AB* s.a. 868, p. 150 (trans. Nelson, p. 151).
103 Thus on cases not being heard outside thprovince: *Brev.* 5 cited in *Expositiones ad Carolum regem* (*PL* 125, col. 1061) and *De causa Teutfridi presbyteri* (*PL* 125, col. 1111), using the main Theodosian text because it uses the word *provincia*, absent from the *interpretatio*; cf.

Brev. Th. 9.1.5.*int.* and *Nov. Marcian.* 1.*int.* in *Opusculum LV capitulorum*, p. 265, c. 28, with greater textual manipulation at *De presbiteris criminosis*, p. 71, c. 7.

104 Devisse, *Hincmar*, II, 635–89; McKeon, *Hincmar of Laon*, p. 92. Note Devisse's defence of Hincmar's adaptation of the Roman texts (*Hincmar*, II, 658, re *Epit. Iul.* CXV c. 462 in *Libellus expostulationis*, MGH *Conc.* IV, p. 457, c. 23).

105 *Brev. Th.* 11.14.2.*int.* in *Antwort der Bischöfe*, MGH *Conc.* IV, p. 558, c. 8.

106 *Brev. Th.* 1.1.2 in *De presbiteris criminosis*, p. 96, c. 25; also in **Y** and **D**.

107 *Brev. Paul.* 5.5.3 in *Antwort der Bischöfe*, MGH *Conc.* IV, p. 558, c. 8.

108 See above, n.96.

109 F. R. Herrmann and B. M. Speer, 'Facing the accuser: ancient and medieval precursors of the confrontation clause', *Virginia Journal of International Law*, 34 (1993–94), pp. 481–552 at 499–503.

110 *Opusculum LV capitulorum*, p. 267, c. 28; cf. *De presbiteris criminosis*, pp. 101–2, c. 28.

111 Thus the Roman rule on contumacy cited in the previous note is endorsed by reference to Celestine I, the Council of Ephesus and Gregory the Great.

112 *Opusculum LV capitulorum*, p. 295, c. 36.

113 For a proper dating clause from the same month, note a charter of Charles the Bald for the Abbey of St Bénigne at Dijon: 'Data XII kalendas augusti, indictione II, anno XXX regnante Karolo gloriosissimo rege. Actum apud Pistas villam. In Dei nomine, feliciter. Amen.' ['Charte Artem/CMJS' no. 787: online 22 November 2014 at www.cn-telma.fr/originaux/charte787/].

114 E.g. minor change from *hac lege* to *sacris legibus* in *Brev. Val. Nov.* 12.*int.* in *De presbiteris criminosis*, p. 103, c. 29; *iudicem* glossed as *id est episcopum suum* in *Nov. Marcian.* 1.*int.* in *De presbiteris criminosis*, p. 71. c. 7.

115 *Expositiones ad Carolum regem*, PL 125, col. 1046; *De presbiteris criminosis*, p. 70, c. 6; *Libellus expostulationis*, MGH *Conc.* IV, p. 473, c. 30.

116 The parallel version in *Sirmondian* 15 (not in **Y** or **D**) reads *miserandae* (deplorable), showing even earlier negative ecclesiastical reaction to this passage.

117 E.g. at *Capitula Angilramni* c.21 (Schon, p. 128), present in **D** f.164[v], and quoted by Hincmar of Laon, *Materialsammlungen vorwiegend pseudo-isidorischen Inhalts*, ed. R. Schieffer, *Die Streitschriften Hinkmars von Reims und Hinkmars von Laon 869–871*, MGH *Conc.* IV, supplementum 2 (Hanover, 2003), 5. Untersammlung, c. 6, p. 43.

118 *Expositiones ad Carolum regem*, PL 125, col. 1038.

119 *The Collection in Seventy-Four Titles: a Canon Law Manual of the Gregorian Reform*, ed. J. Gilchrist (Toronto, 1980), p. 89.
120 See e.g. Anselm of Lucca, *Collectio canonum* 4.13, ed. F. Thaner (Innsbruck, 1906–15), p. 197; Deusdedit, *Collectio canonum* 3.163, ed. V. W. von Glanvell, *Die Kanonessammlung des Kardinals Deusdedit Band 1, Die Kanonessammlung selbst.* (Paderborn, 1905), p. 339, cited as coming from the Justinian Code version (*CJ* 1.3.1), though its MSS do not read *fundos* either. See generally de Wretschko, 'De usu Breviarii', pp. ccclvi–ccclvii and S. Kuttner, 'New studies on the Roman law in Gratian's Decretum', *Seminar*, 11 (1953), 12–50 at 48–9.
121 *Corpus iuris canonici. Pars 1, Decretum magistri Gratiani*, ed. E. Friedberg (Leipzig, 1879), col. 772.
122 *Epit. Iul.* CXV, c. 437, in *Opusculum LV capitulorum*, p. 201, c. 17. For similar canny uses of *et reliqua* in the *Expositiones ad Carolum regem*, see C. West, 'The significance of the Carolingian advocate', *Early Medieval Europe*, 17 (2009), 189–90.

8

Hincmar et la loi revisited: on Hincmar's use of capitularies

Philippe Depreux

The way in which Hincmar used legal texts has long attracted the attention of historians.[1] Heinrich Schrörs noted that the archbishop of Rheims held secular law in great esteem, but he did not think it worthwhile to investigate more closely Hincmar's use of capitularies, the administrative and legal documents promulgated by Carolingian rulers.[2] Drawing on the works of Jean Devisse, to whom we owe the most thorough studies of the subject, this chapter offers a more nuanced, qualitative analysis of how Hincmar made reference to this particular type of normative text.[3] Devisse identified around fifty capitulary citations, of which all those from texts dated before 826 were taken from the collection compiled by Ansegis, abbot of St-Wandrille.[4] Even when Devisse referred to the original capitulary, this was in fact also in Ansegis.[5] This confirms once again the importance of this collection put together under Louis the Pious, which Hincmar knew well, since he had several copies of it made.[6]

Devisse was however more interested in the texts that were cited than in the place where Hincmar cited them. An approach which concentrates not on Hincmar's sources but on the texts in which he cited these capitularies shows that the corpus is one of just a few works. Occasional new discoveries and identifications have had little impact on the general observation that what we are dealing with is a small body of texts.[7] Here is the list:

The acts of the Council of Soissons (853)[8]
The treatise on churches and chapels (857/858)[9]
A letter on the marriage of Count Boso and Engeltrude (860)[10]
The treatise on the divorce of King Lothar II (860)[11]

A letter to Charles the Bald about Hincmar of Laon (868)[12]
A treatise on the defence of the liberties of the Church (868)[13]
A treatise on priesthood and kingship (c.870?)[14]
A letter to Hincmar of Laon about the parish of Folembray (870)[15]
A letter to King Louis the Younger asking him to grant freedom of election to the bishopric of Beauvais (881)[16]
The acts of the Council of Fismes (881)[17]
A treatise on the duties of the bishop concerning ecclesiastical property (881)[18]
An admonition for bishops, concerning King Carloman II (882).[19]

These texts can be grouped chronologically and thematically around the following issues: the status of ecclesiastical property; debates over marriage around 860; the conflict between the archbishop and his eponymous nephew, the bishop of Laon, towards the end of the 860s; and the return of the aged archbishop to the political scene at the time of King Carloman. To this group should be added those texts in which Hincmar made reference to the False Capitularies. These too are not numerous.[20] Apart from the treatise on the divorce of Lothar and the acts of the Council of Fismes, already mentioned, it is a matter of some letters[21] and a treatise on delinquent priests (876–77). However, Benedict Levita's collection is prominent in the latter, for Hincmar's text begins with the citation of a pseudo-capitulary apparently found 'in the first book of capitularies of the august emperor Charles, chapter 34', and there is another citation in the following chapter.[22]

In his treatise *Collectio de ecclesiis et capellis*, written in 857/8, Hincmar made copious reference to papal letters, notably those of Gregory the Great, as well as to other patristic authors and various ancient councils, ecumenical, Visigothic and Merovingian.[23] In contrast, he seldom invoked the conciliar sources of his own day: with the exception of the assembly of summer 829, held at Worms, which played an important role (we shall come back to this), only one decision borrowed from two Carolingian councils is cited, and that tacitly. In the second part of his treatise, which takes the form of episcopal statutes, Hincmar simply cited, in abbreviated form, a canon from the acts of Chalon of 813 (c. 12), itself used again in the acts of the Council of Paris of spring 829 (c. 28): 'That priests should not become *villici*'.[24] Given the brevity of the prohibition in question, one cannot really speak of a citation of the councils of 813 and 829, but rather of Hincmar's revival of a theme to which the bishops of his youth had given particular importance. This really only puts into relief the other, proper, citations.

It is notable that when it came to secular law, Hincmar sheltered behind the authority of Charlemagne and Louis the Pious alone; this is the case in the *Collectio de ecclesiis et capellis*, which is a response to a query from Charles the Bald. In texts where he set out his opinion at the request of bishops or on his own initiative, Hincmar happily referred to synodal decisions and, to a lesser extent, capitularies of kings contemporary to him, but, in this text destined for King Charles, Hincmar seems deliberately to have taken care to draw on older authorities. To make reference to Charlemagne was to inscribe the royal power of his own time into a century-old tradition, in what was rather a familiar discourse, judging by the consistency with which the archbishop addressed both Charles the Bald[25] and his grandson, Carloman.[26]

Devisse rightly noted that Hincmar did not make use of legal texts in every case. He only did so when he addressed two categories of people: the king and the bishops, to which one should add, in the case of the *De ordine palatii*, the councillors of the palace.[27] Yet, while this is true, the observation can be nuanced by looking at how Hincmar 'dressed' his citations, to present them to his readers or listeners. Hincmar thought that human laws had been dictated by God, but what certainly gave a particular force to the capitularies was the consensus required for their promulgation, a consensus whose importance has been rightly emphasised by recent research.[28] This is illustrated by the recommendations that Hincmar, as an experienced political operator, made to King Carloman in his treatise on the ordering of the body politic, designated by the term 'palace'.[29]

Hincmar, who wielded with dexterity the art of selecting citations to garnish his texts, did not hesitate to elaborate a collection of capitularies for the attention of the young king. He made use of this collection in the records of a council held at St-Macre in Fismes in 881, in which he referred to the Gelasian distinction between the royal power (*potestas regia*) and the papal authority (*auctoritas pontificum*) – and denounced the negligence of his time. It is significant that it was precisely in an admonition to the king and the servants of the *respublica*, that is, the auxiliaries of royal power, that Hincmar cited the royal capitularies.[30]

The Council of Fismes collection began with some capitularies from Charlemagne and Louis the Pious on respect for public order, taken from the collections of Ansegis and Benedict Levita. Very unusually, however, Hincmar then continued his enumeration with numerous capitularies of Charles the Bald, citing two chapters on the protection of ecclesiastical property and the summoning of trouble-makers. These chapters were formally borrowed from the treaties of 847 and 851 agreed between Lothar, Louis the German and Charles the Bald at Meerssen, but in fact were of even more recent date, since they were actually cited in the arrangement of these texts produced by the Treaty of Fouron, agreed in 878 between Louis the Stammerer and Louis the Younger.[31]

The text of Hincmar continued with another chapter from the agreement made at Meerssen thirty years earlier, on the extradition of those excommunicated by a bishop for their crimes.[32] The acts of the Council of Fismes were, it seems to me, one of the very rare occasions when Hincmar cited recent law, even though he and the bishops gathered under his leadership hoped to meet the dangers which threatened them by recalling 'the ancient laws promulgated by the Christian emperors and kings' (the other case concerned matters of divorce, to which we shall return).[33] This is probably not accidental: when he cited the capitularies of his own day, it was because he meant to remind his contemporaries of the commitments to which they had themselves agreed.[34]

This power to constrain of capitularies to which Hincmar's contemporaries had subscribed is underlined in a particularly explicit manner in a letter of the archbishop to his recalcitrant nephew Hincmar. The archbishop of Rheims reminded the bishop of Laon that he had himself 'confirmed by his [own] agreement' that which had been constituted by the king during an assembly (*in placito domni nostri regis Caroli apud Pistas constitutum est quod et tua consensione firmasti capitulum*).[35] It is difficult to find a better definition of the way in which a capitulary was promulgated by the joint will of the king and the magnates. Hincmar was only paraphrasing the preamble of the capitulary of Pîtres (869) to which he made reference, thereby giving us yet another proof of the pertinence of his political analysis.[36] It follows that when the archbishop called upon not the authority of the old decisions by those who he liked to remember had been emperors, but instead on the decisions of 'our kings' (without drawing special attention to any king by name), it was because he wanted explicitly to remind everyone of their commitments. What applied to the bishops applied also to the king: in the speech given in front of Charles the Bald in August 868, Hincmar reminded him of the commitments he had made at Coulaines twenty-five years earlier, with the agreement of the bishops.[37] In this speech, Hincmar was able moreover to establish very effectively a line of continuity between older and recent legislation,[38] through the commitment of the king to respect the law, which Charles had promised in 845 at Beauvais[39] and in 851 at Meerssen.[40]

This concern to combine the authority of old capitularies and the constraining power of recent decisions is well illustrated by the texts concerning the matrimonial affairs of Count Boso and King Lothar II.[41] In his *De divortio*, Hincmar created a close link between the *capitula legalia* of the emperors and the kings, their predecessors, and that which had been put into writing at Meerssen in 851 and had just been, or was about to be, confirmed at Koblenz in 860,[42] an agreement labelled by its nature as an autograph document (*cyrographum*).[43] By using this word, Hincmar emphasised the fact that the document bore the marks of their hands.[44]

In some texts, Hincmar referred in a very neutral way to the collection of Ansegis as 'the book of capitularies of Charlemagne and Louis the Pious'. There is not space here to elaborate.[45] But what seems most interesting to me, which some have noted before without however attaching any particular significance to it, is his designation of Ansegis's collection as one of synodal texts. In this respect, Hincmar used two kinds of expressions: either he talked of the synodal capitularies, each time he addressed bishops – whether in full council[46] or when writing to Hincmar of Laon[47] – or he talked of the 'imperial and synodal capitularies', apparently only in the *Collectio de ecclesiis et capellis*,[48] a text in which this expression was used alongside the more neutral 'book of capitularies'.[49]

The reason for this amalgam might rest on the fact that on each occasion it was a question of Book I of Ansegis's collection, in other words the book that was supposed to gather all of Charlemagne's ecclesiastical legislation.[50] But there is something that jars. Hincmar attributed great importance to the council held at Worms in August 829; of all the capitularies, this is indisputably the one that he cited most frequently. True, these citations are concentrated in the *De ecclesiis et capellis*, but one should note the insistence with which Hincmar referred to the assembly in which Louis the Pious intended to make a synthesis of the measures to be taken in the wake of sending

Hincmar et la loi revisited: capitularies

the *missi* throughout the empire, following the meeting of four councils, of which only the acts of Paris have come down to us.[51] Hincmar cited no fewer than six chapters of this capitulary.[52] In other works, Hincmar also cited different chapters of the Worms corpus: a chapter of its *Capitulare missorum* in the collection of capitularies produced during the Council of Fismes,[53] and a chapter from its *Capitulare pro lege habendum* in his *De divortio*. Here, the testimony of Hincmar, a member of the community of St-Denis at the time of the council, is particularly precious because he is the only source for the presence of a papal legate during the *generalis conventus* which took place over the summer of 829 at Worms.[54] Given that one can hardly suspect Hincmar of wanting to mix together that which belonged to ecclesiastical purview with what belonged to the laity, as shown by his account of the trial that took place in 822 at Attigny,[55] it is remarkable that on several occasions he used the term *synodus* to label the Worms assembly.[56] In the ninth century, this word seems to have designated an ecclesiastical assembly more systematically than in the previous century.[57] It is perhaps through this term, which nevertheless remained ambiguous, that the insistence with which Hincmar made reference to the decisions of this assembly can be explained, echoing the same treaty's expression of *liber imperialium ac synodalium capitulorum*,[58] in which reference is explicitly made to the two sources of law, the imperial will and the unanimity of ecclesiastical assemblies.

To summarise the argument of this modest enquiry into the context in which Hincmar referred to capitularies, and the way he did it, one comes away with four points. 1: The archbishop of Rheims adapted to his audience. He invoked the authority of the capitularies chiefly with respect to the magnates, especially the lay ones – beginning with the kings. 2: Hincmar referred chiefly to Charlemagne and the emperor who dominated his youth, Louis the Pious; when he made reference to more recent law, it was essentially to more effectively constrain his contemporaries, who were implicated in the elaboration of that law. 3: Hincmar's way of presenting the decisions taken at the assembly of the summer of 829 at Worms conferred upon this meeting more of an ecclesiastical character than is usually recognised. 4: More generally, regarding the legislation of Charlemagne and Louis the Pious, the way in which Hincmar referred to the collection of Ansegis allows us to suppose that he considered this collection as a true synthesis of secular and ecclesiastical law.

While insisting upon the freedom of tone and the liberty of

thought that Hincmar brought to bear in relation to Charles the Bald, Jean Devisse refused to see in him a precursor to Thomas Becket:[59] Hincmar never moved from complicity to opposition. Even if he was haunted by the feeling of being kept at the margin of things towards the end of his life, despite his various initiatives to continue influencing the politics of his time,[60] Hincmar shared with another great figure of British history, Thomas More, at least the constancy of a demanding conscience. The strong positions he took on various occasions, throughout his episcopacy, made him – to paraphrase Robert Bolt – 'A Man for all Seasons' of Carolingian history.[61]

Notes

1 J. Devisse, *Hincmar et la loi* (Dakar, 1962); Devisse, *Hincmar*; M. Stratmann, *Hinkmar von Reims als Verwalter von Bistum und Kirchenprovinz* (Sigmaringen, 1991).

2 Schrörs, *Hinkmar*, p. 409. On the genre of capitularies, see H. Mordek, *Studien zur fränkischen Herrschergesetzgebung: Aufsätze über Kapitularien und Kapitulariensammlungen, ausgewählt zum 60. Geburtstag* (Frankfurt am Main, 2000).

3 *Capitularia regum Francorum*, ed. A. Boretius and V. Krause, MGH Leges, sectio II, 2 vols (Hanover, 1883–97). A new edition is in preparation: by Michael Glatthaar for the Merovingian capitularies and those dating from the reign of Charlemagne; by Philippe Depreux, Stefan Esders, Steffen Patzold and Karl Ubl for capitularies after 814.

4 Devisse, *Hincmar et la loi*, pp. 11–13. Ansegis's collection is edited as *Die Kapitulariensammlung des Ansegis*, ed. G. Schmitz, MGH *Capitularia regum Francorum*, Nova series 1 (Hanover, 1996).

5 Devisse, *Hincmar et la loi*, p. 12, identifies Hincmar's citation in *Admonitio ad episcopos et ad regem Carolomannum apud Sparnacum facta*, PL 125, col. 1016, c. 14: 'Providendum est ne affligantur in aedificiis superfluis, in exactione hostile, si Deus pacem pro sua misericordia tribuerit, ne contra capitulum domni imperatoris Caroli, ut nemo ad mallum, vel ad placitum cogetur venire, nisi scabini et qui causam suam quaerit, et cui quaeratur' as from 'Capitulaire de Charlemagne, 809, c. 5' = *Capitulare Aquisgranense 809*, MGH *Capit*. I, no. 61, p. 148, c. 5: 'Ut nullus alius de liberis hominibus ad placitum vel ad mallum venire cogatur, exceptis scabinis et vassis comitum, nisi qui causam suam aut quaerere debet aut respondere'. This also appears in Ansegis, *Capitularia*, III, 51, p. 596.

6 They are preserved in the manuscripts of Berlin (Phillipps 1762), Yale University (Beinecke MS 413), Paris (BnF lat. 10758) and St-Gall (Cod.

Sang. 727); cf. *Die Kapitulariensammlung des Ansegis*, pp. 83–5, 109–10, 135–9 and 146–7.
7 R. Schieffer, 'Eine übersehene Schrift Hinkmars von Reims über Priestertum und Königtum', *DA*, 37 (1981), 511–28. This text underlines once again how heavily Hincmar was influenced by the decisions of the Council of Paris of 829.
8 Council of Soissons, 853, MGH *Conc.* III, no. 27, pp. 253–93.
9 *Collectio de ecclesiis et capellis*, ed. M. Stratmann, MGH *Fontes iuris* 14 (Hanover, 1990).
10 Epistula 135, ed. E. Perels, MGH *Epp.* 8, pp. 81–7.
11 *De divortio Lotharii regis et Theutbergae reginae*, ed. L. Böhringer, MGH *Conc.* IV, supplementum 1 (Hanover, 1992).
12 Epistola XV, *PL* 126, cols 94–9 = Schrörs, *Hinkmar*, Reg. 215.
13 *Expositiones ad Carolum regem pro Ecclesiae libertatum defensione*, *PL* 125, cols 1035–70.
14 Schieffer, 'Eine übersehene Schrift Hinkmars', pp. 519–28.
15 *Opuscula et epistolae*, *PL* 126, cols 537–45 = Schrörs, *Hinkmar*, Reg. 278.
16 Epistola XIX, *PL* 126, cols 110–17 = Schrörs, *Hinkmar*, Reg. 504.
17 Council of Fismes, 881, MGH *Conc.* V, no. 15A, *Admonitio ad regem et ministros rei publicae*, pp. 186–90.
18 *De officiis episcoporum* (also known as *Quae exsequi debeat episcopus et qua cura tueri res et facultates ecclesiaticas*), *PL* 125, cols 1087–94 = Schrörs, *Hinkmar*, Reg. 507.
19 *Admonitio ad episcopos et ad regem Carolomannum apud Sparnacum facta*, *PL* 125, cols 1007–18 = Schrörs, *Hinkmar*, Reg. 572.
20 Devisse, *Hincmar et la loi*, p. 34.
21 For instance, the memorandum that Hincmar sent in late 860 to the archbishops Rodulf of Bourges and Frothar of Bordeaux, in which he appears to draw on Benedict Levita in citing the acts of the Council of Estinnes (743): Hincmar, Epistola 136, ed. E. Perels, MGH *Epp.* 8, p. 97. On this text, see G. Fransen, 'La lettre de Hincmar de Reims au sujet du mariage d'Étienne: une relecture', in R. Lievens, E. van Mingroot and W. Verbeke, eds, *Pascua Mediaevali: Studies voor Prof. Dr. J.M. De Smet* (Leuven, 1983), pp. 133–46.
22 *De presbiteris criminosis*, pp. 65–6, cc. 1–2. No authentic capitulary is cited in this treatise.
23 Hincmar, *Collectio de ecclesiis*, pp. 132–3.
24 *Ibid.*, p. 103, from *Concilium Cabillonense*, 813, MGH *Conc.* II, 1, p. 276, c. 12: 'Ut neque presbyteri neque diaconi neque monachi vilici fiant'; repeated in *Concilium Parisiense*, 829, MGH *Conc.* II, 2, p. 630, c. 28: 'Ut presbiteri nullo modo fiant vilici et conductores agrorum vel negotiorum secularium sectatores atque per diversa vagantes; quod et de monachis

similiter convenit observari.' This phenomenon is also denounced in the *Relatio episcoporum* which synthesised the recommendations of the Council of Paris for the attention of the emperor, but in very different terms: *Episcoporum ad Hludowicum imperatorem relatio*, 829, MGH *Capit.* II, p. 33, no. 196, c. 10: 'Similiter de illis presbiteris, qui contra statuta canonum villici fiunt, tabernas ingrediuntur, turpia lucra sectantur et diversissimis modis usuris inserviunt et aliorum domos inhoneste ac inpudice frequentant et comessationibus et ebrietatibus deservire non erubescunt et per diversos mercatus indiscrete discurrunt, observandum iudicavimus, ut abhinc districte severiterque coerceantur, ne per eorum inlicitam et indecentem actionem et ministerium sacerdotale vituperetur et, quibus debuerant esse in exemplum, fiant in scandalum.'
25 Schieffer, 'Eine übersehene Schrift Hinkmars', pp. 525-6: 'Et cum dominus imperator quondam Karolus ex ista causa misericordiae capitula constituit, inter ipsa posuit, ut nemo ad mallum vel ad placitum cogeretur venire, nisi scabini et qui causam quaerit, et cui quaeritur.'
26 Cf. the text cited above, note 5.
27 Devisse, *Hincmar et la loi*, p. 89.
28 J. Hannig, *Consensus fidelium: frühfeudale Interpretationen des Verhältnisses von Königtum und Adel am Beispiel Frankenreiches* (Stuttgart, 1982); J. Nelson, 'Legislation and consensus in the reign of Charles the Bald', in P. Wormald, ed., *Ideal and Reality in Frankish and Anglo-Saxon Society: Studies Presented to J.M. Wallace-Hadrill* (Oxford, 1983), pp. 202-27; B. Schneidmüller, 'Konsensuale Herrschaft. Ein Essay über Formen und Konzepte politischer Ordnung im Mittelalter', in P.-J. Heinig et al., eds, *Reich, Regionen und Europa in Mittelalter und Neuzeit: Festschrift für Peter Moraw* (Berlin, 2000), pp. 53-87; S. Patzold, 'Consensus - Concordia - Unitas. Überlegungen zu einem politisch-religiösen Ideal der Karolingerzeit', in N. Staubach, ed., *Exemplaris imago: Ideale in Mittelalter und Früher Neuzeit* (Frankfurt am Main, 2012), pp. 31-56.
29 Hincmar, *De ordine palatii*, pp. 44-6, c. 7: 'Habent enim reges et reipublicae ministri leges, quibus in quacunque provincia degentes regere debent, habent capitula christianorum regum ac progenitorum suorum, quae generali consensu fidelium suorum tenere legaliter promulgaverunt.' *Ibid.*, pp. 90-2, c. 34: 'Proceres vero praedicti sive in hoc sive in illo praefato placito, qui et primi senatores regni, ne quasi sine causa convocari viderentur, mox auctoritate regia per denominata et ordinata capitula, quae vel ab ipso per inspirationem Dei inventa vel undique sibi nuntiata post eorum abscessum praecipue fuerant eis ad conferendum vel ad considerandum patefacta sunt.' On the political dimension of the *palatium*, see Ph. Depreux, *Prosopographie de l'entourage de Louis le Pieux (781-840)* (Sigmaringen, 1997), pp. 29-39.

30 Council of Fismes, MGH *Conc.* V, no. 15, p. 186: 'Unde quaedam capitula a praecedentibus imperatoribus et regibus statuta in unum collecta subiungere dignum duximus, quae ita se habent.'
31 *Ibid.*, p. 188, cc. 10–11 = *Hlotharii, Hludowici et Karoli conventus apud Marsanam primus*, 847, MGH *Capit.* II, no. 204, p. 70, *Adnuntiatio domni Hludowici*, c. 5, and *Hlotharii, Hludowici et Karoli conventus apud Marsanam secundus*, 852, MGH *Capit.* II, no. 205, p. 73, c. 4. These two chapters are mentioned one after the other in the text of the agreement of Fouron: *Hludowici iunioris et Hludowici Balbi conventio Furonensis*, 878, MGH *Capit.* II, no. 246, p. 170, cc. 7–8, without however taking into account the variants of these texts (a substantial addition at c. 7 and a smaller one at c. 8).
32 Council of Fismes, 881, MGH *Conc.* V, no. 15, p. 188, c. 12 = *Hlotharii, Hludowici et Karoli conventus apud Marsanam secundus*, 852, MGH *Capit.* II, no. 205, p. 73, beginning of c. 5. The first chapters of the agreement of 851 were repeated in 860 at Koblenz: *Hludowici, Karoli et Hlothari II conventus apud Confluentes*, 860, MGH *Capit.* II, no. 242, p. 155.
33 Council of Fismes, 881, MGH *Conc.* V, no. 15, p. 178, Praefatio. On Hincmar's attachment to ancient law, cf. Y. Sassier, *Royauté et idéologie au Moyen Âge: Bas-Empire, monde franc, France (IVe–XIIe siècle)*, 2nd edn (Paris, 2012), pp. 176–7. On divorce, see below, p. 190.
34 The Fouron agreement begins (MGH *Capit.* II, no. 246, p. 169): 'Conventio, quae inter gloriosos reges, Hludowicum filium Karoli imperatoris itemque Hludowicum filium Hludowici regis, in loco, qui vocatur Furonis, Kalendis Novembris, ipsis et communibus fidelibus ipsorum faventibus et consentientibus, facta est, anno incarnationis dominicae DCCCLXXVIII, indictione XI, dicente rege Hludowico filio Karoli.' At Fismes, Hincmar addressed both King Carloman and the *ministr[i] rei publicae* (MGH *Conc.* V, no. 15, p. 186, VI).
35 Hincmar, *Opuscula et epistolae*, PL 126, col. 541: 'Et rectum est ut tu antiquae auctoritati et consuetudini tuae metropoli a tuis praedecessoribus conservatae non deroges: praesertim cum sit constitutum in primo libro capitulorum synodalium tempore Augustorum nostrorum a nostris majoribus conservatorum, ut sine auctoritate, vel consensu episcoporum presbyteri in quibuslibet ecclesiis constituantur, nec expellantur .... et exinde nuper in placito domni nostri regis Caroli apud Pistas constitutum est quod et tua consensione firmasti capitulum, quo dicitur [*Capitula Pistensia*, 869, MGH *Capit.* II, no. 275, p. 335, c. 9] ut si abbates, vel abbatissae, aut comites, seu vassi nostri, aut ceteri laici clericos probabilis vitae et doctrinae episcopis canonice consecrandos, suisque in ecclesiis constituendos obtulerint, nulla qualibet occasione eos episcopi vel ministri eorum rejiciant.'

36 *Capitula Pistensia*, 869, MGH *Capit.* II, no. 275, p. 333: 'Haec, quae sequuntur, capitula constituta sunt a domno nostro Karolo rege glorioso cum consilio et consensu episcoporum ac ceterorum Dei et suorum fidelium, qui adfuerunt, in loco, qui dicitur Pistis, anno incarnationis dominicae DCCCLXIX, anno autem regni sui XXX, indictione secunda, et ab eo denuntiata sunt a se et ab omnibus fidelibus suis secundum uniuscuiusque ordinem et personam inviolabiliter conservanda.' On this capitulary, see R. Schneider, 'Schriftlichkeit und Mündlichkeit im Bereich der Kapitularien', in P. Classen, ed., *Recht und Schrift im Mittelalter* (Sigmaringen, 1977), pp. 257–79, at 274–6.
37 *Expositiones ad Carolum regem pro Ecclesiae libertatum defensione*, PL 125, col. 1066: 'Et hoc cum aliis capitulum quod sequitur, vos ipse manu propria in villa quae dicitur Colonia, consensu episcoporum, et Warini, ac aliorum optimatum vestrorum, anno IV regni vestri confirmastis, et per Ricuinum Ludovico fratri vestro misistis': there then follows the first chapter of the November 843 agreement at Coulaines (*Conventus in villa Colonia*, 843, MGH *Capit.* II, no. 254, p. 255, c. 1).
38 *Expositiones ad Carolum regem*, PL 125, col. 1065: 'Hanc legem decessores et praedecessores vestri reges Ecclesiae servaverunt: quae si aut per excessum principum, aut per negligentiam episcoporum aliquo modo violata fuit, tamen correcta, sicut in eorum capitulis legitur, existit. Vos etiam, decessores vestros sequentes, hanc legem ecclesiasticam servaturos Deo et nobis promisistis, sicut hic continetur. In libro primo capitulorum imperialium, domni Caroli avi, et domni Ludovici patris vestri, in lege ab ipsis confirmata, Ecclesiae et universis episcopis scriptum est'.
39 *Ibid.*, col. 1066: 'Et hoc cum aliis capitulum quod subsequitur, in Belgivaco civitate, anno VI regni vestri coram Deo et angelis ejus, in fide et dextera vestra, per spatam vestram jurantes, sicut praesentes episcopi qui adfuerunt petierant, illis et caeteris episcopis regni vestri ac successoribus suis et eorum ecclesiis cunctis diebus vitae vestrae vos servaturos promisistis, petentibus: [*Synodus Bellovacensis*, 845, MGH *Capit.* II, no. 292, pp. 387–8, c. 1] Ut jus ecclesiasticum et legem canonicam nobis ita conservetis, sicut antecessore vestri, qui hoc bene et rationabiliter observaverunt, juxta quod sciri poterit et Deus vobis posse dederit, nostris praedecessoribus conservaverunt'.
40 *Expositiones ad Carolum regem*, PL 125, col. 1066: 'Et hoc cum aliis capitulum quod subsequitur, anno Incarnationis Dominicae DCCCLI in loco qui dicitur Marsana cum fratribus vestris Waltario [Lothario] et Ludovico manu propria per consilium et consensum fidelium vestrorum communium communiter confirmastis' (=*Hlotharii, Hludowici et Karoli conventus apud Marsanam secundus*, 852, MGH *Capit.* II, no. 205, p. 73, c. 6).
41 Hincmar, Epistola 135, pp. 83–4: 'Et quoniam, sicut ipse Boso dicit, eidem

mulieri, quae caro sua est, nullum crimen inpingit, sed non modicam neglegentiam, quia ab eius se subtraxit servitio et, quantum ex ipsa est, illum mechari fecit, contra auctoritatem atque iustitiam eum dimittens et in aliis regnis circiter per triennium inmorans, contumax mandatis illius adeo extitit, ut nec compellata per tanta temporum spatia ad eum redierit, pro domni apostolici iussione illi paratus est indulgere, restat, ut rex, in cuius regno degit, secundum conscriptionem cyrographi regum nostrorum eam ad viri sui praesentiam adduci faciat, et tu episcopus, in cuius parrochia inmoratur, quia hoc non est regis, sicut sanctus Gregorius de his, qui ad ecclesiam confugiunt, praecipit, si exposcit necessitas, securitatem de aequitate sibi servanda apud virum eius expetas et obtineas, et post hoc missus rei publicae viro uxorem fuga lapsam restituat. Qui vir, si sacramentum fregerit et apostolicis monitis inoboediens extiterit, episcopus, ad cuius curam pertinet, canonicum iudicium in illum proinde exerat. Si autem mulier confessa vel legaliter de adulterio convicta incolomis evaserit, lege ecclesiastica paenitentiae illam isdem episcopus subigat, quia et mundanis legibus cautum atque usitatum esse dinoscitur, ut mala, quae perpetrantur, in illis locis emendentur, in quibus perpetrata fuisse legaliter comprobantur. Praeter haec nihil mihi videtur agendum, nisi aut domni apostolici monita exequamur aut iudicium incurramus.'

42 *Hludowici, Karoli et Hlothari II conventus apud Confluentes*, 860, MGH *Capit*. II, no. 242, pp. 153–8.

43 *De divortio*, Anhang Responsio 5, pp. 244–5: 'Capitula sunt legalia imperatorum et regum praedecessorum suorum, quid sustinere debeat, qui post bannum latronem receperit [cf. Ansegis, *Capitularia*, p. 582: III, c. 23, and p. 596: III, c. 49]. 'Et in cyrographo regum nostrorum hinc expresse decernitur [cf. *Hlotharii, Hludowici et Karoli conventus apud Marsanam secundus*, 852, MGH *Capit*. II, no. 205, p. 73, cc. 4–5; *Hludowici, Karoli et Hlothari II conventus apud Confluentes*, 860, MGH *Capit*. II, no. 242, p. 155, cc. 4–5], cuius ministerium est agere, ut illa observentur, sicut sanctus Ambrosius ad Valentinianum scribit: "Leges enim imperator ferat, quas primus ipse custodiat".'

44 On this term, and on confirmation by touching, see L. Morelle, 'La main du roi et le nom de Dieu: la validation de l'acte royal selon Hincmar, d'après un passage de son 'De Divortio'', in J. Hoareau-Dodinau and P. Texier, eds, *Foi chrétienne et églises dans la société politique de l'Occident du Haut Moyen Age: IVe–XIIe siècle* (Limoges, 2004), pp. 287–318; Ph. Depreux, 'Les Carolingiens et le serment', in M.-F. Auzépy and G. Saint-Guillain, eds, *Oralité et lien social au Moyen Âge: Occident, Byzance, Islam: parole donnée, foi jurée, serment* (Paris, 2008), pp. 63–80, at 77.

45 See *Expositiones ad Carolum regem*, PL 125, col. 1060; *De officiis episcoporum*, PL 125, col. 1088; Epistola XV, PL 126, col. 96; Epistola XIX,

PL 126, cols 111, 112; *De divortio*, Responsio 6, p. 158, Responsio 10, p. 171, Responsio 12, p. 187, Responsio 17, p. 216, Responsio 22, p. 229, Anhang Responsio 5, p. 244.

46 Council of Soissons, 853, MGH *Conc.* III, no. 27, p. 269: 'in libro primo capitulorum synodalium domni Karoli imperatoris'.

47 *Opuscula et epistolae*, *PL* 126, col. 543 (concerning the parish of Folembray, 870): 'scriptum est in libro capitulorum synodalium primo, quae tempore Augustorum nostrorum Caroli et Ludovici fuerunt condita'.

48 *Collectio de ecclesiis et capellis*, pp. 67, 74–5: 'Hinc et in primo libro imperialium ac synodalium capitulorum domni Karoli et Hludowici scriptum est'; *ibid.*, p. 95: 'Unde et in praefato capitulo augustali atque synodali dictum est'.

49 *Ibid.*, p. 94: 'De quo manso in primo libro capitulorum ita scriptum habetur ... Subiunctum est etiam in subnexo praefati libri capitulo'; *ibid.*, p. 95: 'Et in libro primo capitulorum LXXXV capitulo scriptum est'; *ibid.*, p. 108: 'sicut in libro primo capitulorum dicitur'.

50 Ansegis, *Capitularia*, p. 433, Praefatio: 'Sed hoc notum sit lectori, quia praedicta capitula, quae per intervalla temporum a praefatis sunt principibus edita, in quattuor distinxi libellis. Illa scilicet, quae domnus Karolus imperator fecit ad ordinem pertinentia ecclesiasticum, in primo adunavi libello. Ea vero ecclesiastica, quae domnus ac piissimus Hludowicus imperator et Chlotarius caesar filius ipsius ediderunt, in secundo descripsi. Illa autem, quae domnus Karolus in diversis fecit temporibus ad mundanam pertinentia legem, in tertio adunavi. Ipsa vero, quae domnus Hludowicus praeclarus imperator et Chlotarius caesar filius illius fecerunt ad augmentum mundanae pertinentia legis, in quarto congessi.'

51 On this topic, see Ph. Depreux, S. Esders and S. Patzold, eds, *Regnum semper reformandum: Mobiles et enjeux des capitulaires de Louis le Pieux en 829 = Hintergründe und Ziele der Kapitulariengesetzgebung Ludwigs des Frommen im Jahr 829* (Ostfildern, forthcoming).

52 *Capitulare Wormatiense*, 829, MGH *Capit.* II, no. 191, pp. 11–14, is cited in the following passages of *Collectio de ecclesiis et capellis*: p. 84: 'Scriptum est enim in praefata synodo, cuius promulgationes magnopere sunt sequendę, si secundum diffinitionem canonicam perfecta debet haberi synodus, in qua metropolitanus cum suis est suffraganeis, secundo capitulo' (= p. 12, c. 2); p. 93: 'Denique in tercio capitulo praefate synodi tempore domni Hludowici imperatoris habitę ita etiam scriptum est (= p. 12, c. 3); p. 93: 'Et in capitulo VII memoratę synodi dicitur' (= p. 13, c. 7); p. 94: 'Et in eadem synodo capitulum VI legitur' (= p. 13, c. 6); p. 94: 'Sed et in capitulo quarto praedictae synodi scriptum est' (= p. 12, c. 4); p. 95: 'Et item in supramemorata synodo scriptum est' (= p. 12, c. 1).

53 Council of Fismes, 881, MGH *Conc.* V, no. 15, p. 190, VI, c. 22 = *Capitulare missorum Wormatiense*, 829, MGH *Capit.* II, no. 192, pp. 16–17, c. 14.
54 *De divortio*, Responsio 5, p. 138: 'Unde et cum aliis per curricula temporum varia regibus atque imperatoribus iura legalia decernentibus nostri etiam aevi augustus pię memoriae Hludowicus in synodo ac placito generali apud Wormatiam apostolicę sedis et papae Gregorii commeante legato cum aliis plurimis de his, quae episcopi in synodis per quattuor loca sui imperii habitis necessario et utiliter nuper invenerant, de hac, unde agitur, causa omnium tam episcoporum quam et fidelium laicorum votis convenientibus statuit ita decernens: [*Capitulare pro lege habendum Wormatiense*, 829, MGH *Capit.* II, no. 193, pp. 18–19, c. 3] "Quicumque, inquit, propria uxore derelicta vel sine culpa interfecta aliam duxerit uxorem, armis depositis publicam agat poenitentiam; et si contumax fuerit, comprehendatur a comite et ferro vinciatur et in custodiam mittatur, donec res ad nostram notitiam deducatur".'
55 *De divortio*, Responsio 5, pp. 141–2: 'ad memoriam revocare necessarium duximus, quoniam quidam nostrum tempore sanctae memoriae domni Hludowici pii augusti in Attiniaco palatio tunc fuerunt, quando in universali synodo totius imperii etiam cum sedis Romanę legatis et in generali placito femina quaedam non ignobilis genere nomine Northildis de quibusdam inhonestis inter se et virum suum vocabulo Agembertum ad imperatorem publice proclamavit. Quam imperator ad synodum destinavit, ut inde episcopalis auctoritas, quid agendum esset, decerneret. Sed episcoporum generalitas ad laicorum ac coniugatorum eam remisit iudicium, ut ipsi inter illam et suum coniugem iudicarent, qui de talibus negotiis erant cogniti et legibus saeculi sufficientissime praediti, eorumque legalibus iudiciis eadem femina se subiceret et, quod de questione sua decrevissent, sine repetitione teneret'.
56 Cf. above, note 52.
57 D. Eichler, *Fränkische Reichsversammlungen unter Ludwig dem Frommen* (Hanover, 2007), pp. 17–19.
58 Cf. above, note 48.
59 Devisse, *Hincmar*, I, p. 33.
60 S. Patzold, 'Konsens und Konkurrenz: Überlegungen zu einem aktuellen Forschungskonzept der Mediävistik', *Frühmittelalterliche Studien*, 41 (2007), 75–103, at 77–88. See also McCarthy, Chapter 6.
61 I thank Charles West for the translation of my French text into English.

9

The bishop and the law, according to Hincmar's life of Saint Remigius

Marie-Céline Isaïa

Among the works of Hincmar of Rheims, the *Vita Remigii*[1] continues to be regarded as a minor text, a little folkloric recreation that the archbishop permitted himself in old age.[2] Written after his most serious theological and political treatises, the life of Saint Remigius has been seen as a motley compilation, accumulating traditions or inventing them, about a relatively obscure Merovingian bishop. Certainly Saint Remigius, who died around 533/35, did not enjoy a very widespread cult when Hincmar began his work. An extremely short, anonymous and archaic *Vita Remedii* credited the saint with the merit of having resurrected a dead man – but it is a work of slight importance, compared to the *vitae* of other glories of the Gallic sanctoral cycle, such as Germanus of Auxerre.[3] Hincmar toiled to learn more, but in vain, as he recalls in his preface addressed to St-Remi's monks: the older ones remembered that their predecessors 'had seen a very great book, written in an antique script, that recounted Remigius's birth, life, virtues and death … but it had been destroyed … You rightfully wished that I should gather these scattered elements in a single *œuvre* … I would have achieved this a long time ago, if I had not been delayed by a vain hope: I heard, from here and there, that I might succeed in retrieving the great book about the virtues and life of our lord and patron saint; … all was but lies'.[4] So Hincmar filled the gaps as well as he could.

It would however be unfair to see nothing in this hagiographical text but a work of the imagination, isolated from the rest of Hincmar's *œuvre*. The *Vita* is clearly entirely coherent with his political thought – a coherence that for Bruno Krusch proved it had been written *ad hoc*, meaning that it tells nothing but a (forged) truth that served Hincmar.[5] *De facto*, the *Vita* attests to the legend of the Holy Ampoule, and spreads the story in the years when this object became useful for the coronation of Charles the Bald as king of Lotharingia (869).[6]

Historians recognised a long time ago that the *Vita* exposes, in its own words, Hincmar's theory about contractual monarchy and warns Carolingian kings against the temptation to hijack the Church's property.[7] Moreover, the more one explores its composition, the more one realises that Hincmar conceived his *Vita* as a kind of library capable of holding the quintessentials of his theological and pastoral beliefs: intermingled with Saint Remigius's biographical outline, more theoretical developments on predestination or the Trinity directly reflect Hincmar's teachings on these subjects.[8] Furthermore, Hincmar evidently began to write the *Vita* before 852, even if only his death in 882 prevented him from supplementing it again and again: one must conclude that the *Vita Remigii* is not (only) the testament of Hincmar, but (also) the founding text of his episcopacy.[9] Hincmar wanted it to be a constantly enhanced text of self-justification that could warrant all his deeds, from his promotion at Rheims against Ebbo's rights (845) to his actions as kings' counsellor; its main meaning is that the authority of the archbishop of Rheims should not be challenged, since it is based on the precedent of Remigius of Rheims, the greatest apostle that Francia ever had.

The normative effects of a hagiographical text

Hincmar's project followed a long tradition that led him to believe that his *Vita* would contribute to the religious progress of its readers. So he constructed his *Vita* as a dialogue between past and present, between the sixth century of Remigius and his own ninth century, for a moral purpose. After describing some deed of Saint Remigius, Hincmar draws a lesson addressed to all his contemporaries, especially Carolingian bishops, monks and kings. This is why, of all his own works that he cited in the *Vita*, it was his moral treaty, *De cavendis vitiis et virtutibus exercendis* ('Of avoiding sins and cultivating virtues') on which he drew most often.[10] Hincmar quotes this work on at least eighteen occasions, because the *Vita* is the means Hincmar created to exhort his audience to moral and religious improvement.[11] So the *Vita* tends towards being a *speculum*, exactly as the *De cavendis* is a moral guide for King Charles the Bald, and Hincmar reuses useful patristic formulas he found in both. When for example Remigius had dinner at home, as Hincmar tells us following the *Vita Remedii*, he distributed his leftovers to the birds, who ate out of his hand. 'We can receive an excellent moral lesson considering this action of Saint Remigius'[12] continues Hincmar: we can rejuvenate by prayer, by studying, by regretting our sins, even if our flesh grows older.[13] He does not admit that this is a teaching of Pope Gregory the Great[14] that he had already used in the *De cavendis*.[15]

It was not unusual to assign a moral aim to a hagiographical text, which, as many Merovingian *vitae* repeat, should contribute to the edification of each of the *fideles* who hears it read. This is the normal parenetic or hortatory function of hagiography. The only remarkable thing here is the systematic and explicit moral lesson: Hincmar does not let the reader draw his own conclusions, but explains how to interpret the story he tells. For instance, in chapter 17, Remigius saves a certain Eulogius, who was accused of treason; thanks to the intercession of the bishop, Eulogius was not sentenced to death by King Clovis, and even his *villa* of Epernay was not confiscated. Eulogius wanted to thank the bishop by giving him the *villa*, but Remigius refused the gift and bought it instead. Hincmar comments:

> This is a good example that Remigius left all bishops, both his contemporaries in the flesh and those who will come after him in the priesthood: when they help the poor, widows, orphans and all those who seek the refuge of the Church and of their mercy, those who have been wronged, or are condemned to exile or banishment because of their sins, or who are within the scope of any judgment – when they bring them any kind of relief, they should not receive temporal reward in exchange. But, according to the word of the Lord 'Freely you received, freely give' [Matthew 10:8] they must give generously what they have received by the grace of God to those around them, that is what they were given freely – freely indeed meaning without awaiting temporal counterpart.[16]

From a human experience that provides an *exemplum*, and from a saying from the Scriptures, Hincmar generalises: this is the most common homiletical method. The originality of the *Vita Remigii* lies elsewhere, in the definition of the episcopal office it assumes. When adopting a homiletic tone, like many other *vitae*, it immediately justifies this method by portraying the bishop of Rheims as a master whose example *and* teaching must be followed step by step. Hincmar actually blurs the difference between the actions of Remigius on one hand and his own commentaries on the other, assuming that there is a perfect, mystical continuity between them. The *Vita* thereby offers a complete portrait of what Hincmar thinks that a Carolingian bishop must be, a man whose responsibility is to tell others what they have to do. Now this does not only imply a moral standpoint: Hincmar extends the clerical responsibility of teaching to a much broader normative authority. As the example of Eulogius shows, he does not merely tell good from evil, but also defines what is fair, legitimate and permitted. Hence, the *Vita Remigii* must be seen as the very core of Hincmar's *œuvre*: Hincmar, the man who spent his life telling others what they should do or say or believe, chose hagiography to teach dogmatic and theological truths, to impose rules and to reinforce his normative power.

Of course, the life of St Remigius cannot be reduced simply to a series of legal articles; Hincmar also composed his *Vita* to give the episcopal church of Rheims a history, to justify the monastic community of St-Remi's heavy dependence on the successor of Remigius as bishop and to exalt the memory of the saint who baptised Clovis and introduced the Franks into the history of salvation. It seems nevertheless possible to say that Hincmar conceived his *Vita* as both historical and normative – or that he conceived it as a normative text because it is primarily about the past, a Christianised and heavily rewritten past. Nowadays, what we call rules are straightforward, unambiguous texts that set norms, requirements, laws of general scope; such texts are objective ones, or supposed to be, written in the present. Hagiographical texts are exactly the opposite: stories, series of anecdotes, narratives of events, with witnesses, main characters and secondary ones, a biographical logic, sometimes with plots or twists, all necessarily presented in the past and, by definition, not of general scope since it is always the history of an individual, a particular case.

Meetings between the two genres, however, may have been more numerous in the early Middle Ages: their first common point is that both the rules and the *vitae* are supported by a community and a common acknowledgement of a shared past. This is the community that provides the inspiration for the customs, as for the *vita*, by a collective effort of recollection of its past, both of past uses and past events – and it is a community that emerges in the sharing of rules or in the commemoration of its peculiar patron saint. Therefore, Hincmar's choice of hagiography is not totally unexpected. He makes a visible effort to underline that he wrote nothing about Remigius but the story he received from his predecessors. This is not simply the commonplace tune of hagiographical prefaces: the unanimity of the clergy, their participation in both collecting and believing the events Hincmar tells about Remigius, is the very foundation on which the archbishop will base his authority. It justifies the entirely unusual importance of a normative discourse within the *Vita*.

Homiletic moments set apart, the normative strength of the *Vita* sometimes comes from its capacity to include evidence seized elsewhere and embedded in the text, as in the case of a letter of Pope Hormisdas, an authentic letter (though adapted by Hincmar): the archbishop inserted this document as a conspicuous proof that could not be debated. But most of this evidence is slid inside the *Vita*, sewn into it as secretly as possible. Hincmar 'honestly' announced part of this technique in the preface: he would compose his *Vita* from different and heterogeneous origins ... but he almost never indicates which piece is borrowed, or from whom. The heterogeneity he acknowledges is due, if we believe him, to his desire not to modify the different texts he collected about Remigius.[17] There is however a more striking heterogeneity, due to the (sometimes awkward) way in which Hincmar put into the *Vita* words he took from his own previous works. We cannot blame a computer for this frequent copy/paste, so one must understand that Hincmar collected in his treatises the theological convictions he thought most precious, to disseminate them again to a larger audience. In the table of contents that Hincmar included in the beginning of the *Vita*, he explicitly states that episodes from the life of Remigius will be accompanied by lessons.

For example, chapter 8 announces a long speech about predestination, and the heresy of those who misunderstand it:

> Chapter 8: How he [Saint Remigius] rescued the city of Rheims from the fire, this city that the devil had set alight, and how we shall also be rescued by the means of his merits and prayers from the flames of vice and from eternal fire, if we ask faithfully. Hence, by comparison, the error of the heretics of predestination is briefly recalled, who claim that God has predestined some men to eternal fire, and, conversely, the truth of the Catholic faith is demonstrated.[18]

We can conclude that every story in the *Vita* has three steps: a narrative of the facts (Remigius stopped the burning of the city of Rheims), their spiritual meaning for us (with God's and Remigius' help we can fight the devil successfully) and their doctrinal analogue (what we must believe for our salvation). Hincmar improves the technique of the sermon, constructing his text on the various senses of Scripture, literal, moral and anagogical, and playing on similarities, *sumpta similitudine*, here on the word 'fire', which could be real, spiritual or eschatological fire. This is noteworthy in a hagiographical text: the shift from the historical narrative to the admonition is common, but not to this degree, and the third meaning is never or rarely developed so insistently. In chapter 8, there are thirty lines on the 'real' fire, and 215 lines of theological teaching. Why is Hincmar so talkative on the subject? Because his teaching on heresy and its refutation is to be found, in a different order, in his treatise on the same topic, *De praedestinatione Dei*.[19] In a way, Hincmar summarised his treatise for popularisation through the *Vita Remigii*.

The *Vita* admonishes kings as a *speculum* does;[20] the *Vita* publicises truths that a Christian must understand; the *Vita* gives Rheims the past it must have to legitimate its domination of political intrigues. All these achievements are possible because, above all, the *Vita* states that a bishop is a law-giver and the very source of every catholic – that is, universal – norm. Anyone who thinks of Hincmar as conservative will be surprised to discover him claiming, *sotto voce*, complete freedom for bishops in actually creating the norms that the *Vita* promotes; even if he presents the council as an opportune moment for this creation, he does not assert that the definition of norms is a collective action. Indeed, Hincmar's *Vita* appears to represent the moment when Latin hagiography attempts to become a medium for norms rather than an edifying discourse; though perhaps a brief apogee, rather than a successful and durable beginning.

The bishop as law-giver

One of the major innovations of Hincmar's Saint Remigius is his alleged involvement in councils. Anyone looking at the evidence must conclude that there is no sign that Remigius attended any known council in Gaul between 458 and 535, and especially not the exceptional council of Orléans which Clovis organised in 511.[21] He did not call any provincial meetings either, not even the simplest diocesan synod, in more than fifty years. This lacuna did not fit new Carolingian norms, a problem which Hincmar solved in a very subtle way. In chapter 20 of the *Vita* he inserted a letter written by Pope Hormisdas.[22]

It is well known since Krusch's work, followed by Devisse, that the archbishop based his claims to be a kind of papal vicar for the kingdom on this (forged) letter, by asserting for himself the privileges Hormisdas is said to have accorded to Remigius.[23] This letter sums up in a theoretical way what a bishop's mission must be: it is not Christianisation, nor the spiritual life, the correct celebration of the sacraments or the defence of the faith against heresy; it is the observance of rules. More precisely, preaching the faith and constructing the Church may be summarised in a single expression, that is, keeping the tradition expressed in canon law and confirmed by papal authority. In his letter, Pope Hormisdas begins by rejoicing in the election of Remigius as a bishop:

> So we have received by anticipation an omen that our choice [of Remigius as the papal vicar] is judicious, when we learned that you have accomplished what we order tirelessly all others to do, that is that you try to maintain the observance of the rule of the fathers and the authority of the apostolic see in provinces separated by such great distance.[24]

Then the pope makes Remigius his vicar, congratulates him on the baptism of the Franks, and continues with exhortations on the mission of a bishop. That is mainly to maintain the canons:

> Thus we command that the rules of the Fathers and the decrees defined by the most holy councils must be observed by all. We offer brotherly advice and encouragement for your vigilance and concern about these cases. Watch over them with as much reverence as is fitting, let no opportunity for fault be an obstacle to holy observance! That is where we find specified what is lawful and what is unlawful, what is forbidden, to which no one should dare to aspire, and what is allowed, that a mind pleasing to God should seek.[25]

The bishop is thus defined by the authentic letter of Hormisdas as a custodian of canon law, as summarised in the Roman Church tradition: no wonder that the pope insists on this point, because he writes to a bishop of Spain under Visigothic domination.[26] But Hincmar selected this letter, and no other, to forge a brief correspondence between Rheims and Rome: and it is not only a question of contemporaneity, even if Hincmar relies on the fact that Hormisdas and Remigius *could* have exchanged letters. The letter fits both Hincmar's desire and practice to reinforce the normative power of the archbishops, as sustained by papal authority. The letter goes further: it underlines the responsibility of 'Remigius' in maintaining Church tradition, but also his ability to exert normative power over the clergy of his diocese, by means of a council: 'Whenever the defence of religion demands a general council, all your brothers should gather on your summons, and if a particular topic is the occasion of trouble between some of them, then restrain disputes born between them, and find solutions to conflicts by examining the holy Law [the Scriptures, *lex sacra*]'.[27] With such a definition of episcopal ministry, one should not be surprised if, in the *Vita*, Remigius's voice and that of Hincmar combine to formulate real rules and not only encouragement or exhortation. The bishop is a legislator, thanks to his knowledge of Scriptures, patristic tradition and canon law.[28]

Which is the more important: to maintain observance of canon law or to be able to interpret it? Hormisdas openly chose observance, but Hincmar insists on the archbishop's autonomy and ability to create new rules from old ones. Hence, in my opinion, his relatively restrained use of the figure of Moses in the *Vita Remigii*. In the *Vita*, Remigius is compared to many great male figures of the Old and New Testament, including archangels, kings, prophets and apostles.[29] Moses appears in the list, but not at its top, and is mentioned for a fact that is probably not the major feature of his life. Moses is described not as the one who received the Law, nor the law-giver, but as the man whose face was radiant:

> We read this fact about Moses: his face became radiant when the Lord looked upon him. We hear the same about Remigius, who was glorified by a radiant light. That means that, just as Moses was ordained by God to be a legislator for the people of the Old Testament, so the blessed Remigius emerged as the man chosen, by the gift of Christ, to be the bearer of the grace of the gospel to the people who had to be renewed in the baptismal font.[30]

Here Hincmar prefers to oppose the age of Law and the age of Grace rather than insist on the continuity between the two legislators – perhaps because he thinks that a Carolingian bishop does not have to deliver a Law he did not write, but to write laws that had not been transmitted to him.

The council therefore is the place where a bishop is able to reinforce his effective authority over other clergy and his intellectual authority by the commemoration of canonical law.³¹ So it is certainly no coincidence that, in chapter 21, Hincmar imagined a council chaired by Remigius, a chapter he completely invented, without any previous attestation.³² This is a council without place or date, because this is not a historical council, but a staging of the normative authority of the bishop. In the episode's conclusion, Hincmar joins a meditation on the law, from the *De cavendis* and the *Moralia*, to a quite spectacular miracle. The situation is very plain: Remigius chairs a council which also involved an Arian heretic. The heretic refuses to get up when Remigius arrives, so he is reduced to silence. Actually mute, he recovers only to confess the Catholic faith on the order of Remigius:

> Once a proud heretic, now a humble Catholic, he confessed the Catholic faith in the Catholic holy and inseparable Trinity and in the Incarnation of Christ, and promised to persevere in this faith he had confessed. In this way, Saint Remigius, with the power of God, restored the health of soul and body to the man who had lost his soul by his infidelity and had been condemned to the loss of his physical voice by his pride. He showed unambiguously to all the other priests who were present, and to those who would read this passage or hear it, what to do about those who sin by their perverse opinions about Christ, who by His humanity deigned to become our neighbour and our brother, and how they ought to act towards those who sin in themselves or against the Church and who disobey, and towards those who have understood and are repentant.³³

The whole commentary is important, because it is not a mere question of spiritual guidance, a problem of edification for any Christian. Using the example of Remigius, Hincmar asks all the priests to behave in a certain way, or rather imposes a norm, since the duty to forgive sins is addressed to a social or professional category, here the clergy. The incentive to forgive does not depend on the personal behaviour of one priest or another: it is the archbishop of Rheims – that means Remigius as much as Hincmar – who speaks, as he would in a provincial council, and promulgates a rule to all the clergy of his diocese. Indeed, this discourse of Hincmar is staged as part of of a theoretical or ideal council, in which the roles of Hincmar and Remigius are inseparable: there is the example of Remigius on one side, who is able to convince those who attended the scene, then the extension of the work of Remigius by Hincmar, through other means of communication. This is a first response, very clear, to the question of the transmission of norms: as he explained, Hincmar hoped that

Bishop and law: the life of Saint Remigius

the long-awaited hagiographical text would circulate throughout the province, be very widely read in public and be pondered in private, so becoming a very important medium for the dissemination of rules. It is because of the *Vita*'s anticipated wide dissemination that Hincmar chose to mingle more theoretical lessons with the events of the life of Remigius, as he explains in his preface:

> I shall take care to add the words of the Fathers, for the admonition of those who read or listen, to passages that describe the miracles that the Lord carried out through our patron saint, to the extent of my understanding; and I shall try to walk in the footsteps of the blessed Gregory, although I cannot equal him, who, while he described the actions of the saints and the fall of the wicked, drew out an admonition, according to the wisdom that God had communicated to him, and who inserted in his narrative many necessary and useful considerations to those who read them or listen to them.[34]

Hincmar warns us that he will pass from the action of Remigius to exhortations 'for those who read or listen'. In chapter 21, about the speechless heretic, it is Remigius himself who teaches 'to all the other priests who were present, as to those who would read this passage or hear it'; we understand that Hincmar and Remigius are pretty much interchangeable.

The rule that is expressed here – every penitent must be reconciled – is a recurrent matter for Hincmar. What is worth noticing is that he does not justify it by canons, but by the Law, contained in the Scriptures on the one hand and the history of Remigius that embodies justice on the other. Hincmar succeeds in converting a personal belief into an objective norm by the peculiar staging the *Vita* authorises, through an alliance of lived example and imperative discourse. Yet that does not totally explain why Hincmar does not quote any canon on this matter. It is only in his table of contents, on chapter 16, that he alludes to canon law and promises he will devote time to a canonical explanation about the bishop of Laon, Genebaud:

> How one should understand the canonical statement that specifies with extreme insistence that a man subject to penance because of a public sin must not receive ecclesiastical orders or be kept in orders or recover his previous situation.[35]

What is chapter 16 about? A bishop of Laon, Genebaud, had two children with his wife, though they should have separated after his episcopal ordination. Remigius, to whom Genebaud confessed his fault, did not degrade the bishop, but submitted him to a strict penance for seven years before reconciling him.[36] Hincmar tells the story, then raises the question: did Remigius act in accordance with canonical rules? His answer is a typically Hincmarian one, loudly proclaiming that nothing is more essential than the observance of Church's traditions … before concluding that Remigius was well inspired not to follow its sacred rules:[37]

> No one should be bold enough to enunciate novelties in contradiction with the Apostle, revelling in his own words, by claiming that the sacred rules have been established against this example of God's mercy, or that the blessed Remigius acted in this case with respect to Genebaud by divine command against the sacred rules, or that it is against the regular canons that Genebaud was kept in his rank after his sin, since the Catholic Fathers proclaimed by mutual agreement this statement which should be sufficient: 'When it was established in the Church that no one can receive orders after having done penance for a crime, or re-enter the clergy or remain in the orders, this has not been done due to a lack of confidence in forgiveness, but as a result of rigorous discipline. Otherwise it would challenge the power of the keys given to the Church by these words, "Whatever you loose will be loosed" [Matthew 18: 18].' Nothing is excluded or left out by that 'whatever', meaning 'everything'.[38]

Hincmar concludes this passage with a long (though implicit) quotation from Augustine[39] who, and Hincmar after him, finds in the Scriptures the two cases of King David and Peter the Apostle to prove that by true humility, having confessed their sins, they not only obtained their pardon but also retained their functions: David remained king just as Peter remained apostle.

Moreover, the *Vita* directly refers to a canonical text that Hincmar wrote himself and which could be found in his *Capitula episcoporum*.[40] This *capitulum* about the penance of clerics may seem slightly stricter than the *Vita*, insisting on the necessity of a long penance that teaches humility when the *Vita* underlines the perfection of the mercy granted – yet there is no deep contradiction between them, only a difference in the form. The gloss Hincmar added in the *Vita* about the *potestas ligandi* of the Church aims to guarantee her full freedom of decision. The *capitulum* had to be drafted from an accumulation of patristic, explicit and traceable evidences or citations, while patristic quotations are invisible and far fewer in the *Vita*. The important point here is that the hagiographical text comments on the canons: the canons are by definition quite synthesised texts, decisions that do not leave much room for diversity of cases. In the *Vita*, Hincmar restores the legal interpretation that should accompany the canons. A law should not be used blindly but interpreted, adapted to circumstances. The facts are opposed to the principles, especially when the historical example is that of a saint. The hagiographic narrative thus serves as an argument of authority to demonstrate that there may be a difference between laws and judgments.

Finally, we obtain an unexpected answer to the question: Why did Hincmar choose to deliver his most intimate convictions and his most crucial commands via a hagiographic text? Speaking about merely extending the moral improvement assigned to every hagiographical text to incite a more normative and collective progress is not sufficient. Through hagiography, Hincmar creates two levels of language: on a first level, he composes what appears to be a reminder about canonical rules – on penance, on death, on the organisation of a synod – and about doctrinal truths, a reminder which confirms the indisputable authority of the bishop on all these subjects. At the same time, on another level, Saint Remigius's life demonstrates the total independence of the same bishop *vis-à-vis* these previous rules. Hincmar illustrates, supports and embodies in explicit behaviour the idea he does not want to put explicitly: a bishop of Rheims is the source of law and is little constrained by the rules that constrain others.

Back to a stricter definition of hagiography as history

Hincmar counted on the diffusion of the *Vita*, expecting that it would be read in private and in public, broadcast by liturgy and memorised, to be more effective than any synodal act. In this regard, Hincmar's expectations failed: as a brief conclusion, a short study of some specific manuscripts of the *Vita Remigii* proves that this text was not copied in the way the archbishop hoped it would be.

At first sight, Hincmar's hopes would seem to have been fulfilled. After the death of Hincmar in 882, the *Vita Remigii* was often copied in *Francia occidentalis* and, no surprise, especially in the province of Rheims. In fact it had an extraordinary dissemination, with manuscripts that are extremely numerous for a work of the ninth century: Krusch read thirty-one of them, but there are at least eighty-five. However, from these thirty-one, Krusch had to devise six categories to produce a coherent *stemma*, because the transmission of the text is highly volatile: there are only three almost full manuscripts and very few manuscripts are alike. The *Vita Remigii* is indeed a monument, a *vita* so long that it was almost never thoroughly copied after the eleventh century. It is understandable that all its extra matter – the prologue, table of contents, preface or reading guide and documents like the testament of Remigius – was omitted by scribes. But that is also true of the more biographical chapters, which are almost never copied *verbatim*. All copyists seem to have been puzzled by the heterogeneity of the work. They first removed the appendices. But they also cut pieces out of narrative chapters, to rid the *Vita* of all speculative passages. Each manuscript of the life of Saint Remigius therefore provides the chance to examine the shift between the enunciation of rules and their effectiveness. This is an ongoing problem in the study of medieval norms: we know what the rules say, but not whether they were implemented. Starting from consideration of a small part of the dissemination of the *Vita Remigii* in manuscript, we can then assess whether the most normative passages of this text have been preserved, or not. The general structure of the *Vita* is shown in Table 1.

Some faithful scribes kept all the prose and narrative chapters, as in

Table 1: Structure of the *Vita Remigii* in the Bibliotheca Hagiographica Latina (BHL)

BHL 7152	Prologue	Hincmar recounts the circumstances in which he wrote the *Vita* and by what methods
BHL 7153	Table of contents	a very detailed table of chapters (summaries rather than titles)
BHL 7154	*Altera praefatio*	a guide for the reading of the text
BHL 7155	cc. 1–23 (*Vita*)	
BHL 7156	cc. 24–28 (*Miracula post mortem*)	
BHL 7157	c. 29 (*translatio* 852)	
BHL 7158	c. 30	eulogy of *Remigius*: he equals all the other saints
BHL 7159	c. 31	another eulogy of *Remigius*
BHL 7160	c. 32	Remigius' Testament
BHL 7161	Carmen 1	verses written on the saint's shrine by Hincmar
BHL 7162	Carmen 2	other verses written on the saint's shrine

Bishop and law: the life of Saint Remigius

the oldest surviving manuscript, originally from St-Vaast and still in Arras today (Arras, BM MS 199 (189), from the very end of the 10th century). It has been damaged, but once contained most of the *Vita*, as shown in Table 2. The text has been copied with infinite respect by several copyists, without missing a single line. There are even the signs in the margins that Hincmar provided to distinguish the more difficult passages, ones that have to be pondered on, from the ones that everybody can listen to.[41] However, did these indications, which make it so easy to identify the speculative moments of the *Vita*, help later scribes to write an expurgated text, by simply showing them what they had to suppress? A careful reading of some abbreviated manuscripts actually shows that, though scribes did indeed remove the more theoretical passages, they chose them themselves.

For instance, in a manuscript now in Rouen – Rouen, BM MS 1381 (U67) – let us read the chapter 6 of the *Vita*. In this chapter, Hincmar tells how Remigius healed a man who was poor, blind and possessed; he concludes that Remigius, who can give a threefold remedy, manifests the Trinity. Then he underlines the necessity for a Christian to pray and beg constantly, to accord with what he believes and what he practises, to obtain by prayer what is really good for him. In the edition of the text, two moments are clearly distinguished: first, the story of the healing,[42] and second, Hincmar's meditation on the three evils that afflicted the man, reported in the margin by the Greek letter *gamma*.[43] But the Rouen manuscript scribe failed to identify this organisation. He kept the story and its conclusion about the Trinity, but only a part of the meditation that follows.[44] We might suppose

Table 2: Structure of the *Vita Remigii* in Arras, BM MS 199 (189)

BHL 7152	Prologue	now missing
BHL 7153	Table	fols 1–2^v
BHL 7154	*Altera praefatio*	fol. 3
BHL 7155	cc. 1–23 (*Vita*)	fols 3^v–28
BHL 7156	cc. 24–28 (*Miracula*)	fols 28–31^v, with an accidental omission
BHL 7157	c. 29 (*translatio* 852)	fol. 31^v
BHL 7158	c. 30	fol. 32
BHL 7159	c. 31	fol. 33
BHL 7160	c. 32: testament	–
BHL 7161	*Carmen* 1	–
BHL 7162	*Carmen* 2	–

that the scribe simply interrupted his work when he thought that the anecdote of the miraculous healing was completed, rather than selecting the sentences according to a specific purpose.

Another manuscript, again now in Arras, presents a more interesting case, even if it is difficult to draw solid conclusions from a manuscript that has been damaged; this is Arras, BM MS 31 (0823), fols 16–32. The *Vita Remigii* copied here is an abbreviated version of the Hincmarian text. A brief look at chapter 16 about Genebaud gives a good idea of the proportions of this abbreviation: the scribe considered useless more than half of the text,[45] at first sight the most speculative passages, the dogmatic and exegetical teachings. However, not all the theoretical passages are omitted, so the selection does not refer to a more popular or a more liturgical use of the *Vita*, when shortened. The scribe in fact omitted all passages written in the first person plural.[46] Hincmar often uses this rhetorical formula, as if talking directly to the monks of St-Remi as their abbot, or to the clergy as their archbishop: 'We read in the sacred history', 'We have with Bishop Genebaud', 'We heard', 'So, dearest brothers, we have … confidence in the mercy of our Creator', 'Think about what we do, think again about what we did' and so on.[47] All these exhortations, which are brief and easy to understand, have been removed: so the abbreviation does not match a desire to make the text more accessible for the simple, or at least it does not only match that aim.

This abbreviation, stifling the voice of Hincmar and the historical context of the first enunciation of the *Vita*, is the price that was paid for the text to become more than a Rheims history for Rheims readers. As the manuscripts are shortened, the legend of Remigius becomes part of a national history, one that greatly exceeded Hincmar's purpose, one in which the memory of the baptism of Clovis becomes the essential moment of Remigius's career. The hagiography is still considered as a story that can teach something, but it is no longer a question of behaviour or of faith: out of Hincmar's hands, through the copying of scribes, hagiography now teaches the meaning of the political history of the Frankish realm.

Notes

1 Hincmar, *Vita Remigii episcopi Remensis*, [BHL 7152–7164], ed. B. Krusch, MGH *SRM* 3 (Hanover, 1896), pp. 239–341. The *Vita* is referenced here as follows: *VR* chapter, page, line(s).

2 This is notably the opinion of Jean Devisse in *Hincmar*, II, pp. 1004–8. For a recent presentation of the *Vita*, see M.-C. Isaïa, *Remi de Reims: mémoire d'un saint, histoire d'une Église* (Paris, 2010), pp. 465–546.
3 Pseudo-Venantius Fortunatus, *Vita sancti Remedii*, [BHL 7150], ed. B. Krusch, MGH *Auctores antiquissimi* IV, 2 (Berlin, 1885), pp. 64–7; Isaïa, *Remi de Reims*, pp. 373–81.
4 *VR* preface, p. 250, 39–41: 'eos vidisse librum maxime quantitatis manu antiquaria scriptum de ortu ac vita et virtutibus atque obitu beati Remigii sanctissimi patronis nostri. Qui ... deperiit'; p. 253, 12–16: 'Unde bonis vestris desideriis placuit, ut illa mea servitus ... in unum colligeret. Quod etiam diu fecissem, nisi me spes vana deluderet, quibusdam dicentibus, quia in illo et illo loco magnum librum de vita et virtutibus ipsius domni et patronis nostri repperire valerem ... penitus falsa inveni'.
5 Krusch's preface of his edition of the *VR* is a tremendous speech for the prosecution against Hincmar (pp. 239, 2 to p. 240, 7); 'Hincmar ... . a man inflated by a huge desire for domination, and endowed with stupendous guile ... was very disappointed by the extant *Vita brevis*, that did not suit his desires ... The crafty man took a resolution full of cunning [to prove] that the previous *Vita*, [that he needed to assert his views], actually existed. But the *Vita prolixior* that he had forged, if totally destroyed, could not serve him: this is the reason why he thought of a rather clever tale' ('homo nimia dominandi cupiditate inflatus miraque astutia praeditus ... Brevis quae iam extabat V. Remedii eius desideriis minime satisfecit ... Homo autem astutus ... consilium multae calliditatis iniit. Ut probaret, Vitam eam quam desiderabat re vera extitisse ... Prolixior quam finxit Vita, si penitus periisset, proficere ei non potuisset, ideoque fabulam sibi excogitavit satis ingeniosam'). And further (p. 241, 20–21, 43): 'He wants us to believe that all his assertions depend on his documents ... but all the things that Hincmar added from these documents are made up ... Saint Remigius fortunately succeeded in every enterprise that Hincmar failed to achieve' ('Haec igitur ex schedulis suis pendere credi voluit ... atque omnia, quae documentis notis addidit Hincmarus, ficta sunt ... Sanctus igitur ea bono eventu perfecerat, quae sine successu susceperat Hincmarus').
6 *VR* c. 15, p. 296, 31 to p. 297, 4.
7 *VR* c. 14, p. 296, 1–15.
8 See below, n.19. Some important teachings can be read in *VR* c. 8, pp. 281–4 on predestination and in *VR* c. 7, p. 275 about the right understanding of the dogma of the Trinity.
9 Isaïa, *Remi de Reims*, pp. 528–9.
10 Hincmar, *De cavendis vitiis et virtutibus exercendis*, ed. D. Nachtmann, MGH Quellen zur Geistgeschichte des Mittelalters 16 (Munich, 1998). My observation about the reuse of the same citations in both texts does

not contradict Hincmar's ability to adapt his teaching to his audience, an ability Philippe Depreux is right to underline, here in Chapter 8.

11 Krusch did not note the presence of the *De cavendis* inside the *Vita Remigii*, so there may be more quotations than the eighteen important ones I have noticed. Even so, I believe that the *De cavendis* is the most important Hincmarian source of the *Vita*. Hincmar's peculiar use of citations (with explicit citations, allusions, variations, paraphrases and 'textual recycling') is rightly underlined by Simon Corcoran, here in Chapter 7.

12 *VR* c. 5, p. 268, 19-21: 'Sic et de hoc beati Remigii facto maximam instructionis aedificationem ... valemus assumere.'

13 *VR* c. 5, p. 268, 38 to p. 269, 3.

14 Gregory the Great, *Moralia in Job*, XIX, 30, 53, ed. M. Adriaen, CCSL 143-143B, 3 vols (Turnhout, 1979-85), vol. 3, p. 999, lines 15-22.

15 *De cavendis* II, 3, p. 180, lines 13-19.

16 *VR* c. 17, p. 309, 2-10: 'bonum exemplum omnibus episcopis, tam suo tempore in carne viventibus, quam post eum in ordine succedentibus, derelinquens, ut pauperibus aut viduis vel pupillis vel pro his qui ad misericordiam aecclesiae confugiunt, qui iniuriam patiuntur, aut qui peccantes in exilio vel in insulis damnantur, aut certe quamcumque sententiam suscipiunt, iuxta sacros canones subvenientes, vel quaecumque agentes bona pro temporali retributione non faciant; sed iuxta vocem dominicam: "Gratis accepistis, gratis date", quod Dei gratia, id est gratis data, acceperunt, gratis etiam, id est sine retributione temporali, proximis largiantur.'

17 *VR* preface, p. 253, 26-8: 'In the following pages, let the reader not be disturbed by the diversity of style: I put, exactly as I found them, the facts I received from the histories of our ancestors, and those I noticed in old parchments.'

18 *VR* table of contents, p. 255, 7-12: 'Qualiter civitatem Remorum conflagratam per demonem ab incendio liberavit, et nos, si fideliter petierimus, eius meritis et orationibus a viciorum flammis et ab igne perpetuo liberari valebimus. Unde, sumpta similitudine, commemorata est breviter falsitas predestinatianorum hereticorum, qui dicunt, Deum quosdam ad ignem perpetuum predestinasse; et hinc catholicae fidei veritas demonstratur'.

19 Hincmar, *De praedestinatione Dei*. One can notice at least these repetitions: *VR* p. 281, 14-15 = *De praedestinatione Dei*, col. 421; *VR* p. 281, 33-5 = *De praedestinatione Dei*, col. 190 = Gregory the Great, *Homiliae in Hiezechihelem prophetam*, ed. M. Adriaen, CCSL 142 (Turnhout, 1971), I, 9, 2, p. 124; *VR* p. 283, 22-6 and 28-30 = *De praedestinatione Dei*, col. 444; *VR* p. 283, 37-9 = *De praedestinatione Dei*, col. 82; *VR* p. 283, 42 to p. 284, 5 = Leo the Great, *Sancti Leonis Magni romani pontificis Tractatus septem et nonaginta*, ed. A. Chavasse, CCSL 138-138A, 2 vols (Turnhout, 1973), 62, c. 4, vol II, pp. 379-80 with *VR* 283, 42-5 = *De*

Bishop and law: the life of Saint Remigius

praedestinatione Dei, col. 345; *VR* p. 284, 22–7 = *De praedestinatione Dei*, col. 368; *VR* p. 284, 27–9 = *De praedestinatione Dei*, col. 288; *VR* p. 284, 29–30 looks like *De praedestinatione Dei*, col. 283; *VR* p. 284, 30–2 = *De praedestinatione Dei, multi loci* = Leo the Great, Epistola CLXV, c. 4, *PL* 54, col. 1161; *VR* p. 284, 34–7 = *De praedestinatione Dei*, col. 307. For the theological and social issues of the predestination controversy, see Matthew Bryan Gillis here in Chapter 13, and await publication of W. Pezé and J. Delmulle, *La controverse carolingienne sur la prédestination: histoire, textes, manuscrits*. Journées d'étude organisées à Paris les 11 et 12 octobre 2013.

20 I suspect that a first version of the *Vita* was addressed to Louis the German, as a sort of admonition: see Isaïa, *Remi de Reims*, p. 523.
21 We still need a fresh look at the Orléans council of 511, which cannot be reduced to the beginning of a secular and French alliance between the throne and the altar. Gregory Halfond has begun to answer this need, first in G. I. Halfond, *Archaeology of Frankish Church Councils, AD 511–768* (Leiden, 2010) and then with G. I. Halfond, 'Vouillé, Orléans (511) and the origins of the Frankish conciliar tradition', in R. W. Mathisen and D. Shanzer, eds, *The Battle of Vouillé, 507 CE: Where France Began* (Boston, 2012), pp. 151–66.
22 *VR* p. 311, 31 to p. 313, 20, especially p. 311, 34 to p. 312, 30.
23 Krusch, *VR*, pp. 241–2, and Devisse, *Hincmar*, II, p. 652.
24 *VR* c. 20, p. 312, 8–11: 'Praerogativam igitur de nostri sumpsimus electione iudicii, quando id operatum te esse didicimus, quod ceteris agendum obnixius imperamus, ut in provinciis tanta longinquitate disiunctis et apostolicae sedis vigorem et patrum regulis studeas adhibere custodiam'.
25 *VR* c. 20, p. 312, 19–24: 'Paternas igitur regulas et decreta sanctissimis diffinita conciliis ab omnibus servanda mandamus. In his vigilantiam tuam, in his curam, fraternae monita exortationis ostendimus. His ea quanta dignum est reverentia custoditis, nullum relinquit culpae locum sanctae observationis obstaculum. Ibi fas nefasque prescriptum est, ibi prohibitum, ad quod nullus audeat adspirare, ibi concessum, quid debeat mens Deo placitura presumere'.
26 For the context of the correspondence between Hormisdas and Salluste, bishop of Seville, see T. Deswarte, *Une chrétienté romaine sans pape: l'Espagne et Rome (586–1085)* (Paris, 2010), *passim*, but esp. pp. 54–62.
27 *VR* c. 20, p. 312, 24–6: 'Quotiens universale poscit religionis causa concilium, te cuncti fratres evocante conveniant; et si quos eorum spetialis negocii pulsat intentio, iurgia inter eos oborta compesce discussa sacra lege determinando certamina.'
28 On the growing importance of the knowledge of law in the episcopal ministry during Hincmar's career, see L. Jégou, *L'évêque, juge de*

paix: l'autorité épiscopale et le règlement des conflits entre Loire et Elbe (VIIIe-XIe siècle) (Turnhout, 2011) and, more precisely about Hincmar: M.-C. Isaïa, 'Être historien au IXe siècle: Esdras *rerum gestarum scriptor*', in M. Coumert, M.-C. Isaïa, K. Krönert and S. Shimahara, eds, *Rerum gestarum scriptor: Histoire et historiographie au Moyen Age: Mélanges Michel Sot* (Paris, 2012), pp. 67–76.

29 See chapter 30 of the *Vita Remigii* for a good summary of the figures Hincmar used: *VR* p. 326, 24 to p. 328, 5. Archangels and other types of angel are to be found in the beginning of the very rhetorical chapter 31, *VR* p. 328, 6 to p. 331, 11, that heavily depends on Gregory the Great's *Homelium in Evangelia* 34.

30 *VR* c. 14, p. 296, 13–20: 'Quod de Moyse scriptum legimus, quia splendida facta est facies eius, dum respiceret in eum Dominus, hoc et in beatum Remigium luce splendida illustratum factum fuisse audimus; quoniam, sicut Moyses legislator populo veteri erat a Domino constitutus, ita et beatus Remigius euvangelicae gratie lator populo in proximo per fontem baptismatis innovando extitit munere Christi electus.'

31 About the importance of councils as social experiences and occasions for the creation of a self-conscious representation of the Carolingian episcopate, see especially S. Patzold, *Episcopus: Wissen über Bischöfe im Frankenreich des späten 8. bis frühen 10. Jahrhunderts* (Ostfildern, 2008).

32 *VR* p. 313, 21 to p. 314, 10.

33 *VR* c. 21, p. 314, 7–16: 'ante superbus hereticus, humilis iam et catholicus catholicam fidem de sancta et inseparabili Trinitate et de Christi incarnatione catholice confessus est et in eadem confessionis sue fide se permansurum professus est. Sicque anima per infidelitatem perdito et corporali voce propter superbiam condempnato virtute divina sanctus Remigius et animae et corporis reddidit sanitatem, cunctis qui aderant vel lecturi seu haec audituri erant sacerdotibus patenter ostendens de male sentiendo peccante in Christum, qui per humanitatem proximus et frater nobis fieri dignatus est, quomodo erga peccantes in se vel in aecclesiam atque rebelles et erga post recognoscentes et paenitentes debeant agere'.

34 *VR* preface, p. 254, 3–9: 'In his autem, quae descriptis virtutum miraculis, a Domino per beatissimum patronum nostrum operatis, ad exortationem legentium sive audientium pro modulo intellectus mei de catholicorum dictis subiungere studebo, vestigia beati Gregorii, licet non valeam, prosequi moliar, qui describens sanctorum actus pravorumque casus, exortatione inde assumpta, secundum sapientiam sibi a Deo datam multa necessaria et utilia legentibus ac audientibus interposuit'.

35 *VR* preface, p. 256, 21–3: 'et qualiter tenenda sit sententia canonum, quae post lapsum publice paenitentem ad gradum ecclesiasticum non accedere vel in gradu manere aut ad gradum redire sollicitissime precepit'.

36 *VR* c. 16, p. 300, 33 to p. 304, 5. On Genebaud, the most important commentary is now R. Stone, 'Gender and hierarchy: archbishop Hincmar of Rheims (845-882) as a religious man', in P. H. Cullum and K. J. Lewis, eds, *Religious Men and Masculine Identity in the Middle Ages* (Woodbridge, Suffolk, 2013), pp. 28-45.
37 For Hincmar's versatility with the law, see Margaret McCarthy's opinion about the divorce of Louis the Stammerer in Chapter 6, pp. 112-14.
38 *VR*, c. 16, p. 306, 5-15: 'Et ne quis etiam contra apostolum delectans vocum novitates dicere presumat, aut sacras regulas contra hoc misericordiae Domini exemplum constituisse, aut beatum Remigium divina preceptione in hoc opere contra sacras regulas de Genebaudo egisse, aut ipsum Genebaudum contra regularem constitutionem post lapsum in gradu mansisse, satisfaciat illi consona catholicorum patrum sententia: "Ut", inquiens, "constitueretur in aecclesia, ne quisquam post alicuius criminis penitentiam clericatum accipiat, vel ad clericatum redeat, vel in clericatu maneat, non desperatione indulgentiae, sed rigore factum est disciplinae. Alioquin contra claves datas aecclesiae disputabitur, de quibus dictum est: 'Quaecumque solveritis super terram, erunt soluta et in caelo'". In eo enim, quod dicitur: "Quaecumque solveritis, erunt soluta", nihil excipitur, nihil non comprehensum relinquitur'.
39 *VR* c. 16, p. 306, 21-30 = Augustine, Epistula 185, 10, ed. A. Goldbacher, *S. Aureli Augustini Hipponiensis episcopi epistulae*, CSEL 34, 44, 57-8, 5 vols (Vienna, 1895-1923), IV, p. 39.
40 Hincmar, *Capitularia* II, c. 26, Anhang, MGH *Capit. Episc.* II, 1995, pp. 62-6.
41 *VR* Altera praefatio, p. 258, 25-7: 'I took care to distinguish the passages we must read to the people and those that should be kept for more educated and more studious readers' ('quantum inde, populo audiente, legantur, et que instructioribus et studiosioribus, quando sibi licuerit vel libuerit, legenda serventur, designare curavi'). See the whole paragraph: *VR* p. 258, 15 to p. 259, 5.
42 *VR*, c. 6, p. 271, 38 to p. 272, 12.
43 *VR*, c. 6, p. 272, 13 to p. 273, 14.
44 He copies *VR*, c. 6, p. 271, 38 to p. 272, 16.
45 The scribe omitted *VR*, c. 16, p. 300, 25 to p. 301, 31 then *VR* p. 302, 32 to p. 303, 8; *VR* p. 304, 8 to p. 305, 3 and *VR* p. 305, 6 to p. 306, 30.
46 From *VR*, c. 16, p. 303, 5-8.
47 *VR*, c. 16, p. 304, 19; *VR*, c. 16, p. 304, 23; *VR* c. 16, p. 304, 27; *VR*, c. 16, p. 304, 34-40. Perhaps these moments come directly from homilies that Hincmar really preached.

10

Family order and kingship according to Hincmar

Sylvie Joye

The middle of the ninth century appears as the period *par excellence* when theological thought on marriage took shape, and was combined with a new representation of society. It was at this point, as the Carolingian politico-religious model of *ecclesia* reached full maturity, that a treatise on the abduction of women was written (doubtless in the 850s)[1] a treatise which I shall refer to as the *De raptu*.[2] Issued in the name of a synod of bishops, this treatise – in whose elaboration Hincmar played a crucial role (he was its principal instigator and organiser, even if not perhaps its sole author) – is the only moral work which tackles in detail both the abduction of women and marriage. As the bishops clearly indicate at the beginning, its overall argument was for the suppression of *raptus*; but the text shows how this practice became caught up in an increasingly elaborated discourse on the place of marriage in society. In the *De raptu*, abduction is systematically discussed as part of a broader reflection on the ways in which marriage could be undertaken, and on their implications for conjugality.[3] The *De raptu* therefore appears as a key text for interpreting the role of the king, and at the same time, the place of parental authority in Hincmar's social model.[4]

The *De raptu* has many parallels with Hincmar's *De divortio*. But whereas the *De divortio* has a rather composite structure, that of the *De raptu* is clearer.[5] 'A veritable treatise' on abduction,[6] an 'ethical' work according to Pierre Toubert, it seems quite different from the *De divortio*,[7] which Toubert described as a 'case study' and whose canon law approach he underlined.[8] The *De raptu* does not rely on particular facts and evokes contemporary events only seldom and evasively, though it nevertheless deserves the label of 'exhortatory criticism of contemporary life' ('paränetische-zeitkritische ... Schrift') that Letha Böhringer applied to the *De divortio*.[9] In form, therefore, the two works cannot really be compared. As Rachel Stone has shown, it seems difficult to conclude that with it Hincmar succeeded in creating a real 'theology of abduction';[10] in fact this does not seem to have been the goal of Hincmar and his colleagues (or, if it was, they had abandoned it). In any case, although it returns regularly to the theme of abduction, the text of the *De raptu* engages with much broader problems. Though not entering into specific discussions of every religious or moral problem raised by abduction, the text reveals the importance and seriousness of the act. It does so in a synopsis showing the urgent need to preserve the social order of a Christian people, whose organic unity and purity had to be defended at any cost by the king. It was to the king that the bishops addressed their plea, presenting themselves as the true guardians of this social order, ready for the ultimate sacrifice in defence of a model of marriage that had become in their eyes the touchstone of society as a whole.[11]

The king who knows how to judge and to punish

Hincmar began the treatise by noting that the practice of abduction both provokes the wrath of God and brings the peace of the kingdom into doubt.[12] By mentioning the peace of the kingdom, Hincmar and his colleagues instantly show that the king is directly concerned, and must act. Peace is both the form of conduct that everyone should follow, and the ideal state to which society should aspire. Saint Paul, after all, called the faithful to live in peace and purity in order to gain a place in the kingdom of God.[13] If the duty of every Christian is to act in such a way that he does not disturb the peace, and to act with moderation, then without doubt the duty of the king is to guarantee the peace of his kingdom. Yet, while marriage appears as a 'thing of peace, love and concord' (*res pacis, charitatis et concordiae*), abduction in contrast embodies 'discord, violence and impiety' (*discordia, et violentia, et impietas*).[14] For Hincmar, even more than for his contemporaries, peace was the sign of communion and it anchored society.[15] All Carolingian thinkers, however, agreed that the king's role was to guarantee this peace.[16]

As a result, the treatise presents the king's duty as clear: he must severely suppress abduction, in order to save society from disorder by means of *correctio* (correction), an essential concept since the reign of Louis the Pious. The Roman emperors – who, even though pagans, issued good laws against abduction – were examples for the king.[17] He must therefore act vigorously, and tackle abduction head-on, using all the means at his disposal, 'coercing and rooting out' (*coercens et extirpans*) as the treatise's (later) title puts it,[18] but also 'destroying the most shameless recklessness of certain men' (*exterminans quorumdam hominum impudentissimam audaciam*).[19] He must take as his model Christ's chasing out of the merchants from the Temple. Hincmar in fact preceded his call for action, at the very beginning of chapter 4 (the other chapters worked as a kind of introduction), with a description of this biblical scene, borrowing the phrasing to apply it to the king. The king must again take up the zeal for the house of God evoked by Christ[20] and be the 'imitator of the imitation of God' (*aemulator Dei aemulatione*).[21]

Of course, in the biblical text summarised by the *De raptu*, Christ does not content himself with using his voice, but also uses his hands and a whip (*non verbo, quo etiam daemones fugabat, sed manu et flagello*).[22] Speech – or edicts, if one takes the parallel established by the prelates to its logical conclusion – is not enough to drive away either demons or abductors. The demand put to the king, in these troubled times – as Hincmar liked to remind him – was not so much for new capitularies against abduction. There were plenty of these already, clearly showing the place of the suppression of abduction in the systems of representation of royal function and of peace.[23] Rather, it was to take practical action.[24]

As Pierre Toubert noted, the major vices denounced in the Mirror of Princes genre are those which obscure judgement: wrath (*ira*), pride (*superbia*), susceptibility to flattery.[25] But the king must also know how to accept advice offered to him.[26] Hincmar and the other prelates who wrote the *De raptu* seem to have had in mind on this occasion the advice that bishops could offer the king. As abduction slipped into sacrilege, it was the bishops' duty to intervene with the king. As was traditional, the correspondence between divine order and earthly order was linked to the *ministerium* of the king.[27] The bishop portrayed himself thereby as the person who reminded the king of his duties to God.[28] This is indeed just what the text's authors, bishops themselves, did at the end of their treatise, recalling that the king must support episcopal authority, just as God supports royal authority.[29]

The *De raptu* mentions various kings as examples for the Frankish king to follow or avoid. Balthazar, the sacrilegious king, appears clearly as the latter: he scorned religion, and embodied the exact opposite not just of a good king, but of a simple Christian.[30] This example is emphasised so that the recipient of the treatise could not but feel himself set in comparison. The example of Herod is still more significant, used to castigate those who harnessed royal power to violate the laws. The position of the king did not place him above the laws: quite the reverse, he was more guilty than the 'ordinary' Christian if he made use of his powers to accomplish his crimes. It is for this reason that Herod is considered more at fault than an abductor.[31]

He was all the more at fault since the king ought to obey the laws, both human and divine. Hincmar presents here a new moral norm, presented as the expression of a 'natural law', that brings together all other types of norm: judicial, religious and moral.[32] The treatise projects upon the past a series of imaginative interpretations depicting it as the exact opposite of that natural law.[33] Attitudes in support of transgression are designated by the name of 'ancient custom', even in the case of transgressions that are widely accepted, as with abduction. Sources from the Carolingian period are characterised by the theme of rejecting sexuality as the sole basis of marriage. The idea that pagan or 'barbarian' marriage was based on sexual union seems actually to have been a creation of Carolingian clerics, keen to show the superiority of Christian marriage. It seems clear that an insistence on the passive honour of women, linked to notions of pollution and virginity, had not been part of the norms of the Germanic-speaking peoples, and had not played a preponderant role in matrimonial practice.

Hincmar, however, presents things differently: penance is represented as the only way to be rid of the stain produced by abduction, considered as a social but also a sexual failing. The body, the Lord's Temple, had been violated. The image of purificatory washing is evoked almost obsessively. Abduction becomes a sin, not just a crime, as it had been perceived in the preceding period. Whether the woman had consented made little difference to Hincmar, despite his insistence on love (*dilectio*) between spouses:[34] equally, it is not rape that he vigorously attacks with a citation from Paul,[35] but any union considered illegitimate that implies sexual activity, even if it is not violent. This does not undermine Rachel Stone's argument, according to which Hincmar was referring here to the body of the Church; for him, the two entities were linked.[36]

This change in the nature of abduction must be connected to the evolution of incest prohibitions. In the *De raptu*, lust (*libido*) and wantonness (*lascivia*) are always evoked in opposition to reason (*ratio*), which distinguishes humans from animals. The abductor who lets himself be guided by lust, not listening to the divine message, is akin to a beast.[37] With beasts is associated violence, which goes together with the absence of reason. Violence towards women, or at least towards one's wife, is therefore presented as unacceptable. Hincmar goes as far as to present an extreme version, if not a caricature, depicting husbands who send their wives to be slaughtered by the cook, whereas their duty is to save and purify their wives, just as Christ did with the Church.[38] The representation of masculinity no longer had any need to depend on a violent attitude to women, which is henceforth generally criticised in the texts.[39]

The bishop, supporter of the paternalist king

Charlemagne had given fresh energy to legislation on abduction during his reign.[40] Following in this way the example of Constantine and the Visigothic kings, he defended the rights of fathers.[41] The father's authority genuinely was important, but it is all the more emphasised in the sources (particularly the normative ones) because kings hoped to give their own power a paternal, or indeed paternalist, dimension. This paternal image was strengthened under the Carolingians,[42] and Hincmar drew on this image of strong paternal authority, considered the guarantee of social order even more than was the mutual love (*dilectio*) of the couple. It was to a great extent as the 'father over fathers' that the king is represented, as the authority guaranteeing family order and more generally as the guardian of society.

And it was the bishops who were to remind the king of his duties to God. Thus, the *De raptu* does not highlight examples of kings acting alone, but rather the king/counsellor pair. In doing so, the *De raptu* compares bishops with prophets. As always in the work of Hincmar, the most pertinent allusion is drawn from the New Testament. If necessary, bishops are ready to undergo martyrdom just as John the Baptist did, because (like him) they defend truth and holiness. Even faced with a king whose heart is as hardened as that of Herod, they are ready to resist. The affirmation is certainly flattering for the bishops; it is less so for the king.[43]

The other pairing representing the relation between king and bishops was that of Nathan and David from the Old Testament.⁴⁴ Hincmar lingered on the recollection of how David had upset the matrimonial order and offended God by taking Bathsheba, the wife of Uriel. He stated that, though in this matter David cannot be taken as an example, he had realised the need to do penance, and for that reason had been saved. The image of his son, Absalom, is in contrast entirely negative. Not only had Absalom broken the family bond by his rebellion against his father and his king, he had raped the concubines of David; and, what was worse, had done so publicly in front of the Temple. This act of pollution and sacrilege broke the family bond and symbolised a period of chaos.⁴⁵ In this way, throughout his text, Hincmar linked the defence of the family order, both marriage and descent, with the defence of the Church, interweaving themes of purity and repentance.⁴⁶

These examples were also brought up by Hincmar and his colleagues because the abductors themselves seem to have had recourse to the Old Testament to justify their actions. The works of Carolingian moralists indicate that the laity used the authority of the Bible to defend their matrimonial and sexual practices against contemporary prescriptions.⁴⁷ Such debates had doubtless taken place in the margins of Church councils between clerics, but also perhaps with theologically minded laypeople.⁴⁸ What added more fuel to these debates was the existence of a plurality of views within the Church, which cannot be considered as wholly unified at this time; it worked with a stock of contradictory authorities on the subject, even producing mutually contradictory decisions, without doubt useful for abductors.⁴⁹ No wonder then that Hincmar insisted that the Old Testament needed to be explained by clerics and could not be used in a literal sense by the laity, who might otherwise find there examples of illegitimate marriages that had been accepted by God (David and Bathsheba, but above all the account in Judges 21 of the Benjaminites, who had to seize new wives because their own had been decimated). As Hincmar explained elsewhere, Christ had come to liberate the true meaning of the Scriptures, which was confused and obscure in the texts that preceded his arrival. Although Christ had not rejected this ancient heritage, which could always work as a point of reference, he had nevertheless modified its meaning.⁵⁰ The way in which the *De raptu* treats references from the Old Testament corroborates this view; those were the only passages that Hincmar felt obliged to gloss.

For matters of sexuality, the laity were considered by Hincmar as those best able to know the reality and judge it,[51] as he explicitly stated elsewhere (on the topic of the affair of Northild, in his *De divortio*)[52] – but that does not mean that they were to use biblical texts in support. Rather than leaving to the laity the possibility of judging which sexual practices were good and which bad, it was more a question of leaving them to judge the importance of what was permitted to men in their domination over women.[53]

This use of biblical texts to combat the dominant position of churchmen was accompanied by physical attacks against the Church and individual clerics, physically assaulted by abductors who wished to gain their backing for their marriage to be recognised (though marriage could of course take place without the presence of a cleric, and was not considered a sacrament at this time). The authors of the *De raptu* associated these attacks with an attack on the corporate Church (and on the body that was the Christian people), since the abductor denied the unity of the Church by taking communion in one place while he was excommunicated in another.[54] This challenge to the Church and to the social order was expressed in terms of the political and social model of the body: not in itself new, but taken up and elaborated in the Carolingian period. Hincmar and his colleagues did not pose the problem of the duality of powers in this body, preferring to insist on its unity.[55]

In this context, the power of the king, like that of the father, could not be insulted without attacking the order of the world itself, which was therefore a public crime. It was entirely natural for Yan Thomas, in his study of ancient Rome, to move from the study of paternal power to that of sovereignty.[56] Hincmar – who in his annals systematically presented his King Charles the Bald as someone who had been unjustly attacked, who forgave, who tried to retie the bonds of the Carolingian family – further developed in his letters and treatises the image of a sovereign whose position is justified by association with the figure of the father, pivot of a hierarchy presented as sacred and natural (but evidently constructed), and which the king guarantees by the exercise of his judgement.[57]

The king was most readily compared to a father, who played the role within his family that the king played within his kingdom. In the *De raptu*, Hincmar notes that

> The splendour of this glorious dwelling of God, and the place where his glory inhabits, should be most faithfully loved and prized not only by

Family order and kingship

bishops and priests in their sees, but also by kings in their kingdoms and palaces, by counts in their cities, by *vicarii* in their communities, and by all the fathers of families in their dwellings, whether they are rich or poor, in thought and in action.[58]

The kings, and the fathers, who should wield both speech and the whip in their zeal to defend the Church and the body Christian, appear therefore as bearers of an authority intended to maintain unity (with the support of the Church Fathers, evoked in parallel, perhaps as a play on words).[59] In theory, the father was sole authority and all-powerful, even though in practice the mother had a say too, before becoming a model for the mother church,[60] which only gradually became the image of unity, evoking the unity of a family.[61]

Recovering unity through consent and purity

The peace that the king was supposed to institute in his kingdom, like the father in his household, was linked in the logic of the *De raptu* to an ideal of unity. Unity, as conceived there, does not even permit conflict to arise: it is an organic unity, within which every element finds its place and plays its role. The social model that this synodal dossier aimed to promote is clearly hierarchical. The bonds that connected the different elements forming society were carefully defined, and were not to be modified, or at least not in the ideal society imagined by the synod. In reality, it lamented, outside the embrace of the Church, this unity had been reduced to nothing. Abduction, a violent act which tried to break solidly established and clearly defined bonds to create a new though illusory bond, was both evidence for and a consequence of the disunion reigning at the heart of secular power. Marriage, in contrast, instituted a clear contract between two individuals and two kinship groups, creating a unit strongly characterised by unity as understood by Hincmar and his colleagues, and was the means by which society could try to recover its lost unity.

In the early Middle Ages, unanimity – being associated with the concept of consent – was supposed to mean unity in society[62] as well as in marriage. Just as two spouses became joined in one single body, so society was more and more readily thought of as an organic whole: the ideology of conjugality was not only applied in its own domain, but ended up constituting an 'ideal type' in the regulation of social relations beyond the world of the family. According to the *De raptu*, it was about harmonising pre-existing elements, not creating unity from nothing. God would not erase all his work to start again, as he had done in the time of Noah through the Flood, but showed himself as a doctor who would cure society of its ills.[63] The healthy body, which the Christian had not corrupted by sinning, was the Temple of God, the gateway giving access to heaven.[64] Hincmar, far from promoting repugnance for the body, recommended its temperate use. This position corresponded well to the importance Hincmar habitually attributed to the consummation of marriage, up to that point unknown in canon law.[65]

Against a pagan model, which they implicitly disowned (having mostly invented it), Hincmar and his colleagues set up a Christian model, privileging consent (*consensus*) over sexual activity (*concubitus*). A union that had begun with sexual union – a living-together (*contubernium*), properly speaking a mutual soiling (*colluvio*) – could not result in an official marriage. Yet for the bishops, while sexual union is presented as an element that is indispensable but also secondary, the *consensus* of the spouses is not particularly emphasised either.[66] Looking more closely, the term *consensus* is used time and time again in this treatise, but it was the consent of the family – in particular of the father, not of the daughter – which counted in reality, and which was deemed to outweigh the importance of *concubitus*. The only assent involved in the constitution of marriage is that of the parents, while the *consensus* of the young woman is presented only in a negative context: it is the consent that she grants her abductor. Yet marriage in the treatise nevertheless rested on the notion of consent, via the idea of the agreement, the *foedus*.[67] It is clear that for the authors of the *De raptu*, the consent of the young woman does not indicate that she has chosen her spouse, or even given her opinion on the subject, only that she does not feel herself incapable of putting up with him, and above all of respecting and remaining faithful to him.

This unity was not therefore entirely a fleshless one. The identity of the individual is shaped if not determined by sexual relations, and theoretically through the constitution of a couple: this is the famous principle of one flesh (*una caro*), when the spouses share the same flesh (more a matter of kinship than of sexuality, though the latter certainly played an undeniable role).[68] Laurent Barry, at the start of his reflection on *una caro*, which he associates with the 'invention of the couple',[69] underlines the importance of Christian doctrinal efforts to adapt its discourse to reconcile the demands of the Gospels with kinship structures.[70] Fundamental changes were produced through the influence of these doctrinal efforts and the contradictory ideals borne by Christian discourse on marriage from the end of Antiquity,[71] mixing the images of the body of the Christian and that of the Church. The body is a temple of flesh and blood, more precious than the Temple of wood and stone.[72] The physical body is holy, while the figural body is the image of harmony itself. The conjugal unit combined these two qualities: holy and harmonious, the legitimate conjugal unit was the microcosm of society as it ought to be. It was an example and a springboard for the promotion of social stability. The verb 'to procreate' (*procreari*) is always used in a pejorative sense, both in the text of the *De raptu* itself and in the extracts that the authors – without doubt Hincmar himself – selected as illustrations.[73] The bishops were attempting to weld parents together around legitimate children alone, having since the start of the Carolingian age succeeded in lowering the status of children of concubines to that of illegitimate offspring.[74] At the same time, however, the Carolingian period is also the moment it becomes possible to detect the positive impact of hypergamous abduction for children born to a couple whose marriage was eventually, even if reluctantly, acknowledged.

'Faith' (*fides*) in *De raptu* appears explicitly only as conjugal fidelity,[75] as promoted by Augustine, who made it one of the three pillars of the 'good of marriage' (*bonum conjugale*). Already from that point of view, marriage appeared as a model for the whole of society. Fidelity between spouses was now however enriched with a new psychological charge, amalgamating with the vassal's *fides*,[76] an idea Hincmar developed in another of his treatises that worked towards a social morality, the *De cavendiis vitiis*.[77] The notion of contract to which this *fides* makes reference, and the biblical episode of the oaths sworn by the Hebrews never to give their daughters in marriage to a Benjaminite,[78] reminds us that this definition of fidelity rested on implicit contracts that connected the individual to his order (*ordo*), his family and his king. In the face of everything and in all situations, the individual is bound by respect, as indissoluble as the promises sworn by the Hebrews against the Benjaminites. The weight allocated to betrothal too presupposes the indissolubility of the sworn promise. Respect, fidelity, fear – these were the elements that ensured society's stability, eventually allowing it to match the divine order. There could be no fidelity without love (*dilectio*),[79] and no fear of God without vowing obedience, love and honour to the father.[80]

Marriage was then a true *societas*, based on an agreement, the *foedus nuptiale*, just as society itself was based on implicit agreements which link individuals together. Marriage was both an image of society and its foundation. The role of parents was the same as that of the king and queen. They both watched over the family order which gave definitive underpinning to the social order desired by God. In this way marriage, which made spouses into *consortes*, was, as Pierre Toubert put it, 'an elemental society henceforth offered as a miniature model for the *ordo laicorum* [lay order]':[81] but this was a society that could not exist without the fathers' agreement.

In this context, a work like the *De raptu* was both a witness to the turbulence affecting society at the time, and an instrument in the hands of clerics for shaping this changing society. The bishops, among them Hincmar, stood up against the troubles that surrounded them. They sought to give society its stability by promoting only legitimate marriage, and refusing to allow anyone's appetite for power to use abduction as a means of accomplishing upward social mobility. Though closely involved in certain cases of political abduction, Hincmar refused even to mention them here, instead underlining the bestiality of those who practised abduction.

The production of the *De raptu* raises more questions than it answers, but it is highly symptomatic of a state of mind of the Carolingian episcopate, probably grouped around the pre-eminent figure of Hincmar of Rheims. A product of conciliar activity, and setting out to be a real 'instrument of government', this treatise bore the marks of episcopal concern to advise the king, to shape his actions, and to consolidate the unity of the earthly kingdom through the unity of Christian society. In this perspective, abduction appeared as a counter-model of marriage liable to bring down the social pyramid that the Carolingian kings were attempting to construct. It is this that justifies the tone of catastrophe, indeed apocalypse, which can be found in Hincmar's treatise.

Father and emperor were two people who could not be attacked and whose legitimacy could not be brought into question (Stuart Airlie, following Janet Nelson, has insisted on the fact that the Carolingians succeeded in having themselves accepted as 'natural lords').[82] However, this insistence on ideals of marriage and fatherhood cut both ways, from the moment that the Carolingians were affected by abduction and filial rebellion within their own family. The twice-widowed eighteen-year-old daughter of Charles the Bald,

Judith, kept under guard at Senlis, consented to her own kidnap by the ambitious Baldwin of Flanders in 862.[83] Worse, her own brother, the future Louis the Stammerer, was an accomplice. He himself had in the same year married Ansgard, the daughter of a Burgundian count named Harduin, against his father's wishes.[84] His younger brother, Charles of Aquitaine, though less than fifteen years old had already married the widow of count Humbert, also against his father's wishes. In these matters Hincmar was his king's most zealous defender, and a proponent of severity: he was apparently the only person to demand the excommunication of Judith and Baldwin. And in the Annals of St-Bertin, he justified the blinding and subsequent death of Carloman, the rebellious and 'apostate' son of King Charles, by presenting the latter not as a blood-stained tyrant,[85] but as a father and a sovereign who had to maintain order[86] despite the breach of proper relations between the generations.[87]

Notes

1 Dating the *De raptu* is very problematic, but it clearly shares passages with the *De divortio Lotharii regis et Theutbergae reginae* from 860. This chapter follows Letha Böhringer, who has explored the question in greatest depth, and argues from both form and content that the text is a source of the *De divortio*. She proposes a redaction in the 850s, perhaps in 859 (Hincmar, *De divortio*, pp. 68–71). Devisse, *Hincmar*, I, p. 463, suggested a date of 876, seeing in the *De raptu* the 'fruit tardif des dernières enquêtes et des ultimes réflexions du Rémois sur le [mariage]'. This was followed by R. Stone, 'The invention of a theology of abduction: Hincmar of Rheims on *raptus*', *Journal of Ecclesiastical History*, 60 (2009), 437 (though she now accepts Böhringer's view on the priority of *De raptu*: see Introduction p. 34, n.81).
2 The work survives only in an early modern edition by Jan Buys: *Paralipomena Opusculorum Petri Blesensis, et Ioannis Trithemii aliorumque nuper in typographeo Moguntino Editorum a Ioanne Busaeo*, ed. J. Buys (Cologne, 1605), pp. 796–836: *Epistola I, Hincmari Rhemensis Archiepiscopi Epistolae Duae*. The text was reprinted in 1645 by Jacob Sirmond: *Hincmari Archiepiscopi Remensis Opera Duos in Tomos Digesta*, ed. J. Sirmond (Paris, 1645), vol. II, texte XVI, pp. 225–43, with the title *De coercendo et exstirpando raptu viduarum, puellarum ac sanctimonialium*, then again by Migne in *PL* 125, 1017–36. (I shall refer to this edition, as the most accessible; it does not add significant errors to its sources). The text was not included in Buys's edition in 1602 of Hincmar's *epistolae et opuscula*, but added to a volume published in 1605, containing mostly

works by Peter of Blois and Johannes Trithemius. Buys placed two letters by Hincmar at its end, the *De raptu* and a letter on the priest and the king (R. Schieffer, 'Eine übersehene Schrift Hinkmars von Reims über Priestertum und Königtum', *DA*, 37 (1981), 511-28). The provenance of these letters is not specified: a scholar had probably sent them to Buys between 1602 and 1605.

3 See S. Joye, *La Femme ravie: le mariage par rapt dans les sociétés du haut Moyen Âge* (Turnhout, 2012), pp. 405-34.

4 The arguments of this chapter will be further developed in my forthcoming edition and French translation of the *De raptu*.

5 L. Böhringer, 'Der eherechtliche Traktat im Paris. Lat. 12445, einer Arbeitshandschrift Hinkmars von Reims', *DA*, 46 (1990), 18-47, especially pp. 28-31.

6 R. Le Jan, *Famille et pouvoir dans le monde franc (VIIe-Xe siècle): essai d'anthropologie sociale* (Paris, 1995), p. 299.

7 On Lothar II's divorce: S. Airlie, 'Private bodies and the body politic in the divorce case of Lothar II', *Past and Present*, 161 (1998), 3-38; T. Bauer, 'Rechtliche Implikationen des Ehestreits Lothars II: Eine Fallstudie zu Theorie und Praxis des geltenden Eherechts in der späten Karolingerzeit. Zugleich ein Beitrag zur Geschichte des frühmittelalterlichen Eherechts', *Zeitschrift der Savigny-Stiftung für Rechtsgeschichte, Kanonistische Abteilung*, 80 (1994), 41-87; and above all: K. Heidecker, *Kerk, huwelijk en politieke mach: de zaak Lotharius II (855-869)* (Amsterdam, 1997); revised version in English translation: *The Divorce of Lothar II: Christian Marriage and Political Power in the Carolingian World*, trans. T. M. Guest (Ithaca, 2010).

8 P. Toubert, 'La théorie du mariage chez les moralistes carolingiens', *Il Matrimonio nella società altomedievale, 22-28 Apr 1976*. Settimane 24, 2 vols (Spoleto, 1977), I, pp. 233-85 at p. 233, n.2.

9 Böhringer, 'Der eherechtliche Traktat', 31.

10 Stone, 'Invention'.

11 M. Stratmann, *Hinkmar von Reims als Verwalter von Bistum und Kirchenprovinz* (Sigmaringen, 1991), pp. 20-2, for Hincmar's thought, notably from theological and moral perspectives.

12 *De raptu*, col. 1018, c. 2: 'Nihil enim ita omnipotentis Dei iracundiam exasperat, et regni pacem perturbat'.

13 *Ibid.* (citing Hebrews 12:14): 'Pacem sequimini cum omnibus, et sanctimoniam, sine qua nemo videbit Dominum'.

14 *Ibid.*, col. 1020, c. 5. We see here a political vocabulary shared amongst Carolingian authors, particularly during the crisis of Louis the Pious and its aftershocks: W. Wehlen, *Geschichtsschreibung und Staatsauffasung im Zeitalter Ludwigs des Frommen* (Lübeck, 1970); S. Patzold, '*Consensus - Concordia - Unitas*. Überlegungen zu einem politisch-religiösen Ideal

der Karolingerzeit', in N. Staubach, ed., *Exemplaris imago: Ideale in Mittelalter und Früher Neuzeit* (Frankfurt am Main, 2012), pp. 31–56.
15 Devisse, *Hincmar*, II, p. 693.
16 Jonas of Orléans, *De institutione regia*, ed. and trans. A. Dubreucq, *Le métier de roi*, Sources chrétiennes, 407 (Paris, 1995), p. 198, c. 4: 'Regale ministerium specialiter est populum Dei gubernare, et regere cum aequitate et justitia et ut pacem et concordiam habeant studere', repeated in *Concilium Parisiense*, 829, MGH *Conc.* II, 2, no. 50, p. 651, book II, c. 2.
17 *De raptu*, col. 1024, c. 9. See Corcoran, Chapter 7 on Hincmar's use of Roman law. The evocation of *publicae Romanorum leges* refers above all to the constitution of Constantine on abduction (*CTh.* IX, 24, 1), copied in the Breviary (*Brev. Th.* IX, 19, 1), without however citing the emperor. On the latter and his importance in the history of abduction, see most recently Joye, *La Femme ravie*, pp. 272–8.
18 This title was invented by Sirmond.
19 *De raptu*, col. 1019, c. 4.
20 *Ibid.*, col. 1019, c. 3 (Psalm 69:9): 'Zelus domus tuae comedit me'. As for the king, 'arripiat zelum pro domo Dei' (col. 1020, c. 4).
21 *Ibid.*, col. 1019, c. 3 (2 Corinthinians 11:2).
22 *Ibid.*
23 The production of capitularies was the essential instrument of this project for a new *mise en ordre* of society: M. de Jong, '*Admonitio* and criticism of the ruler at the court of Louis the Pious', in F. Bougard, R. Le Jan and R. McKitterick, eds, *La Culture du haut Moyen Âge. Une question d'élites?* (Turnhout, 2009), pp. 315–38 at p. 319. Eight of the thirty capitularies dealing with abduction between 789 and 981 were intended to remind the audience that abduction was liable to the ban, including the *Summula de bannis* (MGH *Capit.* I, no. 110, p. 224). Most of these texts in fact date to the period of Charlemagne: S. Joye, *La Femme ravie*, pp. 362–3; K. Ubl, *Inzestverbot und Gesetzgebung: die Konstruktion eines Verbrechens (300–1100)* (Berlin, 2008), pp. 270–87. Philippe Depreux, Chapter 8, notes that Hincmar hardly ever cited councils from his own period, and seldom capitularies either, which he usually took from the collection of Ansegis.
24 And not to give assistance to abductors when they sought protection: *De raptu*, col. 1031, c. 18: 'Adjiciunt istiusmodi homines malis suis etiam illam nimis, audacem et punidiendam praesumptionem, ut adulterinis et exsecrandis non conjugiis, sed colluvionibus suis, postulando ac supplicando auctoritatem vel mediatorem religiosorum principum acquirant: quod absit a fidelibus et ministris regni Christi principibus, ut cujusquam improbitas eorum interdictis vel interventionibus adjuvetur'. Merovingian edicts in fact already touched on this voluntary restriction of royal power.

25 Toubert, 'Théorie', p. 255.
26 *De raptu*, col. 1024, c. 9.
27 For instance, M. de Jong, *The Penitential State* (Cambridge, 2009), p. 152. In the *De raptu*, the term *ministerium*, used twice, is reserved for bishops.
28 On this topic, and the increasingly confident claims of bishops to advise the king and to judge his conduct from the 820s, see de Jong, *Penitential State*, esp. pp. 112–47; I. H. Garipzanov, *The Symbolic Language of Authority in the Carolingian World (c. 751–877)* (Leiden, 2008), pp. 301–4.
29 *De raptu*, col. 1031, c. 18: 'Oramus itaque et imploramus a vobis auxilium, quod illi sine dubio debetis, cujus munere floretis atque polletis ut ...' (note that the bishops are requesting help from the king, not offering it to him; it is the bishops who have received the task directly from God of protecting the Christian people, and who then turn to the king). S. Patzold, 'Bischöfe als Träger der politischen Ordnung des Frankenreichs im 8./9. Jahrhundert', in W. Pohl and V. Wieser, eds, *Der frühmittelalterliche Staat: europäische Perspektiven* (Vienna, 2009), pp. 255–68.
30 *De raptu*, col. 1020, c. 4. This passage from Daniel, evoking the succession of empires, is often used as a warning to kings in the Carolingian period: S. Shimahara, 'Daniel et les visions politiques à l'époque carolingienne', *Médiévales*, 55 (2008), 19–32. There is also a short passage devoted to Susannah but, though the story is a common point of reference for good royal judgement and good episcopal advice, Hincmar uses it only to evoke the modest and courageous attitude of Susannah, faced by lewd old men.
31 *De raptu*, col. 1032, c. 20: 'quam plusquam raptor, etiam virtute et potentia regiae potestatis, obtinuerat et detinebat'.
32 *Ibid*, col. 1020, c. 5 . This reference to the *lex naturalis* has subtle links to Isidore of Seville's developments of the *ius naturalis* of the Roman lawyers, as modified in his *Etymologiae*.
33 S. Joye, 'Fabrique d'une loi, fabrique d'un peuple, fabrique des mœurs: les lois barbares', in V. Beaulande-Barraud, J. Claustre and E. Marmursztejn, eds, *La Fabrique de la norme: lieux et mode de production des normes au Moyen Âge et à l'époque moderne* (Rennes, 2012), pp. 91–108 at 106–8.
34 See below, p. 198. The consent of the woman, though an element which in practice facilitates a subsequent marriage, is in theory not an extenuating circumstance; anyone who abducts a consenting woman is still considered the principal wrongdoer in both normative and moral texts.
35 2 Corinthians 7:1.
36 Stone, 'Invention', p. 437.
37 *De raptu*, col. 1020, c. 4; col. 1031, c. 18: 'bruta et irrationabilia jumenta et brutae et perniciosae bestiae'.

38 *Ibid.*, col. 1026, c. 11. See A. Pieniądz, 'Incmaro di Reims e i suoi contemporanei sull'uxoricidio: l'insegnamento della Chiesa e la pratica sociale', *Reti medievali rivista*, 12 (2011), 25–52. I am grateful to Simon Corcoran for drawing my attention to this article; and, for a new reference to Roman law, specifically a rescript of Caracalla (Antoninus), see Corcoran, Chapter 7 p. 152, n.83.

39 R. Stone, '"Bound from either side": the limits of power in Carolingian marriage disputes, 840–870', *Gender and History*, 19 (2007), 467–82, at 476–7. Cf. L. Dossey, 'Wife beating and manliness in late antiquity', *Past and Present*, 199 (2008), 3–40.

40 Joye, *La Femme ravie*, pp. 357–8.

41 On Constantine: J. Evans-Grubbs, 'Abduction marriage in Antiquity: a law of Constantine (*CTh* IX. 24. 1) and its social context', *Journal of Roman Studies*, 79 (1989), 59–83. On the Visigothic kings: S. Joye, 'La transcription du droit de la famille et de la propriété, du droit romain à la loi visigothique', *Mélanges de la Casa de Velázquez*, 41/2 (2011), 35–53.

42 It can already be found under the Merovingians: M. Heinzelmann, '*Pater populi*: langage familial et détention de pouvoir public (Antiquité tardive et très haut Moyen Âge)', in F. Thelamon, ed., *Aux sources de la puissance: sociabilité et parenté. Actes du Colloque de Rouen, 12–13 novembre 1987* (Rouen, 1989), pp. 47–56; R. Le Jan, *La société du haut Moyen Âge (VIe–IXe s.)* (Paris, 2003), pp. 224–6.

43 *De raptu*, col. 1032, c. 20.

44 *Ibid.*, col. 1027, c. 13. On the importance of David as a model for Carolingian kings and laity, see A. Graboïs, 'Un mythe fondamental de l'histoire de France au Moyen Âge: le "roi David" précurseur du "roi très chrétien"', *Revue historique*, 287 (1992), 11–31; P. J. E. Kershaw, *Peaceful Kings: Peace, Power and the Early Medieval Political Imagination* (Cambridge, 2011). Thanks to Rachel Stone for these references. For further references on biblical models for the laity, discussed below, see her forthcoming contribution, 'Beyond David and Solomon: Biblical models for Carolingian laymen', in Steffen Patzold and Florian Bock, eds, *Gott handhaben: Religiöses Wissen im Konflikt um Mythisierung und Rationalisierung* (Berlin, forthcoming).

45 Any carnal relations between David and these women became at once impossible, and Hincmar praised him for having renounced any such relation while continuing to provide for them 'as widows'. Hincmar chose not to evoke the case of Tamar (2 Samuel 13): Tamar's demand, that her attacker Amnon, her own half-brother, should redeem himself by marrying her, did not correspond to Hincmar's propositions.

46 Hincmar does not just emphasise this point in theory. In *AB* s.a. 862, pp. 87–8 (trans. Nelson pp. 97–8), as in his correspondence with the pope, he insisted on the necessity of excommunicating Baldwin and

Judith (paying more attention to the attitude of the woman than in his treatise, as always the case in reality as opposed to theory) and deplored the possibility that they could marry without performing any penance (Hincmar, Epistola 169, ed. E. Perels, MGH *Epp.* 8, p. 145: 'Post quae voluimus ... ut iuxta ecclesiasticam traditionem prius ecclesiae, quam laeserant, satisfacerent et sic demum quod praecipiunt iura legum mundialium exequi procurarent. Sed quoniam litteras vestras, quae inde nihil praeceperunt ... sibi sufficere voluerunt'). On penitence, see R. Meens, 'The historiography of early medieval penance', in A. Firey, ed., *A New History of Penance* (Leyden, 2008), pp. 73–95.

47 S. Shimahara, 'L'exégèse biblique et les élites à l'époque carolingienne: qui sont les recteurs de l'Eglise à l'époque carolingienne?', in F. Bougard, R. Le Jan and R. McKitterick, eds, *La Culture du haut Moyen Âge. Une question d'élites?* (Turnhout, 2009), pp. 201–17, and more generally, P. Wormald and J. L. Nelson, eds, *Lay Intellectuals in the Carolingian World* (Cambridge, 2007).

48 Stone, 'Invention', pp. 445–8.

49 These hesitations can also be found in the Carolingian period concerning the other crime affecting marriage, which occupied more and more space in ecclesiastical discourse: incest. On this subject see P. Corbet, *Autour de Burchard de Worms: l'Église allemande et les interdits de parenté, IXe–XIIe siècle* (Frankfurt am Main, 2001), pp. 45ff.

50 Cf. *Opusculum LV capitulorum*, p. 249, c. 25, in which (in 870) Hincmar explains his position.

51 On the competencies of the two jurisdictions: Joye, *La Femme ravie*, pp. 399–405; P. Daudet, *Études sur l'histoire de la juridiction matrimoniale: les origines carolingiennes de la compétence exclusive de l'église (France et Germanie)* (Paris, 1933).

52 Hincmar, *De divortio*, Responsio 5, p. 141 'qui de talibus negotiis errant cogniti et legibus saeculi sufficientissime praediti'.

53 J. L. Nelson, 'England and the Continent in the ninth century: IV, bodies and minds', *Transactions of the Royal Historical Society*, 6th series, 15 (2005), 1–27, especially 20–1; on the affair of Northild, see now J. L. Nelson, 'Du couple et des couples à l'époque carolingienne', *Médiévales*, 65 (2013), 19–32 at 28–30, who rightly says: 'Mais en matière d'histoire du couple, ce qui ressort clairement du cas de Northild, c'est la prédominance et la connivence des "nobles laïcs" et du clergé pour maintenir le patriarcat'.

54 *De raptu*, col. 1022, c. 7.

55 There is a large bibliography on this organic image, known and discussed by Carolingian elites, and on the question of a single or a double representation of the Church and/or the empire as a body. See for instance the summary and study in S. F. Wemple, 'Claudius of Turin's organic

metaphor or the Carolingian doctrine of corporations', *Speculum*, 49 (1974), 222–37, especially 222–4 and 232–3 on Hincmar. In addition to an organic image properly speaking, though, we can note here the interconnection of different communities, evoked just before this passage at the start of chapter 3 of *De raptu*. Order and the defence of the community must be realised at every level, from the diocese and the kingdom to the family, by those who are capable of action: kings and fathers. Suzanne Wemple sees in Hincmar's thought traces of a reflection on two bodies, the Church and the State; but there is only one body here. See also T. Struve, *Die Entwicklung der organologischen Staatsauffassung im Mittelalter* (Stuttgart, 1978).

56 Y. Thomas, 'L'institution de la Majesté', *Revue de Synthèse*, 112 (1991), 331–86. I am grateful to Professor Jacques Chiffoleau for his comments on *Majesté* and the work of Yan Thomas.

57 S. Joye, 'Carolingian rulers and marriage in the age of Louis the Pious and his sons', in J. L. Nelson, S. Reynolds and S. M. Johns, eds, *Gender and Historiography. Studies in the History of the Earlier Middle Ages in Honour of Pauline Stafford* (London, 2012), p. 106.

58 *De raptu*, col. 1019, c. 3: 'Hujus gloriosae domus Dei decorem, et locum habitationis gloriae ejus, fidelissime diligere et zelari debent non solum episcopi et sacerdotes in sedibus, sed etiam reges in palatiis suis, et regum comites in civitatibus suis, et comitum vicarii in plebibus suis, et quicunque patresfamilias in domibus suis, in unum dives ac pauper, in mente et actibus suis'.

59 *Ibid.*, col. 1018, c. 2: 'paternae auctoritatis'.

60 In the affair of the abduction of Judith, Charles the Bald's daughter, the pope exhorted Charles to cede to the Church's maternal love for Baldwin, the repentant sinner, as a substitute for Carolingian paternal love, as a letter sent by Nicholas I to Ermentrude, mother of Judith (24 November 862) suggests – see Nicholas I, Epistola 8, ed. E. Perels, MGH *Epp.* 6, p. 274 (J2704): 'hanc sanctam monium terrarum matrem Romanam ecclesiam … .Quibus multis divinitus fulta auctoritatibus et sanctorum patrum roborata documentis materno amore solamina sumministrat et sugenda ubera consolationis compatiendo inferre recusat'.

61 See the forthcoming article by Raffaele Savigni, 'L'Église et l'épiscopat des temps carolingiens en temps que corps social' in the proceedings of the colloque *La Productivité d'une crise. Le Règne de Louis le Pieux (814–840) et la transformation de l'Empire carolingien* (Limoges, 17–19 March 2011).

62 On the valorisation of the consensus of the magnates, and the sense of belonging to the *gens Francorum*: Garipzanov, *Symbolic Language*, pp. 263–9. On magnate consent at the end of the reign of Charles the Bald, see S. Patzold, 'Konsens und Konkurrenz: Überlegungen zu einem

aktuellen Forschungskonzept der Mediävistik', *Frühmittelalterliche Studien*, 41 (2007), 75–103.

63 K. F. Morrison, '"Unum ex multis": Hincmar of Rheims' medical and aesthetic rationales for unification', in *Nascità dell'Europa ed Europa carolingia: un'equazione da verificare, 19–25 aprile 1979*. Settimane 27, 2 vols, (Spoleto, 1981), II, pp. 583–718 at 594, notes that Hincmar preferred to depict Christ as a doctor, not a miracle worker.

64 *De raptu*, col. 1019, c. 2 (Genesis 28:17): 'Non est hic aliud, nisi domus Dei et porta coeli'.

65 J. A. Brundage, *Law, Sex and Christian Society in Medieval Europe* (Chicago, 1987), p. 136, on Hincmar's 'coital theory' of marriage. Hincmar develops this theme particularly in his letter about Count Stephen, who wanted to annul his marriage on the pretext of having had sexual relations with a cousin of his wife before they were married, and of not having consummated that marriage: Hincmar, Epistola 136, MGH *Epp.* 8, p. 93: 'quando inter ingenuos et inter aequales fit et paterno arbitrio viro mulier ingenua, legitime dotata et publicis nuptiis honestata sexuum commixtione coniungitur'. J. Gaudemet, 'Indissolubilité et consommation du mariage: l'apport d'Hincmar de Reims', *Revue de droit canonique*, 30 (1980), 28–40; G. Fransen, 'La lettre d'Hincmar de Reims au sujet du mariage d'Étienne: une relecture', in R. Lievens, E. Van Mingroot and W. Verbeke, eds, *Pascua Mediaevalia: Studies voor Prof. Dr. J.M. De Smet* (Leuven, 1983), pp. 133–46. Consent is necessary, but not sufficient: Hincmar barely mentions it in *De raptu*, probably because he was trying to combat the idea that *commixtio sexuum* could be at the origin of marriage.

66 I. Weber, '"*Consensus facit nuptias*". Überlegungen zum ehelichen Konsens in normativen Texten des Frühmittelalters', *Zeitschrift der Savigny-Stiftung für Rechtsgeschichte, Kanonistische Abteilung*, 87 (2001), 31–66; A. E. Laiou, ed., *Consent and Coercion to Sex and Marriage in Ancient and Medieval Societies* (Washington DC, 1993).

67 *De raptu*, col. 1021, c. 6: 'foedus et vinculum nuptiarum'.

68 In the *De raptu, una caro* is evoked to make the couple into the image of Christ's union with the Church, of which he is the head: col. 1025, c. 11. See more broadly, F. Héritier, *Les Deux Sœurs et leur mère: anthropologie de l'inceste* (Paris, 2012), pp. 83–5.

69 L. Barry, *La Parenté* (Paris, 2008), pp. 488–93, 523–6, esp. 490 and 525; cf. E. Porqueres i Gené, 'Cognatisme et voie du sang. La créativité du mariage canonique', *L'Homme*, 154/155 (2000), 335–56, esp. 342–3.

70 Barry, *La Parenté*, pp. 488–93, 505–6, 523–6.

71 K. Cooper, *The Virgin and the Bride: Idealized Womanhood in Late Antiquity* (Cambridge MA, 1996).

72 *De raptu*, col. 1020, c. 4.

73 *Ibid.*, col. 1031, c. 18; col. 1033.
74 Le Jan, *Société*, p. 204, n.165. In the earlier period, things were rather vague, like the status of certain royal companions. See e.g. M. Hartmann, 'Concubina vel regina? Zu einigen Ehefrauen und Konkubinen der karolingischen Könige', *DA*, 63 (2007), 545–67; R. Le Jan, 'Le couple aristocratique au haut Moyen Âge', *Médiévales*, 65 (2013), 33–46.
75 *De raptu*, col. 1031, c. 19.
76 Pierre Toubert noted this development in Jonas of Orléans: P. Toubert, 'Le moment carolingien (VIIIe–Xe siècle)', in A. Burguière, C. Klapisch-Zuber, M. Segalen and F. Zonabend, eds, *Histoire de la famille. I, Mondes lointains, mondes anciens*, pp. 333–59 at 337. On the complexity of *fides* in Héric d'Auxerre, see F. Gross, 'La foi de Charles le Chauve', in J. Hoareau-Dodineau and P. Texier, eds, *Foi chrétienne et églises dans la société politique de l'Occident du Haut Moyen Âge (IVe–XIIe siècle)* (Limoges, 2005), pp. 175–86.
77 Toubert, 'Théorie', p. 253. The praise of *fides* is in *De cavendis vitiis et virtutibus exercendis*, ed. D. Nachtmann, MGH Quellen zur Geistesgeschichte des Mittelalters 16 (Munich, 1998), I, 9, pp. 162–70.
78 *De raptu*, col. 1029, c. 15.
79 On this subject, see the forthcoming article by Régine Le Jan, 'Amitié, haine, famille et politique à l'époque de Louis le Pieux', in *La Productivité d'une crise. Le Règne de Louis le Pieux (814–840) et la transformation de l'empire carolingien* (conference held at Limoges, 17–19 March 2011).
80 Hrabanus Maurus, *Liber de Reverentia filiorum erga patres et subditorum erga reges* addressed to Louis the Pious after 833 (Epistola 15, ed. E. Dümmler, MGH *Epp.* 5, pp. 403–15). The influence of Pseudo-Cyprian, *De duodecim abusivis saeculi*, who placed the *rex iniquus* and the *adolescens sine oboedientia* among the worst kinds of people, is evident in the period.
81 Toubert, 'Théorie', p. 258.
82 S. Airlie, '*Semper fideles*? Loyauté envers les Carolingiens comme constituant de l'identité aristocratique', in R. Le Jan, ed., *La Royauté et les élites dans l'Europe carolingienne (début du IXe aux environs de 920)* (Villeneuve d'Ascq, 1998), pp. 129–43.
83 S. Joye, 'Le rapt de Judith par Baudoin (862): un "*clinamen sociologique*"?', in F. Bougard, L. Feller and R. Le Jan, eds, *Les Élites au haut Moyen Âge: crises et renouvellements* (Turnhout, 2006), pp. 361–79.
84 *AB* s.a. 862, p. 91 (trans. Nelson, p. 100). C. Brühl, 'Hinkmariana II: Hinkmar in Widerstreit von kanonische Recht und Politik in Ehefragen', *DA*, 20 (1964), 55–77.
85 Charles's reputation as a vengeful father surfaces even in some modern authors: H. Sproemberg, 'Judith. Koenigin von England, Graefin von

Flandern', *Revue belge de philologie et d'histoire*, 15 (1936), 397–428, 915–50 at 917.

86 Liable to capital punishment according to the *sacrae leges*, according to Hincmar in *AB* s.a. 873, p. 190 (trans. Nelson p. 181), in other words the laws of Christian Roman emperors, as Simon Corcoran, Chapter 7, reminds us.

87 S. Joye, 'Gagner un gendre, perdre des fils? Désaccords familiaux sur le choix d'un allié au haut Moyen Âge', in M. Aurell, ed., *La parenté déchirée: les luttes intrafamiliales au Moyen Âge* (Turnhout, 2010), pp. 79–94 at 92–3.

11

'The praetor does concern himself with trifles': Hincmar, the polyptych of St-Remi and the slaves of Courtisols[1]

Josiane Barbier

The monastery of St-Remi of Rheims produced in the ninth century a remarkable and detailed estate survey or polyptych. Even though this polyptych survives only in later copies, I shall try to show in what follows that Archbishop Hincmar of Rheims left his trace on the lost original manuscript, in the shape of a *nota* mark in the margin of the description of the monastery's estate of Courtisols (Marne), and then try to discern the reasons for the prelate's personal involvement in the management of the Rheims estates, as revealed by this graphical element.

The manuscript tradition of the polyptych of St-Remi

There has been considerable recent progress in our understanding of this polyptych and its surviving copies. The 1980s were marked by a renewal of interest in Carolingian polyptychs generally, and other accounting documents of the early Middle Ages. This interest focused on the codicological and palaeographical critique of the manuscripts in which these documents were transcribed, and revolved around the detailed textual analysis of their contents. New editions of polyptychs were produced, accompanying or leading to a renewal of research on Carolingian administration, communication and rural history.[2] The polyptych of St-Remi of Rheims did not escape this trend. Within a decade, a study by Britta Lützow (1979), a new edition by Jean-Pierre Devroey (1985) and a substantial article, co-written by François Dolbeau and Pierre Desportes (1986), transformed the understanding of this Carolingian monument, until then known largely though the edition of Benjamin Guérard (1853).[3]

The original manuscript of the polyptych of St-Remi of Rheims has been lost since 1774,[4] but at least three copies of it had been made before then. Two these go back to at least the beginning of the seventeenth century: one is in the Bibliothèque Inguimbertine in Carpentras (MS 1779, fols 260–321), the other at the Bodleian Library in Oxford (MS Eng. Hist. c.242, fols 5–60, 66–70).[5] Both of these remained unknown until François Dolbeau and Pierre Desportes revealed their existence in 1986. The third copy is at the Bibliothèque nationale de France (Paris BnF lat. 9903); it had been found in the holdings of the library (at that point the Bibliothèque Imperiale) by Benjamin Guérard, who attributed it to the diligence of Dom Poirier (end of the eighteenth century), though François Dolbeau put its date back to the years 1680–1720.[6] This Paris copy served as the basis for the editions of B. Guérard and Jean-Pierre Devroey.

All we know about the original manuscript depends on what scholars of the Ancien Régime observed and on what the graphical particularities in these three copies allow us to work out. The issue that has most stimulated discussion is the date of the lost manuscript. During the Ancien Régime, the manuscript was variously attributed to the ninth century (Peiresc, Dom Baluze, Dom Tassin), the tenth (Dom Mabillon) or even the eleventh century (Dom Vincent).[7] The composite nature of the manuscript, revealed by the scribe of the Paris copy – who indicated three different hands, of which one used a 'much more modern script' – doubtless did not help those trying to date it.[8]

The argument of Dom Vincent in favour of attributing the original manuscript to the eleventh century, though apparently based on palaeographical considerations, was in fact wholly founded on the assumption that the manuscript was the work of a single compiler, allowing the text to be dated by its most recent parts.[9] In the preface to his edition, Guérard pointed out the weaknesses of this dating; working from palaeographical elements noted by the Paris copyist and from the content of the polyptych, he proposed dating the manuscript to the ninth century, and then identified additions from the tenth, eleventh and twelfth centuries.[10] Trying to reconcile these findings with the philological evidence, Auguste Longnon a little later suggested that what was lost had been a composite manuscript of the eleventh century.[11] Devroey, based on elements of textual critique, gave his support to this opinion, suggesting that the Rheims polyptych might have been copied in the eleventh century and then received an addition, before another element was added in the twelfth century.[12] This was the best way of harmonising the different theories advanced up to that point. But this did not take into account the copies at Carpentras and Oxford, whose discovery allowed Dolbeau and Desportes to offer a different conclusion to this long debate.

These two scholars showed that, unlike the Paris copy, the copies at Carpentras and Oxford reproduced the ex-libris and the colophons of the original, which were on the upper and lower margins of the manuscript.[13] Two colophons of a scribe named Adam, attested elsewhere, allowed the attribution of an essential part of the lost manuscript to the 'second third of the ninth century'.[14] For Devroey, the presence of these colophons did not in any way contradict the solution he had proposed: 'nothing prevents us imagining that the redactor could have included a copy of the colophon of the scribe Adam in his work, in admiration of a good hexameter, or, more simply, to perpetuate the pious invocation of the author'.[15] One detail, not noticed to my knowledge, confirms nevertheless the earlier dating of the manuscript attributed to the scribe Adam, and can perhaps be put into relation with the activity of Hincmar.

This detail is a monogram drawn in the lateral margins of the copies of Paris, Carpentras and Oxford.[16] In the Paris manuscript, this monogram is on the left part of folio 21^r, at lines 12–15. It takes the form (shown in Figure 4) of a mirror image of an abbreviation of the word *nota* ('Take note!'): the oblique stroke of the N is backwards, the T is placed on the left and not on the right. It should therefore be reconstructed as shown in Figure 5.

In the Carpentras manuscript, this same sign is found on the left margin of fol. 277^r, at line 5. Unlike that in the Paris manuscript, this monogram is not reversed and is as seen in Figure 6. The monogram of the Oxford manuscript, which is not reversed either, is found on the right-hand margin of folio 40^v, at line 18 (see Figure 7).

The existence of this monogram in three copies which, according to Dolbeau, have no relation to each other is an indication of its presence in the original. Moreover, the fact that this monogram had been copied in the Paris manuscript allows this manuscript's rehabilitation, because the discovery of the colophons of Adam only in the manuscripts of Carpentras and Oxford could have led to doubts over the Paris copyist's diligence. If the Paris copyist did not copy the colophons of Adam, it is doubtless because they had disappeared from the original manuscript: the top and bottom margins of this manuscript

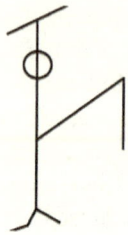

4 *Nota* mark from Paris, BnF lat. 9903, fol. 21ʳ (redrawn).

5 Reconstructed *nota* mark.

6 *Nota* mark from Carpentras, Bibliothèque Inguimbertine, MS 1779, fol. 277ʳ (redrawn).

7 Bodleian Library, MS Eng. Hist. c.242, fol. 40ᵛ – an early modern copy of the polyptych of St-Remi, showing a *nota* mark next to the list of the Courtisols witnesses (with permission of The Bodleian Library, University of Oxford)

had perhaps been cropped between the moment when Peiresc saw it and had it copied, and when the Paris copyist did his work.

In all three copies, the *nota* mark relates to a passage of the polyptych that describes a very important Rheims property, Courtisols (see appendix, pp. 221–2, for the overall structure of the entry).[17] Like other sections of the polyptych, the section on Courtisols begins by describing the land there run directly by the monastery, then sets out in detail the holdings of tenants with their obligations, before giving a concise summary of this information. The Courtisols description also has, however, some more unusual features. The *nota* mark draws the reader's attention to one of these, just before the summary: a list of names of 'witnesses to the aforementioned matter' (*testes pręscriptae rei*) whose precise function must be determined.[18] The concordance between the three traditions leads one to think that that, although reversed in the Paris copy, the monogram was in this place in the original manuscript.[19]

The *nota*, being alongside the list of the *testes pręscriptae rei*, must have been written by someone interested in the identity of these witnesses. This was most likely someone involved in the management of Courtisols shortly after the description of the estate was put into writing. That moment can be quite closely dated thanks to the insertion, after the estate summary, of another unusual feature of the Courtisols description, the record of a judgment given against the estate's slaves (*mancipia*) on 13 May 847.[20] Since in the description of Courtisols, a little higher up, there is a list of 'slaves, male and female, recently repressed' (*servi et ancillę noviter repressi*), some of whom had been returned to their original status by this judgment, one can suggest without great risk that the description of Courtisols must have been put into writing shortly after May 847.[21] It cannot have been long afterwards that the *nota* mark was added in the margin beside the list of witnesses.

The existence and the dating of this marginal abbreviation confirm that this part of the original was indeed, as Dolbeau proposed, from the middle of the ninth century. For even if one can admit (following Devroey) that the colophons of Adam could have been reproduced by an eleventh-century copyist impressed by his predecessor's demand for prayer, it is much less likely that this copyist would have transcribed so exactly an earlier annotation that drew attention to out-of-date information, a mark whose use was as unremarkable in his time as in the ninth century, when the witnesses were alive and someone needed their names.

The 'aforementioned matter' (pręscripta res) and its witnesses

To understand the significance of the list of 'witnesses of the aforementioned matter', we must first identify the 'matter' (*res*) in question. The first hypothesis that comes to mind is that it was the estate description itself, whose summary (*summa praescriptae Augutiore curte*) immediately follows the listing of the *testes pręscriptae rei*.[22] According to this hypothesis, one would expect to find the term 'witness' (*testis*) in the other estate descriptions of the polyptych. Yet the word *testis* occurs only three times in the polyptych, in all the layers of redaction taken together. The first time is here.[23] The second comes a few lines further down, in the account of the May 847 public judgment (*placitum publicum*) already mentioned, concerning the slaves of Courtisols, in which the testimony of very old witnesses (*testes senissimi*) served to defeat the accused.[24] The third time is in the record of the granting (*traditio*) of Condé-sur-Marne by a royal representative (*missus*) to the representatives (*missi*) of Archbishop Hincmar: the *testes* were those who had observed this grant, and whose witnessing would help (if necessary) defend at court the rights of St-Remi.[25] So, in the polyptych of St-Remi, the term *testes* does not designate the people who witnessed the estate inquiry: these were not given any title except that of 'swearer' (*juratus*), as they simply took an oath.[26]

As a result, one is led to conclude that, in the passage examined here, the 'witnesses' cannot be these 'swearers', and so the *pręscripta res* cannot refer to the estate description of Courtisols. This matter (*res*) must instead have been of the same nature as the *placitum* and the *traditio* – that is, a public legal process – and probably, according to the technical sense of *res*, a judicial matter. And it must also be something already mentioned. The only matter of this nature – and the only event – that one can find in the description of Courtisols is the recent 'repression' of the *servi* and *ancillae* listed a few lines before, even though the act of 'repression' is only present implicitly through the expression *servi et ancillę noviter repressi* that heads the list of names.[27]

So the 'witnesses of this aforementioned matter' were people who had in one way or another participated in this 'repression'. As a second hypothesis, therefore, one might wonder whether this repression was part of the judgment of May 847; in which case these witnesses were those of that legal process, or had been involved in the return of the *mancipia* to their original status after the judicial defeat. If that were so, the names of these *testes* would have been identical to those witnesses called upon during the process, or those who signed the record of the judgment.

But this is not the case either. The record of the judgment does indeed name 'very old witnesses' (*testes senissimi*) whose testimony proved so damaging for the slaves (*mancipia*) in May 847, but none of these names can be found among the nine *testes prescriptae rei*.[28] The May judgment was also subscribed by twenty-six named individuals, but of these only the mayor Adroinus (the fifth subscriber) and a certain Betto (the ninth subscriber) can be found among the *testes prescriptae rei*.[29] The seven other *testes prescriptae rei* were the estate deacon Hagroinus, who did not appear at all in the May judgment, and the first six jurors (*scabini*) mentioned by the judgment. Along with two other jurors, these six pronounced the judgment condemning the *servi* and *ancillae* brought before them to be returned to their servile condition.[30] In other words, the nine *testes prescriptae rei* were the two estate officers of Courtisols, six jurors of the archiepiscopal tribunal of Courtisols and one subscriber of the judgment of 847. These local notables were undoubtedly honourable 'witnesses', whose word would carry weight in law in a defence of the rights of Rheims. Nevertheless, they had not been witnesses, properly speaking, during the judgment of 847.

As a result, one must question whether the *prescripta res* was that judgment. In any case, just nine *servi* and *ancillae* were named as 'repressed' by the *placitum*, whereas the list of 'recently repressed' *servi et ancillae* lists forty-two people returned to servile status.[31] It is therefore likely that after the legal process of 847, which had brought into the open the attempt of the grandchildren of two slaves, Berta and Avila, to escape their condition, the Rheims authorities began a complementary enquiry to clarify the status of all the dependants of St-Remi at Courtisols.[32] It was this enquiry that led to the 'repression' of the forty-two individuals listed separately and to the establishment of an exhaustive list of their names and family connections.[33] It must have been this complementary enquiry, and probably a new judgment, indispensable to return the *mancipia* unmasked in this way to their original status, to which the expression *prescripta res* refers.[34] The *testes prescriptae rei* were those who participated in this new judicial action, strengthened by what had happened before the representatives of Hincmar in May 847.

The reader who entered the *nota* mark against the list of the *testes pręscriptae rei* wanted therefore to be able easily and rapidly to find in the manuscript the names of people whose testimony had returned all Saint Remigius's *mancipia*, and whose involvement guarded against any potential repeat. One can see here, quite specifically, how the St-Remi polyptych could have been used by the agents of the lord of Courtisols. That lord was none other than Archbishop Hincmar, because the monastery of St-Remi was part of the Rheims *episcopium* between the end of the seventh century and 945.[35]

Hincmar and the slaves of Courtisols

Hincmar devoted much time and energy, at the beginning of his archiepiscopate, to restoring Rheims's property, damaged by several years of vacancy of the see.[36] In particular, he ensured the production of estate inventories of his Church's properties as well as, it seems, a general polyptych covering the properties of the bishopric of Rheims and its dependent monasteries.[37] It is to his initiative that we owe a large part of the polyptych of St-Remi, which one might suppose was created for the restoration of the monastery's temporal and the elevation of the relics of Saint Remigius on 1 November 852.[38]

Using manuscripts from the Rheims library of Hincmar, Jean Devisse painstakingly reconstituted the way in which the archbishop worked, reviewing the methods which allowed the prelate to produce such a considerable body of writing.[39] In the documentation which Hincmar gathered together while composing his treatises and his letters, the passages from the authorities that were most important for his argument were signalled in the margin by a *nota* (or *notandum*) mark. These graphical signs, which allowed this workaholic to find essential information rapidly, and which Devisse found in many manuscripts, were written by the archbishop's secretaries or by Hincmar himself.[40]

This tracking technique is the same as that used in the polyptych of St-Remi for the Courtisols affair. Its graphic design – even though it is known only through copies – links it closely to the *nota* marks identified by Devisse in Hincmar's autograph manuscripts.[41] If a more thorough investigation confirmed this identification, we would have evidence of the prelate's personal, direct involvement in the inventory and management of his church. This would only really confirm what is already known of his activities as an administrator.[42] But it would also demonstrate that the archbishop paid particular attention to the Courtisols affair.

Indeed, the tribunal of the estate of Courtisols, part of the Rheims judicial immunity,[43] had been summoned on his order (*ordinante Ingmaro archiepiscopo*) and had been presided over by two members of his entourage sent for this purpose, the priest Sigloard and the aristocrat Dodilo.[44] These *missi* of Hincmar were not people of little consequence. Sigloard was the schoolmaster of the cathedral – he later became an archdeacon often called upon by the prelate in diocesan administration – and Dodilo was a vassal of the archbishop.[45] These close associates of Hincmar were accompanied by another person also probably from his entourage, the 'chancellor' Heronodus.[46] They had all been convened following a legal complaint brought against the nine *mancipia* (*sonum de istis et his mancipiis*).[47] It is possible that the author of this complaint was the monk Leidradus – the only subscriber to the judgment labelled as *monachus* – who could have been the monk of St-Remi entrusted with the administration of Courtisols.[48]

Was the Hincmarian eagerness to deliver the solemn 'justice of Saint Remigius' just a manifestation of the rigorous way in which Hincmar normally acted?[49] Did the recently appointed archbishop seize this opportunity to affirm his insistence on taking back into his hands his church's property, and his determination to make sure the law (his law) was respected? Or was the Courtisols affair genuinely worrying?

The Courtisols affair must have unsettled the archbishop when he realised the proportion of the *mancipia* at Courtisols who had apparently almost succeeded in changing their status, given that their 'obligations had been unjustly held back and neglected for a long time' (*servicium multis diebus injuste retentum vel neglectum*).[50] There were forty-two of them, almost a third of the estate's slaves.[51] What must also have unsettled him were the mechanisms which had permitted these unfree dependants to slide towards freedom. It was probably thanks to their settlement on holdings (*mansi*), and because the great majority of these holdings were held by free men (*ingenui*), that the slaves had been able to claim to be free. A minority among tenants of servile holdings (only 19% of the tenants of servile holdings were *mancipia*) and a tiny minority among tenants of free holdings (just 2.4% of tenants of free holdings were *mancipia*), it was all the easier for them to state that they were free, since their co-tenants – those who shared the holdings with them – were.[52] One can see that at

Courtisols in the middle of the ninth century, the distinction between *mancipia* and *ingenui* was purely legal, and in practice fragile, and that it tended to fade away in favour of an improvement of status: only a mark of discrimination, like an obligation to *servicium* guaranteed by strict seigneurial control, could distinguish the two conditions in everyday life.[53]

There may have been another source of worry for Hincmar: it is not impossible that the 'repressed' *mancipia* had benefited from the tacit complicity of their neighbours. For, of the free co-tenants of the repressed *mancipia* named in the description of the estate, none witnessed or took part in either the judgment of May 847 or the *repressio* that followed, abstaining whether from ignorance, indifference, caution or sympathy.[54] This apparent village apathy was perhaps a form of passive resistance to the power of the Rheims lord (and to the *descriptio* itself). It is equally possible that episcopal authority thought it best (because of this resistance?) to rely only on those free men of Courtisols who had no shared interests with *mancipia*:

> the judicial process ... left to one side all the free men living in a community of exploitation with the *servi* and *ancillae* on the holdings ... whether their servile associates were included or not in the category of *servi noviter repressi*'.[55]

The witnesses, the jurors and the subscribers to the judgment (and thus the *testes prescriptae rei* too), all of whom were *ingenui* at the head of holdings or plots of land (*accolae*), represented in the end less than 15% of the tenants of Courtisols.[56]

Whatever the case, the situation required the solemn affirmation of the right of the lord, and the decisive re-establishment of 'the justice of St Remigius', by law and by writing.[57]

Conclusion: the stakes for Hincmar's documentation

As the question of the status of the *servi* and *ancillae* of Courtisols had clearly come up in relation to establishing who had holdings on the estate,[58] it is likely that the problem had arisen in the course of putting together a description of the estate's tenures. This shows that the production of the polyptych of St-Remi was already under way in May 847.[59] The inventory of the rights of St-Remi, a precondition to their description, had led to a local mini-revolution, which showed itself, conforming to the etymology of revolution, to be a return to the past.

The polyptych of St-Remi and the slaves of Courtisols

Hincmar's way of preventing any new social outburst seems to have been to produce, as he habitually did, as complete a written record as possible,[60] extending the sections of the estate descriptions that listed dependants along with their precise status. The remarkably detailed form of the descriptions of Courtisols and Viel-Saint-Remi in this regard may have been a direct consequence of this affair.[61] The scrupulous transcription into the polyptych of these lists, with the record of the judgment of 847 and the list of 'witnesses of the aforementioned affair' specially convened for this reason,[62] completed these preventative measures at Courtisols. Finally, the *nota* mark added to the margin of the list of *testes prescriptae rei* – perhaps added by the archbishop as he read over the polyptych – served to draw the attention of his agents to the people best placed to watch over and, if necessary, constrain the *mancipia* of the estate.

The polyptych of St-Remi undeniably carries the stamp of Hincmar's personality and preoccupations in those sections compiled in the middle of the ninth century. This administrative tool in the service of Rheims's rights was supposed to guarantee the integrity of monastic property and conserve the social order desired by God.[63] Through the care given to its redaction, it was supposed to permit efficient management of the patrimony of St-Remi. But the thoroughness of its details was also supposed to reassure a prelate who kept an eye on everything, and whose fundamental character trait, according to Devisse, was uneasiness.[64]

Appendix: The *nota* and the structure of the entry for Courtisols in the Paris manuscript

NOMINA OMNIUM SERVORUM VEL ANCILLARUM interius et exterius de eadem villa ... *[beginning of the list of the Courtisols slaves]*

SERVI ET ANCILLĘ NOVITER REPRESSI ... *[beginning of the list of 'recently repressed' slaves]*

Major ... *[beginning of the description of the tenures and obligations of the mayor and the cellarer]*

	Est in praescripta villa ecclesia ... *[beginning of the description of the church]*
[Nota in margin]	TESTES PRESCRIPTAE REI ... *[beginning of the list of 'witnesses of the aforementioned affair']*
	SUMMA PRAESCRIPTAE Augutiore curte ... *[beginning of the summary of the estate of Courtisols]*
	ORDINANTE INGMARO ARCHIEPISCOPO ... *[beginning of the record of the court judgment of 13 May 847]*

Notes

1 This article is an updated version of my '*De minimis curat praetor*: Hincmar, le polyptyque de Saint-Remi de Reims et les esclaves de Courtisols', in G. Constable and M. Rouche, eds, *Auctoritas: mélanges offerts à Olivier Guillot* (Paris, 2006), pp. 267–79.

2 On this: Y. Morimoto, 'État et perspectives des recherches sur les polyptyques carolingiens', *Annales de l'Est*, 40 (1988), 99–149; Y. Morimoto, 'Autour du grand domaine carolingien: aperçu critique des recherches récentes sur l'histoire rurale du haut Moyen Âge (1987–1992)', in A. Verhulst and Y. Morimoto, eds, *L'Économie rurale et l'économie urbaine au Moyen Âge* (Ghent, 1994), pp. 25–79; Y. Morimoto, 'Aperçu critique des recherches sur l'histoire rurale du haut Moyen Âge: vers une synthèse équilibrée (1993–2004)', in Y. Morimoto, *Études sur l'économie rurale du haut Moyen Âge: historiographie, régime domanial, polyptyques carolingiens* (Brussels, 2008), pp. 133–88. Most recently: É. Renard, 'Administrer des biens, contrôler des hommes, gérer des revenus par l'écrit au cours du premier Moyen Âge', in X. Hermand, J.-F. Nieus and É. Renard, eds, *Décrire, inventorier, enregistrer entre Seine et Rhin au Moyen Âge: formes et usages des écrits de gestion* (Paris, 2012), pp. 7–36.

3 B. Lützow, 'Studien zum Reimser Polyptychum sancti Remigii', *Francia*, 7 (1979), 19–99; *Le polyptyque et les listes de cens de l'abbaye de Saint-Remi de Reims (IXe–XIe siècles)*, ed. J.-P. Devroey (Rheims, 1984); P. Desportes and F. Dolbeau, 'Découverte de nouveaux documents relatifs au Polyptyque de Saint-Remi de Reims. À propos d'une édition récente', *Revue du Nord*, 68 (1986), 575–607; *Polyptyque de l'abbaye de Saint-Remi de Reims ou dénombrement des manses, des serfs et des revenus de cette abbaye vers le milieu du neuvième siècle de notre ère*, ed. B. Guérard (Paris, 1853).

4 Desportes and Dolbeau, 'Découverte', 576.

5 *Ibid.*, 576–81.

6 *Polyptyque*, ed. Guérard, p. III; Desportes and Dolbeau, 'Découverte', 581.
7 *Ibid.*, 590-1; Dom Vincent, 'Notice d'un ancien polyptique', *Le Journal des Sçavans pour l'année MDCCLXX*, juin, vol. II (Paris, 1770), 415-21, at 416-17.
8 Bibliothèque nationale de France (BnF) lat. 9903, fols 12^v, 40^r.
9 Vincent, 'Notice', 416-17.
10 *Polyptyque*, ed. Guérard, pp. vii-xii.
11 A. Longnon, *Étude sur les* pagi *du diocèse de Reims* (Paris, 1872), appendice A, pp. 111ff.
12 *Le polyptyque*, ed. Devroey, pp. xl-xli.
13 Desportes and Dolbeau, 'Découverte', 583.
14 *Ibid.*, 583-5. The colophon of Adam is this hexameter: *Adam sydereum mereatur scandere regnum*. The same colophon signed a manuscript [BnF lat. 10911] dated by Bernard Bischoff to 828-50, a dating which means that chapters XI-XII and XIV-XXVI in Guérard's edition (= pp. 73-6, 9-62, ed. Devroey) might have been copied by Adam.
15 Observations of J.-P. Devroey on the article of P. Desportes and F. Dolbeau, appended to that article, pp. 605-7 (here at 607).
16 I am grateful to Charles West, who consulted the copy at Oxford and obtained the photograph which illustrates this article.
17 The description of Courtisols corresponds to chapter XVII of Guérard's edition. It occupies pp. 16-29 in the Devroey edition.
18 These *testes* are named at p. 28, at ll. 1-3 in the Devroey edition. On their function, see below, pp. 216-17.
19 The Paris copyist could have reversed the monogram by tracing it backwards.
20 The *testes prescriptae rei* are cited at p. 28, ll. 1-3; the *summa* is at ll. 4-17; it precedes the record of the *placitum* of 13 May 847, copied at ll. 18-44 (and p. 29, ll. 1-19). The use of the judgment to estimate the date of the Courtisols description goes back to Guérard: *Polyptyque*, ed. Guérard, p. vii; see also Lützow, 'Studien', 74-80, *Le Polyptyque*, ed. Devroey, p. xli. The judgement is dated as III ides of May (13 May) in the sixth year of King Charles the Bald (846) and the third year of Archbishop Hincmar (847). The accepted date is sometimes 847 (M. Stratmann, *Hinkmar von Reims als Verwalter von Bistum und Kirchenprovinz* (Sigmaringen, 1991), p. 12), sometimes 848 (Lützow, 'Studien', 28; *Le Polyptyque*, ed. Devroey, p. xli, following Schrörs, *Hinkmar*, p. 48), but 847 seems more likely, because the counting of the years of the episcopate might be more reliable than that of the regnal years in a Rheims church document. J.-P. Devroey, 'Libres et non-libres sur les terres de Saint-Remi de Reims: la notice judiciaire de Courtisols (13 mai 847) et le polyptyque d'Hincmar', *Journal des Savants*, 1 (2006), 65-103, at 65, n.1 adopted that date: a

judicial assembly cannot have been summoned for 13 May 848, since it was a Sunday, and what is more, the feast of Pentecost.

21 Lützow, 'Studien', 80; *Le Polyptyque*, ed. Devroey, p. xli (after 848). The list of *servi et ancillę noviter repressi* (*Le Polyptyque*, ed. Devroey, p. 27, ll. 3–18) is transcribed before the description of the holdings and obligations of the mayor and cellarer (*ibid.*, p. 27, ll. 19–26); this is in turn followed by a description of the village church (*ibid.*, p. 27, ll. 27–45), itself followed by the list of *testes pręscriptae rei* (*ibid.*, p. 28, ll. 1–3): see appendix at end of chapter.

22 Lützow, 'Studien', 74; *Le Polyptyque*, ed. Devroey, p. lxi.

23 *Le Polyptyque*, ed. Devroey, p. 28, l. 1.

24 *Ibid.*, p. 28, l. 34.

25 *Ibid.*, p. 71, l. 41, p. 72, l. 4.

26 There are only three references to these oaths: *ibid.*, p. 71, l. 5; p. 88, l. 16 (in both cases, one finds the expression 'isti juraverunt'); p. 76, l. 33 ('jurati dixerunt'). The terms *jurati* and *jurare* are used in the same way in the polyptych of St-Germain-des-Prés (the references are given in *Polyptyque de l'abbaye de Saint-Germain des Prés rédigé au temps de l'abbé Irminon*, tome II: *Texte du polyptyque*, ed. A. Longnon, Paris, 1886): descriptions of Palaiseau (II. *De Palatiolo*, § 120, p. 28: 'Isti juraverunt'); Épinay-sur-Orge (VI. *De Spinogilo*, § 56, p. 74: 'Isti juraverunt'); Villemeux (IX. *De Villamilt*, § 295, pp. 148–9: 'Isti jurati dixerunt de decania Warimberti ... De decania Acledulfi similiter dixerunt ... De decania Grivoldi similiter dixerunt'); Boissy-Maugis (XIII. *De Buxido*, § 111, p. 201: 'Isti sunt qui juraverunt'), Thiais (XIV. *De Theodaxio*, § 89, p. 216: 'Isti juraverunt') and Chavannes (XXIII. *De Cavannas vel de Lodosa*, § 28, p. 316: 'Isti dixerunt jurati').

27 *Le Polyptyque*, ed. Devroey, p. 27, l. 3. Devroey, 'Courtisols', 93, n.65, maintains that conclusion.

28 *Le Polyptyque*, ed. Devroey, p. 28, l. 34–6. Guérard was the first to compare the names of the *testes praescriptae rei* with those appearing in the *placitum* of 847 (*Polyptyque*, ed. Guérard, p. VII); see the more systematic inquiry in Lützow, 'Studien', 74–80.

29 *Le Polyptyque*, ed. Devroey, p. 29, ll. 9–10, p. 28, l. 1; p. 29, l. 11, p. 28, l. 3.

30 *Ibid.*, p. 28, ll. 43–4.

31 *Ibid.*, p. 28, ll. 29–30, p. 29, l. 16; p. 27, ll. 3–18.

32 *Ibid.*, p. 28, ll. 25–6, 36–9.

33 Here I depart from the interpretation of J.-P. Devroey (in his edition, p. xli), who attributes the difference between the list of *mancipia* repressed after the May 847 *placitum* and the list of *servi et ancillę noviter repressi* to a chronological gap, noting the reference to new children.

34 F.-L. Ganshof, 'Charlemagne et l'administration de la justice dans la monarchie franque', in W. Braunfels, ed., *Karl der Grosse, Band I: Persönlichleit und Geschichte* (Düsseldorf, 1965), pp. 394–419 at p. 402: disputes over personal status were usually investigated by the comital court, presided over by the count.
35 *Le Polyptyque*, ed. Devroey, p. xciv.
36 J. Devisse, *Hincmar, Archevêque de Reims 845–882*, 3 vols (Geneva, 1975–76), I, pp. 105–13; Stratmann, *Hinkmar als Verwalter*, pp. 45–53; M. Sot, *Un historien et son église au Xe siècle: Flodoard de Reims* (Paris, 1993), pp. 493–7 (and pp. 478–84 for Ebbo's deposition, in 835/41).
37 *Le Polyptyque*, ed. Devroey, pp. lvi–lvii; Stratmann, *Hinkmar als Verwalter*, p. 46.
38 On Hincmar's involvement with St-Remi: Stratmann, *Hinkmar als Verwalter*, p. 54; Sot, *Un Historien*, p. 502.
39 Devisse, *Hincmar*, II, pp. 917 ff.
40 *Ibid.*, II, pp. 924–6.
41 *Ibid.*, II, p. 925.
42 See Stratmann, *Hinkmar als Verwalter*.
43 On the court of the immunity and the problems of jurisdiction it generated, see Stratmann, *Hinkmar als Verwalter*, pp. 12, 25 and esp. 41. On the jurors created by the immunity-holder, see Ganshof, 'Charlemagne', p. 401, n.49.
44 *Le Polyptyque*, ed. Devroey, p. 28, ll. 19–21. From the manuscripts of Paris and Carpentras, Sigloardus's subscription is 'omnibus his veris indiciis regiius [*corr.* rogitus] interfui et manu propria subscripsi.' The term *rogitus*, derived from the verb *rogare*, indicates a witness or a notary; it emphasises that the person thus labelled had acted on behalf of a third party (here, Hincmar). See B.-M. Tock, *Scribes, souscripteurs et témoins dans les actes privés en France (VIIe–début du XIIe siècle)* (Turnhout, 2005), pp. 216–17.
45 For Sigloard, see Flodoard, *HRE* III-28, pp. 354–6; Stratmann, *Hinkmar als Verwalter*, pp. 25–7.
46 His rank can be deduced from his place among the subscribers of the judgment (*Le Polyptyque*, ed. Devroey, p. 29, ll. 7–8), after the priest Sigloardus (first subscriber) and before Dodilo (third subscriber). This chancellor is said to have written the judgment (*scripsi*; but should one not correct this to [*sub*]*scripsi*?); he is distinct from the notary of the court record, the 'chancellor' Hairoaldus, who authenticated and signed it. Hairoaldus should probably be identified with a monk of St-Remi deposed in 853 at the Council of Soissons for having been ordained by Ebbo (Flodoard, *HRE* III-11, p. 211; Devisse, *Hincmar*, I, pp. 91–6).
47 *Le Polyptyque,* ed. Devroey, p. 28, l. 23.
48 *Ibid.*, p. 29, l. 9.

49 Devisse, *Hincmar*, II, pp. 861, 964.
50 *Le Polyptyque*, ed. Devroey, p. 29, ll. 1–2.
51 *Ibid.*, p. 26, ll. 16–41 and p. 27, ll. 1–2: not including the *repressi*, there were eighty-one *servi* and *ancillae* at Courtisols.
52 Of the nine *servi* 'repressed' by the May 847 judgment (*Le Polyptyque*, ed. Devroey, p. 28, ll. 29–30, p. 29, l. 10), seven were men and two women. From the list of *servi et ancillę noviter repressi*, we learn that the latter were the sister and niece of one of the men (*ibid.*, p. 27, ll. 7–8). Of the seven men, six can be found in the description of Courtisols (had the seventh one died?). All had holdings (*mansi*); four had free holdings (*ibid.*, p. 17, ll. 30–1, p. 18, l. 14), two servile ones (*ibid.*, p. 19, ll. 21–2). The four *servi* who were tenants of free holdings were the only *servi* with this kind of holding: they all claimed to be free. Two of them were moreover co-tenants of *ingenui* (*ibid.*, p. 17, ll. 30–1). The two *mancipia* who were tenants of servile holdings were also co-tenants of *ingenui*. More generally, a quarter of *mancipia* with servile holdings had claimed to be *ingenui* (percentage established from the list of *servi et ancillę noviter repressi* and the list of tenants of servile holdings, *ibid.*, p. 19): this is half of those slaves who were co-tenants of servile holdings with *ingenui*. Among the *servi et ancillę noviter repressi* (forty-two names), nine cannot be found elsewhere in the Courtisols record: among them were a shepherd and six women, who perhaps did not have holdings. The proportions given above are based on the lists of tenants of free and servile holdings (*ibid.*, pp. 16–8 and p. 19). This does not include the list of 'women and of some men with holdings in the afore-mentioned estate' (*Haec nomina feminarum et quorundam virorum in praefata curte mansa tenentium*, *ibid.*, pp. 20–2), the nature of whose holdings is unknown and who were all anyway free (labelled as *ingenui*, except one *franca* woman, *ibid.*, p. 21, l. 1, an *accola* without status [copyist error? *ibid.*, p. 21, l. 3] and an *ingenuilis* man, *ibid.*, p. 21, l. 13). On the use of the polyptych's demographic information, especially the notice of Courtisols, see Lützow, 'Studien', 92–9.
53 On the question of 'servitude', see the well-founded perspectives of H.-W. Goetz, 'Serfdom and the beginning of a "seigneurial system" in the Carolingian period: a survey of the evidence', *Early Medieval Europe*, 2 (1993), 29–51. On the 'unfree' of Courtisols, see now Devroey, 'Courtisols'.
54 References at n.52.
55 Devroey, 'Courtisols', 98 and n.74.
56 All can be found in the lists of tenants of free and servile holdings cited above at note 52. One can also find them among the tenants of *accolae* (*Le Polyptyque*, ed. Devroey, pp. 19–20). On these 'coqs de village': Devroey, 'Courtisols', 93–5, 98–9. As above (n.52), the percentage has been estab-

lished without taking into account the list of 'women and of some men with holdings in the afore-mentioned estate'.
57 *Le Polyptyque*, ed. Devroey, p. 28, l. 22.
58 The first *mancipia* convicted of lying, in May 847, were all tenants of holdings, whether free or servile (see n.52).
59 Lützow, 'Studien', 80, also thought that the conflict over the status of the *mancipia* was caused by the estate *descriptio*. According to her, it could have been the listing of these people as *servi* and *ancillae* which sparked things off.
60 Devisse, *Hincmar*, II, p. 828; Stratmann, *Hinkmar als Verwalter*, pp. 5–19.
61 In this hypothesis, the description of Viel-St-Remi could have been carried out in parallel to that of Courtisols, or very soon afterwards. J.-P. Devroey (*Le Polyptyque*, ed. Devroey, p. lxxi) saw in 'la tentative de dénombrement des hommes qui est menée après 848' the evidence for a 'glissement progressif du système domanial pur vers la seigneurie'. The explanation we have proposed, less seductive from a theoretical perspective, seems to us better suited to the local context. The increase in the weight of seigneurial power over these people that followed this census is of course incontestable.
62 Stratmann linked the care given to detailing the names of accusers and witnesses in the May 847 judgment to the norms fixed by Hincmar (for judicial process and how judgments should be written up) in a letter written doubtless only slightly later: Stratmann, *Hinkmar als Verwalter*, p. 12, using Flodoard, *HRE* III–28, pp. 354–5, a letter about a judicial inquiry concerning a priest, addressed to several of his agents, and notably the archpriest Sigloard. In this letter, the archbishop demanded, among other things, that 'a list should be made of all those who were present at the court, priests and laymen, as seemed necessary' (*ibid.*, p. 355: *Describantur quoque omnes, qui in ipso placito fuerint, tam de presbiteris quam de laicis, prout necessitas esse visa fuerit*). It could well be that the names of the *testes prescriptae rei* were noted down after considerations of this kind.
63 On Hincmar's attitudes to Church property: Devisse, *Hincmar*, I, pp. 500ff.; on the social order: *ibid.*, I, pp. 492–3.
64 *Ibid.*, II, pp. 1100–3.

12

Hincmar's parish priests[1]

Charles West

Archbishop Hincmar of Rheims wrote voluminously about the parish and its priest during his long episcopacy (845–82). Author of a treatise dedicated to the status of rural churches, the *Collectio de ecclesiis et capellis*, Hincmar also issued several sets of instructions traditionally labelled 'episcopal capitularies' or 'statutes' to rural priests in his diocese, became involved in fierce controversies over particular churches and touched on related issues in many other texts. His interest in the topic represents an important part of his activities as a pastorally engaged Carolingian bishop, an aspect of his life and work that should not be forgotten amid the attention to his political influence.[2]

If the parish was important for the archbishop, it is also true that the archbishop is important for the history of the parish. This remarkably long-lasting institution was one of the defining elements of the Latin Church in the Middle Ages – and, by extension, of medieval Europe more broadly – and its significance has been underlined by recent research. It lay at the heart of perhaps the most important medieval tax in the shape of the ecclesiastical tithe, it created in its priests a local elite right across Europe and, through the work of those priests, it helped fold scattered and disparate populations into larger cultural and religious networks. Within the historiography of this institution, the Carolingian period often features as a point of origin, for it was then that the parish's economic, social and cultural dimensions began to unfurl: this was when the ecclesiastical tithe was first imposed on the countryside in theory and in practice too in some areas, when we first see rural priests in substantial detail and when, for some historians anyway, the Christianisation of the general rural populace began in earnest. And whenever the Carolingian parish is mentioned, references to Hincmar are bound to follow, for he was the figure with the most developed notion of the parish at the time, or at least the one who wrote the most about it.[3]

His prominence in the narrative of the rise of the parish brings with it the familiar perils of teleology. It can be difficult to see Hincmar's parish as anything other than the embryonic form of an institution that would only later reach full maturity, and this encourages assessment of the Carolingian parish by the standards of later times, according to which it will inevitably be found wanting (for instance in the degree to which it was territorially defined).[4] This approach obscures its existence as a lived and complex reality of the time. To loosen that teleological straitjacket, this chapter does not seek to collate Hincmar's writings to reconstruct a seamless, coherent body of emergent Carolingian thought about a parish system whose subsequent spread throughout the medieval west was either glacial or swift, according to preference, but instead concentrates on tensions and inconsistencies. For Hincmar, the parish was at once timeless and historical, its priest was both part of local society and separated from it, and it was a structure that was simultaneously threatened and dominant. In acknowledging and exploring these three tensions, the intention is to not to belittle Hincmar's role in the history of the medieval parish, but to show how his ideas should be understood with reference to their context and not simply assessed according to their contribution to grand historical narratives.

The parish in time

For Hincmar of Rheims, the parish, understood as a rural church serving the sacramental needs of a defined body of parishioners under the supervision of the bishop, was essentially timeless, a part of the Church from its earliest history. This was proved by texts purporting to be correspondence from the successors of St Peter in Rome: for example, a decree supposedly issued by Pope Denis (d. 268) which declared that every *ecclesia parrochiana* ('parish church') was to be protected and maintained intact. Though Hincmar notoriously had doubts about the authenticity of the Pseudo-Isidorian decretals from which this text was drawn – and with good reason, since they had actually been compiled earlier in the ninth century – he chose not to express them in this context.[5]

In any case, there was plenty of other entirely authentic Late

Antique canon law that talked about *rusticae parrochiae*, which Hincmar took to mean 'rural parishes'.[6] Historians now tend to read these texts differently, though. There were no parishes as such in Late Antiquity, because the churches tasked with pastoral duties in that early period, the *rusticae parrochiae*, were usually owned and run by the bishop, effectively as outposts of the cathedral. This was quite different from parish churches in the Carolingian period and later, which could be owned or controlled by anyone without major consequence for their role in the diocesan network of pastoral care under the local bishop's regulatory supervision.[7] Hincmar himself was, in general, very conscious that the canon-law tradition, already ancient by his day, needed careful interpretation. Indeed, the *Collectio de ecclesiis et capellis*, which he wrote around 858, is chiefly devoted to teasing out exactly what was meant when canon law talked about the *potestas* of the bishop over rural churches.[8] Hincmar was nevertheless confident that, properly interpreted, these texts about the parish meant what they had always meant: a confidence that led him on occasion to adjust the wording of canon law to bring out that meaning more clearly.[9]

Insistent that the structures of parish care, built upon this firm foundation of canon law, should not be changed unnecessarily, Hincmar was however equally aware that the parish was a developing reality that moved with the times, in particular as new churches were constructed.[10] This is made quite clear by a linked pair of disputes between Hincmar and his nephew, Bishop Hincmar of Laon, which intensified in 869–70 as relations between the two worsened. The disagreements concerned churches at Folembray and *Attolae curtis*, of which the former was owned by Rheims but lay in the diocese of Laon, while the latter was owned by Laon but lay in the diocese of Rheims. The disputes turned on the question of whether these churches should be considered as mere chapels dependent upon other churches, at Coucy and *Iuviniaca villa* respectively, or whether they were themselves autonomous and independent parish churches in their own right, as Hincmar of Rheims argued for Folembray, and Hincmar of Laon for *Attolae curtis*.[11] The two cases mirrored each other, and in fact Hincmar of Laon probably targeted Folembray as revenge for Hincmar of Rheims's intervention at *Attolae curtis*.[12] These were not affairs without repercussion. Each bishop placed the church whose status he doubted under interdict, prohibiting the sacraments from being dispensed there. Hincmar of Rheims could name two men, Erleher and Gislehard, who had as a result died without communion at Folembray, while Hincmar of Laon claimed to have compiled a similar list for *Attolae curtis*.[13]

Where Bishop Hincmar of Laon treated the disputes as primarily matters of law – the bishop's authority over churches in his diocese – the archbishop gave questions of history considerable weight too. This was not merely a matter of chronological reckoning. Hincmar of Rheims in fact conceded that the church at *Attolae curtis*, which he maintained was merely a chapel, might well be older than its alleged mother church at *Iuviniaca villa*.[14] But Archbishop Hincmar argued that the date of foundation was not the whole story: circumstances changed over time, and the parish organisation needed to take this into account.[15] While the structure of the parish network should be preserved against arbitrary change, and new churches should not be allowed to thrive at the expense of older ones by taking over their tithes, Hincmar accepted that a degree of adaptation was necessary for the parish to be able to fulfil its remit of providing pastoral care.

Such adaptation did not concern only the shape of the parish network either, for the very rules too might evolve. Hincmar acknowledged that issues could arise in his time and place that had not arisen in the times and places in which the canon law had been decreed. In such cases, he believed a more contemporary Church council could temper the rigidity or severity of the canon law, as appropriate. A good example is the question of whether it was permissible for there to be burials within a church. This was something that a number of influential earlier texts quite clearly forbade, statements which other bishops were using as a pretext to demolish churches. Hincmar's response was that customs could change.[16] Another example of Hincmar's willingness to adapt the parish to the requirements of his age is his innovation in dividing up his diocese into archdeaconries, with an archdeacon in each responsible for monitoring the parishes in his area. This was a way of organising the parish network with a very bright future ahead, but it was largely without precedent.[17]

The parish and its priest

Alongside Hincmar's concern to preserve the parish network without freezing it, a second tension in his ideas about the parish concerned the place of its priest.[18] On the priest fell the weighty responsibility of ministering the sacraments and other requirements of the Christian faith to the villagers, and of ensuring that they took communion regularly. Hincmar understood that, for this to happen effectively, the rural priest had to be part of Frankish rural society, even to the point of being personally involved in agricultural work (*opus rurale*).[19] Rural priests in northern Francia certainly had plenty of time to integrate themselves in their communities, as they could be in position for quite literally decades. The village of Coucy, for instance, was served for twenty years by a priest named Nodalbert; his successor Gozmar acted as Coucy's priest for thirty years until he became too old to carry out his duties and agreed to a replacement; Ermenric, the priest at *Iuviniaca villa*, had also served for over thirty years; the priest Otteric had, it was claimed, served at Folembray for over sixty years, spanning the pontificates of five bishops of Laon.[20] Such a length of service contributed to the stability of the parish system, though at the same time it may well have impeded efforts at reform.

Hincmar sought to ensure that priests like Gozmar and Otteric were not merely embedded in local society, but acted to some degree as its leaders, whatever their origins: horse-riding, property-owning members of the elite who were enjoined to dispense patronage at the Church's expense, in the form of alms and lunches at their own tables.[21] Hincmar encouraged village residents to bring gifts to the church, which the priest could then give away later to those who needed them, making the local church into the focal point of village-level redistribution. While it was not acceptable for priests to be offered bribes or to be paid for their services, it was perfectly all right for them to take thank-you presents – free gifts, so to speak.[22] That this was not merely a hypothetical issue is shown by the church at *Attolae curtis*, which Hincmar noted, without criticism, had benefited from donations of little patches of land by grateful local residents.[23]

Given how entangled these priests were in Frankish society, it is no surprise that Hincmar gave due consideration to their secular legal status. This was an issue that emerged in the dispute concerning Folembray. Priests were meant to be legally free, according to royal and ecclesiastical legislation, but the status of the man that Hincmar had sent to become priest of Folembray, Senatus, was at best ambiguous. Hincmar noted that Senatus was 'from the *potestas*' of Rheims, and described him as a *mancipium* of the Church, a word with an unmistakable ring of dependence. Perhaps heading off a line of attack, Hincmar of Rheims brought this up himself, and even tried to use it as ammunition, criticising his nephew Hincmar of Laon for having prematurely ordained Senatus as an acolyte without waiting for him to be granted 'ecclesiastical' or 'canonical' freedom or manumission.[24] The younger Hincmar wondered in his reply why his uncle had permitted an unfree man to become a cleric, and further accused him of truncating canon law to support his case.[25] Hincmar of Rheims's somewhat unconvincing response was that he had omitted certain sections of a royal capitulary because these sections concerned dependants of individuals, whereas Senatus was a dependant of a church.[26] As in their other confrontations, uncle and nephew fired off tailored legal citations at each other, leaving the facts somewhat obscure (had Senatus actually been ordained as a priest yet?); both however agreed that Senatus's secular legal status had consequences for his status as a priest.

No matter what their formal legal position, many of these priests were caught up in networks of patronage, and owed their position to influential backers. Hincmar of Rheims was, perhaps surprisingly, quite relaxed about these more informal mechanisms of integration into broader Frankish society. He made it quite clear that it was reasonable for the local priest to be appointed at the recommendation of the patrons of the church, and in fact admitted that he had appointed Senatus to Folembray on the request of the lay aristocrat, Sigibert, who held the village as a benefice, just as a previous benefice-holder had recommended an earlier priest. Hincmar insisted that this was not only legitimate and 'according to ancient custom' and 'following the tradition of my predecessors', but cited capitulary legislation to the effect that Sigibert's wishes could not be gainsaid without good reason.[27] Hincmar specified that Sigibert did not personally have anything to gain or lose from whether the church at Folembray was autonomous or not, or whether Senatus was appointed or not. It was simply a matter of showing him the appropriate respect.[28]

In short, Hincmar recognised that priests were and ought to be an integrated part of the local community. Yet he was simultaneously determined that rural priests were to be separated from the communities in which they lived, a separation that was no invention of the eleventh century.[29] Erudition represented one of the crucial mechanisms of this differentiation. Hincmar's rural priests had to be knowledgeable, and capable of transmitting that knowledge.[30] He insisted that they had to possess books, learn their contents by heart and understand them too.[31] Though we have no idea where the books came from, there is reason to believe that these instructions were followed. Quite apart from the evidence of rural church book lists preserved in the polyptych (estate survey) of the monastery of St-Remi that was compiled during Hincmar's archiepiscopate, we know that Senatus of Folembray's own predecessor, a priest named Bertfrid, complained that the priest of Coucy had taken away one of his books, along with other objects, perhaps as a ritual of deconsecration.[32] Failure to live up to these requirements had potentially harsh consequences: in one case, Hincmar ordered a priest in his diocese, who had forgotten what he had learned about his responsibilities, to be imprisoned, in order to teach him a lesson.[33]

Hincmar was clear that rural priests were to be distinct in their behaviour, too. Permitting no more than three rounds of drinks at local gatherings, he sternly warned priests in his diocese against allowing drinking games or dancing bear shows to take place in their presence.[34] They were also urged not to use their local prominence to promote their own family, since their primary obligation was now to the Church.[35] As priests, they were to be considered legally separate, no longer answerable to secular courts but only to ecclesiastical ones.[36] Above all, Hincmar was absolutely insistent on the question of priests' chastity, relentlessly stressing the vital importance of avoiding contact with women, and even devising special purgatory oaths for priests under suspicion.[37] Clearly not all priests shared Hincmar's preoccupation. Godbald, a priest in Hincmar's diocese, was deposed for his relations with a woman named Doda (he took flight, which for Hincmar proved his guilt).[38] Yet there is strikingly little evidence for married priests in Carolingian Francia as a whole, and some priests at least do seem to have internalised anxieties about sexuality (Hincmar offered advice to the bishop of Cambrai about one priest who had castrated himself).[39] And there are hints too that local communities held their priests to these high standards. For instance, Hincmar observed without comment that Bertfrid, Senatus's predecessor at Folembray, had had to leave the village because of rumours about him.[40]

For Hincmar, it was enough for priests to be suspected of erring for them to be brought before an inquiry. Some remarkable passages in Hincmar's second set of episcopal capitularies, which he requested not to be given to rural priests directly, justify the superficially surprising rule that priests might be irrevocably deposed for having committed some sin if it were widely known, but merely subjected to penance if it were not. This was partly a question of practicality, because Hincmar doubted whether it would be easy to prove sins like fornication on the part of priests.[41] It was also however a matter of sensitivity to reputation, concern about bringing the special status of priests into disrepute. Public breaches of the boundary between the priest and the community he served were punished with severity, and ultimately with deposition.

The parish and its enemies

The third tension in Hincmar's ideas about the parish lay in its viability as an institution within the Frankish world. To read Hincmar's works on the matter, one might think the parish structure had enemies all around, against whom vigilance and resolute action were continually required. Lay aristocrats did not always do what they were meant to, for instance by not asking bishops' permission when appointing priests to serve in churches they controlled, and intimidating or corrupting the priests in question.[42] Sometimes local communities fell short of their obligations, for instance in not paying tithes, not listening to the sermons or simply, 'the hardness of the undevout', not making donations to their local churches.[43] Sometimes, it was popes who introduced unwelcome confusion, notably by supporting priests who went to Rome to complain about their bishop, thereby undermining that bishop's authority.[44]

Problems did not only stem from those outside the Frankish Church, though. As we have seen, the rural priests themselves needed to be kept carefully under surveillance. To Hincmar's dismay, they persisted in having fights, drinking too much, not knowing enough, committing usury, not respecting their lords or their peers, conspiring against their bishop and bribing their way into positions.[45] Finally, sometimes it was Hincmar's colleagues, other Frankish bishops, who stepped out of line in their dealings with the parish. Their motives were diverse. Hincmar hinted that the bishop of Laon's actions at Folembray were linked to a personal vendetta against the benefice-holder Sigibert, who happened to be his own brother-in-law. In other cases, though, the root of the matter was that bishops like Prudentius of Troyes, and in fact very plausibly Hincmar of Laon too, understood the existing canon law about rural churches differently from Hincmar of Rheims (who thought they interpreted the canon law 'inconveniently').[46]

To Hincmar, the parish was constantly threatening to slip into disarray. Yet these difficulties need to be understood against the backdrop of a consensus in late Carolingian Francia about the parish church that ultimately reflected a widely shared consensus on what the role of bishops was, details of internal hierarchies aside.[47] Hincmar did not see the parish as struggling against any rival system of pastoral care. The only hint in Hincmar's work of something like the 'minster system' notorious for Anglo-Saxon historians, based around teams of priests serving large areas from central sites, comes in one of his episcopal capitularies. Here, with particular reference to Montfaucon, a house of canons near the River Meuse, Hincmar warned canons and monks against taking over parish churches 'on account of the profits of the tithe'. This is certainly an indication of how lucrative tithes and other revenues from rural churches might be (and Hincmar elsewhere conceded that money could be an inducement for people to become parish priests).[48] He did not however consider this as a rival method of delivering pastoral care, still less a relic of an older system. It was just a potential complication that needed to be avoided, since he doubted whether those based in monasteries would really be able to respond to routine pastoral crises in the middle of the night. Nor for that matter did Hincmar's opponents conceive of rural pastoral care as based around anything other than rural priests in dispersed churches, subjected to proper episcopal scrutiny; disagreements arose simply from diverging notions of what that episcopal scrutiny should be.[49] Not only was there was no viable alternative to the parish in the late Carolingian countryside, no alternative was truly thinkable, whether by Hincmar or anyone else.

The parish in Hincmar's conception of the Church

In Hincmar's view, then, parishes were a timeless, stable feature of the Church, their priests an inviolably separate caste, the institution itself universal and part of the natural order of things. Yet at the same time, he knew that the shape of the parish network was constantly in flux, that priests were necessarily closely involved in local society and that almost all parts of the parish mechanism were vulnerable to breakdown. What should historians make of these tensions framing Hincmar's vision of the parish and its priest?

It might be tempting to ascribe these tensions to a gap between over-reaching ideal and intransigent reality that is sometimes invoked by historians in Carolingian contexts. Whatever the value of this trope in other circumstances, it certainly will not do here.[50] The parish was not merely a theoretical construction confined to Hincmar's scriptorium, it was part of lived reality – and not simply for Hincmar, but for the people who lived in the countryside around Rheims. The parishioners at Folembray and *Attolae curtis*, for example, were active participants in parish life, who not only made donations to their churches, but acted when their community's access to communion, baptism and the last rites was threatened or removed by the absence of a priest. The residents of Folembray lobbied Hincmar over the delayed ordination of Senatus, and did so again following Hincmar of Laon's interdict in February 870; a previous generation had lobbied Pardulf of Laon (d. 857).[51] These communities cherished long-lived memories of previous incumbents, memories upon which Hincmar of Rheims relied to create a list of Folembray's parish priests stretching back around a hundred years to the days of Archbishop Tilpin.

It is true that the cases of Folembray and *Attolae curtis*, often referred to above, are exceptional: no other Carolingian parishes are so well known. But that speaks less to their circumstances than to the great care taken to preserve the correspondence that concerned them by both Hincmar of Rheims and Hincmar of Laon, as they marshalled their textual arsenals against one other. For instance, Hincmar saw to it that the letters about Folembray were copied in a manuscript as background to another sprawling text illuminating his nephew's many defects.[52] Even so, we know that more was written about them that has not been transmitted (and perhaps we should be grateful, given how Hincmar later summarised one lost pamphlet's contents).[53] Given the numerous references to now vanished correspondence about quite different parishes that are registered in Flodoard of Rheims's *Historia Remensis ecclesiae*, we should lament what has been lost as much as rejoice in what has been preserved.[54] What the cases of Folembray and *Attolae curtis* do make clear is that parish churches were immensely important to the ordinary lives of people in the countryside around Rheims, as they probably were elsewhere in Francia too.[55] As Hincmar put it, 'no member of the faithful in our diocese wants to be without a priest in his church'.[56] And, as we have seen, northern Frankish villagers were not apparently satisfied either if their priest fell short of the standards expected of him.[57]

In view of this mass of evidence, we should accept that the tensions that characterised Hincmar's ideas about the parish were not generated simply by a stubborn gap between theory and application, between the world as it really was and the world as he wanted it to be, but were deeply rooted in his conception of the parish itself, a complex interplay between that reality and a set of divergent legal and theological imperatives. These tensions are not paradoxes that can be neatly resolved if only we look at them properly; they were knotty problems that tested Hincmar's powers of conceptual and organisational synthesis. What underpinned that complexity, leading Hincmar to expend so much effort in wrestling with the parish, and what therefore represents the key to Hincmar's ideas about it, was the place the parish occupied in his view of the Church (*ecclesia*) as a whole.

Hincmar's view of the Church, his ecclesiology, was one that saw it as a layered structure, defined by its pastoral engagement with the laity and its fidelity to tradition, with authority dispersed throughout.[58] He tended to emphasise the homologies between bishops like himself and priests, even lowly priests in the countryside, noting that they had the same origin in the early Church. For Hincmar, both were members of the *ordo ecclesiasticus*, as opposed to the *ordo laicus*: even the lowly priest should remember that he was a successor to the seventy-two disciples of the Apostles.[59] The difference was one of scale and place in a hierarchy, not in essence. The priest was to his parish what the bishop was to his diocese, which, Hincmar argued, was what the metropolitan was to his province.[60] It is no coincidence that Hincmar used the same word, *parrochia*, for both parish and diocese. Though he sometimes talked of *rusticani parrochiae* to avoid ambiguity, he also deliberately played upon that ambiguity.[61]

As a consequence of this view, not only were priests held to high standards, but principles and norms could migrate easily between the different levels of the Church. Hincmar considered that procedures designed for the accusation of bishops were, up to a point, relevant to priests too (and some priests in the diocese of Laon agreed, probably more enthusiastically than Hincmar would have liked); relevant too were ideas about the deference owed to patrons, whether these patrons were kings or the founders or owners of a small local church; so too were rules about 'translation', that is moving from one church to another.[62] Just as the great abbeys and cathedrals of the Carolingian Empire were sanctified places, so Hincmar considered that modest parish churches were holy buildings too, whose materiality was of great symbolic significance and therefore needed to be monitored.[63]

If the issues raised by the parish were both major and irresolvable, it was because they were simply the local articulation of the very same issues that affected the Carolingian Church in general.

This view of the Church was widespread in the ninth century, in part due to Hincmar's influence, though it was not universal, and other bishops (and monks) thought differently.[64] However, it was certainly not the way that reformers in the eleventh and twelfth centuries saw the Church.[65] Their view of the Church as an institution, one that privileged the Roman centre in a quite uncompromising way, was bound to provide quite a different perspective on distant rural parishes. As a consequence, even as the parish continued to extend its sway over the rural population, reformers associated with Pope Leo IX or Pope Gregory VII paid it scant attention, despite their concerns over priestly celibacy. The major exception to this only further underpins the point. The eleventh- and twelfth-century concern to make sure that 'altars', the shorthand term for the revenues accruing from the exercise of sacramental activities as opposed to revenues from tithes, were held by clerics, not by laymen, suggests a perspective on the parish community rather different from Hincmar's, revolving around simplified notions of ownership rather than moralised ideas of reciprocity and community.[66] Quite simply, the parish did not matter so urgently to Church leaders later as it had to Hincmar. Its tensions seemed less acute, because they understood the Church in a different sense.

There can be no doubt that the development of the parish in the ninth century, in which Hincmar played a leading role, set parameters for its later history, foreclosing on some possibilities while leaving others open. The challenge for the historian is to acknowledge the significance of this development without transforming that significance into a measure of assessment that anachronistically dwells on the absence of later features (for example, emphasis on precise boundaries) at the expense of the Carolingian parish's meaning in its own context. This chapter has attempted to square this circle not by dismissing the tensions inherent in Hincmar's ideas about how the parish should work, but by drawing attention to them. These tensions show that the history of the Carolingian parish cannot be confined to a point of origin of something pristine that would later be corrupted, or of something primitive that would be later perfected: it was a messy, and sometimes controversial, part of everyday life in northern Francia 'already' in the ninth century.

More than that, though, what these tensions also reveal is the centrality of the parish to the Carolingian Church. For Hincmar, at least, the parish was not merely an aspect of his pastoral duties, it was a kind of miniature of the God-given ecclesiastical order. That centrality placed it at the intersection of different forces at work in Frankish society: developing practices of episcopal authority, a steadily growing population and economy, intensifying processes of social differentiation and, above all, debates about how best to bring traditions of often incompatible texts written in quite different social and cultural contexts to bear on contemporary society. As a result, the parish raised thorny issues about the relations between property and authority, between tradition and change, between the clerical and the lay orders, because these were crucial issues for the Church as a whole as it attempted to realise its mission.

By paying attention to these difficulties, both practical and theoretical at the same time, it becomes easier to view the ninth-century parish in a way that sidesteps the worst dangers of teleology, without diminishing our awareness of the long-term importance of the parish as economic, social and religious formation, and of the place of the ninth century in the formation of a 'parochial Christianity'. The basic anatomy of the parish community and its priest in which Hincmar was so interested would have been easily recognisable in later periods. Yet to approach Hincmar's parish and its priest solely or primarily through a concern to identify the roots of the parish system of the High Middle Ages impoverishes our understanding of its place in the specific patterns of interaction between the 'dominant institution' of the Church and society at large that characterised the Carolingian world.[67] Only once we have approached Hincmar's parish in its own terms, and understood its place in his view of the world, can its later history be properly appreciated.

Notes

1 My thanks to Erik Niblaeus, Mayke de Jong and Rachel Stone for their comments on this chapter. I am also grateful to the audience at the IMC in Leeds in 2012 for their questions on an early draft of this paper.
2 Cf. M. Stratmann, *Hinkmar von Reims als Verwalter von Bistum und Kirchenprovinz* (Sigmaringen, 1991), and of course J. Devisse, *Hincmar*, II, pp. 829–46 and 862–85.
3 A selection of the most significant recent work on parishes, all of which

come with ample further references, must include: D. Iogna-Prat and E. Zadora-Rio, eds, 'La Paroisse, genèse d'une forme territoriale', [themed issue of] *Médiévales*, 49 (2005); M. Lauwers, ed., *La Dîme, l'Église et la société féodale* (Turnhout, 2012); N. Kruppa, ed., *Pfarreien im Mittelalter: Deutschland, Polen, Tschechien und Ungarn im Vergleich* (Göttingen, 2008); and S. Wood, *The Proprietary Church in the Medieval West* (Oxford, 2006). Forthcoming work by Erik Niblaeus will further improve our understanding of the parish's later and comparative development.

4 See S. Reynolds, *Kingdoms and Communities in Western Europe, 900–1300* (London, 1984), pp. 79–100. For (perhaps excessive) emphasis on territorial discontinuity in early medieval church networks, see J-P. Devroey, 'L'introduction de la dîme obligatoire en Occident: entre espaces écclesiaux et territoires seigneuriaux à l'époque carolingienne', in Lauwers, *La Dîme*, pp. 87–106.

5 Hincmar, *Collectio de ecclesiis et capellis*, p. 67, citing Pseudo-Isidore (Ps. Dionysius, c. 3). On Pseudo-Isidore, and Hincmar's use of it, see D. Jasper and H. Fuhrmann, *Papal Letters in the Early Middle Ages* (Washington DC, 2001), pp. 135–95.

6 For instance, Council of Chalcedon (451), canon 17. In his *Collectio de ecclesiis et capellis*, p. 69, Hincmar cited the council from a canon-law collection known as the 'Dacheriana' – *Collectio Dacheriana*, ed. L. d'Achery, *Spicilegium, sive, Collectio veterum aliquot scriptorum qui in Galliae bibliothecis delituerant*, 3 vols (Paris, 1723), I, pp. 509–64 – where it appears as canon 68, p. 540.

7 On territoriality (a key concern of much recent French work), M. Lauwers, 'Paroisse, paroissiens et territoire. Remarques sur parochia dans les textes latins du Moyen Âge', *Médiévales*, 49 (2005), 11–32. S. Patzold, 'Den Raum der Diözese modellieren? Zum Eigenkirchen-Konzept und zu den Grenzen der *potestas episcopalis* im Karolingerreich', in Ph. Depreux, F. Bougard and R. Le Jan, eds, *Les Élites et leurs espaces: mobilité, rayonnement, domination (du VIe au XIe siècle)* (Turnhout, 2007), pp. 225–45, offers a brisk demolition of the old *Eigenkirche* concept, with Hincmar of Rheims as his key witness.

8 As Hincmar put it, 'This is the *ordinatio* and *potestas* of bishops over parish churches': *Collectio de ecclesiis et capellis*, p. 112. For a commentary, Ph. Depreux and C. Treffort, 'La paroisse dans le *De ecclesiis et capellis* d'Hincmar de Reims. L'énonciation d'une norme à partir de la pratique?', *Médiévales*, 48 (2005), 141–8.

9 For instance, Hincmar interpreted the *ecclesias vel plebes* mentioned in the Council of Carthage (418) as referring to parish churches, and in his citation altered the text accordingly, adding the word *parrochia* (*Collectio de ecclesiis et capellis*, p. 70).

10 As emphasised by Devisse, *Hincmar*, II, pp. 829–46.

11 The identification of *Attolae curtis* and *Iuviniaca villa* is problematic. Traditionally they have been identified as Aguilcourt and Juvincourt. Devroey, 'L'introduction de la dîme obligatoire', accepts the new identifications proposed by J.-C. Malsy, *Les Noms de lieu du département de l'Aisne*, 3 vols (Paris, 1999–2001), vol. I, pp. 47–9 and 508–14, of *Iuviniaca* as Juvigny (Aisne), and *Attolae curtis* as St-Martin, a small hamlet nearby. However, these places were in the diocese of Soissons in the Middle Ages, yet Hincmar clearly states that both *Iuviniaca villa* and *Attolae curtis* were in the diocese of Rheims: *Opusculum LV capitulorum*, p. 143, Praefatio (*Habes enim quandam villam in mea parrochia*), p. 146, c. 1 (the priest of *parrochiae nostrae*), p. 147, c. 1 (*pars parrochiae nostrae, in qua ipsa capella consistit*). For this reason, Malsy's proposed identifications do not seem to me conclusive, and I have left the place-names in Latin.

12 For the tit-for-tat, see Hincmar, *Opuscula et epistolae*, PL 126, col. 544. The *PL* edition of these letters has many problems (for example, DCCCLXX is erroneously transcribed as 860); I have checked the text against the manuscript, Vatican, Pal. lat. 296.

13 Hincmar of Rheims's list: *Ibid.*, col. 540. Hincmar of Laon's list: Hincmar, *Opusculum LV capitulorum*, p. 143, Praefatio.

14 Hincmar, *Opusculum LV capitulorum*, p. 148, c. 1.

15 As Hincmar put it in *Opuscula et epistolae*, PL 126, col. 545, repeated in his *Opusculum LV capitulorum*, p. 148, c. 1: 'a longo tempore, certis eventuum ac necessitatum causis accidentibus'.

16 On tempering earlier laws, Hincmar, *Collectio de ecclesiis et capellis*, pp. 79–80. On previous burial customs, *ibid.*, p. 82. More broadly, see B. Kötting, *Der frühchristliche Reliquienkult und die Bestattung im Kirchengebäude* (Cologne, 1965).

17 Stratmann, *Hinkmar als Verwalter*, pp. 24–6. See also C. Mériaux, 'Ordre et hiérarchie au sein du clergé rural pendant le haut Moyen Âge', in F. Bougard, D. Iogna-Prat and R. Le Jan, eds, *Hiérarchie et stratification sociale dans l'Occident médiéval (400–1100)* (Turnhout, 2008), pp. 117–36, emphasising the personal importance of Hincmar in developing these intermediary roles.

18 Research on the rural priest in the Carolingian period has been put on a new footing by C. van Rhijn, *Shepherds of the Lord: Priests and Episcopal Statutes in the Carolingian Period* (Turnhout, 2007). A forthcoming volume on rural priests, edited by her and Steffen Patzold, contains a number of important articles: of particular relevance here is Charles Mériaux's discussion of priests in northern Francia (I am grateful to Dr Mériaux for showing me his article ahead of publication).

19 Hincmar, *Capitularia* I, MGH *Capit. Episc.* II, p. 38, c. 9. See also Devisse, *Hincmar*, I, pp. 510–15.

20 For Nodalbert, Gozmar and Otteric, see *Opuscula et epistolae*, PL 126, col. 538; for Ermenric, *Opusculum LV capitulorum*, p. 148, c. 1.
21 For the horse riding, *Collectio de ecclesiis et capellis*, p. 76, and Hincmar, *Capitularia* II, MGH *Capit. Episc.* II, p. 52, c. 20. On patronage, Hincmar, *Capitularia* I, MGH *Capit. Episc.* II, p. 39, c. 10. See also J. L. Nelson, 'Making ends meet: wealth and poverty in the Carolingian church' in W. J. Shiels and D. Wood, eds, *The Church and Wealth. Papers read at the 1986 Summer Meeting and the 1987 Winter Meeting of the Ecclesiastical History Society* (Oxford, 1987), pp. 25–35.
22 On the oblations, Hincmar, *Capitularia* I, MGH *Capit. Episc.* II, p. 37, c. 7; on additional gifts, *Capitularia* I, p. 43, c. 16; on acceptable little gifts, *Capitularia* I, p. 40, c. 12 and *Capitularia* III, p. 74, c. 2.
23 Hincmar, *Opusculum LV capitulorum*, p. 147, c. 1.
24 Hincmar, *Opuscula et epistolae*, PL 126, cols 542–3. On clerical manumission, see Thomas Faulkner, *Law and Authority in the Early Middle Ages: The Frankish Leges in the Carolingian Period* (Cambridge, forthcoming).
25 Hincmar of Laon, Epistola I, *PL* 124, col. 984.
26 Hincmar, *Opuscula et epistolae*, PL 126, col. 562. Cf. Flodoard, *HRE* III–27, p. 352, where Hincmar adopts a similar line of argument.
27 For Sigibert's request, Hincmar, *Opuscula et epistolae*, PL 126, col. 539; citation of legislation, col. 561. Devisse, *Hincmar*, II, p. 750, n.193, wondered whether this Sigibert might have been the Sigibert *de Trepallo* mentioned in the polyptych of St-Remi. For the previous benefice-holder, Osver, and the priest Wulfger, see Hincmar, *Opuscula et epistolae*, PL 126, col. 538.
28 Hincmar, *Collectio de ecclesiis et capellis*, p. 91. On Sigibert's lack of direct interest, Hincmar, *Opuscula et epistolae*, PL 126, col. 564: *cura non est*. Devroey, 'L'introduction de la dîme obligatoire', suggests that laymen benefited from church tithes, via an exemption for demesne land, from their inception under Charlemagne; but the evidence for this is fragile, and Hincmar strongly implies that Sigibert, the benefice-holder of the *villa*, had no link to the tithe at all. Cf. also Hincmar, *Opusculum LV capitulorum*, p. 146, c. 1, mentioning that the *Iuviniaca villa* priest had collected some of the harvest *de terris dominicatis*.
29 Cf. R. I. Moore, 'Family, community and cult on the eve of the Gregorian reform', *Transactions of the Royal Historical Society*, 5th series, 30 (1980), 49–69. It must of course be acknowledged that urbanisation may have raised the stakes. For the Carolingian (and to some extent Merovingian) precedent, see Mériaux, 'Ordre'.
30 Hincmar, *Capitularia* I, MGH *Capit. Episc.* II, pp. 34–5, c. 1, and more broadly van Rhijn, *Shepherds*, pp. 107–9.
31 Hincmar, *Capitularia* II, MGH *Capit. Episc.* II, p. 47, c. 5, enquiring

'Which and how many books he has, and whether they are read out properly'.
32 Hincmar, *Opuscula et epistolae*, *PL* 126, col. 539. On the polyptych, see the editorial comments in MGH *Capit. Episc.* II, p. 7, and Josiane Barbier, Chapter 11. See more broadly C. van Rhijn, 'The local church, priests' handbooks and pastoral care in the Carolingian period' in *Chiese locali e Chiese regionali nell'Alto Medioevo*, Settimane 61 (Spoleto, 2014), 689–706 (I am grateful to Dr van Rhijn for showing me this ahead of publication).
33 Flodoard, *HRE* III-28, p. 355.
34 Three rounds of drinks: Hincmar, *Capitularia* I, MGH *Capit. Episc.* II, p. 43, c. 15. Dancing bears and drinking games: *ibid.*, p. 41, c. 14.
35 *Ibid.*, p. 50, cc. 17–18.
36 Flodoard, *HRE* III-28, p. 354; cf. *De presbiteris criminosis*, pp. 105–6, c. 31.
37 E.g. Hincmar, *Capitularia* II, MGH *Capit. Episc.* II, pp. 51–9, cc. 19–21, including abundant citations from canon law; *Capitularia* IV, pp. 83–4, c. 3. The oaths are conveniently edited in *De presbiteris criminosis*, pp. 30–1.
38 Hincmar, *De iudiciis et appellationibus episcoporum et presbyterorum*, edited as Epistola XXXII, *PL* 126, cols 230–44.
39 Castration: Flodoard, *HRE* III-23, p. 312. Other Frankish bishops sharing Hincmar's concerns. Bishop Rothard of Soissons deposed a priest named Adelold (*in stupro fuerat deprehensus*): see Rothad of Soissons, *Libellus proclamationis*, Council of Rome, 864 and 865, MGH *Conc.* IV, no. 20B, pp. 182–7 at 183.
40 Rumours: Hincmar, *Opuscula et epistolae*, *PL* 126, col. 539 (*fama de eo vulgata*).
41 Practicalities: Hincmar, *Capitularia* II, MGH *Capit. Episc.* II, pp. 58–9, c. 21; the difference in punishment: *ibid.*, pp. 62–70, c. 26, Anhang (this capitulary was directed to the archdeacons).
42 Making priests: Flodoard, *HRE* III-26, p. 336. Corrupting priests: Flodoard, *HRE*, III-26, p. 337. Intimidating priests: Flodoard, *HRE* III-26, p. 338.
43 Refusal to pay tithe (in the neighbouring diocese of Troyes): Flodoard, *HRE*, III-23, p. 316. For the *indevotorum duritia*: *Collectio de ecclesiis et capellis*, p. 76.
44 Hincmar, *De iudiciis et appellationibus*, *PL* 126, col. 231. See de Jong, Chapter 14, pp. 272–3, 279–281.
45 On usury, see Gerhard Schmitz, 'Wucher in Laon. Eine neue Quelle zu Karl dem Kahlen und Hinkmar von Reims', *DA*, 37 (1981), 529–58. On bribery: Hincmar, *Capitularia* IV, MGH *Capit. Episc.* II, p. 85, c. 5.
46 Vendetta: Hincmar, *Opuscula et epistolae*, *PL* 126, col. 540. On alternative interpretations: *Collectio de ecclesiis et capellis*, p. 76.

47 Recently and magisterially explored by S. Patzold, *Episcopus: Wissen über Bischöfe im Frankenreich des späten 8 bis frühen 10 Jahrhunderts* (Ostfildern, 2008). These matters of hierarchy, notably the question of metropolitan authority, of course loomed large for some contemporaries: see below, n.64.
48 Hincmar, *Capitularia* IV, MGH *Capit. Episc.* II, p. 81, c. 1. On the attraction of growing rich from tithes, *Collectio de ecclesiis et capellis*, p. 92. On the minster system, see now C. Cubitt, 'The clergy in Anglo-Saxon England', *Historical Research*, 78 (2005), 273–87.
49 *Collectio de ecclesiis et capellis*, notably pp. 88–9 and 111.
50 Devisse, *Hincmar*, was decidedly pessimistic about the efficacy of Hincmar's pastoral efforts, e.g. II, pp. 880–1. On the historiographical topos of a gap between ideal and reality, see the penetrating comments of S. Airlie, ' "For it is written in the law": Ansegis and the writing of Carolingian royal authority', in S. Baxter, C. E. Karkov, J. L. Nelson and D. Pelteret, eds, *Early Medieval Studies in Memory of Patrick Wormald* (Farnham, 2009), pp. 219–35.
51 Hincmar, *Opuscula et epistolae*, *PL* 126, col. 538. The parishioners of Trising also complained to Hincmar: see de Jong, Chapter 14.
52 Hincmar's report of the Council of Attigny 870 (MGH *Conc.* IV, no. 33, pp. 380–95, at 384) specifies that the letters concerning Folembray were copied alongside the *Opusculum LV capitulorum*, and so they are in the manuscript Vatican, Pal. Lat. 296, one of several dossiers aimed at Hincmar of Laon.
53 Both Hincmars wrote texts about *Attolae curtis* which are now lost (see *Opuluscum LV capitulorum*, p. 143, n.9 and n.11). Hincmar of Laon also wrote a now-lost text about Folembray (Council of Attigny, 870, MGH *Conc.* IV no. 33, p. 384), which Hincmar of Rheims refrained from discussing in detail, 'lest its ravings cause you boredom' (*ne vobis tedium deliramenta sua inferant*): see *Libellus expostulationis*, Council of Douzy, 871, MGH *Conc.* IV, pp. 420–87 at 436, c. 13.
54 For example, Flodoard, *HRE* III-21, p. 277 (Tours-sur-Marne); III-21, p. 281 (unnamed *parrochia*, disputed between bishops of Senlis and Soissons); III-23, p. 308 (unnamed *parrochia*, disputed between bishops of Soissons and Beauvais); III-23, p. 318 (complaint from a parish priest in the diocese of Thérouanne); III-28, p. 356 (about the church at Vendresse and its *parrochiani*). Beyond Flodoard, see Hincmar's fleeting reference to a dispute with Hincmar of Laon over the tithes of a church at Antenaco, Hincmar, *Opuscula et epistolae*, *PL* 126, col. 545.
55 For a related discussion, see my 'Unauthorised miracles in mid-ninth-century Dijon and the Carolingian Church reforms', *Journal of Medieval History*, 36 (2010), 295–311.
56 Hincmar, *Capitularia* IV, MGH *Capit. Episc.* II, p. 85, c. 5.

57 See n.40 above. Another example, from the neighbouring diocese of Châlons, is provided by a letter of Bishop Mancio, concerning Grimma and the priest Angelric: *PL* 131, col. 23.
58 Devisse, *Hincmar*, II, pp. 566–80; P. R. McKeon, *Hincmar of Laon and Carolingian Politics* (Urbana, 1978), pp. 88–98.
59 Joint origin in early Church: *Opusculum LV capitulorum*, p. 175, c. 10. Heirs of the 72 apostles: Hincmar, *De ordine palatii*, p. 40, c. 4; and *Admonitio ad episcopos et ad regem Carolomannum apud Sparnacum facta*, *PL* 125, cols 1007–18, at 1009 (borrowing from Bede).
60 *Collectio de ecclesiis et capellis*, p. 66: *sicut episcopus ... ita unusquisque presbiter*. Cf. *ibid.* p. 108. On the metropolitan, see Hincmar's *De iure metropolitanorum*, *PL* 126, cols 189–210.
61 As noted by Depreux and Treffort, 'Paroisse'.
62 Accusation: *De presbiteris criminosis*, pp. 88–90, c. 19. Deference to patrons: *Collectio de ecclesiis et capellis*, p. 64. Laon clerics: K. Zechiel-Eckes, *Rebellische Kleriker?: eine unbekannte kanonistisch-patristische Polemik gegen Bischof Hinkmar von Laon in Cod. Paris, BNF, nouv. acq. lat. 1746*, MGH Studien und Texte 49 (Hanover, 2009), though the priests in question might have been those of the cathedral of Laon. Translation: *Collectio de ecclesiis et capellis*, p. 68.
63 Monitoring: Hincmar, *Capitularia* II, MGH *Capit. Episc.* II, p. 49, cc. 13–15. On the materiality of the church, see most recently, with a full bibliography, M. Czock, *Gottes Haus: Untersuchungen zur Kirche als heiligem Raum von der Spätantike bis ins Frühmittelalter* (Berlin, 2012).
64 For a broad-brush treatment of Carolingian ecclesiologies, see K. Morrison, *The Two Kingdoms: Ecclesiology in Carolingian Political Thought* (Princeton, 1964); a more recent and very rich analysis is provided by R. Savigni, 'La *communitas christiana* dans l'ecclésiologie carolingienne', in Bougard, Iogna-Prat and Le Jan, *Hiérarchie et stratification sociale*, pp. 83–104.
65 On the Gregorian Reform, see the special edition of *Revue d'histoire de l'église de France*, 96 (2010), with seven articles devoted to the topic.
66 W. Petke, 'Von der klösterlichen Eigenkirche zur Inkorporation in Lothringen und Nordfrankreich im 11 und 12 Jahrhundert', *Revue d'histoire ecclésiastique*, 87 (1992), 34–72, 375–404; more broadly, Wood, *Proprietary Church*. On the debates surrounding tithes in the later eleventh century, though with little discussion of the parish as such, see J. Eldevik, *Episcopal Power and Ecclesiastical Reform in the German Empire: Tithes, Lordship and Community, 950–1150* (Cambridge, 2012).
67 For the church as a 'dominant institution', see J. Baschet, *La Civilisation féodale: de l'an mil à la colonisation de l'Amérique* (Paris, 2004), pp. 149–227, following here A. Guerreau, *Le féodalisme: un horizon théorique* (Paris, 1980), pp. 201–10.

13

Heresy in the flesh: Gottschalk of Orbais and the predestination controversy in the archdiocese of Rheims

Matthew Bryan Gillis

The controversy over divine predestination hit the archdiocese of Rheims like an unforeseen storm in late 848 and troubled the region repeatedly through the 850s.[1] The origin of this conflict was the missionary priest Gottschalk of Orbais, whose interpretation of Augustine's teachings on predestination caused scandal first in Italy and then in the eastern Frankish realm. Emphasising the utter sinfulness of humanity and the need to turn to God with absolute humility for salvation, Gottschalk saw himself as a vessel of divine grace in the face of episcopal opposition and called Christians to repentance after decades of scandal and civil war. His attempts at Christianisation in Francia, however, failed and his doctrine of grace was condemned as heresy at Church councils in Mainz in 848 and then Quierzy in the archdiocese of Rheims in 849. Despite this condemnation, Gottschalk refused to recant and spurned episcopal authority in the process, showing himself to be a Carolingian rarity: an actual heretic in the flesh. He was severely punished and placed in perpetual monastic confinement, where he remained an inveterate opponent to those bishops who condemned his teachings, foremost among them Archbishop Hincmar of Rheims.

Hincmar first sought to contain the danger of Gottschalk's heresy and restore order to the Church, threatened by Gottschalk's resistance to episcopal correction. Yet the archbishop soon found himself in the position of trying to resolve the doctrinal conundrum of predestination as kings, bishops and intellectuals from other kingdoms became involved in the controversy. The two-fold problem of Gottschalk the unrepentant heretic and the mystery of divine predestination proved severe obstacles for Hincmar who sought to keep order and maintain the legitimacy of his position. The archbishop struggled to defend Gottschalk's condemnation and his own articulation of predestination against the attacks of episcopal opponents within and outside his see while Gottschalk won over more followers, who carried on subterranean theological discussions and presented a latent threat to the archbishop's authority until Gottschalk's death in 868. The phenomenon of Gottschalk and the predestination controversy represent a remarkable case of defiance of episcopal authority and an unusual occurrence of heresy in the Carolingian world, both of which exposed Hincmar's limitations as a defender of doctrine and ecclesiastical discipline in his own archdiocese.

A missionary of grace

Theological controversy came to the archdiocese of Rheims in 848 when Gottschalk, a priest from the archdiocese and former monk of the abbey of Orbais, returned after a decade of travels through the Carolingian empire, Dalmatia, Bulgaria and possibly Pannonia.[2] Gottschalk's chief activity during his absence seems to have been missionary work outside the empire, although he also developed a reputation in Italy as a theologian for his teachings on divine grace and predestination.[3] Gottschalk conceptualised salvation as possible only through grace, saying that God granted it to the elect while withholding it from the damned.[4] It was up to human sinners to beg for that grace with a penitent heart, as Gottschalk emphasised in his penitential hymns.[5] The deity's act of giving and refusing grace was wholly indivisible from divine omniscience, which enabled God from eternity to see into the nature of every human creature living within time and thus to discern penitent sinners from impenitent ones. Accordingly, God mercifully and freely bestowed the grace made available through Christ's sacrifice on the repentant, but denied it to the unrepentant, whom he justly damned for their sins.[6] Gottschalk's teachings on grace articulated a novel kind of cosmic holism in terms of the mysteries of divine omnipotence and immutability on the one hand and of human sinfulness and salvation on the other. He presented his doctrine as the logical understanding of revelation and patristic thought on the subject of grace, drawing on biblical and patristic (especially Augustinian) writings as authorities.[7] Gottschalk called his doctrine 'twin predestination' (*praedestinatio gemina*), a term borrowed from Isidore of Seville, since he thought it best captured the complexity of divine grace in a single concept.[8]

Gottschalk developed his doctrine during the Carolingian world's troubled 830s and early 840s. It was difficult for rulers, bishops and the nobility to be certain who held legitimate authority to rule and correct, as one crisis followed another: rebellions against Louis the Pious by his sons and their supporters; Louis's dethronement, atonement and dramatic recovery of power;[9] and then Louis's death followed by civil war and the division of the empire.[10] In this atmosphere of existential uncertainty, Gottschalk's teachings offered a clear message of what was expected of every believer: true humility for one's utter sinfulness and belief in the absolute need for grace. Gottschalk's message grew as much out of the penitential culture of the 820s and 830s, when even Louis the Pious performed a public penance for his sins, as it did out of his reading of Augustine.[11] In particular the new monastic emphasis on frequent, daily prayer and confession played a central role in Gottschalk's calls for repentance.[12] Rather than momentary expressions of remorse for particular sins, however, Gottschalk saw repentance as a permanent mode of Christian existence: absolute penitence and humility were meant to frame one's every activity so as to avoid sin and avert God's wrath, which had seemed to plague the realm so often in recent years. Such a way of life was the very enacting of grace and evidence of one's election by God.

Gottschalk's doctrine of predestination brought him into conflict with Archbishop Hrabanus Maurus of Mainz.[13] Gottschalk had originally been a child oblate at the monastery of Fulda, but in 829 he won a lawsuit against Hrabanus (then abbot of Fulda) at a reform synod in Mainz, where the council ruled that Hrabanus had wrongly coerced Gottschalk into taking the monastic vow and forcibly tonsured him as a boy.[14] While Gottschalk was absolved of his vow, he earned the enmity of Hrabanus, who in his *Liber de oblatione puerorum* labelled Gottschalk a vicious rebel spreading heresy about monastic life and child oblation in particular.[15] Hrabanus also emphasised the fact that Gottschalk's Saxon ethnicity contributed to his tendency to heresy, since the Saxons had only recently been forced to accept Christianity by the conquering Franks.[16] Though the accusations of heresy seem to have fallen on deaf ears, Hrabanus watched his former pupil's career from a distance in the 830s and then began denouncing him when his fame as a theologian in Italy grew in the 840s.[17] Hrabanus chastised the powerful marcher lord, Eberhard of Friuli, for hosting and supporting

Gottschalk, claiming that the former Fulda monk was a false teacher and 'know-it-all' (*sciolus*) and that his doctrine transformed God into a cruel tyrant, who refused the possibility of redemption for many.[18] Believers would either think they were absolved of the need to do good works because of grace or they would simply despair over the possibility of achieving salvation at all without it.[19]

In 848 the confrontation between Gottschalk and his old abbot happened at Mainz once again, but this time with Hrabanus presiding over the synod as archbishop in the presence of his king, Louis the German.[20] Gottschalk had prepared a *libellus* to present his doctrine to the council and to refute Hrabanus's criticisms, but to no avail.[21] The archbishop persuaded the bishops to condemn Gottschalk's teachings as heretical.[22] Since Gottschalk was now a priest and monk from the archdiocese of Rheims, he was sent to Hincmar for punishment, but only after he had suffered a beating at the synod and taken an oath never to return to Louis's kingdom.[23] In his letter to Hincmar, Hrabanus warned the archbishop of Rheims that the dubious priest and 'wandering monk' (*monachus gyrovagus*) Gottschalk was spreading 'new superstitions' and seducing those of weak faith into error.[24] Hrabanus described Gottschalk's doctrine as claiming that God's predestination made some people incorrigible sinners from the beginning and automatically subject to the punishment of eternal death, since they could not reform themselves from error and sin. Whether the archbishop of Mainz understood the subtleties of Gottschalk's doctrine or not, his portrayal of it made God rather than the unrepentant sinners the cause of their damnation, which was an obviously untenable and heretical position meant to discredit Gottschalk in Hincmar's eyes.

When Hincmar received Hrabanus's letter and placed Gottschalk in monastic custody, he suddenly found himself and his archdiocese thrust into the middle of a dangerous and unforeseen theological controversy at a time when the western kingdom had already seen its share of disquiet.[25] Carolingian theologians and rulers had traditionally emphasised the need for correct faith, divine grace and good works as a complete apparatus of salvation.[26] There is evidence that some eighth- and early ninth-century theologians emphasised the importance of grace, as Gottschalk did, although there were no in-depth debates between theologians exploring the mysterious inter-relationship of faith, grace and works.[27] During the anxious reform councils of 829, the Council of Paris warned that profession of

Christian faith alone without good, heavenly works to replace earthly vanities was not enough for salvation. The bishops emphasised genuine participation in Christian life with the help of grace (*Christi adiuvante gratia*) as they called for reform among the faithful.[28]

Consensus and co-operation between rulers and bishops had ensured that doctrinal conflicts were largely attributed to foreigners, so that contemporary heretics were chiefly Spanish or Greek (or Saxon in Hrabanus's case), or an 'imagined other' for Carolingian theologians and biblical commentators to employ when defining the boundaries of the faith.[29] The exception that proves the rule was the Frankish Amalarius of Metz, who quickly abandoned his liturgical reforms after they were condemned.[30] Yet, with Gottschalk, Hincmar was forced to deal with an actual heretic who had been canonically condemned at Mainz in 848, but who was from Hincmar's own archdiocese and wholly unrepentant.

The archbishop soon discovered that Gottschalk was determined to convince the world that the Council of Mainz was wrong about his doctrine. With the help of the monks of Orbais, where he was temporarily housed, Gottschalk began sending out confessional treatises and leaflets (*schedulae*) to bishops, monks, scholars and old friends in the archdiocese.[31] In these documents Gottschalk presented his doctrine to readers with biblical and patristic excerpts (especially from Augustine's writings) as authorities, but without Hrabanus' misleading and damaging distortions. Gottschalk claimed he believed and confessed twin predestination because he was 'divinely inspired, disposed and armed', and he warned readers against misrepresenting his teachings as Hrabanus had done: 'a false witness is he who corrupts either the meaning or the appearance in anyone else's writings'.[32] Gottschalk denounced the bishops at the Council of Mainz as heretical 'Hrabanians' (*Hrabanici*) and urged his correspondents to confess and believe the truth about divine grace towards their own salvation.[33] Such were the very workings of grace in the world.[34]

No doubt, Gottschalk expected to find support among his correspondents; he had been known as a teacher in the archdiocese before his journey south and had studied at Corbie. He now sent works to the missionary monk Gislemar and the scholar Ratramnus there; Ratramnus eventually composed a treatise on predestination with a position comparable to Gottschalk's.[35] It is possible that Gottschalk's stay at Corbie was formative in his development as an intellectual and missionary. Since the beginning of the Scandinavian mission in

Louis the Pious' reign, Corbie had been famed as a centre for preparing and sending forth missionaries, including Gislemar, to northern Europe.[36] Corbie monks may have helped to develop the missionary strategies that emphasised one's submission to the Christian God as essential to salvation, and these may have been an important influence on Gottschalk's teachings on predestination. Rimbert's *Vita Anskari*, written probably in the 860s, emphasises divine inspiration and grace at key moments in Anskar's mission to Scandinavia, and Rimbert's correspondence with Ratramnus suggests continued links between Corbie and the northern mission.[37] In this tradition, submission to baptism and confession might be seen as signs of grace, which made faith and good works possible. With conversion as a hallmark in this process, such teaching might have helped make Christianity intelligible and even attractive to potential converts.

In an unprecedented way, however, Gottschalk's refusal to accept his condemnation and his attacks on the bishops contradicted established Carolingian rules of hierarchy and practices for solving doctrinal conundrums. Traditionally, kings selected learned advisers to examine particular theological questions through a study of scripture and patristic authorities, and then episcopal synods under royal direction ruled on doctrine.[38] Ninth-century bishops had grown particularly keen to prevent anyone from usurping their role as arbiters of the faith, and since Gottschalk was neither a bishop nor a royal adviser on doctrinal matters his preaching had occurred without sanction.[39] His condemnation at the Council of Mainz, on the other hand, had been the result of this very canonical process. Archbishop Amolo of Lyons, one of Gottschalk's correspondents, sent a letter warning Gottschalk to accept the bishops' judgment and to stop defaming them as heretics.[40] But Amolo's admonition had little effect on Gottschalk. Even Gottschalk's supporters, such as Ratramnus, whose doctrinal position echoed his friend's, did not openly support his actions.

While we cannot outright explain Gottschalk's stunning behaviour, there are several possible reasons why he acted as he did. First, he had developed a maverick and combative approach to preaching and defending Christian truth as a missionary. He was used to advising Frankish and Slavic leaders and nobles on matters of Christian doctrine and prophecy, and perhaps even anticipated becoming a bishop to the Slavs as a result of his work.[41] Gottschalk was an expert disputant and he was known in Italy, the staging ground of his Slavic mission, for vigorously defending his doctrine in debates with fellow

Christians. Being steeped in patristic discussions of grace and able to draw on texts with a remarkable memory, Gottschalk also employed the logic of syllogisms to force his opponents to agree with him or fall silent.[42] Quite likely Gottschalk viewed his doctrine as fundamental to his mission and for this reason fiercely defended it in Italy and then north of the Alps. Second, Gottschalk probably viewed his condemnation at Mainz in 848 as Hrabanus' revenge for his defeat in their earlier confrontation in 829. In this sense, Gottschalk understood his conviction for heresy as the result of Hrabanus' personal enmity, the archbishop's unfamiliarity with Augustine's later writings favouring grace over free will, and the synod's willingness to follow Hrabanus' direction as archbishop and a respected theologian.[43] Hrabanus had even caused Gottschalk's aristocratic patron Eberhard of Friuli to abandon him, so that Gottschalk was without any protection whatsoever. His writing campaign was meant to overcome these upsets and win over new supporters on his old home ground in the archdiocese of Rheims. Third, and certainly not least, Gottschalk's doctrine of grace required believers to recognise and admit their absolute dependence on divine aid for truth and salvation. To believe and confess the truth was a sign of grace, and for Gottschalk to recant would be to show that he was condemned to eternal punishment.

Gottschalk sent his most dramatic and perhaps his most important appeal for support to Archbishop Hincmar himself, in the form of his so-called *Longer confession* (*Confessio prolixior*).[44] Written in a poetic confessional style and condemned by the archbishop as a work 'small in size, but greatest in impiety',[45] Gottschalk's *Longer confession* is a remarkable document meant to clear his name of heresy and to convince the archbishop either that his doctrine was true or at least that another synod should be called where Gottschalk might prove his doctrine before the king, clergy and nobles of western Francia. Drawing on penitential strategies to shape his position as a doctrinal authority, Gottschalk emphasised that as a sinner he was only a vessel of divine truth and grace and he was not the originator of the doctrine of twin predestination.[46] He quoted from numerous biblical and patristic sources, incorporating those sources into his personal confession of faith and stressing that the doctrine came from the divine Word itself and was taught by Augustine and other ancient authorities.[47] Gottschalk stressed that he avoided all heresy out of fear of eternal damnation and that others must believe and confess the truth of the mystery of divine predestination towards salvation, in much the same way that Christians believed and confessed the truth of the Trinitarian mystery.[48]

Anticipating that Hincmar might refuse him, Gottschalk also prayed that he be allowed to undergo a test (*examen*) at a new synod to prove the truth of twin predestination. In this test, Gottschalk would submerge himself into four barrels of boiling, scalding liquids – water, oil, lard and pitch – and then be set aflame. He prayed that God's right hand would lead him through these physical dangers and protect him, so that when the synod witnessed his miraculous survival, then heresy would be banished from the Frankish realm.[49] This was, to say the least, an unprecedented request and one meant to emphasise Gottschalk's role as a vessel of divine grace suffering persecution for the truth. His *examen* seems to have been crafted in imitation of the trials of the martyrs Crispin and Crispinian who were believed in the ninth century to have suffered their passions – including being thrown into boiling pitch, lard and oil – at nearby Soissons.[50] Gottschalk, as a missionary-turned-Christianiser now persecuted within the Frankish empire for defending divine truths, seems to have viewed himself as much like these ancient martyrs who endured Roman persecution. As Ian Wood has shown, Carolingian hagiographers such as Alcuin and Rimbert emphasised the miraculous in conversions and Gottschalk envisioned this miracle as a means of converting the Franks to his correct doctrine.[51]

By presenting himself as a martyr, Gottschalk intended to place his reader in the indefensible position of refusing divine truth as it was revealed through its humble, human vessel. Gottschalk concluded his plea to Hincmar by asking his reader to accept his requests with 'dove-like love' rather than 'raven-like envy' – an obvious jibe at Hrabanus and his supporters, since the archbishop of Mainz's Germanic name meant 'raven'.[52] This clever slight, however, was also meant to suggest that the name of Gottschalk's condemner revealed a person of wicked, jealous and ultimately self-interested nature, whereas Gottschalk – whose Germanic name means 'God's servant' – described himself simply and humbly as 'Gottschalk the sinner' (*Godescalcus peccator*) as someone in need of his reader's prayers and only desiring to speak the truth. We might also translate *Godescalcus peccator* as 'God's servant the sinner', a reading which eerily emphasises Gottschalk's humble claim to be nothing more than a vessel of grace: a strangely anonymous and selfless voice uttering authoritative divine mysteries. The possible effects of such remarkable strategies would not have been lost on an experienced missionary and gifted author such as Gottschalk.

The Council of Quierzy, 849

Gottschalk's wish for another synod was granted, although it did not happen as he hoped. Some six months after his condemnation in Mainz, Gottschalk was brought before the Council of Quierzy and questioned about his doctrine to see whether he persisted in his condemned views and whether he would accept the bishops' correction.[53] Present at the gathering were King Charles the Bald, Archbishop Hincmar, numerous bishops and several abbots. The royal notary Aeneas appears to have taken a leading role in the interrogation, and at one point explained how logic dictated that Gottschalk's reading of Augustine was wrong – the greatest of the Church Fathers simply could not have taught that God predestined the damned.[54] Frustrated by his prosecutor's ignorance of Augustine's anti-Pelagian writings, Gottschalk exploded in abuse and even insulted the bishops, since they refused to see the logic of twin predestination and to accept it as divine truth.[55] Shocked by Gottschalk's disrespect and finding him a depraved heretic and reprobate, the bishops passed sentence: Gottschalk was stripped of his priestly status, whipped as a monk for stirring up civil and Church affairs, placed in monastic custody in the stronghouse (*ergastulum*) at the monastery of Hautvillers and condemned to perpetual silence.[56]

The bishops perceived Gottschalk to be a dangerous source of disorder and perversion.[57] First, the bishops were concerned to punish him for not respecting them as his superiors and for usurping their authority as the arbiters of correct doctrine, claiming that his behaviour displayed 'irrevocable contumacy' and 'incorrigible obstinacy' in the face of their rightful authority.[58] They also wrote that Gottschalk had 'irregularly usurped' his ordination through the chorbishop Rigbold (rather than receiving it from his bishop) and had abused the priestly office with depraved acts and perverse doctrines. The sentence of perpetual silence was to prevent him from further usurping the doctrinal office. Second, Gottschalk was restored to the monastic order. As a wandering or 'headless' monk, Gottschalk was subjected to corporeal punishment for wrongly causing scandals and disputes in the world and was returned to the cloister, from which it was found he had departed 'irregularly', that is (allegedly) without his bishop's permission.[59]

In this way, the western Frankish episcopate restored the order and discipline of the Church and ended Gottschalk's perverse depredations. After suffering the rod, Gottschalk was forced to burn those writings he brought to the synod to defend his doctrine in what the bishops must have seen as a symbolic act of purifying the Church of his perverse teachings.[60] The severity of Gottschalk's punishment shocked some, including Florus of Lyons who, writing from Lotharingia, later said that he had learned how Gottschalk was beaten 'nearly to death' at the request of the abbots for having insulted the bishops.[61] While Florus did not condone Gottschalk's disrespectful behaviour, he condemned the bishops for following the advice of the lower-ranking abbots and deplored Gottschalk's sentence as an 'unheard-of example of irreligiosity and cruelty', claiming that ancient Church councils won over heretics through argument rather than violence. Gottschalk's unheard-of solitary confinement and silence, Florus contended, could lead him to nothing but despair.

Doubtless Florus was not the only critic of the synod's decision. In the 850s and 860s, Hincmar repeatedly found himself defending Gottschalk's condemnation as canonical; he even listed the chief sources, the Benedictine Rule and the canons of the Council of Agde, for his punishment.[62] In the tense atmosphere of the decade-long predestination controversy following Gottschalk's condemnation, Hincmar's direction of the proceedings seemed questionable to some – especially opponents of Hincmar's rule and those sympathetic to Gottschalk's doctrine.

The limits of an archbishop's authority

During the 850s and 860s the twin issues of containing the condemned heretic Gottschalk and resolving the matter of predestination remained central concerns for Archbishop Hincmar. The archbishop sought to establish an alternative to Gottschalk's conceptualisation of predestination for the Frankish Church, but winning episcopal consensus for his articulation of this divine mystery proved extremely controversial. Partly this was due to the dynastic politics of the divided empire, in which each realm's bishops might compete over defining Frankish orthodoxy. But it was also due to the complexity of the mystery of predestination and the Carolingian abundance of riches when it came to learned theologians in the 850s: the western realm in particular contained a formidable body of thinkers keenly interested in debating doctrine.[63] Yet even after an episcopal consensus on predestination was reached in 860, Gottschalk's continued presence in the monastery of Hautvillers until his death in 868 served as a threat to unleash heresy into the Church again. For after his condemnation Gottschalk transformed himself into something of an underground sage, and Hincmar viewed Gottschalk's followers as a dangerous, subterranean force waiting for any opportunity to emerge from the shadows.

Not long after the Council of Quierzy, Hincmar received a request from Gottschalk for the Eucharist, possibly because of the severity of his beating at the synod.[64] The archbishop then discovered that, with the help of monks at Hautvillers, Gottschalk was still circulating texts in the hope of finding support among the archdiocese's monks and clerics.[65] Gottschalk repeatedly encouraged his readers to believe and confess twin predestination for salvation. Drawing on Paul's classic dictum, Gottschalk wrote that believing the truth in one's heart was not enough, for everyone must confess it with their mouth.[66] In order to prevent Gottschalk's heresy from spreading, Hincmar composed his first treatise on predestination, his so-called *Ad reclusos et simplices*, in which he warned all of the religious in his jurisdiction to avoid Gottschalk's canonically condemned teachings.[67] Hincmar claimed that the Gottschalk they had known in the 830s as a respectable teacher and religious figure was actually a dangerous charlatan who filled his writings with 'mutilated and corrupted' passages from scripture and the fathers in order to win praise and in the process lead others into error.[68]

Yet Hincmar quickly found his theological arguments in *Ad reclusos et simplices* challenged. Ratramnus immediately criticised the treatise, and when the archbishop contacted other scholars for support, he found little forthcoming. Lupus of Ferrières avoided siding with either Gottschalk or Hincmar, emphasising the importance of grace for salvation and the sinner's evil will for damnation. Bishop Prudentius of Troyes argued that God did not wish to save the wicked and seemed closer to Gottschalk's position than the archbishop's. Charles the Bald's favourite John Eriugena produced a novel and troubling interpretation of predestination that was soon condemned by Prudentius and others. No doubt horrified by the explosion of learned opinions produced by his calls for aid, Hincmar must have been equally troubled when Charles requested more substantial treatises on predestination from both Lupus and Ratramnus – two scholars inclined to show little support for the archbishop's position. These authors took strong positions that accounted for Augustine's teachings on predestination, although they did not openly condone Gottschalk's defiance of the bishops.[69]

In the face of these criticisms, Hincmar contacted Hrabanus in the spring of 850 for guidance, sending along his own treatise and writings from Gottschalk, Ratramnus and Prudentius. Hrabanus responded in two letters, the first of which was brief and only warned Hincmar not to let Gottschalk accept the Eucharist unless he recanted his heresy.[70] But Hrabanus's second letter soon followed, in which he offered numerous criticisms. The archbishop of Mainz wrote that Gottschalk's unheard-of request for a fiery trial indicated his continuing pride, obstinacy and error. He contrasted Gottschalk's blasphemous proposal with the trial of the three humble boys in Nebuchadnezzar's fiery furnace.[71] Hrabanus reassured Hincmar that Ratramnus's criticisms of his *Ad reclusos et simplices* were unfounded, yet Hrabanus strongly chastised Hincmar for allowing Gottschalk to write at all, since such communications being passed around among the religious could cause such great harm.

In the spring of 851 at an assembly in Meerssen, King Charles the Bald, King Louis the German and the Emperor Lothar and their nobles resolved to prevent men like Gottschalk from disturbing the peace of the realm again. They agreed to pursue any dangerous and wandering individuals fleeing reason and needing correction, and to reform them or eliminate them from the realm.[72] Yet Hincmar and Charles the Bald realised that Gottschalk's containment alone was not a solution for the controversy in the western realm, and in the spring of 853 they resolved to put an end to the controversy and some other troubling matters in the archdiocese at a pair of synods. At the Council of Quierzy, a small gathering of carefully selected bishops and abbots accepted Hincmar's Four Chapters as a definitive understanding of predestination: there was a single predestination to grace or rightful justice, though no one was predestined to punishment; all have free will thanks to Christ's sacrifice; God wills all to be saved, though not all are; and Christ died for all, though not all are redeemed.[73] At the Council of Soissons, Hincmar deposed several clerics ordained by his controversial predecessor, Archbishop Ebbo of Rheims in order to replace them with men loyal to himself, and the synod also condemned as heretical the term 'triune deity' (*trina deitas*), which was found in monastic hymns.[74] According to the bishops, praying to the triune God was orthodox, but not to the triune deity.

The synods' actions were intended to bring order to the Church and to purify it from heresy, but instead they stirred up discontent and counter-accusations of heresy. Gottschalk and Ratramnus defended the term 'triune deity' as orthodox, and Ebbo's clerics seem to have found common cause with Gottschalk's supporters in resisting Hincmar's authority.[75] Also, the churches and monasteries around Rheims seem to have buzzed with underground discussions about predestination. The question of predestination was really a question of the Christianisation of the realm, of defining what separated the elect from the damned, and Gottschalk's surviving texts show that these underground disputes between lesser monks and clerics could be heated. Among Gottschalk's surviving texts are collections of leaflets (*schedulae*) that could easily be transported and passed between readers unnoticed. In these leaflets, Gottschalk encouraged his readers to believe and confess twin predestination 'all the way unto death' and to debate with those who denied the truth of his doctrine.[76] He composed models for doctrinal debate that amounted to barrages of questions that would overwhelm opponents until the beleaguered victims were forced either to profess twin predestination or simply to fall silent.[77] Gottschalk's emphasis was always on the logic of twin predestination (as well as triune deity) as opposed to the illogical and untenable positions of opponents.[78] Gottschalk encouraged defiance towards opponents 'no matter how great their talent, authority, fame, holiness or character'.[79] He also developed (from an Augustinian sermon) a rationale for going over the heads of ecclesiastical superiors, claiming that petty, earthly powers must be defied when they resisted and contradicted the divine power.[80]

Hincmar's actions confirmed that Gottschalk had numerous supporters in the archdiocese among the younger monks and clergy, and like their leader these ambitious and wrongheaded fellows were more interested in appearing right by winning arguments than in being right in the eyes of episcopal superiors. The archbishop characterised Gottschalk's 'school' as a heretical sect of dissolute and rustic accomplices and followers who acted like *doctores* but were really just know-it-alls.[81] Gottschalk, Hincmar claimed, wanted most of all to seem like a 'teacher of his own teachers' (*suorum doctorum doctor*), and in the process led the young and foolish into error.[82] If Gottschalk had followers who needed to know how to win debates, then Hincmar certainly also had opponents among the lesser religious of the archdiocese. The activities of these two anonymous groups show how the archdiocese's religious of all levels saw the predestination controversy as an important struggle over the nature of the Church and the salvation of souls.

Episcopal opposition to the Council of Quierzy's Four Chapters also soon followed. In Valence in 855, Lotharingian bishops condemned the Four Chapters, widening the controversy to include the middle realm and placing Hincmar on the defensive.[83] Within Charles the Bald's realm, Prudentius of Troyes also came out against the Four Chapters in 856, demanding that Aeneas, the former royal notary and now bishop-elect of Paris, agree to four different chapters strongly contradicting those of Quierzy: free will only functions with the help of divine grace, predestination is twin, Christ's blood was only for those believing in him, and no one could be saved who was not destined by God.[84] As a result of Prudentius' attack on Hincmar, the archbishop composed his second treatise on predestination, a long work attacking Gottschalk, Ratramnus and Prudentius. This text is now lost, but it seems likely that it was an earlier version of Hincmar's third and final work on the subject – *De praedestinatione* – a massive tome containing over 1,100 excerpts from 150 works that he had evidently been collecting for some time.[85] Hincmar was also particularly furious about the Valence bishops, for the synod had been organised by Ebbo, bishop of Grenoble, who was Ebbo of Rheims' nephew.[86] He viewed the younger Ebbo's opposition to the Four Chapters as a political attack in retribution for his conflict with his Rheims predecessor and the deposition of Ebbo's clerics, whom Hincmar identified as sympathetic to Gottschalk.

The issue of predestination remained contentious for a few years until the Council of Savonnières in 859, where forty-two bishops gathered in the presence of Charles the Bald, Lothar II of Lotharingia and Charles of Provence.[87] The gathering sought to restore concord between the churches of the different realms, on the issue of predestination in particular. At this council, Remigius of Lyons presented decrees from the Council of Langres of the same year, decrees which attacked Eriugena's position, but did not explicitly condemn the Council of Quierzy of 853.[88] Charles the Bald, however, demurred so that Hincmar could offer a response, which came in the form of his *De praedestinatione*. In this work, Hincmar attacked Gottschalk (who, he claimed, the Council of Quierzy of 849 had rightfully condemned), the *capitula* of Valence, the writings of Florus of Lyons and the position of Prudentius.[89]

The episcopal debate on predestination came to an end in 860, when bishops from the kingdoms of Charles the Bald, Lothar II and Charles of Provence met at the Council of Tusey and formed a consensus: there was predestination to salvation, and both human free will and grace were necessary for salvation.[90] Although the need for grace had been accepted, some of the most contentious issues (such as the predestination of the damned) were carefully left unmentioned. With this agreement, Gottschalk's condemnation was tacitly confirmed. This was the final synod to address the issue of predestination, which had continued for seven years after the Council of Quierzy in 853, and eleven years since Gottschalk's conviction.

Yet Hincmar's concerns about Gottschalk remained and he soon learned that Pope Nicholas was willing to offer support to the archbishop's various opponents. In 864 Bishop Rothad of Soissons, whom Hincmar had deposed for failing to obey Church rulings and for being a lover of 'novelties' (suggesting he may have been a Gottschalk supporter), petitioned Pope Nicholas and was restored to his office.[91] Then in 866 Gottschalk's disciple Guntbert fled from Hautvillers to ask Pope Nicholas's aid in Gottschalk's case in Rome. Guntbert had seemingly learned of the pope's apparent sympathy for Gottschalk's doctrine in an entry written in Prudentius's annals, and joined several of Ebbo's clerics who followed Rothad's path to Rome to seek reinstatement in that same year.[92] In several letters, Hincmar again defended Gottschalk's condemnation as canonical and explained that Gottschalk was too dangerous to be released out of captivity – even for a new synod – since he could recite scripture and the fathers all day long without taking a breath and could twist these texts to his own purposes. The danger of releasing Gottschalk even to plead his case again was that the 'greatest sickness' (*maxima nausea*) would afflict the Church in the form of renewed heresy, and his hidden followers would emerge to cause worse crimes.[93] Whatever Nicholas's response to the question of predestination and Gottschalk's treatment, he died in 867 and the issue went no further.

Just before Gottschalk died in 868, Hincmar offered him the Eucharist should he recant his heresy.[94] Gottschalk refused and died surrounded by the monks of Hautvillers, who honoured him by preserving his 'pious memory' (*pia memoria*) in the *necrologium*, recording that he had been 'falsely accused, hastily judged, and unjustly condemned' (*falso criminatus, praecipitanter iudicatus, et iniuste damnatus*).[95] Such an epitaph highlights the limitations of Hincmar's ability to keep order in his own see. The fact that the sole surviving manuscript of most of Gottschalk's theological writings was probably copied around Rheims in the late ninth century also attests to continued interest in his ideas.[96] Although Gottschalk was never released from Hautvillers, Hincmar was never able to silence him or to prevent his followers from openly espousing views contradictory to those mandated by their episcopal superiors. Hincmar's attempts to wrestle with the mystery of grace and salvation put him on the defensive numerous times, jeopardising his authority as a theologian and as archbishop, and causing his various opponents to band together in common cause against him. Hincmar certainly weathered these storms, yet only after more than a decade of persistent anxiety about his enemies, intense intellectual effort to solve the strange mystery of predestination and fierce political wrangling with bishops and kings.

Notes

1 This chapter condenses and adds new insights to some of the findings of my dissertation, 'Gottschalk of Orbais: a study of power and spirituality in a ninth-century life' (PhD dissertation, University of Virginia, 2009), which I am transforming into a monograph. Among previous examinations of this controversy the following are especially important: D. Ganz, 'The debate on predestination', in M. T. Gibson and J. L. Nelson, eds, *Charles the Bald: Court and Kingdom*, 2nd revd edn (Aldershot, 1990), pp. 283–302; and C. M. Chazelle, *The Crucified God in the Carolingian Era: Theology and Art of Christ's Passion* (Cambridge, 2001), pp. 165–208. See also the translations in V. Genke and F. X. Gumerlock, *Gottschalk and a Medieval Predestination Controversy: Texts Translated from the Latin* (Milwaukee, 2010).
2 *AB* s.a. 849, pp. 56–7 (trans. Nelson, p. 67).
3 Hrabanus Maurus, Epistolae 22 and 44, ed. E. Dümmler, MGH *Epp.* 5, pp. 428, 490.
4 Gottschalk, Fragmentum 15, ed. C. Lambot, *Œuvres théologiques et grammaticales de Godescalc d'Orbais* (Louvain, 1945), p. 38.
5 See, for example, Gottschalk, Carmen I (*Christe, mearum*), ed. L. Traube, MGH *Poetae* III (Berlin, 1896), pp. 724–5.
6 Chazelle, *Crucified God*, pp. 173–7.
7 See, for example, Gottschalk, *Confessio brevior*, ed. Lambot, pp. 52–4.

8 *Ibid.* and Isidore of Seville, *Sententiae*, II, 6, 1, ed. P. Cazier, CCSL 111 (Turnhout, 1998), p. 103.
9 P. E. Dutton, *The Politics of Dreaming in the Carolingian Empire* (Lincoln NE, 1994), pp. 81–112; M. de Jong, *The Penitential State: Authority and Atonement in the Reign of Louis the Pious, 814–840* (Cambridge, 2009).
10 Dutton, *Politics*, pp. 113–56; M. Costambeys, M. Innes and S. MacLean, *The Carolingian World* (Cambridge, 2011), pp. 379–88.
11 de Jong, *Penitential State*, pp. 228–34.
12 M. Driscoll, 'Penance in transition: popular piety and practice', in L. Larson-Miller, ed., *Medieval Liturgy: A Book of Essays* (New York, 1997), pp. 121–63; and J. Black, 'Psalm uses in Carolingian prayerbooks: Alcuin's *Confessio peccatorum pura* and the seven penitential psalms (use 1)', *Mediaeval Studies*, 65 (2003), 1–56.
13 On Hrabanus' career, see L. Coon, *Dark Age Bodies: Gender and Monastic Practice in the Early Medieval West* (Philadelphia, 2011), pp. 17–41.
14 M. de Jong, *In Samuel's Image: Child Oblation in the Early Medieval West* (Leiden, 1996), pp. 77–91; M. B. Gillis, 'Noble and Saxon: the meaning of Gottschalk of Orbais' ethnicity at the Synod of Mainz, 829', in R. Corradini, M. Gillis, R. McKitterick and I. van Renswoude, eds, *Ego Trouble: Authors and Their Identities in the Early Middle Ages* (Vienna, 2010), pp. 197–210.
15 Hrabanus Maurus, *Liber de oblatione puerorum*, PL 107, cols 419–40.
16 *Ibid.*, cols 431–2.
17 See n.3.
18 Hrabanus Maurus, Epistola 42, MGH *Epp.* 5, pp. 481–7.
19 For Hrabanus on predestination, see G. Schrimpf, 'Die ethischen Implikationen der Auseinandersetzung zwischen Gottschalk und Hraban um die Prädestinationslehre', *Archiv für Geschichte der Philosophie*, 68 (1986), 153–73; G. Schrimpf, 'Hraban und der Prädestinationsstreit des 9. Jahrhunderts', in R. Kottje and H. Zimmermann, eds, *Hrabanus Maurus: Lehrer, Abt und Bischof* (Mainz, 1982), pp. 145–53; and Chazelle, *Crucified God*, pp. 181–7.
20 *Annales Fuldenses*, s.a. 848, ed. F. Kurze, MGH SRG 7 (Hanover, 1891), pp. 37–8 (trans. T. Reuter, *The Annals of Fulda* (Manchester, 1992), p. 28, n.7).
21 Hincmar, *De praedestinatione Dei*, PL 125, col. 84, c. 2.
22 *Annales Fuldenses*, s.a. 848, ed. Kurze, pp. 37–8 (trans. Reuter, *Annals of Fulda*, p. 28, n.7).
23 *Ibid.* and *Annales Xantenses*, s.a. 848, ed. B. von Simson, MGH SRG 12 (Hanover, 1909), p. 16.
24 Hincmar, *De praedestinatione*, PL 125, cols 84–5, c. 2.
25 D. Ganz, 'Debate', pp. 283–7; J. L. Nelson, *Charles the Bald* (London, 1992), pp. 132–59.

26 D. Ganz, 'Theology and the organisation of thought', in R. McKitterick, ed., *The New Cambridge Medieval History, c.700–c.900*, volume 2 (Cambridge, 1995), pp. 758–85, at 758–62.
27 F. X. Gumerlock, 'Predestination in the century before Gottschalk (part 1)', and 'Predestination in the century before Gottschalk (part 2)', *Evangelical Quarterly*, 81 (2009), 195–209 and 319–37.
28 *Concilium Parisiense*, 829, MGH *Conc.* II, 2, no. 50, pp. 656–9, II, c. 7.
29 Mayke de Jong, 'Religion', in R. McKitterick, ed., *The Early Middle Ages*, Short Oxford History of Europe (Oxford, 2001), pp. 131–64, at 144–5; and M. Innes, '"Immune from heresy": defining the boundaries of Carolingian Christianity', in P. Fouracre and D. Ganz, eds, *Frankland: The Franks and the World of the Early Middle Ages. Essays in Honour of Dame Jinty Nelson* (Manchester, 2008), pp. 101–25.
30 Ganz, 'Theology', pp. 777–8.
31 Gottschalk, *Confessio brevior*, ed. Lambot, pp. 52–4; Amolo, Epistola 2, ed. E. Dümmler, MGH *Epp.* 5, pp. 368–78; and Hincmar, *Ad reclusos et simplices*, ed. W. Gundlach, 'Zwei Schriften des Erzbischofs Hinkmar von Reims', *Zeitschrift für Kirchengeschichte*, 10 (1889), 258–310, at 261–2.
32 Gottschalk, *Confessio brevior*, ed. Lambot, p. 54.
33 Amolo, Epistola 2, MGH *Epp.* 5, p. 377.
34 W. Kagerah, *Gottschalk der Sachse* (Inaug.-Diss, Greifswald, 1938), pp. 76–7 and Chazelle, *Crucified God*, pp. 174–5. G. Schrimpf, 'Die ethischen Implikationen', pp. 169–70, and 'Hraban und der Prädestinationsstreit', pp. 147–8, makes a similar argument, emphasising that moral life was a sign of election.
35 Hincmar, *Ad reclusos et simplices*, ed. Gundlach, pp. 260–2; Hincmar, *De praedestinatione Dei*, PL 125, cols 84–5, c. 2.
36 J. Palmer, 'Rimbert's *Vita Anskarii* and Scandinavian mission in the ninth century', *Journal of Ecclesiastical History*, 55 (2004), 235–56.
37 I. Wood, *The Missionary Life: Saints and the Evangelisation of Europe, 400–1050* (London, 2001), pp. 123–32, and Palmer, 'Rimbert's *Vita Anskarii*'.
38 T. Noble, 'Kings, clergy and dogma: the settlement of doctrinal disputes in the Carolingian world', in S. Baxter, C. E. Karkov, J. L. Nelson and D. Pelteret, eds, *Early Medieval Studies in Memory of Patrick Wormald* (Farnham, Surrey, 2009), pp. 237–52.
39 de Jong, *Penitential State*, pp. 179–80; M. Moore, *A Sacred Kingdom: Bishops and the Rise of Frankish Kingship, 300–850* (Washington DC, 2011), pp. 328–67.
40 Amolo, Epistola 2, MGH *Epp.* 5, p. 377.
41 Gottschalk, *Responsa de diversis*, ed. Lambot, p. 169; and Gottschalk, *De corpore et sanguine domini*, ed. Lambot, p. 325. See also F. Curta, *Southeastern Europe in the Middle Ages, 500–1250* (Cambridge, 2006),

pp. 139–40; and P. Kershaw, 'Eberhard of Friuli, a Carolingian lay intellectual', in P. Wormald and J. L. Nelson, eds, *Lay Intellectuals in the Carolingian World* (Cambridge, 2007), pp. 77–105, at 91–7.

42 Hincmar, Epistola 169, ed. E. Perels, MGH *Epp.* 8, pp. 144–63, at 162; J. Jolivet, *Godescalc d'Orbais et la Trinité: la méthode de la théologie à l'époque carolingienne* (Paris, 1958), pp. 94–8, 170; and see n.76.
43 Schrimpf, 'Hraban und der Prädestinationsstreit', pp. 145–53.
44 Gottschalk, *Confessio prolixior*, ed. Lambot, pp. 55–78. The dating of this text is unclear, but not long after the Council of Quierzy Hincmar had a copy from Gottschalk himself, who most likely sent it before the gathering in order to influence the archbishop.
45 Hincmar, *Ad reclusos et simplices*, ed. Gundlach, p. 262.
46 Gottschalk, *Confessio prolixior*, ed. Lambot, pp. 55–6.
47 *Ibid.*, pp. 56–71.
48 *Ibid.*, pp. 71–3.
49 *Ibid.*, pp. 74–5.
50 Hrabanus Maurus, *Martyrologium*, ed. J. McCulloh, CCCM 44 (Turnhout, 1979), p. 108.
51 Wood, *Missionary Life*, pp. 83–5, 129–32.
52 Gottschalk, *Confessio prolixior*, ed. Lambot, pp. 76–7.
53 Hincmar, *De praedestinatione Dei*, PL 125, col. 85, c. 2.
54 Gottschalk, *Responsa de diversis*, ed. Lambot, pp. 156–7.
55 Florus of Lyons, *Libellus de tribus epistolis*, ed. K. Zechiel-Eckes, *Opera polemica*, CCCM 260 (Turnhout, 2014), c. 24, pp. 320–2.
56 Council of Quierzy, 849, MGH *Conc.* III, no. 18, pp. 198–9.
57 A. Diem, 'Een verstoorder van de *ordo*: Gottschalk van Orbais en zijn leer van de dubbele predestinatie', *Utrechtse historische cahiers*, 16 (1995), 115–31.
58 Council of Quierzy, 849, MGH *Conc.* III, no. 18, pp. 198–9.
59 For the sources of Gottschalk's sentence, see n.62.
60 *AB* s.a. 849, pp. 56–7 (trans. Nelson, p. 67).
61 Florus, *Libellus de tribus epistolis*, ed. Zechiel-Eckes, c. 25, pp. 366–8.
62 Hincmar, *De praedestinatione Dei*, PL 125, col. 85. The sources: Benedict of Nursia, *Regula monachorum*, ed. and trans. P. Schmitz, *Règle de saint Benoît*, 5th ed. (Turnhout, 1987), c. 2, ll. 28–9 (pp. 16–18); c. 23 (p. 70); c. 25, ll. 1–2 (p. 72); *Concilium Agathense*, 506, in C. Munier, ed., *Concilia Galliae a. 314–a. 506*, CCSL 148 (Turnhout, 1963), pp. 189–228, at cc. 27, 50, pp. 205, 225; (not indicated by Hincmar) Council of Meaux-Paris, 845–46, MGH *Conc.* III, no. 11, p. 111, c. 57; (not indicated by Hincmar) Siricius, *Epistola ad Himerium episcopum Tarraconensem*, cc. 6–7, ed. K. Zechiel-Eckes and D. Jasper, *Die erste Dekretale: der Brief Papst Siricius' an Bischof Himerius von Tarragona vom Jahr 385 (JK 255)*, MGH Studien und Texte (Hanover, 2013), pp. 94–102.

63　Ganz, 'Debate', p. 283.
64　Flodoard, *HRE* III-28, pp. 358-9.
65　Hincmar, *Ad reclusos et simplices*, ed. Gundlach, pp. 260-2.
66　See, for example, Gottschalk, Carmen VII (*Age, quaeso*), MGH *Poetae* III, pp. 733-7, at 736.
67　For Hincmar on predestination, see Devisse, *Hincmar*, I, pp. 214-68; Chazelle, *Crucified God*, pp. 181-95.
68　Hincmar, *Ad reclusos et simplices*, ed. Gundlach, pp. 260-1.
69　For an excellent discussion of Ratramnus, Lupus, Eriugena and Prudentius and their works, see Ganz, 'Debate', pp. 288-94.
70　Hrabanus Maurus, Epistola 43, MGH *Epp.* 5, pp. 487-9.
71　Hrabanus Maurus, Epistola 44, MGH *Epp.* 5, pp. 490-9.
72　*AB* s.a. 851, pp. 61-2 (trans. Nelson, pp. 70-1).
73　*AB* s.a. 853, p. 67 (trans. Nelson, pp. 76-7).
74　Council of Soissons, 853, MGH *Conc.* III, no. 27, pp. 253-93; G. H. Tavard, *Trina deitas: the Controversy between Hincmar and Gottschalk* (Milwaukee, 1996), pp. 35-8. On the Ebbo clerics, see Screen, Chapter 4, p. 77.
75　Tavard, *Trina deitas*, pp. 59-82; Nelson, *Charles the Bald*, pp. 168-9.
76　Gottschalk, *De praedestinatione*, ed. Lambot, p. 229; Gottschalk, *Opusculum primum*, ed. Lambot, p. 412.
77　Gottschalk, *De praedestinatione*, ed. Lambot, pp. 229-31.
78　Genke and Gumerlock, *Gottschalk*, pp. 62-3.
79　Gottschalk, *De praedestinatione*, ed. Lambot, p. 251.
80　Gottschalk, *De trina deitate*, ed. Lambot, p. 96; Augustine, Sermo 62, c.8, §13, *PL* 38, cols 420-1.
81　Hincmar, *De praedestinatione Dei*, *PL* 125, col. 106, c. 10; col. 125, c. 14; col. 130, c. 16; col. 162, c. 17; col. 165, c. 17; col. 271, c. 26, col. 289, c. 29.
82　Hincmar, Epistola 169, MGH *Epp.* 8, pp. 162-3.
83　Ganz, 'Debate', p. 298.
84　Prudentius, *Epistola tractoria ad Wenilonem*, *PL* 115, cols 1365-8.
85　Devisse, *Hincmar*, I, pp. 223-4; Ganz, 'Debate', p. 299.
86　Ganz, 'Debate', p. 298.
87　Council of Savonnières, 859, MGH *Conc.* III, no. 47, pp. 447-89.
88　*Ibid.*, pp. 473-6; Ganz, 'Debate', p. 298.
89　Devisse, *Hincmar*, I, pp. 224-68.
90　Council of Tusey, 860, MGH *Conc.* IV, no. 3, pp. 22-34; P. R. McKeon, 'The Carolingian councils of Savonnières (859) and Tusey (860) and their background', *Revue bénédictine*, 84 (1974), 74-110, at 76-84, 105-9.
91　Devisse, *Hincmar*, I, pp. 201, II, pp. 583-600; Hincmar, Epistola 169, MGH *Epp.* 8, pp. 144-63.
92　*AB* s.a. 859, p. 82 (trans. Nelson, p. 91); Devisse, *Hincmar*, II, pp. 582-635.
93　Hincmar, Epistolae 187-8, MGH *Epp.* 8, pp. 194-6, 200-1.

94 Hincmar, *De una et non trina deitate*, PL 125, cols 473–618 at col. 618.
95 J. B. Manceaux, *Histoire de l'abbaye et du village d'Hautvillers* (Épernay, 1880), p. 253, citing A. de Yepes, *Chroniques générales de l'Ordre de S. Benoist*, 2 vols (Toul, 1646–84), II, p. 387.
96 The manuscript is Burgerbibliothek Bern 584, on which see Lambot, ed., *Œuvres théologiques et grammaticales*, p. xii; and B. Bischoff, *Katalog der festländischen Handschriften des neunten Jahrhunderts (mit Ausnahme der wisigotischen)*, 2 vols (Wiesbaden, 1998–2004), vol. 1, p. 130.

14

Hincmar, priests and Pseudo-Isidore: the case of Trising in context

Mayke de Jong

Trising returns from Rome

In the autumn of 871, Archbishop Hincmar of Rheims sent a long and indignant letter to Pope Hadrian II, defending himself against the accusations of his nephew, Bishop Hincmar of Laon. Almost as an afterthought, he added a report on a delinquent and violent priest named Trising.[1] Well over two years previously, Trising had failed to appear in front of a synod to account for himself; instead, without Hincmar being aware of it, he had gone off to Rome to take his case to the pope. Now he had returned, at a highly inconvenient moment, for in his place another priest had already been ordained. The contents of the papal letter brought back home by Trising are not revealed, but it is clear that the case was not shut, as Hincmar had assumed. It was still wide open. The pope demanded that the archbishop of Rheims present his side of the matter, so the pope could make a well-informed decision. That Trising's successor had already been appointed was embarrassing, to say the least. Hincmar's exasperation transpires towards the end of his reply to Hadrian: the pope knew very well indeed (*sufficientissime*) that one could not leave a parish without a priest for such a long time.[2]

Trising's conduct as depicted by Hincmar was outrageous indeed. The priest's brother had married a woman who already had a daughter from an earlier marriage. She also had a brother called Livulf. All these relatives lived in the same village (*villa*). Allegedly, Trising had slept with his brother's stepdaughter. After Livulf and Trising went drinking in a tavern, the two men started arguing about Trising's behaviour towards Livulf's niece. The verbal fight turned nasty, with Livulf hitting Trising, who then, having snatched a sword from

Livulf's son (apparently also present), set upon his adversary. He wanted to kill him but got no further than cutting off two fingers of the hand Livulf raised to shield himself. Livulf fainted and fell off his horse while Trising, thinking that he had killed his adversary, jumped on the latter's mount and rode home. Livulf turned out to be very much alive, however, for along with others from the village he accused Trising of all the above. In his letter, Hincmar explained to Hadrian that 'he heard this from many people', leaving no doubt that the affair had become public and needed to be dealt with accordingly: it was a 'manifest crime' (*crimen manifestum*), about which more below.

Commenting on Hincmar's report on Trising, Carine van Rhijn has underlined the central role of the local community in this affair. The men and women of a *villa* could make or break the reputation of their priest; they provided the kind of bottom-up *correctio* that could be just as effective, or even more so, than the distant control exercised by exercised by (arch)bishops.[3] In practice, the two corrective forces worked together, for the ecclesiastical authorities largely depended on the information of local men and women who lodged a complaint. Yet, from the perspective of Hincmar and his colleagues, a delicate balance had to be observed. Inevitably, some accusations were partly or wholly unfounded, or even downright malicious; accepting every allegation at face value meant encouraging slander, undermining the reputation of the rural priesthood. Ugly rumours, true or not, could develop into a scandal and make the crimes in question 'manifest', which required a public trial in a (provincial) synod and removal from office if the accusation were proven. The priest in question might try to purge himself with the aid of oath-helpers, but in any case, his reputation (*fama*) would be damaged. In other words, there was a lot of incentive to deal with sexual transgressions by means of a secret confession and penance, amends that would allow the culprit to remain in office and atone for his sins away from the public eye. But, as Hincmar's letter stresses, this was not an option in Trising's case; everyone was talking of it, and the priest himself had confessed openly to his murderous intent. Given the public nature of the affair, deposition and excommunication were the likely outcome.

Trising's case was by no means exceptional but, thanks to Hincmar's reply to Pope Hadrian, rather more is known about it than most, so it provides a good vantage point for the topic on which I focus here: priests who appealed to Rome, hoping to overturn the verdict of their local superiors. Hincmar's strongly worded account of the wayward priest should be handled with care, for he was writing himself out of a tight spot. On the other hand, only a few years earlier, the archbishop had backed up a papal verdict on a wrongly punished priest, ordering the bishop of Noyon to obey the instructions from Hadrian II. This was another case of a priest who returned from Rome bearing a papal letter restoring him to his parish, but in this case Hincmar did his utmost to effectuate the papal verdict.[4] Thus it was not a matter of an archbishop who automatically resisted papal interference, though the increasing proximity of the papacy did create some special problems, as we shall see.

By the 870s some resourceful priests seem to have been relying on precepts from the Pseudo-Isidorian Decretals in order to escape from local ecclesiastical justice. This in turn raises other questions, for scholars agree that the False Decretals were meant to safeguard the authority and independent status of bishops, first and foremost; priests travelling to Rome to have their bishop's verdict overturned were hardly an obvious part of this scheme. But priests appropriating the principles of Pseudo-Isidore for their own purposes were part of a larger development that occurred during Hincmar's tenure as archbishop, namely a growing interdependence between the West Frankish Church and the Roman pontiff. To a large extent, this *rapprochement* was fuelled by a series of internal conflicts within Hincmar's archdiocese, in which successive popes were increasingly implicated. This papal involvement was mostly generated by a demand from clashing parties north of the Alps, rather than by initiatives on the part of Rome itself. Of this trend, the affair of the priest Trising was a minor yet revealing part.

Trising's predicament

Hincmar's version of events, as mentioned already, is far from objective. On the other hand, his report to Pope Hadrian provides much information that should not be ignored, one-sided though it may be. To begin with, it states in no uncertain terms that Trising's sins qualified as manifest crimes. Their public nature should be reflected in the subsequent judicial procedure. Apart from his much talked-about affair with his brother's stepdaughter, there was public drunkenness; likewise, his shouting match with Livulf and violent attack on the man were committed openly, in front of witnesses. That killing rather than

Pseudo-Isidore: the case of Trising

maiming had been Trising's intention, he had made patently clear when he left Livulf lying there for dead and went home. Hincmar had heard about it from many people,[5] and it can safely be assumed that there was no lack of accusers, beginning with Livulf himself, whose testimony is cited in the letter. The notoriety of this priest had made him so infamous that Hincmar called him to account.[6] The publicity of the case was maintained in the subsequent judicial procedure, and Hincmar's own report to Hadrian added to this.[7]

Trising appeared in front of Hincmar in the presence of the latter's clerics and priests. This was not a provincial synod, attended by the bishops of the archdiocese, but a gathering of Hincmar and his Rheims clergy. Trising's sexual sins remained hidden, in that they were not the object of a formal accusation or confession, so these were left to God's judgment, but 'what was not allowed to remain hidden', the public violence and the obviously intended homicide, Hincmar subjected to his judgment. In the presence of Hincmar and his clerics Trising confessed that he had intended to kill Livulf; presumably he saw no point in denying it since public opinion had unified against him. He was removed from his priestly office, pending the provincial synod that would deal with his case. In Hincmar's view, the only legitimate ground to depose a priest was if he had confessed publicly and was then convicted *legaliter ac regulariter*, that is by a provincial synod convened by the archbishop.[8] There, Trising would have to repeat his confession in public, and the accusation against him would have to be supported by the oath of seven trustworthy witnesses, the canonical number required, according to Hincmar, to make a deposition legitimate.[9]

Given Trising's dismal standing in his own parish, these seven *testes* would not have been difficult to find. In the face of this inevitable outcome, the priest decided to travel to Rome and put his case to the pope. He and other priests who did so were clearly no poor and downtrodden rural clerics; they had the resources to pay for the long journey to Rome as well as their stay in this foreign and no doubt expensive city.[10] Altogether, Trising was gone for a year and nine months. Given that his successor was already in place, it is unlikely that he managed to regain his parish, but he certainly managed to embarrass his archbishop. Hadrian never replied to Hincmar's strongly worded explanation and Trising's fate is unknown, but he was neither the first nor the last priest from Hincmar's archdiocese who decided on this course of action.

Transalpine affairs

Throughout Hincmar's career, the question how to discipline his clergy in a truly canonical way was a central aspect (and major headache) of his office. His second episcopal statute of 852 already contains an extensive section on how to deal with priests and deacons who had incurred *mala fama*;[11] this text was partly incorporated in *De presbiteris criminosis*, a text that dates from the mid-870s.[12] Its central issue was how to proceed *legaliter ac regulariter* when accusations and rumours ran rife, but proof was lacking. How to depose a manifestly criminal priest?[13] Not much later, in 877, Hincmar drafted an extensive memorandum in the name of Charles the Bald to Pope John VIII (*r.* 872–82), directed against clerics, and especially priests, who had appealed to Rome without the knowledge or permission of their superiors.[14]

By then, the problem was apparently of such magnitude that consultation at the highest level was needed, namely between King Charles, crowned emperor in 875, and Pope John VIII. This is why Hincmar acted as Charles's ghost-writer, in a long and learned text known as *De iudiciis et appellationibus*. It was composed as if the emperor resided in Rome, and commented from this southern vantage point on the affairs of his transalpine kingdom. The high-level exchange that Hincmar envisaged never took place, for Charles died on 6 September 877, before he ever reached Rome. Still, this eminently imperial document may also have been meant to impress audiences closer to home. If so, they would be informed that relations between Charles/Hincmar and Pope Hadrian were at an absolute nadir, and that the pope's support for priests who challenged Hincmar's verdict was a major bone of contention.

'Charles' opened by referring to the exemplary way in which his illustrious forebears had once dealt with priests accused of crimes; since his nephew Louis reigned in Italy, however, papal letters had been received that were so intemperate that they could not be ascribed to the apostolic see.[15] The issue at hand was then presented: it had come to Charles's imperial attention that priests from the regions north of the Alps, who had been deposed and subjected to penance by their bishops for certain crimes, came 'here' (that is, to Rome) without the permission or knowledge of their archbishops or bishops. They then took back home from Rome letters that went against any known canonical precept. Of course all this did not happen on the orders of the pontiff himself, the king and emperor explained, but because of the many judicial complaints and petitions he had to cope with; it was no different for a ruler in his *respublica*. Underlings, on the pretext of earnest compassion, had become far too proactive. This was the opinion of the bishops of 'that region' (Charles's kingdom) and of the king himself.[16]

Although this document mentioned bishops who had appealed to Rome, it was priests *(presbyteri)* that received by far the most attention. In both cases justice should be done in the place where the crime and accusation had occurred, rather than in faraway Rome. If a bishop had deposed or excommunicated a priest in anger and with haste, this did not give the priest the right to turn to Rome. Hincmar gathered a formidable canonical dossier for the emperor to present, with the central argument that it was the provincial synod that should be the final instance of appeal for bishops, priests and deacons accused of manifest crimes. This had been the case under Charles's predecessors and should be strictly maintained; otherwise any priest could act with impunity, and go off to Rome when he was convicted.[17] Particularly priests who had lived with women and had been punished for it by their bishop went to Rome 'regularly' *(regulariter)*, without their bishop's knowledge, and returned home with papal letters that not only overturned the bishop's verdict, but also compelled him and his colleagues to travel to the papal court in order to argue his case, something not found in any ancient law or canonical precept.[18]

Heinrich Schrörs gathered a small dossier of priests and laymen who appealed to Rome during Hincmar's tenure as archbishop. This is the tip of an iceberg, and far too scanty to firmly support any trends. Still, we may note that the first appeal by a priest dates to the pontificate of Leo IV (*r.* 844–55) and that their number seems to have risen significantly during the pontificate of Nicholas I (*r.* 858–67).[19] This was the pope who first claimed that grievous accusations against bishops *(causae episcoporum)* should be judged in Rome. In this, he followed the Pseudo-Isidorian Decretals, which he knew since 864/65 at least, when he supported the appeal of Bishop Rothad of Soissons against Hincmar.[20]

Pseudo-Isidore and the priesthood

Although the so-called Pseudo-Isidorian forgeries consist of a larger corpus of texts, the Decretals are the largest and most important constituent part. When in what follows I refer to 'Pseudo-Isidore' for short, I mean the False Decretals, which are in fact a mixture of forged and authentic canonical material: the letters of early popes, mostly forged, as well as the often genuine canons of influential synods of the western Church.[21] In *De presbiteris criminosis*, his treatise on manifestly criminal priests written in the mid-870s, Hincmar turned upon 'certain people' (*quidam*) who claimed that a layman could not bring a complaint against a cleric, nor a priest against a bishop, a deacon against a priest, a subdeacon against a deacon, an acolyte against a subdeacon, an exorcist against an acolyte, or a doorkeeper against a lector; bishops could only be condemned with seventy-two witnesses, and the pope not at all. According to Pseudo-Isidore, the condemnation of a cardinal priest in Rome required forty-four witnesses, that of a cardinal deacon twenty-six, and accusations against all lower ecclesiastical ranks had to be supported by at least seven witnesses. Lay witnesses and accusers should not suffer from any kind of infamy, must possess wives and children and declare their loyalty to Christ. Finally, the testimony of a cleric against a layman was invalid in all circumstances.[22]

This remarkable canon, ascribed to the sainted Pope Sylvester himself, could put a spanner in the works of any ninth-century Frankish judicial procedure, with the additional complication that the Roman *testes* would be understood as oath-helpers who swore to the guilt or innocence of the accused.[23] The text had already been circulated from the sixth century onwards as a part of the so-called Symmachian forgeries, but Hincmar cited it as an excerpt from the Acts of Saint Sylvester 'which Isidore, the Spanish bishop, compiled together with the letters of the pontiffs of the Roman see from Saint Clement to the blessed Gregory'. In other words, in the form in which Hincmar knew this precept, it had been transmitted as part of the Pseudo-Isidorian decretals.[24] In the archbishop's view, anyone in his right mind and with knowledge of sacred law could see that this went against the *canones*. He questioned the authority of the *Gesta sancti Sylvestri*, and derided the notion that witnesses would be more suitable if they had wives and children. Of course those who lived chastely would be more pure and trustworthy. Yet his main objection to the 'certain people' who spread this text was about the practicalities of administering justice. How could this ever be done *legaliter et regulariter*[25] if no layman could accuse a cleric, no cleric a layman, or a cleric a cleric? If a priest could not be proved guilty or innocent except by such an enormous amount of suitable oath-helpers, how could anything be proved? There were villages in his diocese which did not even have the necessary number of suitable *testes*, that is, men with wives and children who held a *mansus*. Given that Pseudo-Sylvester required a minimum of forty-four witnesses in the case of a priest, this was a pertinent observation.

This was one of the texts on which Trising and like-minded priests might have relied when they contested the verdict of their (arch) bishops. Whether they also resorted to Pseudo-Isidore to justify their appeal to Rome is another matter. Whether Trising did so remains unknown, and in the case of the laymen who appealed to the pope this forgery surely did not play a direct part. Moreover, there is a broad agreement that False Decretals were meant to protect bishops, rather than priests, against arbitrary accusation and deposition on the part of their metropolitans and secular rulers. The right to appeal to Rome was one part of the strategy, while the demand for an impossible amount of impeccable witnesses – seventy-two in the case of a bishop – was another.[26]

Over the past decade, views on the date and origins of the False Decretals have changed. Until quite recently, the forgery used to be seen as the product of conflicts between Hincmar and his clergy, to be dated to 847–52; nowadays it is thought to have originated in the monastery of Corbie, in the direct aftermath of the rebellions against Louis the Pious in 830 and 833.[27] Although the discussion still continues, the first direct reference to the Decretals remains the one in Hincmar's *Second episcopal statute*, issued on 1 October 852. The few citations Hincmar took from Pseudo-Isidore were hardly sensational: they forbade priests to pawn sacramental vessels, and ordered penance for lapsed clerics whose sins had remained undetected.[28] They are a reminder that much of this compilation was concerned with humdrum aspects of ecclesiastical life, rather than with the high-level clerical infighting for which it has become infamous. Yet it may not be entirely accidental that these citations occurred in Hincmar's first extensive discussion of how to secure canonical proof if priests were accused of manifest crimes.[29]

In this same text, Hincmar insisted that clerics whose crimes had been manifest should be deposed and remain deposed, against those who claimed that such major cases (*negotia maiora*) should be referred for final judgment to the pope.[30] This precept too was much older than Pseudo-Isidore so it could have been cited via another tradition, but all the same it was included in the Decretals, and the fact that this discussion on *negotia maiora* flared up with regard to priests should give us pause for thought. The very first case known to me of a priest from Hincmar's archdiocese who appealed to Rome dates to this very time, 852/53. It is a sad but revealing story of one priest ousting another from his parish. The victim's indignant relatives revenged him by blinding his adversary, without his knowledge; nevertheless, he had been excommunicated by the bishops of Senlis and Beauvais. Pope Leo IV ordered the bishops to lift this excommunication as soon as possible.[31]

Clearly Hincmar was aware of the compilation, of which he thought Isidore of Seville was the author, and he occasionally cited it, but it never became the central plank of his argument; he preferred the *Dionysio-Hadriana* and the *Hispana*, along with dossiers of texts that were of his own making. But he had to become more involved in 862–65, the years of his confrontation with Bishop Rothad of Soissons, who successfully appealed to Rome against his deposition; it was then, most likely, that Pseudo-Isidore became known in Rome. Hincmar's fierce clash with his nephew Bishop Hincmar of Laon in 869–71 moved the Decretals even more centre stage for, like Rothad, the younger Hincmar used Pseudo-Isidore as his means to escape from his archbishop's juridical grasp. This eminently public row between the two Hincmars has rightly been called 'a struggle over the circulation and validity of Pseudo-Isidorian canonical norms'.[32] The struggle was won by the uncle, who in 870 at the synod of Attigny presented his *Opusculum LV capitulorum*, a brilliant critique of the Pseudo-Isidorian attempts to render bishops unassailable. His nephew left the synod under a cloud, and, accused of disloyalty, was deposed in August 871 by Charles the Bald. Shortly thereafter, he was blinded, rendered unable to act in episcopal office or any other kind of royal service.[33]

The confrontations of the tempestuous Hincmar of Laon with his archbishop and his king went a long way towards making Pseudo-Isidore known in West Frankish kingdom. It is in sources from this context that one can observe the use of this compilation by priests, who evidently took a leaf from their bishop's book. In July 868 the bishop of Laon denounced Charles the Bald to Pope Hadrian II as a usurper of Church property. The pope reacted quickly, siding with King Charles and Archbishop Hincmar; a first attempt by Charles's leading men to arrest the contrarian bishop in January 869 failed, for he positioned himself next to the altar of his cathedral, surrounded by his clergy.[34] He was then summoned to account for himself at a synod at Verberie on 25 April of this year but, before attending, he took precautions. On 19 April he convened the clergy of his diocese to a synod. Having lectured them on the might of episcopal authority, he had all those present subscribe a compilation of forged papal letters taken from the Pseudo-Isidorian Decretals, selected because they made bishops unassailable and undermined the authority of archbishops.[35] On the same occasion, he also declared that if he were to be prevented from appealing to the pope, or be taken captive, his entire clergy would have to go on strike: no sacraments should be administered, and no pastoral care should be given, until he, the bishop, was at liberty again and a papal verdict could be obtained.[36] Towards the end of May, when Charles did have Hincmar of Laon arrested, this became effective. Only days later his uncle received a delegation of clerics from Laon who complained about the disastrous consequences for their entire diocese. Only by late June did Hincmar of Rheims manage to get the episcopal interdict lifted; presumably, by then his nephew had regained his liberty of movement.[37]

By this time there was dissatisfaction and anger among the clergy of Laon, as transpires from an anonymous collection of Pseudo-Isidorian and other texts compiled by and for 'maltreated clerics'. Klaus Zechiel-Eckes has argued convincingly that this treatise was a response to the bishop of Laon, who had not only put his clerics through a harrowing confrontation with the king, but was also a strict disciplinarian who had cracked down, in writing and practice, on his 'rebel clerics'.[38] In their compilation these clerics extended Pseudo-Isidore's stipulations in favour of bishops to the lower clergy; for example, 'bishops' that were driven out became 'bishops, priests and deacons' that had been expelled.[39] In the turbulent years 869–71, the clergy of Laon had ample opportunity to familiarise themselves with Pseudo-Isidore, not least by having to swear allegiance to a selection from its precepts.

No doubt the maltreated men who put together the compilation against their bishop came from the learned cathedral clergy with a good library at their disposal. All the same, it would be overly cautious to assume that rural priests such as Trising remained completely outside the *milieu* where such knowledge circulated, be it in written or oral form.[40] The diocesan synod, to be held twice a year, was meant to involve and discipline precisely these rural priests; this was the most likely occasion to meet each other and exchange information. When Hincmar of Laon convened such a gathering on 19 April 869, he intended as many clerics as possible from his diocese to be present, so that all would be bound by their promise to effectuate his interdict, if need be. Furthermore, the fact that their bishop resisted the authority of his archbishop and king, and considered only the papacy the final and legitimate instance of appeal, cannot have gone unnoticed either; this was a high-level and notorious political conflict. Trising came from the diocese of Rheims, not from Laon, but distances between the relevant places of action were not all that great; Mouzon, where Trising and Livulf got drunk, was a little over 100 km from Rheims, and less than 10 km from Douzy, where Hincmar of Laon was deposed in 871.

The nephew's shameful downfall presumably worked as a disincentive to other bishops, who became less eager to base their claims on this apparently weak foundation.[41] According to Horst Fuhrmann, once the controversy with Hincmar of Laon had subsided, the brief Carolingian heyday of Pseudo-Isidore was over. But how does this correspond with the 'explosive expansion of manuscripts' of the False Decretals in West Francia up to 900, as Fuhrmann called it? He pointed out that the mechanical copying of manuscripts was not the same as explicit references in the context of intellectual reflection.[42] Yet this distinction is not very helpful when it comes to assessing the influence of a text, for copying also expresses interest; and, without in-depth investigations of the manuscripts in question, we do not know whether it was 'mechanical' or not. The fact that at least thirty complete or partial manuscripts survive from the late ninth century means that the False Decretals were thought worth the attention.[43]

Recent research has concentrated almost entirely on the question of the Decretals' origins and authorship, with the basic assumption that Pseudo-Isidore was all about protecting bishops against kings and archbishops. This may have well been an initial incentive, but not necessarily the only one, and it looks as if by c.870 priests and deacons were also discovering the collection's uses. It is no coincidence that Hincmar's two substantial treatises on criminal priests discussed above, *De iudiciis et appellationibus* and *De presbiteris criminosis*, were both written in the decade after his highly public confrontation with the bishop of Laon. That priests appealed against their bishops to the pope need not be a direct consequence of knowing the basic tenets of the False Decretals, but some familiarity must certainly have helped, and the same holds true for knowledge and acceptance of the Decretals in Rome since the 860s. When Trising made his appeal in 869, he encountered Pope Hadrian II, who treated the Decretals as an authoritative collection of genuine canon law. In short, the possibility that Trising and like-minded colleagues who appealed to Rome were at least partly influenced by Pseudo-Isidorian notions is not as far-fetched as it may seem.

The growing proximity of Rome

Hincmar of Rheims had to contend with an increasingly independent-minded priesthood, in combination with a papacy that was ever more ready to assert its authority. At first glance, this is a story of a formidable archbishop who used his vast knowledge of canon law in order to fend off papal interference, while the popes in question successfully managed to expand their influence, especially during the pontificate of Nicholas I. The role of Pseudo-Isidore in this process was insignificant; after all, Pope Nicholas did not need this forgery in order to exert his authority, and the way in which Hincmar of Rheims made mincemeat of both Pseudo-Isidore and his nephew in 869–71 taught bishops to think twice before they relied on this collection.

This is one way of looking at it, but one might also see such conflict as an effective way to communicate. Hincmar's tenure as archbishop was punctuated by a series of major upheavals and the papacy was ever more drawn into them, not because popes took the initiative but because members of the West Frankish elite – the king and his most powerful archbishop to begin with – involved the popes in their quarrels and treated them as the font of all authority. And this was what the successors of St Peter were, according to Hincmar's most cherished authentic canons as well as the Pseudo-Isidorian forgeries: claims to papal primacy go back as far as Leo I (r. 440–46) and his fifth-century successors. Still, the major role played by popes like Nicholas I and Hadrian II in the great political affairs of the West Frankish kingdom and Church was in many ways novel. When in May 833 Pope Gregory IV travelled north to mediate between Louis the Pious and his three rebellious sons, only a minority of the Frankish episcopate welcomed this intervention; the majority saw him as an uninvited meddler, who had just come to further the rebels' interests.[44] When two years later Louis, together with his bishops, turned Ebbo of Rheims into the scapegoat for the rebellion of 833, removing him from his archiepiscopal see and turning him into a penitent, he felt no need to ask for the pope's formal permission.[45]

By contrast, in 867, with the controversy about Ebbo's deposition still dragging on after the latter's death in 851, the Council of Troyes that tried to solve the matter simply assumed that there must have been some correspondence with Rome about it, and asked Pope Nicholas I to produce it from the papal archives.[46] From that same year there dates a letter from Charles the Bald to Pope Nicholas, apologising for having made the court cleric Wulfad archbishop of Bourges without notifying the pope beforehand.[47] This was also meant to take the wind out of Hincmar's sails, since he had furiously opposed the appointment of an 'Ebbo cleric' whom he had deposed as a bishop in 853.[48] As in the case of Hincmar of Laon, who blackened the name of his king in angry letters to the pope, such epistles were also (perhaps especially) intended for an audience at home. This also holds true for the long and complicated conflict over the divorce of Lothar II and Theutberga (855–69), in which Pope Nicholas became an ever stronger player, mainly because different parties in the north invoked his authority for their own purposes.[49]

This is the context in which priests appealing to Rome should be understood, and it is also the context for the spread of Pseudo-Isidore. If they indeed originated in the early 830s, the False Decretals – with their emphasis on supreme papal authority – represented very much a minority view at that time, but this changed in the course of the 850s and 860s. This is not to say that the famous forgery was the main cause of the increasing interdependence between the West Frankish Church and Rome, or of the growing self-confidence of successive popes. Created by a Rome-oriented minority of learned Frankish clerics, it offered a huge collection of texts that could legitimate the notion of supreme papal justice in future generations.

More importantly, the False Decretals evoked a commanding world of pristine and authentic Christianity, and provided a missing link in canonical tradition: the authoritative pronouncements of the very first popes. The Decretals were contested throughout the ninth century, first and foremost by Hincmar of Rheims, whose arguments against Trising's departure to Rome make eminent sense from a pastoral point of view. Manifest crimes by priests should be judged in the location where they were committed and could be proved, and a parish should not be left unstaffed for years on end because its priest was busy appealing in Rome. Yet like those who created Pseudo-

Pseudo-Isidore: the case of Trising

Isidore, Hincmar himself also looked for authority and canonicity in the written tradition of the early Church, and creatively adapted this when he saw fit.

This was a society in which good law was by definition old law, and Rome had very strong and even biblical claims to ancient authority: here the apostles Peter and Paul had been martyred and buried, among hosts of other martyrs. A vision of centuries of sacred history that stretched behind St Peter's successor inspired the awe in which many north of the Alps held Rome and the papacy, even at times when the popes themselves were involved in contentious and less than savoury Roman and West Frankish politics. In spite of their fierce clashes and disagreements, this vision of ideal Christian communities, located in an authoritative past that ought to be recreated in the present, was shared by all the main protagonists of this chapter. It helped to shape Hincmar's view of what a parish should be,[50] and his notion of what canonical authority amounted to, as well as Pseudo-Isidore's meticulous evocation of this past, and Trising's conviction that better justice could be found in Rome. Even Archbishop Hincmar had to bow before that, making a long voyage with an uncertain outcome worth all the trouble.

Appendix: Letter from Hincmar of Rheims to Pope Hadrian II, spring 871

This is the last section of an epistle that otherwise deals with Hincmar of Laon (*PL* 126, cols 0646C–0648C).

> Furthermore, the Authority of Your Paternity recently sent me a letter about a priest of our parish named Trising, commanding that I would send you an extensive written report on this affair. About which I write to your Authority, as the truth of the matter stands.
>
> Some free woman, the sister of a man called Livulf, from the same village in which the aforesaid Trising had been ordained priest, accepted as husband the brother of this Trising; and through this familiarity, the same Trising began to frequent the house of his brother. And, as Livulf who lives in this village and the parishioners and neighbours of this priest said, he [Trising] began to sleep with the daughter of his brother's wife whom she had from another husband. And one day this priest and the aforesaid Livulf went to the fortress named Mouzon, and got drunk in some tavern, against our episcopal prohibition: for in all synods we forbid this to our priests, as the African councils formulate

it: 'Let clerics and priests not enter taverns, except when forced by the needs of travel'.[51] And this priest went into the tavern in order to get drunk, because of gluttony, not because of the needs of travel, for the very same fortress is not more than four miles away from the house of this priest. Returning drunk from the said fortress, the self-same priest and Livulf began to argue with each other, as drunks usually do, and their argument got to the point that he [Livulf] reproached the priest about his niece; and in return this priest hurled any taunt at Livulf that he could think of. Then the same Livulf twice hit the priest Trising with the stick he had in his hand. Then this priest rushed up to Livulf's son, who was girded with a sword, and removed this very sword; and while he [Trising] wanted to split his head in two in order to kill him, this Livulf lifted his hand against the sword and received the sword's blow, and two fingers of the same hand were cut off. And when he fell off his horse, the priest thought he was dead, and jumping on the man's horse he went back to his house.

When I heard this from many people, I summoned him, in the presence of clerics and our fellow ministers, and I interrogated him, and the truth. As for the woman who was talked about, he denied that he had slept with her. But of his intention that he wanted to kill that man, in the way I have just explained, he made a confession; and according to the word of John the Apostle he is convicted of homicide.[52] As the blessed Augustine wrote to his metropolitan *(primatus)* Xantippus about a priest from his bishopric, however, what he denied, I left to God;[53] what was not allowed to be hidden, I submitted him to my judgment, and I removed him from his priestly office until he would appear in front of a provincial synod, and, as the canons of Carthage prescribe,[54] would get a certain outcome of his case. Yet this very same man did not come to any synod, even though we held several synods in our archbishopric *(provincia)*. I expected him for one year and six months, and he made no effort on behalf of himself. And this while the sacred canons decree that 'whenever clerics are convicted of and confess any kind of crime, if they perchance wish to be present at their trial to declare their innocence, they should do so within one year after their excommunication. If within one year they disdain to justify themselves, let the voice of none of them be heard thereafter'.[55] Meanwhile, after a year and six months the members of the parish in which the priest in question had been ordained, complained that they did not have a priest; for that he had travelled to Rome, I did not know until three months later, when, after a priest had been ordained in his place, he came from Rome and brought me Your Holiness's letter.

In the canons of the fourth provincial council of Africa chapter 67, about rebels and usurers, what clerics should not do is formulated as follows: 'rebels should never be ordained, or those who revenge the injuries done to them'.[56] And if such men are not to be ordained, it can be deduced what those deserve who have no fear to admit to such things after their ordination. And the ancient canons of the fathers in the synod in which several metropolitans were together with their suffragans – and the council of Antioch decided that the perfect council is this council where the metropolitan is present – pronounced clear decrees: 'Let clerics who have been found willing to take up arms in some revolt or other, be taken off to a monastery for penance, having lost the rank of their ordination'.[57] And Pope Zachary wrote to Boniface, the bishop of Mainz, that he should remove bishops, priests and deacons who were found to have spilt the blood of Christians or pagans, from these ecclesiastical orders.[58] And now that I send you this report, as you commanded, it is already more than two years since the aforesaid Trising wanted to kill the above-mentioned Livulf and mutilated him. And that the people cannot be left for so long without a priest without danger, Your Wisdom knows very well indeed. May God Almighty deign to preserve Your Holiness for the instruction and correction of His Holy Church through the course of many years, in the service of Him that has only just begun, most holy lord, and most reverend Father of Fathers in the Lord.

Notes

1 Hincmar, *Ad Adrianam papam, Opuscula et epistolae*, PL 126, cols 641–8; see the appendix for my translation of the relevant section. H. Schrörs, *Hinkmar*, Reg. 315; M. Stratmann, 'Briefe an Hinkmar von Reims', *DA*, 48 (1992), 37–81 at 63, n.136.

2 Hincmar, *Ad Adrianam papam*, PL 126, col. 648: 'Et quia populus sine presbytero tandiu manere sine periculo dimitti non potest, vestra sapientia sufficientissime novit.'

3 C. van Rhijn, *Shepherds of the Lord: Priests and Episcopal Statutes in the Carolingian Period* (Turnhout, 2007), pp. 200–9; C. Mériaux, 'Ordre et hiérarchie au sein du clergé rural pendant le haut Moyen Âge', in F. Bougard, D. Iogna-Prat and R. Le Jan, eds, *Hiérarchie et stratification sociale dans l'Occident médiéval (400–1100)* (Turnhout, 2009), pp. 117–36, at 122–3. On priests and their integration in local communities, see also recently C. West, *Reframing the Feudal Revolution: Political and Social Transformation Between Marne and Moselle, c. 800–c.1100* (Cambridge, 2013), pp. 34–8, and West, Chapter 12, pp. 231–4.

4 Flodoard, *HRE* III-23, p. 313. The letter dates from 868–70: Schrörs, *Hinkmar*, Reg. 262 and p. 578, n.108.

5 *Ad Adrianam papam*, PL 126, col. 647: *Ego vero per multos hoc audiens*.

6 On *infamia* and *infamare*, see Hincmar, *Capitularia* II, MGH *Capit. Episc.* II, p. 60, cc. 23, 24; Hincmar, *De presbiteris criminosis*, p. 68, l. 3, c. 4 (Council of Carthage 419), and p. 91, ll. 14 and 24, c. 7 (Pseudo-Isidorian Decretals). Only from Gratian onwards would this develop into a more well-defined notion of clerical *infamia* with specific juridical consequences; the early medieval meaning ranged more widely: see P. Landau, *Die Entstehung des kanonischen Infamiebegriffs von Gratian bis zur Glossa ordinaria* (Cologne, 1966), esp. pp. 17–19.

7 As was the case with public penance; see M. de Jong, 'What was *public* about public penance? *Paenitentia publica* and justice in the Carolingian world', in *La giustizia nell'alto medioevo (secolo ix–xi)*, Settimane 44, 2 vols (Spoleto, 1997), II, pp. 863–904. On written documents that heightened the publicity of an already public penance, see M. de Jong, *The Penitential State: Authority and Atonement in the Age of Louis the Pious, 814–840* (Cambridge, 2009), pp. 235–6.

8 Hincmar, *Capitularia* II, MGH *Capit. Episc.* II, p. 70, c. 29. On the expression *legaliter ac regulariter*, see *ibid.* p. 57, and n.102.

9 *Ibid.*, p. 59, c. 21; *De presbiteris criminosis*, p. 81, c. 4, uses the same text; see also Hincmar's letter to John of Cambrai, Epistola XXIV, *PL* 126, col. 253 (Schrörs, *Hinkmar*, Reg. 344) which refers to the same in different words. Witnesses and oath-helpers are all *testes* in Hincmar's terminology.

10 On priests and wealth, see van Rhijn, *Shepherds*, pp. 193–200.

11 Hincmar, *Capitularia* II, MGH *Capit. Episc.* II, pp. 45–70, especially cc. 21–26 (see above, n.6).

12 *De presbiteris criminosis*, pp. 4–5 on the date; see the informative introduction, and van Rhijn, *Shepherds*, pp. 206–12.

13 *De presbiteris criminosis*, pp. 4–5, citing Schrörs, *Hinkmar*, p. 373, n.72; *ibid.*, Reg. 420.

14 Hincmar, *De iudiciis et appellationibus*, Epistola XXXII, *PL* 126, cols 230–44; see *De presbiteris criminosis*, pp. 3–6; Schrörs, *Hinkmar*, pp. 372–6; *ibid*, Reg. 420. Another instance of Hincmar writing for Charles is the very angry letter of February/March 872 to Pope Hadrian II: Schrörs, *Hinkmar*, Reg. 325, in response to the pope's stiff letter to the king (Hadrian II, Epistolae, 35, ed. E. Perels, MGH *Epp.* 6, pp. 691–765 at pp. 741–3 (J2946)).

15 Hincmar, *De iudiciis et appellationibus*, *PL* 126, col. 231, cc. 1–2; the letters referred to are by Hadrian II, protesting against Charles' appropriation of Lotharingia: Epistolae 16–17, MGH *Epp.* 6, pp. 717–20 (J2917–18); cf. J. L. Nelson, *Charles the Bald* (London, 1992), p. 223. The royal capitularies cited are taken from Benedict Levita I, cc. 35–36: see *De presbiteris criminosis*, p. 3.

16 Hincmar, *De iudiciis et appellationibus*, *PL* 126, col. 231, c. 3: 'Et quoniam

pravis saepius prava quam recta innotesci solent, nata hinc occasione, Transalpinarum regionum presbyteri, a suis episcopis de certis criminibus regulariter ab ordine sacerdotali dejecti, et poenitentiae subacti, sine licentia et conscientia primatum et episcoporum suorum, huc venire, et hinc epistolas, quae regulis non conveniunt, referre coeperunt. Quas non jussione apostolica, sed, ut assolet etiam in republica, propter multiplicia reclamatorum negotia, quorumcunque ministrorum quasi pia miseratione factas, et nos illius regionis putant episcopi.' Please note Hincmar's use of the plural *primatus* to refer to the level of the metropolitans; the *primas* is an invention of Pseudo-Isidore, where it refers to a level above the metropolitans, equal to patriarchs: see H. Fuhrmann, *Einfluß und Verbreitung der pseudoisidorischen Fälschungen: von ihrem Auftauchen bis in die neuere Zeit*, 3 vols (Stuttgart, 1972–74), I, pp. 121–2.

17 Hincmar, *De iudiciis et appellationibus*, PL 126, cols 239–40, c. 19: 'Haec itaque Transalpinis ecclesiis, earumque rectoribus, a sede apostolica, de appellatione episcoporum ad hanc sedem apostolicam, et de presbyterorum ac diaconorum appellatione, si de judiciis episcoporum suorum questi fuerint, ad comprovinciales synodos, et dijudicatione regulari eorum in iisdem synodis, ante longissimae aetatis annos usque ad nostra tempora servata, et a decessoribus ac praedecessoribus eorum secuta et exsecuta fuerunt. Quae si etiam illis servata, et ab eis secuta et exsecuta non fuerint, nihil prodest eos secundum sacros canones et decreta sedis Romanae pontificum, pro accusatis presbyteris de manifestis criminibus comprovinciales episcoporum synodos frequentare, sed faciet licenter quisque presbyterorum quodlibet, unde si fuerit redargutus, veniat Romam.'

18 *Ibid.*, col. 240, c. 20: 'Maxime de subintroductione contra regulas mulierum: pro qua ab episcopis Transalpinis presbyteri regulariter judicati ad hanc sanctam Romanam sedem insciis suis episcopis veniunt, et eis epistolas eorum refragantes judicia deferunt, eosque vel comministros illorum ad hanc sedem ad conquerendum contra eos venire praecipiunt, quod nullis antiquorum legibus vel patrum regulis decretum fuisse legimus.'

19 Schrörs, *Hinkmar*, p. 372, n.69, assembled a small dossier from Jaffé's *Regesta Pontificum Romanorum* comprising laymen as well as priests who appealed to Rome. The priests involved are in *Regesta Pontificum Romanorum* J2624 (Leo IV); J2839, J2854, J2855 (Nicholas I); J2935 (Hadrian II), J2937 (Hadrian II; the case of Trising); other examples are in Schmitz's introduction to *De presbiteris criminosis*, pp. 9–10, nn.33–5. Laymen are the culprits in Jaffé J2837, J2840, J2850, J2852 (Nicholas I); J3056–3058 (John VIII). The complaint of Archbishop Liutward of Mainz to John VIII concerning two men who married consecrated women and then appealed to Rome also

concerned laymen: *Collectio Sangallensis* no. 42, *Formulae Merowingici et Karolini aevi*, ed. K. Zeumer, MGH *Formulae* (Hanover, 1886), pp. 424–5.
20 Furhmann, *Einfluß und Verbreitung*, II, pp. 257–61.
21 For a brief survey of the entire Pseudo-Isidorian forgeries, see D. Jasper and H. Fuhrmann, *Papal Letters in the Early Middle Ages* (Washington DC, 2001), pp. 137–69; on the Decretals, see *ibid.*, pp. 153–69.
22 *De presbiteris criminosis*, pp. 90–1, c. 21.
23 Hincmar used the expression *adprobari*, which seems to denote oath-helpers rather than witnesses.
24 See *De presbiteris criminosis*, p. 91, c. 21, and the commentary of Schmitz on p. 33; *Decretales pseudo-Isidorianae et Capitula Angilramni*, ed. P. Hinschius (Leipzig, 1863), p. 449.
25 This is one of Hincmar's set expressions, taken from an often cited letter by Augustine; cf. *De presbiteris criminosis*, p. 94, n.147; see also *ibid.*, p. 77, n.63.
26 Jasper and Furhrmann, *Papal Letters*, pp. 142–3, 180.
27 The standard work is Furhmann, *Einfluß und Verbreitung*; the best introduction in English is also by Fuhrmann, in D. Jasper and H. Furhrmann, *Papal Letters*, pp. 135–95. For an overview of all the Pseudo-Isidorian forgeries, see *ibid.*, pp. 137–9. In a series of publications, the late Klaus Zechiel-Eckes revolutionised Pseudo-Isidorian research: K. Zechiel-Eckes, 'Ein Blick in Pseudoisidors Werkstatt. Studien zum Entstehungsprozess der falschen Dekretalen. Mit einen exemplarischen Editorischen Anhang (Pseudo-Julius an die orientalischen Bischöfe, JK † 196)', *Francia* 28 (2001), 37–90; K. Zechiel-Eckes, 'Auf Pseudoisidors Spur. Oder: Versuch, einen dichten Schleier zu lüften', in W. Hartmann and G. Schmitz, eds, *Fortschritt durch Fälschungen? Ursprung, Gestalt und Wirkungen der pseudoisidorischen Fälschungen* (Hanover, 2002), pp. 1–28. Horst Fuhrmann commented cautiously in 'Stand, Aufgaben und Perspektiven der Pseudoisidorforschung', in *Fortschritt durch Fälschungen?*, pp. 227–62; some of the recent discussion is summarised in M. de Jong, 'Paschasius Radbertus and Pseudo-Isidore', in V. L. Garver and O. M. Phelan, eds, *Rome and Religion in the Medieval West: Studies in Honor of Thomas F.X. Noble* (Farnham, Surrey, 2014), pp. 149–77.
28 Hincmar, *Capitularia* II, MGH *Capit. Episc.* II, pp. 39–40, c. 11, and c. 26, Anhang, p. 68; cf. Jasper and Fuhrmann, *Papal Letters*, pp. 174–5; on Hincmar and his use of Pseudo-Isidore, see Furhmann, *Einfluß und Verbreitung*, I, pp. 200–24. The manuscript tradition of the Decretals begins c. 860; cf. Jasper and Fuhrmann, *Papal Letters*, 156–9.
29 See the discussion in van Rhijn, *Shepherds*, pp. 204–9.
30 Hincmar, *Capitularia* II, MGH *Capit. Episc.* II c. 26, Anhang, pp. 62–3; *Decretales pseudo-Isidorianae et Capitula Angilramni*, pp. 39, 74, 204.

31 Leo IV, Epistola 38, ed. A. de Hersch-Gereuth, MGH *Epp.* 5, p. 606 (J2624).
32 Jasper and Fuhrmann, *Papal Letters*, p. 178. The documents of this controversy have been edited by R. Schieffer, *Die Streitschriften Hinkmars von Reims und Hinkmars von Laon, 866-871*, MGH *Conc.* IV, supplementum 2 (Hanover, 2003); Fuhrmann, *Einfluß und Verbreitung*, II, pp. 664-72.
33 Hincmar of Laon died in 879; on his downfall and last years, see P. R. McKeon, *Hincmar of Laon and Carolingian Politics* (Urbana, 1978), pp. 132-64. On blinding, see G. Bührer-Thierry, '"Just anger" or "vengeful anger"? The punishment of blinding in the early medieval West', in B. H. Rosenwein, ed., *Anger's Past: the Social Uses of Emotion in the Middle Ages* (Ithaca, 1998), pp. 75-91.
34 *AB* s.a. 869, p. 152 (trans. Nelson, pp. 152-3).
35 K. Zechiel-Eckes, 'Frühe Pseudoisidor-Rezeption bei Hinkmar von Laon. Ein Fragment des verloren geglaubten 'Unterschriftswerk' vom Juli 869', *DA*, 66 (2010), 19-54.
36 Hincmar, *Letter to the diocese of Laon* (after 3 June 869), *Opuscula et epistolae*, PL 126, col. 512: 'Sed quia credebat in ipsa synodo, quod mos haud exposcit canonicus, aliquam violentiam sibi illegaliter et contra leges canonum a quocunque fieri, sermone contestatorio et auctoritate sancti Petri, quod si ei licentia eundi Romam prohiberetur, aut ipse captus obtineretur, omnes sacerdotes totius parochiae suae colligavit, ut nemo eorum in ea sacerdotali ministerio tandiu uteretur, usque dum ille ipse nobiscum iterum viva voce loqueretur; aut litterae ex ipsa sancta sede beati Petri apostoli nobis mitterentur.'
37 See Zechiel-Eckes, 'Frühe Pseudoisidor-Rezeption', pp. 20-2.
38 K. Zechiel-Eckes, *Rebellische Kleriker?: eine unbekannte kanonistisch-patristische Polemik gegen Bischof Hinkmar von Laon in Cod. Paris, BNF, nouv. acq. lat. 1746*, MGH Studien und Texte 49 (Hanover, 2009), pp. 39-52; the treatise was composed between May/June 869, when the interdict was effective, and August/September 871, when the Council of Douzy was held where Hincmar of Laon was deposed. For the maltreated clerics, see *ibid.*, p. 59, c. 6.
39 *Ibid.*, p. 59, c. 7: *episcopos, presbiteros et diaconos eiectos*.
40 On Laon, see J. J. Contreni, *The Cathedral School of Laon from 850 to 930: Its Manuscripts and Masters* (Munich, 1978). On rural priests' education, see West, Chapter 12, pp. 232-3 and Steffen Patzold, 'Bildung und Wissen einer lokalen Elite des Frühmittelalters: das Beispiel der Landpfarrer im Frankenreich des 9. Jahrhunderts', in F. Bougard, R. Le Jan and R. McKitterick, eds, *La Culture du haut Moyen Âge. Une question d'élites?* (Turnhout, 2009), pp. 377-91.
41 Jasper and Fuhrmann, *Papal Letters*, p. 181; Fuhrmann, *Einfluß und Verbreitung*, II, pp. 219-24, 232-4.

42 Jasper and Fuhrmann, *Papal Letters*, p. 185.
43 *Ibid.*, pp. 184–6; S. Williams, *Codices Pseudo-Isidoriani: a Palaeographico-historical Study* (New York 1971), pp. 1–80; H. Mordek, 'Codices Pseudo-Isidoriani. Addenda zu dem gleichnamigen Buch von Schafer Williams', *Archiv für katholisches Kirchenrecht*, 147 (1978), 471–8; L. Kéry, *Canonical Collections of the Early Middle Ages (ca. 400–1140): a Bibliographical Guide to the Manuscripts and Literature* (Washington DC, 1999).
44 de Jong, *Penitential State*, pp. 214–24.
45 *Ibid.*, pp. 252–9.
46 Council of Troyes, 867, MGH *Conc.* IV, no. 24A, pp. 232–8.
47 *Ibid.*, no. 24B, pp. 239–42.
48 Wulfad was one of the clerics ordained by Ebbo during his brief reinstatement (840–1) as archbishop of Rheims; if these ordinations were recognised as valid, this in turn would mean that Hincmar's succession to the see had been invalid. Hincmar's anger about Wulfad's advancement in 866 is palpable in *AB* s.a. 866, pp. 128–30 (trans. Nelson, pp. 132–4).
49 On the successive stages of this conflict, see K. Heidecker, *The Divorce of Lothar II: Christian Marriage and Political Power in the Carolingian World*, trans. T. M. Guest (Ithaca, 2010).
50 See West, Chapter 12, pp. 228–46.
51 *Conc. Carthag.* III, c. 27, *Collectio Hispana*, ed. C. Munier, *Concilia Africae a. 345–a. 525*, CCSL 149 (Turnhout, 1974), p. 134.
52 *Apocalypsis Iohannis* 21:8: 'Timidis autem, et incredulis, et execratis, et homicidis, et fornicatoribus, et veneficis, et idolatris, et omnibus mendacibus, pars illorum erit in stagno ardenti igne et sulphure: quod est mors secunda.'
53 Augustine, Epistola 65 (a. 402), ed. A. Goldbacher, *S. Aureli Augustini Hipponiensis episcopi epistulae*, CSEL 34.1 (Vienna, 1895), pp. 232–4.
54 *Conc. Carthag.* V, c. 11, *Collectio Hispana*, ed. Munier, p. 358.
55 *Conc. Carthag.* V, c. 12, *Collectio Hispana*, ed. Munier, p. 358 (quoted in part).
56 *Conc. Carthag.* IV, c. 67 (55), *Collectio Hispana*, ed. Munier, p. 350.
57 *Conc. Tolet.* IV (a. 633), c. 45, ed. J. Vives, *Concilios visigóticos e hispanico-romanos* (Barcelona, 1963), p. 207. In Hincmar's letter the expression *in monasterio contradantur* has become *in monasterio retrudantur*. *Retrudere* and *retrusio* are the usual ninth-century expressions for involuntary penance in a monastery.
58 Boniface, Epistola 51, ed. M. Tangl, MGH *Epistolae selectae* 1 (Hanover, 1916), p. 88.

Bibliographies

Primary sources

Ambrose *see* Pseudo-Ambrose
Amolo of Lyons, *Epistolae*, ed. E. Dümmler, MGH *Epp.* 5, pp. 361–78
Annales Bertiniani, ed. F. Grat, J. Vielliard, and S. Clémencet, *Annales de Saint-Bertin* (Paris, 1964); English translation: J. L. Nelson, *The Annals of St-Bertin* (Manchester, 1991)
Annales Fuldenses, ed. F. Kurze, MGH *SRG* 7 (Hanover, 1891); English translation: T. Reuter, *The Annals of Fulda* (Manchester, 1992)
Annales regni Francorum, ed. F. Kurze, MGH *SRG* 6 (Hanover, 1895); English translation: B. W. Scholz, *Carolingian Chronicles. Royal Frankish Annals and Nithard's Histories* (Ann Arbor, 1970)
Annales Vedastini, ed. B. von Simson, MGH *SRG* 12 (Hanover, 1909)
Annales Xantenses, ed. B. von Simson, MGH *SRG* 12 (Hanover, 1909)
Anon., Polemic against Hincmar of Laon, ed. K. Zechiel-Eckes, in *Rebellische Kleriker?: eine unbekannte kanonistisch-patristische Polemik gegen Bischof Hinkmar von Laon in Cod. Paris, BNF, nouv. acq. lat. 1746*, MGH Studien und Texte, 49 (Hanover, 2009)
Ansegis, *Capitularia*, ed. G. Schmitz, *Die Kapitulariensammlung des Ansegis*, MGH *Capitularia regum Francorum, Nova series* 1 (Hanover, 1996)
Anselm of Lucca, *Collectio canonum*, ed. F. Thaner (Innsbruck, 1906–15)
Augustine, *De adulterinis coniugiis*, ed. J. Zycha, *Sancti Aureli Augustini opera sect. V, pars. III*, CSEL 41 (Vienna, 1900), pp. 347–410
Augustine, *De civitate Dei*, ed. B. Dombart and A. Kalb, CCSL 47–48, 2 vols (Turnhout, 1965)
Augustine, *Enarrationes in Psalmos*, ed. E. Dekkers and J. Fraipont, CCSL 38–39, 2 vols (Turnhout, 1956)
Augustine, *Epistulae*, ed. A. Goldbacher, *S. Aureli Augustini Hipponiensis episcopi epistulae*, CSEL 34, 44, 57–58, 5 vols (Vienna, 1895–1923)

Bibliographies

Augustine, *In Iohannis Evangelium tractatus CXXIV*, ed. R. Willems, CCSL 36 (Turnhout, 1954)

Augustine, *Sermo* 62, *PL* 38, cols 415–23

Benedict of Nursia, *Regula monachorum*, ed. and trans. P. Schmitz, *Règle de saint Benoît*, 5th ed. (Turnhout, 1987)

Benedict Levita, ed. G. H. Pertz, MGH *Leges* II (Hanover, 1837), Part 2, pp. 39–158; a new edition under preparation by G. Schmitz is available at www.benedictus.mgh.de/haupt.htm

Boniface, *Epistolae*, ed. M. Tangl, *Die Briefe des Heiligen Bonifatius und Lullus*, MGH *Epistolae selectae* 1 (Berlin, 1916); English translation: E. Emerton, *The Letters of Saint Boniface* (New York, 2000)

Breviary of Alaric: see *Lex Romana Visigothorum*

Capitularia regum Francorum, ed. A. Boretius and V. Krause, MGH *Leges, Sectio II*, 2 vols (Hanover, 1883–97)

Collectio Dacheriana, ed. L. d'Achery, *Spicilegium, sive, Collectio veterum aliquot scriptorum qui in Galliae bibliothecis delituerant*, 3 vols (Paris, 1723), I, pp. 509–64

Collectio Hispana, *PL* 84, cols 93–848

[*Collectio in LXXIV titulos:*] *Diversorum patrum sententie sive Collectio in LXXIV titulos digestos*, ed. J. Gilchrist (Vatican City, 1973); English translation: J. Gilchrist, *The Collection in Seventy-Four Titles: a Canon Law Manual of the Gregorian Reform* (Toronto, 1980)

Collectio Quesnelliana, *PL* 56, cols 353–746

Concilia aevi Karolini [742–842], ed. A. Werminghoff, MGH *Conc.* II, 2 vols (Hanover, 1906–8)

Concilia aevi Karolini, ed. W. Hartmann, I. Schröder and G. Schmitz, *Die Konzilien der karolingischen Teilreiche*, MGH *Conc.* III–V, 3 vols (Hanover, 1984–2012) [III: 843–859, IV: 860–874, V: 875–911]

Concilia Africae: a. 345–a. 525, ed. C. Munier, CCSL 149 (Turnhout, 1974)

Concilia Galliae a. 314–a. 506, ed. C. Munier, CCSL 148 (Turnhout, 1963)

Concilios visigóticos e hispano-romanos, ed. J. Vives (Barcelona, 1963)

Corpus legum ab imperatoribus Romanis ante Iustinianum latarum, quae extra constitutionum codicas supersunt, ed. G. Haenel (Leipzig, 1857)

Cyprian *see* Pseudo-Cyprian

Deusdedit, *Collectio canonum*, ed. V. W. von Glanvell, *Die Kanonessammlung des Kardinals Deusdedit. Band 1, Die Kanonessammlung selbst* (Paderborn, 1905)

[Epitome of Julian:] *Iuliani epitome latina Novellarum Iustiniani*, ed. G. Haenel (Leipzig, 1873)

Flodoard of Rheims, *Historia Remensis ecclesiae*, ed. M. Stratmann, MGH *SS* 36 (Hanover, 1998)

Bibliographies

Florus of Lyons, *Capitula ex lege et canone collecta*, PL 119, cols 419–22
Florus of Lyons, *Libellus de tribus epistolis*, ed. K. Zechiel-Eckes, *Opera polemica*, CCCM 260 (Turnhout, 2014), 317–417
Formulae Merowingici et Karolini aevi, ed. K. Zeumer, MGH *Formulae* (Hanover, 1886)
Gelasius, *Epistolae*, ed. A. Thiel, *Epistolae romanorum pontificum genuinae, et quae ad eos scriptae sunt a S. Hilario usque ad Pelagium II. Tomus I: A S. Hilario usque ad S. Hormisdam: Ann. 461–523* (Braunsberg, 1868), pp. 285–510
Gottschalk and a Medieval Predestination Controversy: Texts Translated from the Latin, trans. V. Genke and F. X. Gumerlock (Milwaukee, 2010)
Gottschalk, *Carmina*, ed. L. Traube, MGH *Poetae* III (Berlin, 1896), pp. 707–37
Gottschalk, *Confessio brevior*, ed. Lambot, *Œuvres*, pp. 52–4
Gottschalk, *Confessio prolixior*, ed. Lambot, *Œuvres*, pp. 55–78
Gottschalk, *De corpore et sanguine domini*, ed. Lambot, *Œuvres*, pp. 324–37
Gottschalk, *De praedestinatione*, ed. Lambot, *Œuvres*, pp. 180–350
Gottschalk, *De trina deitate*, ed. Lambot, *Œuvres*, pp. 81–130
Gottschalk, *Fragmenta*, ed. Lambot, *Œuvres*, pp. 5–44
Gottschalk, *Œuvres théologiques et grammaticales de Godescalc d'Orbais*, ed. C. Lambot, Spicilegium Sacrum Lovaniense 20 (Louvain, 1945)
Gottschalk, *Opusculum primum*, ed. Lambot, pp. 353–420
Gottschalk, *Responsa de diversis*, ed. Lambot, pp. 130–79
Gratian, *Corpus iuris canonici. Pars 1, Decretum magistri Gratiani*, ed. E. Friedberg (Leipzig, 1879)
Gregory the Great, *Homiliae in Hiezechihelem prophetam*, ed. M. Adriaen, CCSL 142 (Turnhout, 1971)
Gregory the Great, *Moralia in Iob*, ed. M. Adriaen, CCSL 143–143B, 3 vols (Turnhout, 1979–85)
Gregory the Great, *Registrum epistularum*, ed. D. Norberg, CCSL 140–140A, 2 vols (Turnhout, 1982)
Gregory the Great, *Regula Pastoralis*, ed. B. Judic, F. Rommel and C. Morel, *Grégoire le Grand, Règle pastorale*, Sources Chrétiennes 381, 2 vols (Paris, 1992)
Hadrian II, *Epistolae*, ed. E. Perels, MGH *Epp*. 6, pp. 691–765
Hincmar of Laon, *Materialsammlungen vorwiegend pseudoisidorischen Inhalts*, ed. R. Schieffer, *Die Streitschriften Hinkmars von Reims und Hinkmars von Laon 869–871*, MGH *Conc*. IV, supplementum 2 (Hanover, 2003), pp. 1–55
Hincmar of Laon, *Pittaciolus*, ed. R. Schieffer, *Die Streitschriften Hinkmars von Reims und Hinkmars von Laon 869–871*, MGH *Conc*. IV, supplementum 2 (Hanover, 2003), pp. 57–97

Hincmar of Laon, *Rotula prolixa*, ed. R. Schieffer, *Die Streitschriften Hinkmars von Reims und Hinkmars von Laon 869–871*, MGH *Conc.* IV, supplementum 2 (Hanover, 2003), pp. 363–408

Hincmar of Rheims, *Admonitio ad episcopos et ad regem Carolomannum apud Sparnacum facta*, *PL* 125, cols 1007–18

Hincmar of Rheims, *Ad reclusos et simplices in Remensi parrochia contra Gothescalcum*, ed. W. Gundlach, 'Zwei Schriften des Erzbischofs Hinkmar von Reims', *Zeitschrift für Kirchengeschichte*, 10 (1889), 258–310

Hincmar of Rheims, *Capitularia*, ed. R. Pokorny and M. Stratmann, *Capitula episcoporum*, MGH *Capit. Episc.* II (Hanover, 1995), pp. 3–89

Hincmar of Rheims, *Collectio contra haereticos et de privilegiis multarum sedium*, ed. M. Hartmann, '"Collectio contra haereticos et de privilegiis multarum sedium": ein bislang übersehenes Werk Hinkmars von Reims in der Centuriatoren-Handschrift ÖB Basel O II 29', in A. Mentzel-Reuters and M. Hartmann, eds, *Catalogus und Centurien: Interdisziplinäre Studien zu Matthias Flacius und den Magdeburger Centurien* (Tübingen, 2008), pp. 211–31

Hincmar of Rheims, *Collectio de ecclesiis et capellis*, ed. M. Stratmann, MGH *Fontes iuris*, 14 (Hanover, 1990)

Hincmar of Rheims, *De causa Teutfridi presbyteri*, *PL* 125, cols 1111–16

Hincmar of Rheims, *De cavendis vitiis et virtutibus exercendis*, ed. D. Nachtmann. MGH Quellen zur Geistesgeschichte des Mittelalters 16 (Munich, 1998)

Hincmar of Rheims, *De coercendo et exstirpando raptu viduarum puellarum ac sanctimonalium*, ed. J. Buys, *Epistola I, Hincmari Rhemensis Archiepiscopi Epistolae Duae, Paralipomena Opusculorum Petri Blesensis, et Ioannis Trithemii aliorumque nuper in typographeo Moguntino Editorum a Ioanne Busaeo...* (Cologne, 1605) pp. 796–836; also J. Sirmond, ed., *Hincmari Archiepiscopi Remensis Opera Duos in Tomos Digesta* (Paris, 1645), vol. II, texte XVI, pp. 225–43; also *PL* 125, 1017–36

Hincmar of Rheims, *De divortio Lotharii regis et Theutbergae reginae*, ed. L. Böhringer, MGH *Conc.* IV, supplementum 1 (Hanover, 1992); English translation: R. Stone and C. West, *On the divorce of King Lothar and Queen Theutberga* (Manchester, forthcoming)

Hincmar of Rheims, *De fide Carolo regi servanda*, *PL* 125, cols 961–84

Hincmar of Rheims, *De institutione regia (Ad Carolum III imperitum)*, *PL* 125, cols 989–94

Hincmar of Rheims, *De iudiciis et appellationibus episcoporum et presbyterorum* = Epistola XXXII, *PL* 126, cols 230–44

Hincmar of Rheims, *De iure metropolitanorum* = Epistola XXX, *PL* 126, cols 189–210

Hincmar of Rheims, *De officiis episcoporum (Quae exsequi debeat episcopus, et qua cura tueri res et facultates ecclesiasticas) PL* 125, cols

Bibliographies

1087-94

Hincmar of Rheims, *De ordine palatii*, ed. T. Gross and R. Schieffer, MGH *Fontes iuris* 3 (Hanover, 1980)
English translation: P. E. Dutton, *Carolingian Civilization: a Reader* (Peterborough, Ontario, 1993), pp. 485-99

Hincmar of Rheims, *De praedestinatione Dei*, *PL* 125, cols 65-474

Hincmar of Rheims, *De presbiteris criminosis. Ein Memorandum Erzbischof Hinkmars von Reims über straffällige Kleriker*, ed. G. Schmitz, MGH Studien und Texte 34 (Hanover, 2004)

Hincmar of Rheims, *De regis persona et regio ministerio ad Carolum Calvum regem*, *PL* 125, cols 833-56

Hincmar of Rheims, *De una et non trina deitate*, *PL* 125, cols 473-618

Hincmar of Rheims, *De villa Novilliaco*, ed. H. Mordek, 'Ein exemplarischer Rechtsstreit: Hinkmar von Reims und das Landgut Neuilly-Saint-Front', *Zeitschrift der Savigny-Stiftung für Rechtsgeschichte, Kanonistische Abteilung* 83 (1997), 86-112, at 100-112

Hincmar of Rheims, *Epistolae*, ed. E. Perels, MGH *Epp.* 8 (Berlin, 1939)

Hincmar of Rheims, *Epistolae*, *PL* 126, cols 9-280

Hincmar of Rheims, *Expositiones ad Carolum regem pro ecclesiae libertatum defensione*, *PL* 125, cols 1035-1070

Hincmar of Rheims, *Juramentum quod Hincmarus Archiepiscopus edere jussus est apud Pontigonem*, *PL* 125, cols 1125-8

Hincmar of Rheims, *Libellus expostulationis*, ed. W. Hartmann, MGH *Conc.* IV, no. 37B, pp. 420-87

Hincmar of Rheims, *Novi regis instructio ad rectam regni administrationem*, *PL* 125, cols 983-90

Hincmar of Rheims, *Opuscula et epistolae quae spectant ad causam Hincmari Laudunensis*, *PL* 126, cols 279-648

Hincmar of Rheims, *Opusculum LV capitulorum*, ed. R. Schieffer, *Die Streitschriften Hinkmars von Reims und Hinkmars von Laon 869-871*, MGH *Conc.* IV, supplementum 2 (Hanover, 2003), pp. 99-361

Hincmar of Rheims, *Über Priestertum und Königtum*, ed. R. Schieffer, 'Eine übersehene Schrift Hinkmars von Reims über Priestertum und Königtum', *DA*, 37 (1981), 511-28

Hincmar of Rheims, *Visio Bernoldi*, ed. M. van der Lugt, 'Tradition and revision: the textual tradition of Hincmar of Reims' "Visio Bernoldi" with a new critical edition', *Archivum latinitatis medii aevi* 52 (1994), 109-49

Hincmar of Rheims, *Vita Remigii episcopi Remensis*, ed. B. Krusch, MGH *SRM* 3 (Hanover, 1896), pp. 239-341

Hrabanus Maurus, *Epistolae*, ed. E. Dümmler, MGH *Epp.* 5, pp. 379-516

Hrabanus Maurus, *Liber de oblatione puerorum*, *PL* 107, cols 419-40

Hrabanus Maurus, *Martyrologium*, ed. J. McCulloh, CCCM 44 (Turnhout, 1979)

Innocent I, *Epistolae et decreta*, PL 20, cols 463–612
Isidore of Seville, *Isidori Hispalensis episcopi Etymologiarum sive originum libri XX*, ed. W. M. Lindsay, 2 vols (Oxford, 1911)
Isidore of Seville, *Sententiae*, ed. P. Cazier, CCSL 111 (Turnhout, 1998)
Isidore of Seville see also Pseudo-Isidore
Iuliani epitome see Epitome of Julian
John VIII, *Registrum*, ed. E. Caspar, MGH *Epp.* 7, pp. 1–272
Jonas of Orléans, *De institutione regia*, ed. and trans. A. Dubreucq, *Le métier de roi*, Sources chrétiennes, 407 (Paris, 1995)
Leo the Great, *Epistolae*, PL 54, cols 581–1218
Leo the Great, *Sancti Leonis Magni romani pontificis Tractatus septem et nonaginta*, ed. A. Chavasse, CCSL 138–138A, 2 vols (Turnhout, 1973)
Leo IV, *Epistolae*, ed. A. von Hirsch-Gereuth, MGH *Epp.* 5, pp. 581–614
Lex Dei: see *Mosaicarum et Romanarum legum collatio*
Lex Romana canonice compta: testo di leggi romano-canoniche del sec. IX pubblicato sul ms. paragino Bibl. Nat. 12448, ed. C. G. Mor (Pavia, 1927)
Lex Romana Visigothorum, ed. G. Haenel (Leipzig, 1849)
Liber Pontificalis, ed. L. Duchesne, 2 vols (Paris, 1886–92); English translation (in part): R. Davis, *The Lives of the Ninth-century Popes (Liber pontificalis): the Ancient Biographies of Ten Popes from A.D. 817–891* (Liverpool, 1995)
Lothar, see also *Urkunden Lothars I. und Lothars II.*
Lothar I, *Epistola* 46, ed. A. von Hirsch-Gereuth, MGH *Epp.* 5, pp. 609–11
Mancio of Châlons, *Epistola ad Fulconem Rhemensem episcopum*, PL 131, col. 23
Mosaicarum et Romanarum legum collatio, ed. M. Hyamson (London, 1913); also edited in *Fontes iuris Romani antejustiniani. Pars altera, Auctores*, ed. J. Baviera, 2nd edn (Florence, 1940), pp. 541–89
Nicholas I, *Epistolae*, ed. E. Perels, MGH *Epp.* 6, pp. 257–690
Nithard, *Historiarum libri quattuor*, ed. P. Lauer, *Nithard, Histoire des fils de Louis le Pieux* (Paris, 1964); English translation: B. W. Scholz, *Carolingian Chronicles. Royal Frankish Annals and Nithard's Histories* (Ann Arbor, 1970)
Origen, *Homiliae in Jeremiam*, PG 13, cols 253–543; Latin translation: Jerome, *Translatio homiliarum Origenis in Jeremiam et Ezechielem*, PL 25, cols 583–786
Polyptyque de l'abbaye de Saint-Germain des Prés rédigé au temps de l'abbé Irminon, tome II: *Texte du polyptyque*, ed. A. Longnon (Paris, 1886)
Polyptyque de l'abbaye de Saint-Remi de Reims ou dénombrement des manses, des serfs et des revenus de cette abbaye vers le milieu du neuvième siècle de notre ère, ed. B. Guérard (Paris, 1853)
Le polyptyque et les listes de cens de l'abbaye de Saint-Remi de Reims (IXe-XIe siècles), ed. J.-P. Devroey (Reims, 1984)

Bibliographies

Prudentius of Troyes, *Epistola tractoria ad Wenilonem*, *PL* 115, cols 1365–8
Pseudo-Ambrose, *De lapsu virginis consecratae*, ed. I. Cazzaniga, *De lapsu Susannae (De lapsu virginis consecratae) incerti auctoris* (Turin, 1948)
Pseudo-Cyprian, *Pseudo-Cyprianus: De XII abusivis saeculi*, Texte und Untersuchungen zur Geschichte der Altchristlichen Literatur, 3rd series, 4/1, ed. S. Hellmann (Leipzig, 1909)
Pseudo-Isidore, *Die Capitula Angilramni: eine prozessrechtliche Fälschung Pseudoisidors*, ed. K.-G. Schon, MGH Studien und Texte 39 (Hanover, 2006)
Pseudo-Isidore, *Decretales pseudo-Isidorianae et Capitula Angilramni*, ed. P. Hinschius (Leipzig, 1863) [A new edition under preparation by K.-G. Schon is available at www.pseudoisidor.mgh.de/].
Pseudo-Venantius Fortunatus, *Vita sancti Remedii* [BHL 7150], ed. B. Krusch, MGH *Auctores antiquissimi* IV, 2 (Berlin, 1885), pp. 64–7
Recueil des actes de Charles II le Chauve, roi de France, ed. A. Giry, M. Prou and G. Tessier, 3 vols (Paris, 1943–55)
Recueil des actes de Louis II le Bègue, Louis III et Carloman II, rois de France (877–884), ed. F. Grat, J. de Font-Réaulx, G. Tessier and R.-H. Bautier (Paris, 1978)
Regesta Pontificum Romanorum ab condita ecclesia ad annum post Christum natum MCXCVIII, 2nd ed. ed. P. Jaffé *et al.*, 2 vols (Leipzig, 1885–8)
Regino of Prüm, *Chronicon*, ed. F. Kurze, MGH *SRG* 50 (Hanover, 1890); English translation: S. MacLean, *History and Politics in Late Carolingian and Ottonian Europe: the Chronicle of Regino of Prüm and Adalbert of Magdeburg* (Manchester, 2009)
Rothad of Soissons, *Libellus proclamationis*, ed. W. Hartmann, MGH *Conc.* IV, no. 20B, pp. 182–7
Siricius, *Epistola ad Himerium episcopum Tarraconensem*, ed. K. Zechiel-Eckes and D. Jasper, *Die erste Dekretale: der Brief Papst Siricius' an Bischof Himerius von Tarragona vom Jahr 385 (JK 255)*, MGH Studien und Texte, 55 (Hanover, 2013)
Die Streitschriften Hinkmars von Reims und Hinkmars von Laon 869–871, ed. R. Schieffer, MGH *Conc.* IV, supplementum 2 (Hanover, 2003)
Theodosiani libri XVI cum Constitutionibus Sirmondianis et leges novellae ad Theodosianum pertinentes, ed. T. Mommsen and P. M. Meyer, 2 vols (Berlin, 1905)
Theodosiani libri XVI cum Constitutionibus Sirmondianis et leges novellae ad Theodosianum pertinentes. Tabulae et narratio tabularum, ed. L. Traube (Berlin, 1905)
Die Urkunden Lothars I. und Lothars II., ed. T. Schieffer, MGH *Diplomatum Karolinorum* III (Berlin, 1966)
Venantius Fortunatus *see* Pseudo-Venantius Fortunatus

Select bibliography of secondary literature

Airlie, S., 'Private bodies and the body politic in the divorce case of Lothar II', *Past and Present*, 161 (1998), 3-38

Anton, H. H., *Fürstenspiegel und Herrscherethos in der Karolingerzeit* (Bonn, 1968)

Bartlett, R., *Trial by Fire and Water: the Medieval Judicial Ordeal* (Oxford, 1986)

Beck, H. G. J., 'The selection of bishops suffragan to Hincmar of Rheims, 845-882', *Catholic Historical Review*, 45 (1959), 273-308

Böhringer, L., 'Der eherechtliche Traktat im Paris. Lat.12445, einer Arbeitshandschrift Hinkmars von Reims', *DA*, 46 (1990), 18-47

Brühl, C., 'Hinkmariana II: Hinkmar im Widerstreit von kanonischen Recht und Politik in Ehefragen', *DA*, 20 (1964), 55-77

Buc, P., 'Text and ritual in ninth-century political culture: Rome, 864', in G. Althoff, J. Fried and P. J. Geary, eds, *Medieval Concepts of the Past: Ritual, Memory, Historiography* (Cambridge, 2002), pp. 123-38

Calvet, G., '*Cupiditas, avaritia, turpe lucrum*: discours économique et morale chrétienne chez Hincmar de Reims (845-882)', in J.-P. Devroey, L. Feller and R. Le Jan, eds, *Les élites et la richesse au Haut Moyen Âge* (Turnhout, 2011), pp. 97-112

Carey, F. M., 'The scriptorium of Reims during the archbishopric of Hincmar (845-882 A.D.)', in L. W. Jones, ed., *Classical and Mediaeval Studies in Honor of Edward Kennard Rand* (New York, 1938), pp. 41-60

Chazelle, C. M., *The Crucified God in the Carolingian Era: Theology and Art of Christ's Passion* (Cambridge, 2001)

Congar, Y., *L'Ecclésiologie du haut Moyen âge: de Saint Grégoire le Grand à la désunion entre Byzance et Rome* (Paris, 1968)

Costambeys, M., M. Innes and S. MacLean, *The Carolingian World* (Cambridge, 2011)

Depreux, Ph., and C. Treffort, 'La paroisse dans le *De ecclesiis et capellis* d'Hincmar de Reims. L'énonciation d'une norme à partir de la pratique?', *Médiévales*, 48 (2005), 141-8

Devisse, J., *Hincmar, Archevêque de Reims 845-882*, 3 vols (Geneva, 1975-6)

Devisse, J., *Hincmar et la loi* (Dakar, 1962)

Devroey, J.-P., 'Libres et non-libres sur les terres de Saint-Remi de Reims: La notice judiciare de Courtisols (13 Mai 847) et le polyptyque d'Hincmar', *Journal des Savants*, 1 (2006), 65-103

Dutton, P. E., *The Politics of Dreaming in the Carolingian Empire* (Lincoln NE, 1994)

Ganz, D., 'The debate on predestination', in M. T. Gibson and J. L. Nelson, eds, *Charles the Bald: Court and Kingdom*, 2nd revd edn (Aldershot, 1990), pp. 283-302

Bibliographies

Gaudemet, J., 'Indissolubilité et consommation du mariage: l'apport d'Hincmar de Reims', *Revue de droit canonique*, 30 (1980), 28–40

Gillis, M. B., 'Gottschalk of Orbais: a study of power and spirituality in a ninth-century life' (PhD dissertation, University of Virginia, 2009)

Goldberg, E. J., *Struggle for Empire: Kingship and Conflict under Louis the German, 817–876* (Ithaca, 2006)

Goudesenne, J.-F., 'La musique de l'ancien office de saint Remi retrouvée (VIIIe–IXe siècles)', in M. Rouche, ed., *Clovis, histoire et mémoire*, 2 vols (Paris, 1997), II, pp. 103–28

Haller, J., *Nikolaus I. und Pseudoisidor* (Stuttgart, 1936)

Hartmann, W., *Die Synoden der Karolingerzeit im Frankenreich und in Italien* (Paderborn, 1989)

Heidecker, K., *The Divorce of Lothar II: Christian Marriage and Political Power in the Carolingian World*, trans. T. M. Guest (Ithaca, 2010)

Heidecker, K., 'Gathering and recycling authoritative texts: the importance of marginalia in Hincmar of Reims' treatise about king Lothar's divorce', in M. Mostert, ed., *Organizing the Written Word: Proceedings of the First Utrecht Symposium on Medieval Literacy, Utrecht 5–7 June 1997* (Turnhout, forthcoming),

Isaïa, M.-C., *Remi de Reims: mémoire d'un saint, histoire d'une Église* (Paris, 2010)

Jasper, D. and H. Fuhrmann, *Papal Letters in the Early Middle Ages* (Washington DC, 2001)

Jong, M. de, *The Penitential State: Authority and Atonement in the Age of Louis the Pious, 814–840* (Cambridge, 2009)

Joye, S., *La Femme ravie: le mariage par rapt dans le sociétés occidentales du haut Moyen Âge* (Turnhout, 2012)

Laehr, G., 'Ein karolingischer Konzilsbrief und der Fürstenspiegel Hincmars von Reims', *Neues Archiv der Gesellschaft für ältere deutsche Geschichtskunde*, 50 (1935), 106–34

Lauwers, M., ed., *La Dîme, l'Église et la société féodale* (Turnhout, 2012)

Lesne, E., 'Hincmar et l'empereur Lothaire', *Revue des questions historiques*, NS 34 (1905), 5–58

McCarthy, M. J., 'Power and kingship under Louis II the Stammerer, 877–879' (PhD dissertation, University of Cambridge, 2012)

McKeon, P. R., *Hincmar of Laon and Carolingian Politics* (Urbana, 1978)

Meyer-Gebel, M., 'Zur annalistischen Arbeitsweise Hinkmars von Reims', *Francia*, 15 (1987), 75–108

Mordek, H., 'Ein exemplarischer Rechtsstreit: Hinkmar von Reims und das Landgut Neuilly-Saint-Front', *Zeitschrift der Savigny-Stiftung für Rechtsgeschichte, Kanonistische Abteilung*, 83 (1997), 86–112

Nees, L., 'The fastigium of Saint-Remi ("the Tomb of Hincmar") at Reims', in R. A. Maxwell, ed., *Representing History, 900-1300: Art, Music, History* (University Park PA, 2010), pp. 31-52, 211-21

Nees, L., *A Tainted Mantle: Hercules and the Classical Tradition at the Carolingian Court* (Philadelphia, 1991)

Nelson, J. L., 'The "Annals of St Bertin"', in M. T. Gibson and J. L. Nelson, eds, *Charles the Bald: Court and Kingdom*, 2nd revd edn (Aldershot, 1990), pp. 23-40

Nelson, J. L., *Charles the Bald* (London, 1992)

Nelson, J. L., 'The intellectual in politics: context, content and authorship in the capitulary of Coulaines, November 843', in L. Smith and B. Ward, eds, *Intellectual Life in the Middle Ages: Essays Presented to Margaret Gibson* (London, 1992), pp. 1-14

Nelson, J. L., 'Kingship, law and liturgy in the political thought of Hincmar of Rheims', *English Historical Review*, 92 (1977), 241-79

Nelson, J. L., 'Legislation and consensus in the reign of Charles the Bald', in P. Wormald, ed., *Ideal and Reality in Frankish and Anglo-Saxon Society: Studies Presented to J.M. Wallace-Hadrill* (Oxford, 1983), pp. 202-27

Nelson, J. L., 'A tale of two princes: politics, text and ideology in a Carolingian annal', *Studies in Medieval and Renaissance History*, 10 (1988), 105-41

Patzold, S., *Episcopus: Wissen über Bischöfe im Frankenreich des späten 8. bis frühen 10. Jahrhunderts* (Ostfildern, 2008)

Patzold, S., 'Konsens und Konkurrenz: Überlegungen zu einem aktuellen Forschungskonzept der Mediävistik', *Frühmittelalterliche Studien*, 41 (2007), 75-103

Rhijn, C. van, *Shepherds of the Lord: Priests and Episcopal Statutes in the Carolingian period* (Turnhout, 2007)

Schmitz, G., 'Hinkmar von Reims, die Synode von Fismes 881 und der Streit um das Bistum Beauvais', *DA*, 35 (1979), 463-86

Schmitz, G., 'Wucher in Laon. Eine neue Quelle zu Karl dem Kahlen und Hinkmar von Reims', *DA*, 37 (1981), 529-58

Schneider, O., *Erzbischof Hinkmar und die Folgen: der vierhundertjährige Weg historischer Erinnerungsbilder von Reims nach Trier* (Berlin, 2010)

Scholz, S., *Politik — Selbstverständnis — Selbstdarstellung. Die Päpste in karolingischer und ottonischer Zeit* (Stuttgart, 2006)

Schrörs, H., *Hinkmar, Erzbischof von Reims: sein Leben und seine Schriften* (Freiburg im Breisgau, 1884)

Sieben, H. J., *Die Konzilsidee des lateinischen Mittelalters (847-1378)* (Paderborn, 1984)

Sommar, M. E., 'Hincmar of Reims and the canon law of episcopal translation', *Catholic Historical Review*, 88 (2002), 429-45

Sot, M., *Un historien et son église au Xe siècle: Flodoard de Reims* (Paris, 1993)

Bibliographies

Staubach, N., *Das Herrscherbild Karls des Kahlen: Formen und Funktionen monarchischer Repräsentation im früheren Mittelalter* (Münster, 1982)

Stone, R., '"Bound from either side": the limits of power in Carolingian marriage disputes, 840–870', *Gender and History*, 19 (2007), 467–82

Stone, R., 'Gender and hierarchy: Archbishop Hincmar of Rheims (845–882) as a religious man', in P. H. Cullum and K. J. Lewis, eds, *Religious Men and Masculine Identity in the Middle Ages* (Woodbridge, Suffolk, 2013), pp. 28–45

Stratmann, M., 'Briefe an Hinkmar von Reims', *DA*, 48 (1992), 37–81

Stratmann, M., *Hinkmar von Reims als Verwalter von Bistum und Kirchenprovinz* (Sigmaringen, 1991)

Stratmann, M., 'Zur Wirkungsgeschichte Hinkmars von Reims', *Francia*, 22 (1995), 1–43

Tavard, G. H., 'Episcopacy and apostolic succession according to Hincmar of Reims', *Theological Studies*, 34 (1973), 594–623

Tavard, G. H., *Trina deitas: the Controversy between Hincmar and Gottschalk* (Milwaukee, 1996)

Toubert, P., 'La théorie du mariage chez les moralistes carolingiens', in *Il Matrimonio nella società altomedievale, 22–28 Apr 1976*, Settimane 24, 2 vols (Spoleto, 1977), I, pp. 233–85

Ubl, K., *Inzestverbot und Gesetzgebung: die Konstruktion eines Verbrechens (300–1100)* (Berlin, 2008)

West, C., 'The significance of the Carolingian advocate', *Early Medieval Europe*, 17 (2009), 186–206

Zechiel-Eckes, K., *Fälschung als Mittel politischer Auseinandersetzung: Ludwig der Fromme (814–840) und die Genese der pseudoisidorischen Dekretalen* (Paderborn, 2011)

Index

Note: literary works can be found under authors' names

abduction, *see raptus*
Actard, bishop of Nantes 17, 68
Adalard, count of the palace 53
Adalard, cousin of Charlemagne 3, 20, 45, 54
Adalhard, seneschal 83
Adam, scribe 213, 215
Aegidian Epitome, *see* Roman law
Aeneas, bishop of Paris 255, 260
Ambrose, saint 99–100
Amolo, archbishop of Lyons 79, 252
annals 49
   see also Hincmar of Rheims: *Annales Bertiniani*; Prudentius: *Annales Bertiniani*
Ansegis, abbot of St-Wandrille 156, 159, 160
Ansegis, archbishop of Sens 18, 53, 116
Ansgard, wife of Louis the Stammerer 11, 112–13, 201
archdeacons 231, 244 n.41
   see also Sigloard
Attolae curtis, parish in Rheims diocese 230–2, 237
Augustine 259
   on predestination 247, 251, 253, 255, 258
   source for Hincmar 17, 44, 99–100, 140, 180, 282, 286 n.25
   see also Hincmar of Rheims: *Capitula diversarum sententiarum*
Avenay, convent 79–80

Baldwin, *see* Judith
bears, dancing 234
Benedict Levita 157, 159, 284 n.15
Bernard of Autun 116–17
Bernard of Gothia 116–17, 120
Bernard of Italy 3, 70
Bernard of Septimania 46
Bernard of Toulouse, relative of Hincmar 46, 52
Bertha, daughter of Lothar I 79–80
Bertram of the Tardenois, relative of Hincmar 52
biblical models 142, 177, 180, 192–9 *passim*
   see also David
bishops 61–2, 69–71, 236, 252
   deposition 8, 13, 15, 60, 62
      see also Ebbo; Hincmar of Laon; papacy: appeals to; Rothad
   disputed successions 5, 13, 19, 157
   relations with kings 3, 15–16, 63–67, 69
      see also Charles the Bald; Lothar I;
   translation, *see* Actard
   see also Hincmar of Rheims: on bishops

Index

blinding 3, 17, 60-1, 69-71, 201, 276
Boso, husband of Engeltrude, *see* Engeltrude
Boso of Provence 16, 17, 60, 116-17, 122
Breviary of Alaric, *see* Roman law

canon law 12, 15, 71, 93, 143-4, 176-181, 190, 233
   source for Hincmar 28, 131-2, 229-230, 241 n.6, 272-3, 282-3
   see also Collectio Hispana; Collectio Quesnelliana; councils; Pseudo-Isidore
Capitula diversarum sententiarum, *see* Hincmar of Rheims: *Capitula diversarum sententiarum*
capitularies 46, 81, 142, 156-62, 192, 233
   Capitulary of Coulaines (843) 45-6, 160
   Capitulary of Pîtres (864) 14, 136
   Capitulary of Quierzy (877) 18, 118
   see also Benedict Levita
Carloman II, king of West Francia 19, 54, 113-14, 122, 157, 158
Carloman, son of Charles the Bald 16-17, 61, 70-1, 201
Carloman, son of Louis the German 17, 96
celibacy 234, 239
Charlemagne 20, 26, 158-9, 194
Charles Martel 28, 94
Charles of Provence, king 9, 11, 260
Charles the Bald, king of West Francia 18, 46, 101, 136, 200-1, 257-8, 260
   invasions by 11, 16-18, 51
   relations with Hincmar of Laon 60-1, 63-70
   relations with Hincmar of Rheims 5-6, 9-10, 14-16, 45, 50-2, 71, 79-80, 95-6, 102, 110-14 *passim*, 158, 160, 196, 201, 272
      see also Hincmar of Rheims: *De fide Carolo regi servanda*; Hincmar of Rheims: Quierzy letter
   relations with Lothar I 79-80, 83
   relations with Louis the Stammerer 11, 18, 113, 114
Charles the Fat, emperor 108 n.54
Charles the Younger, son of Charles the Bald 11, 113, 201
Church, the 12, 239
   as body 193, 196, 199
   property 9, 16, 17, 60, 63-4, 94, 139, 143-4, 157, 159, 171
      see also Hincmar of Rheims: *Collectio de ecclesiis et capellis*; Hincmar of Rheims: *Expositiones ad Carolum regem pro ecclesiae libertatum defensione*; proprietary churches; Rheims, church of
   see also archdeacons; bishops; Hincmar of Rheims: on Church; papacy; parishes
Clovis, Frankish king 51, 172, 184
coinage 14, 50, 136
Collectio Britannica, *see* manuscripts
Collectio Hispana 148 nn.39-40, 276, 288 n.51
Collectio Quesnelliana 135
concubines 16, 199
   see also marriage
consensus 12-13, 27, 45, 115, 158, 159, 161, 197-8
Constantine, Roman emperor 144, 194
Corbie, monastery 8, 153 n.94, 275
   see also Adalard, cousin of Charlemagne; Ratramnus of Corbie
coronations 9, 15, 50, 51, 115, 116, 171
correctio 191-2
Coucy, parish in Laon diocese 230, 232, 234
councils 10-11, 69, 97-8, 160, 175-8, 252
   Aachen (860) 10
   Aachen (862) 11
   Agde (506) 256
   Attigny (822) 3, 44-5, 161
      see also Northild
   Attigny (870) 16, 61, 65, 75n.58, 245 nn.52-3, 276
   Beauvais (845) 160

Index

councils (*cont.*)
  calling of 12-13
  Chalon (813) 157
  Douzy (871) 17, 66-8, 74 n.43, 75 n.53, 75 n.58, 146 n.10, 148 n.37, 151 n.67, 152 n.87, 153 n.93, 153 n.95, 154 nn.104-5, 154 n.107, 154 n.115, 245 n.53
  Douzy (874) 17
  Fismes (881) 19, 23, 112, 157, 158-9, 161
  Francia (846) 81
  Langres (859) 260
  Mainz (829) 249
  Mainz (848) 250, 253
  Meaux-Paris (845-846) 265 n.62
  Orléans (511) 57 n.19, 175
  papal confirmation 12, 15, 36 n.118, 68, 80, 83
  Paris (829) 3, 95, 157, 250-1
  Paris (846) 80
  Ponthion (876) 18
  provincial 142, 178, 269, 271, 273, 282
  Quierzy (849) 48, 50, 255, 260
  Quierzy (853) 8, 49, 258, 260
  Quierzy (857) 9
  Quierzy (858) 9-10, 94
    see also Hincmar of Rheims: Quierzy letter
  Savonnières (859) 260
  Soissons (853) 8, 15, 35 n.96, 36 n.118, 83-4, 156, 168 n.46, 258
  Soissons (862) 14
  Soissons (866) 15
  Thionville (835) 5
  Troyes (867) 15-16, 280
  Troyes (878) 70, 119, 120-1
  Tusey (860) 10, 163 n.21, 261
  Valence (855) 7, 260-1
  Verberie (869) 65, 277
  Ver (844) 6
  Worms (829) 157, 160-1
  Yütz (844) 78
Courtisols, estate of Rheims church 215-22
courts 3, 7, 18-19, 44-5, 72 n.5, 79, 118-19
  as audience 50-1, 53, 62, 63, 69

  see also Hincmar of Rheims: *De ordine palatii*
custom 141, 193, 231

David, biblical king 101, 180, 194-5, 205 n.44
Devisse, Jean 2, 21, 33 n.62, 34 n.80, 44, 81, 93, 115, 124 n.4, 129-32 *passim*, 156, 158, 162, 185 n.2, 218, 221, 245 n.50
drinking 234, 268
Drogo, archbishop of Metz 79, 81

Eberhard of Friuli 83, 149 n.49, 249-50
Ebbo, archbishop of Rheims 5-6, 47-8, 78, 80
  clerics ordained by 5-6, 15, 47, 83, 86, 225 n.36, 258-9, 261
    see also Wulfad
  deposition 4-5, 8, 15, 279-80
  political networks 7, 47, 260
Ebbo, bishop of Grenoble 7, 260
Engelberga, wife of Louis II of Italy 52, 58 n.42
Engeltrude, wife of Boso 10-11, 13, 91 n.61, 156
Epitome of Julian, *see* Roman law
Ermengard, wife of Lothar I 7, 79-80
Ermentrude, wife of Charles the Bald 15, 16, 51, 58 n.42, 207 n.60
excommunication 82-3, 86, 100, 120, 159, 196, 201, 205 n.46, 273

False Decretals, *see* Pseudo-Isidore
fathers 194-201
fides (fidelity/faith) 26-7, 80, 84-5, 98, 100-3, 199
Flodoard of Rheims 1, 4, 5, 31 n.30, 45, 77, 237
Florus of Lyons 137, 256, 261
Folembray, parish in Laon diocese 157, 168 n.47, 230-5, 237
Fontenoy, battle (841) 5, 46
forgeries 21, 23, 77, 85-6, 176
  see also Benedict Levita; Hincmar of Rheims: manipulation of texts; Pseudo-Isidore

Index

Fouron, meeting at (878) 119, 121, 159
Fulcric, vassal of Lothar I 8, 82–3

Gauzlin, abbot of St-Denis 19, 53, 113–14, 116–18, 122
Gelasius I, pope 102, 158
Genebaud, bishop of Laon 179–180, 184
Giselbert, abductor 79–80
Gottschalk 7, 247–62
  as missionary 248, 252–3
  claims to authority 24, 251–5, 259
  condemnation and punishment 48–9, 250–2, 255–6, 261
  political networks 25, 50, 251, 257, 259–60
  relations with Hincmar of Rheims 48–9, 250, 253–4, 256–61
  writings 250–1, 253, 256–9
grace of God 248–53 *passim*, 258–61
Gregorian Code, *see* Roman law
Gregory I ('the Great') pope 101, 105 n.18, 139, 152 n.83, 157, 172, 178, 188 n.29
Gregory IV, pope 4, 279
Gunther, archbishop of Cologne 13, 62

Hadrian II, pope 17, 36 n.118, 268, 270, 272, 276, 279, 281–3
hagiography 170, 181, 184
  see also Hincmar of Rheims: *Miracula sancti Dionysii*; Hincmar of Rheims: *Vita Remigii*
Hautvillers, monastery 48, 255, 257, 261–2
heresy 26, 174–5, 178, 249–51, 253–4, 261–2
  see also Gottschalk; Hincmar of Rheims: *Collectio contra haereticos*; predestination
Hetti, archbishop of Trier 79, 91 n.58
Hilduin, abbot of St-Denis 3–5, 44–5, 49, 55 n.7
Hilduin, archchancellor of Lothar I 83
Hincmar of Laon
  conflicts with Hincmar of Rheims 16–17, 60–71, 132, 142–3, 159,

230–7 *passim*, 245 n.54, 268, 276–8
  deposition 68
  political networks 25, 70
  writings 8, 16, 62, 65, 132, 140
Hincmar of Rheims
  Admonitio ad episcopos et ad regem Carolomannum apud Sparnacum facta 157, 162 n.5, 246 n.59
  Ad reclusos et simplices in Remensi parrochia contra Gothescalcum 7, 48–9, 257–8, 264 n.31, 264 n.35, 265 n.45, 266 n.65, 266 n.68
  afterlife of works 28, 181–4
  Annales Bertiniani 11, 49–54, 62–71, 117, 120–1, 123, 196, 201
  audiences for 51, 63, 69, 96–7, 158, 173, 179, 181–2, 184, 187
  see also courts
  on bishops
    authority 12, 24, 47, 67, 171–3, 255
    behaviour 64–9
    deposition 68, 273
    fidelity to king 18, 80
    see also De fide Carolo regi servanda; Hincmar of Rheims: on kings
    role 67, 117, 175–8
    as successors to the apostles 12, 67, 100, 177, 238
    see also Actard; Hincmar of Laon; Hincmar of Rheims: *De officiis episcoporum*; Hincmar of Rheims: on metropolitans; Hincmar of Rheims: on priests; Rothad
  Capitula diversarum sententiarum 5, 17
  on Church 193, 196, 238–9
  see also church property; Rheims, church of
  Collectio contra haereticos et de privilegiis multarum sedium 39 n.164, 151 n.68
  Collectio de ecclesiis et capellis 9, 44, 47, 156–8, 160, 228, 230, 241 nn.5–6, 241 nn.8–9, 242 n.16, 243 n.21, 243 n.28, 244 n.43, 244

303

Hincmar of Rheims (*cont.*)
n.46, 245 nn.48–9, 246 n.60, 246 n.62
Collectio de raptoribus 9
on counsellors 7, 18–19, 49–51, 53–4, 84, 95, 100, 111, 115–16, 192, 194
De causa Teutfridi presbyteri 153 n.103
De cavendis vitiis et virtutibus exercendis 28, 40 n.169, 171–2, 178, 199
De coercendo et exstirpando raptu viduarum puellarum ac sanctimonialum, see *De raptu*
De divortio Lotharii regis et Theutbergae reginae 10, 125 n.20, 140, 141–2, 146 n.15, 149 n.45, 150 n.58, 150 n.63, 152 n.83, 152 n.87, 156, 160, 161, 167 n.45, 190–1, 196
see also Northild
De fide Carolo regi servanda 18, 93, 96–102
De institutione regia 108 n.54
De iudiciis et appellationibus episcoporum et presbyterorum 244 n.38, 244 n.44, 272–3, 278
De iure metropolitanorum 88 n.16, 92 n.82, 149 n.51, 151 n.73
De officiis episcoporum 157, 167 n.45
De ordine palatii 19–20, 26, 32 n.45, 45, 54, 94, 153 n.93, 158, 246 n.59
De praedestinatione Dei 7, 52, 131, 135, 146 n.10, 146 n.22, 150 n.58, 175, 260–1, 263 n.21, 263 n.24, 264 n.35, 265 n.53, 265 n.62, 266 n.81
De presbiteris criminosis 146 n.11, 148 n.37, 150 n.63, 151 nn.67–8, 153 n.93, 154 nn.103, 154 n.106, 154 n.110, 154 nn.114–15, 157, 244 nn.36–7, 246 n.62, 272, 274, 278, 284 n.6, 284 n.9
De raptu 22, 34 n.81, 140–1, 146 n.14, 190–200
De regis persona et regio minsterio ad Carolum Calvum regem 17
De una et non trina deitate 266 n.94
De villa Noviliaco 112
diplomacy by 10, 19, 33 n.62, 82–3, 121
early life 3–6, 44–5, 79
episcopal capitularies 8, 17, 131, 140, 146 n.21, 152 n.79, 180, 228, 234, 236, 242 n.19, 243 nn.21–22, 243 nn.30–1, 244 n.34, 244 n.37, 244 n.41, 244 n.45, 245 n.48, 245 n.56, 246 n.63, 272, 275, 284 n.6, 284 nn.8–9
Expositiones ad Carolum regem pro ecclesiae libertatum defensione 16, 146 n.10, 146 n.12, 148 n.37, 149 n.51, 151 n.68, 151 n.70, 151 n.75, 152 n.86, 153 n.95, 153 nn.102–3, 154 n.115, 154 n.118, 155 n.122, 157, 166 nn.37–40, 167 n.45
as historian 20, 44–5, 49–55, 173, 184, 193
see also Hincmar of Rheims: *Annales Bertiniani*
Juramentum quod Hincmarus Archiepiscopus edere jussus est apud Pontigonem 30 n.19, 38 n.140
on kings
authority of 10, 22, 196–7, 200–1
contractual monarchy 18, 101, 171
relations with bishops 18–20, 39 n.157, 71, 77, 94–103 *passim*, 111, 144, 158, 192, 194
see also Hincmar of Rheims: on bishops
relations to law 141, 142, 159–60 193
role 39 n.157, 190–4
see also Charles the Bald; Hincmar of Rheims: *De regis persona et regio minsterio ad Carolum Calvum regem*; Lothar I; Louis the Stammerer
on laity 21, 26, 195–6, 200
see also Hincmar of Rheims: *De cavendis vitiis et virtutibus exercendis*

on law 21, 47, 93, 141, 156, 175–7, 180–1, 193
  see also canon law; capitularies; custom; Hincmar of Rheims: on kings; norms; Roman law
letters by 1, 6–7, 8–9, 13, 16, 18, 52, 79–84 passim, 112, 114, 119, 149 n.51, 152 n.83, 156–7, 167 n.45, 237, 258, 261, 268, 281–3
  see also Flodoard of Rheims; Hincmar of Rheims: Opuscula et epistola
Libellus expostulationis, see Council of Douzy (871)
manipulation of texts 21, 50, 51, 63–71, 137, 142–4, 170–1, 230, 233
manuscripts owned 28, 132
  see also manuscripts: Berlin SB Phillipps 1741; manuscripts: Paris BnF lat. 12445; Rheims, church of:
marginalia by 39 n.164, 49–50, 132, 136–7, 183, 213–15, 218, 221
on metropolitans 12–14, 16, 64–9, 142, 271, 273, 276, 285 n.16
  see also De iure metropolitanorum; Opusculum LV capitulorum
Miracula sancti Dionysii 5
Novi regis instructio ad rectam regni administrationem 53–4, 56 n.13, 111, 115–16, 117
old age 19–20, 53–54, 122, 162, 170
Opuscula et epistolae quae spectant ad causam Hincmari Laudunensis 74 n.35, 157, 165 n.35, 168 n.47, 242 n.12, 242 n.15, 243 n.20, 243 n.24, 243 nn.26–8, 244 n.32, 244 n.40, 244 n.46, 245 n.51, 245 n.54, 283 n.1, 287 n.36
Opusculum LV capitulorum 65, 72 n.4, 74 n.37, 146 n.11, 151 n.68, 151 n.72, 153 n.93, 151 n.95, 154 n.103, 154 n.110, 154 n.112, 155 n.122, 206 n.50, 242 n.11, 242 n.13–15, 243 n.20, 243 n.23, 243 n.28, 245 nn.52–3, 246 n.59, 276

on papacy 12–13, 64, 176–7, 270, 279
  see also Nicholas I
on parishes 229–40
personality 44–5, 50, 54–5, 77, 81, 116, 123, 171, 221
political networks 52, 79, 83
on predestination 48–9
  see also Hincmar of Rheims: Ad reclusos et simplices in Remensi parrochia contra Gothescalcum; Hincmar of Rheims: De praedestinatione Dei
on priests 8, 26, 178–9, 228, 231–5
  authority 238
  chastity 234–5, 268
  control of by bishops 18, 46, 177–8
  deposition 14, 17, 234–5, 271, 273
  education 233–4
  legal status 232–3
  misbehaving 18, 22, 234–5, 269–76 passim
  reputation 234–5, 269, 271–2
  see also Ebbo: clerics ordained by; Hincmar of Rheims: De iudiciis et appellationibus episcoporum et presbyterorum; Hincmar of Rheims: De presbiteris criminosis; jurisdiction over clerics; papacy: appeals to; Trising
Pro ecclesiae, see Expositiones ad Carolum regem pro ecclesiae libertatum defensione
Quae exsequi debeat episcopus, see De officiis episcoporum
Quierzy letter 10, 94–5, 112
sources used by 5, 21, 95, 98–9, 129, 142, 157, 170, 180, 195
  see also Ambrose, Augustine, canon law, capitularies, Gelasius, Gregory I, Isidore of Seville, Jerome, Leo I, Pseudo-Cyprian, Pseudo-Isidore, Roman law
tomb 27–8
Über Priestertum und Königtum 157

Hincmar of Rheims (*cont.*)
  Visio Bernoldi 18
  Vita Remigii 8, 19, 24, 28, 170–81
    manuscripts 181–4
  working methods 23, 49–50, 63, 68, 99, 130–2, 141, 174–5, 218
  writings, *see* titles of individual works *and also* Capitulary of Coulaines (843); Capitulary of Pîtres (864); coronations; Council of Douzy (871); Council of Fismes (881); Council of Soissons (853); Council of Troyes (867)
history-writing 24
  see also annals; Hincmar of Rheims: as historian
holy oil 28, 51, 171
Hormisdas, pope 174, 176–7
Hrabanus Maurus 7, 49, 85, 209 n.80, 249–51, 253, 254, 258
Hugh the Abbot 116–17, 119–20, 122

incest 8–9, 10, 17, 194, 206 n.49
infamia 271, 274
interdict 65–6, 67, 230–1, 237, 277–8
invasions, *see* Charles the Bald; Louis the German; Saracens; Vikings
Isidore of Seville 130, 138, 204 n.32, 248, 276
Iuviniaca villa, parish in Rheims diocese 230–2
ivories 18, 42 n.227

Jerome 106 n.33
John VIII, pope 18, 70, 96, 120–1, 272
John Scottus Eriugena 257, 260
Jonas of Orléans 5, 203 n.16
Judith, daughter of Charles the Bald 9, 11–12, 13, 50, 53, 200–1, 205 n.46, 207 n.60
jurisdiction over clerics 16, 142, 234–5, 274
Justinian, *see* Roman law

kingship, *see* Hincmar of Rheims: on kings
kinship 59 n.50, 72 n.4, 198–9
  see also fathers; marriage; mothers

laity, *see* Hincmar of Rheims: on laity; Hincmar of Rheims: on parishes; magnates; papacy: appeals to; proprietary churches
law 15, 21, 141–2
  see also canon law; capitularies; custom; Hincmar of Rheims: on law; jurisdiction over clerics; norms; Roman law
Leo I ('the Great'), pope 5, 186 n.19
Leo IV, pope 76, 80, 85–6, 273, 276
Lex Dei, *see* Roman law
lordship over churches, *see* proprietary churches
Lothar I, emperor 3–6, 84, 258
  relations with Ebbo 78
  relations with Hincmar of Rheims 7, 76–86
  personality 81
  relations with papacy 81–2, 83
Lothar II, king of Middle Kingdom 9, 260
  divorce 10–12, 13, 14, 20, 36 n.118, 141, 202 n.7
  death 16, 51
Louis the German, king of East Francia 4–6, 11, 14, 16, 51, 101, 113, 187 n.20, 250, 258
  invasion by (858) 9–10, 93
  invasion by (875) 17–18, 93, 96
  relations with Ebbo 78
Louis II, emperor of Italy 9, 12, 17
Louis III, king of West Francia 19, 54, 112, 113–14, 122, 157
Louis the Pious, emperor 3–5, 26, 44–5
  capitularies 20, 158–9, 160–1
Louis the Stammerer, king of West Francia 159
  marriages 11, 112–14, 201
  relations with Hincmar 11, 18–19, 53–4, 110–23
Louis the Younger, king of East Francia 19, 52, 113, 119, 159
Lupus of Ferrières 6, 32 n.42, 257–8

magnates 6, 9, 27, 44–5, 46, 52, 76, 93–5, 117–18

Index

manuscripts
  Arras, BM MS 31 (0823) 184
  Arras, BM MS 199 (189) 183
  Berlin SB, lat. fol. 269 152 n.89
  Berlin SB, Phillipps 1741 (Y) 131-7, 143-4
  Berlin SB, Phillipps 1745 147 n.34
  Berlin SB, Phillipps 1762 162 n.6
  Bodleian Library, MS Eng. Hist. c. 242 212-14
  British Library, Additional MS 8873 (*Collectio Britannica*) 85-6
  Burgerbibliothek Bern 584 267 n.96
  Carpentras, Bibliothèque Inguimbertine MS 1779 212-14
  Cologny, Fondation Martin Bodmer, col. Bodmer 107 147 n.35
  Ivrea breviary 133, 135, 143
  Leiden Universiteitsbibliotheek BPL 114 150 n.57
  Paris BnF lat. 3838 152 n.80
  Paris BnF lat. 3846 152 n.80
  Paris BnF lat. 9903 212-15
  Paris BnF lat. 10758 162 n.6
  Paris BnF lat. 10911 223 n.14
  Paris BnF lat. 12097 150 n.54
  Paris BnF lat. 12445 (D) 131-9, 143-4
  Paris BnF lat. nouv. acq 1632A 5
  Rheims, BM 425 150 n.59
  Rheims, BM 426 150 n.59
  Rouen, BM MS 1381 (U67) 183-4
  St-Gallen Stiftsbibliothek, Cod. Sang 727 162 n.6
  Utrecht Psalter 42 n.227, 48
  Vatican, Pal. Lat. 296 245 n.52
  Vatican, Reg. lat 886 136, 143
  Vatican, Reg. lat 1128 138
  Vatican, Reg. lat. 1283 146 n.17
  Yale University Beinecke MS 413 149 n.48, 162 n.6
marriage 10-11, 113, 141, 157, 190-1, 193, 195, 197-201
  consummation 198
  see also concubines; incest; Judith; Lothar II; Louis the Stammerer; Northild; *raptus*; Stephen

Martin, saint 51, 100, 101
masculinity 194
  see also patriarchy
Meerssen
  meeting (847) 80-1, 82, 159
  meeting (851) 85, 87 n.2, 159-60, 258
Middle Kingdom 6, 9, 16, 51, 77-8, 83, 96
  see also Lothar I; Lothar II
ministerium 3, 18, 192
  see also Hincmar of Rheims: on bishops; Hincmar of Rheims: on kings
miracles 170, 178, 179, 183, 254
missionaries 251-2
mothers 197, 200

Nicholas I, pope 10, 12, 113, 207 n.60, 280
  on papal authority 12-13, 24, 36 n.116, 273
  relations with Gottschalk 13, 49
  relations with Hincmar 13-15, 86, 261, 273, 279
  norms 23-4, 61-2, 93, 141, 173-9 *passim*, 182, 193, 238
Northild 55 n.4, 196
  see also Council of Attigny (822)
Novels, *see* Roman law

oaths 18, 26-7, 52, 61, 65-6, 69, 101, 199, 216, 234, 271, 274-5
  see also Hincmar of Rheims, *Juramentum quod Hincmarus Archiepiscopus edere jussus est apud Pontigonem*
oblates 3, 249
Orbais, monastery 251
ordeals 141

pallium 16, 80, 85-6
papacy
  appeals to 13, 27, 36 n.116
  by bishops 14-15, 64-5, 270, 277
  by laity 13, 83, 113, 285 n.19
  by priests 235, 268-72, 277-9
  authority of 12-13, 280-1

Index

papacy (*cont.*)
   see also Hincmar of Rheims: on papacy; Nicholas I
   papal legates 12, 13, 14, 51, 161
   papal vicariate 18, 81, 85–6, 176
   relations with Francia 12–13, 15–16, 270
   see also Gelasius I; Gregory I; Gregory IV; Hadrian II; John VIII; Leo I; Leo IV; Nicholas I
parishes 228–9, 239–40
   see also Attolae curtis; Coucy; Folembray; *Iuviniaca villa*
patriarchy 25–6, 196
Paulus, Roman jurist, *see* Roman law
peace 82, 102, 191–2, 197
penance 3, 4, 9, 13, 15, 71, 179–80, 193, 205 n.46, 234, 248–9, 253, 284 n.7
Pippin I, king of Aquitaine 3–4
Pippin II, king of Aquitaine 6, 7, 14, 46, 79, 83
political culture 23–5, 61–2, 123, 202 n.14
   see also consensus; norms
political networks 117–18, 122
   see also Ebbo; Gottschalk; Hincmar of Laon; Hincmar of Rheims
pollution 193, 195
polyptychs 40 n.172, 211
   see also St-Remi
predestination 7–8, 22, 47–9, 171, 174–5, 247–61
   see also Augustine; Gottschalk; Hincmar of Rheims: on predestination
priests, *see* Hincmar: on priests; Pseudo-Isidore; Senatus; Trising
proprietary churches 26, 47–8, 230, 233, 235, 238
Prudentius, bishop of Troyes
   Annales Bertiniani 48–50
   conflicts with Hincmar 9, 47–50, 235, 257, 260–1
Pseudo-Cyprian 105 n.18, 209 n.80
Pseudo-Isidore 24, 132, 140, 280
   dating and origin 8, 275
   Hincmar on 229, 274–6, 279, 280
   manuscripts 278
   use by bishops 16, 65
   use by priests 75 n.45, 275, 277–8
   see also Benedict Levita
punishment, *see* blinding; Gottschalk

queens, *see* royal women

raptus 11, 21–2, 79, 190–7, 200
   female role in 193, 198, 205 n.46
   see also Giselbert; Judith
Ratramnus of Corbie 251, 257–8, 259
Regino of Prüm 113–14
Remigius, saint 28, 51, 100, 171–81, 184
   cult of 8, 20, 170
   see also Hincmar of Rheims: *Vita Remigii*; holy oil
respublica 45, 158, 165 n.34
Rheims, church of 1, 5–6, 7–8, 20, 27–8, 51, 77, 96, 116, 119, 173, 259
   manuscripts 1, 42 n.227, 138
   see also Hincmar: manuscripts owned
   property 6–7, 22, 47–8, 50, 64, 77–8, 80–1, 83, 112, 172, 218, 221
   see also Courtisols; Folembray
Richildis, wife of Charles the Bald 16, 51, 115
rituals 3, 62
   see also coronations
Roman empire 141, 192
   see also Constantine
Roman law
   Aegidian Epitome 137–8, 144
   Breviary of Alaric 130, 131, 133–8, 141, 144, 203 n.17
   Breviary Gregorianus 140
   Epitome of Julian 130, 131, 135, 138–40, 141, 144
   Epitome of Ulpian 138
   Gregorian Code 131, 140
   Justinian Code 131, 138–9
   Lex Dei 131, 140–1, 144
   Lex Romana canonice compta 151 n.76
   Novels 131, 133–6, 138, 139, 148 n.44

Paulus, *Sentences* 131, 134, 137–8
Sirmondian Constitutions 133, 137
source for Hincmar 129–41
Theodosian code 130, 131, 133–8, 141, 149 n.51, 203 n.17
Rothad, bishop of Soissons 8, 9, 13–14, 35 n.97, 244 n.39, 261, 273, 276
royal women 58 n.42
see also Ansgard; Bertha; Engelberga; Ermengard; Ermentrude; Judith; Richildis; Theutberga;
rules, *see* norms

St-Denis, monastery 3–5, 45, 136
see also Gauzlin, Hilduin
St-Remi, monastery 170
polyptych of 211–13, 215–18, 221–2, 234
Saracens 81
Schrörs, Heinrich 2, 29 n.2, 81, 273
Senatus, priest 232–3, 237
sexual behaviour 193, 195–6, 234, 269
see also celibacy; incest; marriage; *raptus*
Sigibert, aristocrat 233, 235
Sigloard, archdeacon 219, 227 n.62
sin 3, 4, 26, 81–2, 100, 172, 178–80, 192, 193
see also Hincmar of Rheims: *De cavendis vitiis et virtutibus exercendis*; penance
Sirmondian Constitutions, *see* Roman law
slaves 143, 215–17, 219–21, 232–3

social order 3, 25–6, 61, 101, 102–3, 190–201 *passim*, 219–21, 238, 240, 256
Stephen, Count of the Auvergne 10, 163 n.21, 208 n.65
synods, *see* councils

Theoderic, bishop of Cambrai 77, 83
Theodosian Code, *see* Roman law
Theutberga, wife of Lothar II 10–12, 13, 14
Theutgaud, archbishop of Trier 7–8, 13, 62
tithes 235, 236, 243 n.28, 245 n.54
Trinity, doctrine of 171, 183, 258–9
Trising, priest 268–71, 275, 279, 281–3

unfree, *see* slaves
unity, concept of 102, 191, 196–8
see also consensus
usury 244 n.45

Verdun, Treaty of (843) 6, 76, 94, 102
Vikings 6, 9, 14, 20, 52–3, 54, 95, 102–3, 112
violence 9, 268–71 *passim*
against women 141, 194
see also blinding; Gottschalk; Trising

women, *see* Engeltrude; marriage; Northild; patriarchy; *raptus*; royal women; violence: against women
wrath of God 10, 81–2, 191, 195, 249
Wulfad, archbishop of Sens 14–16, 280

EU authorised representative for GPSR:
Easy Access System Europe, Mustamäe tee 50,
10621 Tallinn, Estonia
gpsr.requests@easproject.com

www.ingramcontent.com/pod-product-compliance
Lightning Source LLC
Chambersburg PA
CBHW030116240426
43673CB00041B/1305